The TRIUMPHAL ENTRY

Of *ALEXANDER* into *Babylon*.

With DANCING

By Mr. GRANIER, Miss HILLIARD, &c.

To which will be added a FARCE, call'd

The Double Disappointment.

Loveless by Mr. LOWE,

Gripe by Mr. COLLINS,

The Marquiss of *Fanfaron* by Mr. HOLTOM,

Isabella by Miss YOUNG,

PHELIM O-BLUNDER by Mr. BARRINGTON.

Boxes 5 *s.* Pit 3 *s.* First Gallery 2 *s* Upper Gallery 1 *s.*

On *Monday* next, A *BURLETTA*, call'd

Gli AMANTI GELOSI.

Some of the Ladies-who-came-first figure in this unique playbill of Theatre Royal, in Covent Garden.
The probable date of the bill is 1754–5.

Anne

With love

from

Kathleen

Xmas 1952.

To Anne Haggel

who loves the Theatre
& who is a friend of
mine on that account —
& on her own charming
account too.

Every Good Wish

W Macqueen Pope

12/11/ 1952

Ladies First

Other books by W. Macqueen-Pope

IVOR

THEATRE ROYAL DRURY LANE

HAYMARKET: THEATRE OF PERFECTION

GAIETY: THEATRE OF ENCHANTMENT

THE MELODIES LINGER ON: THE STORY OF MUSIC HALL

CARRIAGES AT ELEVEN

TWENTY SHILLINGS IN THE POUND

AN INDISCREET GUIDE TO THEATRELAND

GHOSTS AND GREASEPAINT

LADIES FIRST

By

W. Macqueen Pope

THE STORY OF
WOMAN'S CONQUEST OF THE
BRITISH STAGE

W. H. ALLEN
LONDON
1952

Made and printed in Great Britain by The Camelot Press,
London and Southampton, for the publishers W. H. Allen & Co. Ltd.
Essex Street, London, W.C.2.

To

SYLVIA GREY

A Great Lady of Our Theatre
Who Came First and Unrivalled in her Art
When our Days and Nights were Golden;
Who, during her Career, Filled the Stage of
the Gaiety with Radiance
And who now Sheds Radiance by means of her
Kindly Understanding and Fadeless Charm
over the Greater Stage of Life

Contents

Illustrations

Author's Explanation

THIS is a book about the Actresses who have graced the stage of our country, a stage whose history is without rival in the world and which today still holds its premier position. For the English Theatre still leads the way as it always has. I use the word English advisedly. Although our Profession owes very much to those whose talent and art derived from the sister isle of Eire—it was Ireland then—from which so much amazing genius has come, and, in a lesser degree, to Scotland and Wales, it was here in England, and more particularly in the city of London, that it blossomed like the rose, the English Rose. Indeed, it was when the Tudor Rose was our emblem that our Theatre came into full flower. At that time, when we had our Renaissance, but when we were still poor in many of the Arts, when painters and sculptors hardly existed amongst us, when composers were the merest and smallest handful, we had a Theatre, actors and dramatists without equal in the world. Here, in Shoreditch, the first real theatre in Europe was built, and that meant the first real theatre in the world. The Grecian and Roman amphitheatres were not playhouses in the theatrical sense; our Shoreditch "Theatre" and "Curtain" were the genuine article—roofless, yes, but theatres nevertheless.

We were, in those days, awakening to new beauties. The spirit of liberty was sweeping over our land, which had always had more freedom than any other part of the world, in a greater and all embracing wave. Old walls were down, old restrictions swept away; there was sense of adventure, which led our pioneers in their tiny ships right round the world, showing what great hearts and the spirit of free men could do against overwhelming odds.

There was a thirst for knowledge; printing had placed the inscribed thoughts of the geniuses of the past within reach of everyone who could read. But they were still the few; the many were still illiterate. But they were just as eager, just as inspired by this reawakening of the awareness of the lovelier things of Life. If they could not read, they nevertheless loved to listen. They were avid for words, and those words, strung like necklets of glittering jewels by master craftsmen, were supplied by the Theatre.

England led, and the rest followed. As the years went by in one thing only did this country's Theatre lag behind. Being English, it had formed a Tradition. That was unavoidable; wherever the English are, there Tradition arises. Two Englishmen wrecked on a desert island, without hope of rescue, would form a tradition of their own. It is one of the reasons and probably one of the best reasons why we have always been unconquerable. So long as it survives, so shall we. For Tradition is foundation: and a house built upon sand cannot continue to stand.

So our Theatre built a tradition. This was the belief that it was a purely male preserve in which the female had no place. The plots of the plays must perforce have female characters, but Tradition ordained that these must be played by men or boys. Women belonged to the Home, not to the public places. The other nations of Europe considered it right and proper to have female parts played by females. The conservative English Theatre refused to share this view. It had never been done here; therefore it could never be done. So for eighty-five years, if we fix (somewhat arbitrarily maybe, but of necessity) the opening of The Theatre which Burbage built as the beginning, until the year 1661, the stage of England remained without women upon it. The Continent had had women players years before that date, even before a real theatre had appeared outside this island. And the foreigners, so despised by the English, had found that the women helped. They had brought something new, something credible. But it was not to be thought of here: it was immoral, it was untraditional, perish the thought.

It took a revolution to bring women into our Theatre. It took a civil war, the beheading of a King, a King's son in exile, and a period of exhausting religious austerity. Had Charles I not lost his head, had Charles II not spent so much of his youth in exile and seen so much of the way of life in other lands, there is no knowing how long it would have been before women came upon our stage. For the Theatre is the most conservative thing in this most conservative country. Our Theatre still clings to the old and obsolete phrases and customs. There is still a linkman outside each playhouse, there is still talk of Green Room gossip, though no more links are used and no more Green Rooms exist. Up to a few years ago, ladies' hats were referred to on programmes, as "bonnets." Who wears bonnets today, or who wore them even when that phrase was still flourishing in the Theatre?

The Revolution and the period of Puritan austerity shut down the theatres. When the King came into his own again—a travelled, experienced, and broad-minded king—he re-opened them. At the same time he opened the door to women, and the English actress arrived.

It is the story of those women pioneers which this book seeks to tell. It is no new story. But the author hopes that he may have brought to the tale what our newspapers now demand and insist upon—a new angle. For one thing, the book is written from the inside and not from the outside of the playhouse. Its author has been a very humble member of the profession, whose inadequate historian he strives to be, all his life. That life, not a short one now, has covered many changes. Consequently what is sought here is not a technical appraisement of the talents of those actresses, not a critical review of their performances and a record of the parts they played, but rather a picture of the women themselves: how they lived and how they worked in the life they led behind the scenes rather than before them, and what manner of creatures they were. The story also strives to show what the Theatre in which they worked was like, the sort of life which surrounded them, and how they made their impacts each in their own way.

In some cases, it was more their own personalities and their way of life, rather than their art, which made the impression. In other cases it was sheer, inherent talent for the stage. But, one and all, they were Actresses; they brought the incalculable allure, mystery and charm of femininity to the illusion and glamour of the acting profession and to that institution known as the Theatre. Often the glamour was entirely their own—there is precious little in real theatrical life—but it had been lacking before, when our stage was a purely male domain.

Could we endure their banishment today? Would our Theatre still live if there were no women to colour it? Have those people who clamour for the return of the Elizabethan Theatre ever considered the point? We hear so much talk, we read so much pleading, for a return to the days of Elizabeth, but would those champions go the whole hog and banish the actresses? Of course they would not. Then why moan for the Elizabethan days in the Theatre, when even they, its champions, would falsify it with women players? Let us keep our perspective. And let us cherish our actresses.

This book is called "Ladies First" for two reasons. In my previous books, I fear I have always devoted the major space to the men, most ungallantly putting the ladies second. Well, I am entirely a man myself, and proud of it. So I am apt to put men first. I believe in them. But I am no anti-feminist, not by any means. Although I am old-fashioned enough to believe that the running of the world is better done by men than by women, I never under-rate the powers possessed by the feminine sex, and I never cease to deplore the fact that today they are not held in the same respect as they were when I was young.

To me, it is still not right that a woman should pay her own fare, carry her own parcels, walk on the outside, suffer any discomfort which is the privilege of the male. It is also abhorrent to me that any woman should stand treat or pay the bill in a restaurant. Those are masculine duties. I like to see women on a pedestal, not pushing with the crowd. Absurd and old-fashioned, of course, but so far as I am concerned, Tradition. But the power and importance of women are very real to me. I have been a happily married man for many years, I have a daughter of my own and two grandchildren, one a girl. So I know something about women. Also I was born in the Theatre and have served in it for nearly half a century, full time. I have served part time too.

But, being an old-fashioned man, I fear I am still apt to put men first. So here, in this book, I try to make amends. It is "Ladies First." And the story mainly concerns those Ladies Who Came First upon the Stage of England. It is of them that I speak mostly, for they were the forerunners of so much that was to come; they blazed the trail which their successors, the Ladies of the stage today, follow with such brilliance and beauty. They, the Ladies Who Came First, were the makers of Tradition. Need much more be said?

So, do not be disappointed if you fail to find in these pages a life story of your favourite actress of today, or even of yesterday. Not only has space to be considered, but I have to consider my own safety. I do not want to write about my contemporaries and friends whom I meet so often and with whom I still work. That I leave to the modern critics, who are separated from those they criticise by the safety of the footlights, and who are not in that extraordinary proximity which life in the Theatre enforces. I am not a critic, never have been one, and never expect to be one. I prefer praise to condemnation. I believe in chronicling the bright rather than the dark. I am told, very often, that I indulge in superlatives. Of course I do. So do all theatrical people. We live a life which is all superlative, otherwise we should, like old soldiers, just fade away. But I believe in fact and I believe in telling the truth. To me success is more important than failure, and the best success is that which has met failure and conquered it. There is much of that in the Theatre. I write of what I have learned by experience, gained by participation and not by book knowledge. I have had a lot of experience of all kinds in the Theatre and perhaps that may serve to bring to life those ladies who came first—whom neither I nor any other living writer knew—by understanding from the inside what they did, how they did it, why they did it and what they felt whilst they were doing it. One delves into old books, old records, and reads what is there inscribed. They give facts and they sometimes try to explain them. But either they were compiled by men who were just onlookers —as are most critics—or else they were written under the eye and at the behest of the subjects themselves. So they can be only a bare skeleton. Actual experience must do the rest, must put the flesh on the bones, the thoughts into the heads long since mere skulls, and supply the motive force to limbs long crumbled away.

But the Ladies of the Stage who came first were women, and they were actresses. Of all the people in the world, actors and actresses change the least. They are the least subject to machinery:

theirs is still a handicraft, they still do the job themselves. Consequently they change little in their manners and their thoughts, although, be it said at once, they have changed their method of life and their code of morals. But they still have to do their job personally, as they always did it. There is no mass production for them. They are the creators, not just a series of die stamps. They remain men and women of that completely mad world which is the Theatre, in which we are all lunatics or we could not survive, in which we all lead topsy-turvy lives, and where Illusion is the only Reality. The Ladies who came first had that in common with their descendants today.

They were pretty tough, those ladies; they had to be. They were part of a tough world, and a very tough Theatre. They endured things which would send their modern counterparts screaming from the stage door. They were part of a profession—or calling—which had no claim to respectability (and which may have been none the worse for that). In their lives, they reflected the manners and customs of their times. Yet, amongst the crowd of women fair and frail, there gleam the rays of those who were chaste and constant. Some were women first and actresses afterwards; in some the mixture was equal; and in a small sprinkling the actress transcended everything else.

It has not been possible to give the story of them all. It must, perforce, be a selection; not always of the most famous, not always of the best-remembered but, it is hoped, always of those who, down the centuries, built up the tradition of the English Stage, which they, the first of their sex to do so, trod in equality with men.

I have tried, most inadequately perhaps but very sincerely, to present a portrait gallery of those wonderful women who are the foundations of such glory. So, in this book, it is "Ladies First."

April, 1952.

PRELUDE

The Fabulous Days

THERE really was a time, and it was not so long ago, when the phrase "Ladies First" was in constant use. Many such phrases were just platitudes, or even jokes, getting a laugh because of the antithesis which the words actually implied. But not "Ladies First"—that was absolute fact. Ladies did come first. No man with the slightest pretension to being a gentleman—and in his heart every man is quite sure he is a gentleman—ever disputed or doubted it. There was probably that tiny minority of irreconcilables who found their pleasure in being in the opposite camp on all occasions, but even they, who scorned to be gentlemen, would have had to bow to the custom of ladies being first in public, whatever they might have done in the privacy of their homes. Had they done otherwise, scorn would have withered them and even violence might have overtaken them.

Fifty years ago, no man would have gone out of a door ahead of a lady. He would, moreover, have been most active in getting to that door and holding it open for her, whether he knew her or not. No man in a public vehicle would have remained seated whilst a lady stood. It was a point of honour. And it made no difference if she was plain or past her youth. There might have been a brighter and more ingratiating smile, a slightly deeper bow for a young and pretty woman, but—"Ladies First." No man would have remained seated whilst conversing with a lady who was standing. He rose and did not resume his seat until she was seated, or gave him such permission. Even then, he saw to it, before he sat down again himself, that her chair was properly adjusted and that she had all she wanted. No man would have dreamed of wearing his hat in the presence of ladies. He raised it when they just passed by, but if there was a stop for conversation he would hold it in his hand for some moments before putting it on again. Some old diehards did not cover their heads again, in the presence of ladies, until requested so to do. In the street, no man walked on the inside of a lady; he always took the outside, the side of the kerb. And no woman accompanied by a male carried her own parcels. That was a man's job. "Allow me," he would say; and she allowed him to burden himself. Strange to say, he did not mind.

At table, ladies were not only served first but always had the titbits: the liver wing of a chicken was a woman's prerogative and she never had the dark meat. Permission was always sought before a cigar or cigarette was lighted, and for a time no men smoked when ladies were present. Pipes were always taboo, unless at home. Gentlemen in shining "toppers" held umbrellas over the heads of ladies when caught in a shower of rain, sacrificing their own vulnerable headgear with stoicism. The lady must not get herself or her finery wet. Sir Walter Raleigh's chivalry was the standard. Also, the lady must be helped in or out of any vehicle; even on a staircase an arm was proffered. And despite what the melodramas said, the man always paid when it came to bills, refreshments, meals, fares or the like. No man would have allowed a woman to stand him a dinner or a drink, unless he were a guest in her own house.

All this may be, probably will be, regarded by the younger generation as a lot of foolish affectation and time-wasting courtesy. But it was not so. It was sincere. There was no question in any man's mind. It was always "Ladies First."

Indeed, women ruled the world, even if today they may not think so. They were supreme, they were the bosses. The little girls were taught from their cradles that men existed for the purpose of being their slaves, their breadwinners, and their luggage porters. They were taught that their ultimate achievement was Marriage so that they would have a slave completely of their own. That was Woman's destiny.

Little boys were taught that women must be respected, revered and that ladies always came first. They accepted this without question. But they usually revolted in the case of their sisters.

They knew them too well: there was too much familiarity, too much equality. Yet these boys were taught the superiority of women even in their nursery days for it was legendary that they, the boys, were made of slugs and snails and puppydog tails in contrast with the sugar and spice and everything nice which went, allegedly, to the manufacture of their sisters. There it was in black and white, in the nursery-rhyme books and vouched for by Nannie. Later, the boys found out that this idea had taken hold and that other people's sisters were indeed made of those delectable ingredients that had by some unaccountable means been omitted from the mixture which formed their blood relations. Their own sisters were presumed, therefore, to be the exceptions which proved the rule.

Petticoat government was at once a sneer and a verity. Women ruled from behind the Throne, just because they were women. Chivalry set them on a pedestal. Gallant knights fought each other for a prize from the Queen of Beauty. They wore her tokens on their helms, they upheld her honour and beauty against all comers. Knights-errant roamed about looking for a damsel in distress so that they could kill the recreant who oppressed her. The highest order of Chivalry in this land—the most coveted order in the world—was founded on a woman's accessory garment, a garter. Earls might be belted, knights gold spurred, but the garter was supreme. It was feminine; it belonged to the superior sex.

And yet women were called "the Weaker Sex." Whilst this was generally physically true, it was a very clever move on the part of women to foster the idea. It awoke all the better instincts, the protective sense, in the male. Woman must be kept from the evil things of life—the grossness, the storm and strife, the battle for existence. It was man's job to protect her. A woman had no rights. She did not need them. She was omnipotent by merely being a woman. Had man for one moment regarded her as an equal, she could well have fended for herself. And, in those days, she knew it.

So she cultivated the feminine arts; she preserved modesty, chastity, beauty. At least, she did so outwardly. She knew the value of concealment. When Ladies came first there was no such exhibitionism as is seen today on every beach and by every swimming-pool. No masses of feminine flesh were exposed to the rays of the sun, with pristine whiteness turning to parboiled pink and then angry sullen red. No lady, taking the sun, exposed all her physical drawbacks, nor tried to enhance her charm by oiling herself like a railway engine.

When Ladies came first they enhanced their charms by veiling them. Their legs were not common property for anyone to view but, strange to say, their complexions were mostly their own and did not come out of jars and bottles. Yet they had a complete armoury wherewith to subjugate the male and keep him on tenterhooks of suspense, thereby ensuring his enslavement. They were women and they behaved as women. Their object in life was the subjection of the male; and they succeeded.

Yet, when they married, they had no legal right to property, no income of their own. But it was a dull woman indeed who did not hold the purse strings. Those who were, after marriage, cheated by their husbands—cads, of course—suffered through their own fault. Their descendants today are swindled in just the same way, legal rights notwithstanding. Throughout History, so long as men regarded women as something different from themselves, women had power and used it. They got men important posts, they swayed governments, they put men into high places and often toppled them out too.

Men were conscious of their subjugation though they never admitted it openly. They knew and they feared the power of women. That was our reason for the establishment of clubs in which men took refuge and from which women were excluded. There men had a stronghold in which they could please themselves, do as they liked, keep their own secrets, and let their masculine selves have a real fling. There are few such strongholds today. Even when there were, the feminine influence managed to infiltrate. Many of the quarrels and resultant duels were about women. Not even in his exclusive club was a man quite safe.

When Queens sat on the Throne, this country always added lustre and greatness to its history. The Queens not only reigned, they really ruled, for men were inspired to render service and excelled themselves. They were much more malleable and less obstructive than they would have been to a King, a mere man anyway.

If proof is wanted that women ruled men when they were not

regarded as equals, Western civilisation supplies it. Left to themselves, men tend to become primitive. They get untidy, they don't shave, they live in conditions which women would not tolerate but which men find quite pleasant. It is the women who civilised men. Now, in these days of equality, men are nothing like so spruce and well turned out. They are slipping back. . . .

Man is naturally polygamous, and that, we have learned, is a barbaric state. Various causes went to establish monogamy, but it was the women who really clinched it. As one of a mass of wives and concubines they had little chance of getting their man under control. Even a man's chief wife had much competition with which to contend. Women felt that, in a state of polygamy, they did not come first. So they fought against it, and in the more enlightened parts of the world, or what are regarded as such, they won. A man might be master of the house, but the woman became master of him.

In the days when Ladies came first, Woman was the inspiration of most poems and a multitude of songs. She was glorified; she was an angel; she was semi-divine; she was a goddess. She was SHE, the unpredictable, the desired. There was one very popular ballad which epitomised the position. It glorified womanhood and motherhood together. Men sang it and believed it. It was called "Queen of the Earth" and ran thus:

QUEEN OF THE EARTH

(Man's Guardian Angel)

An angel in all but name is she
O'er life her vigil keeping,
Whose wings are spread, o'er each cradle bed
Where the hopes of earth lie sleeping.
The Heroes that vanquish amid the strife
And write their names on the scroll of Life,
Have fought for the fadeless laurels of fame
To lay their crowns on her sacred name.

Wide as the world is her kingdom of power,
Love is her sceptre, her crown and her dower,
In every heart she has fashioned her throne,
As Queen of the Earth she reigneth alone.

An angel in all but name is she
'Mid scenes of shade and sorrow,
She weaves through each night, a ladder of light
That leads to a bright tomorrow;
She launches each life on the sea of Time
And guides each helm to the far-off clime,
Her pinions of love are spread in each sail
Till she casts the anchor within the vale.

Wide as the world, etc.

H. L. D'Arcy Jaxone.
Music by Ciro Pinsuti.

There were hundreds of similar songs about women and about mothers. They were always angels and charmers. Mothers alone had a whole library of songs. Nobody wrote about poor old Father. There was a song, it is true, called "Daddy," a piece of vast sentimentality, but Daddy only got his chance because Mummy was dead. Nowadays songs are about pistol-packing Mommas, strawberry blondes and girls whose hair hangs down in ring-a-lets and who are of the roving kind. Songs now tend to be more about places than about women—which goes to show. But these are the days of equality.

Yet, even in those fabulous days, there was a leaven working. There were women who wanted their Rights. Those rights included a vote. They were not content to see men doing all the fighting, handling all the big jobs, and keeping women out of the hurly-burly. They were not content with marriage as the ultimate ambition.

They did not sweep the board at first. But quite early on they showed their hand. A Mrs. Bloomer started a campaign for wearing bifurcated garments. Women were to shed their shackling skirts and to show that they were as good as men, inasmuch as they could wear trousers. What this proved was never clear. This business died, partly from ridicule, from women as much as men, and partly because the garments were not attractive. All that remained was a word in the language—bloomers—which always got a laugh. That word afterwards became synonymous with a bad mistake, a "frightful bloomer." So it was. When bicycling became a fashionable craze a few women wore bloomers, but they never caught on. How the shade of Mrs. Bloomer must chuckle! It never dawned on any of them—it does not now—that the wearing of trousers by women was mere plagiarism and that such things were worn habitually by women in the Orient, who were slaves of the harem and had no equality at all. Women so keen-witted and adroit when it came to female fashions—although the leading creators of female fashions are men—did not succeed in evolving a nether garment which could challenge masculinity and remain feminine at the same time. They have not done so yet.

Women got into Commerce, however, by means of machinery. It was the typewriting machine which gained her a foothold. At first she was not very welcome. She was still treated with respect but she was never admitted to the inner circle. She exercised a repressive tendency in the world of men. No secretary-typist of the fabulous days would have dreamt of going into a bar or a pub and "knocking back a beer," nor would any of her male colleagues have thought of inviting her so to do. She still came first, she still had to be respected. Men did not swear in her presence, nor tell risqué stories; women were not supposed to know about such things. Hardly any women smoked, and never in public. To do so was "fast," and by a paradox the ladies who were fast were not the ladies who came first in the eyes of men.

Still, women wanted equality and emancipation and after many years and a great world war they got them. They did not realise that equality meant that men would henceforth treat them as equals and not as superior people to be respected, served and given first consideration. Maybe they did not care—maybe they do not care. They wanted to enter the professions and now they have succeeded in that. Yet, even in the fabulous days, there was one profession which they had already entered and it should have warned them of what was to come.

For in that profession—the Stage—they stood on equality with men. There they enjoyed equality and there they certainly did not come first, even when they arrived—and they were a long time arriving. For into the English Theatre they came very late. In that queer democracy which exists in the Land of Illusion they at once took their place beside and as equals of men.

Now, the Theatre has its roots in religion and in religious ritual priestesses performed rites which might be classed as theatrical performances, for they impersonated the goddesses who were being worshipped. It was acting of a sort, although it was miming and was not done to provide amusement. Women also played a large part in the rhythmic dancing and chanting in honour of Dionysos, from which the Greek Theatre grew. But it was a man who invented the art of acting, one Thespis. When the great Greek dramas arrived, women found no place in this new and, in Greece, exalted profession. The immense roles in the tragedies were all played by men. It is not even certain if women were allowed in the Chorus. There were women musicians, dancers, and entertainers, but no actresses.

When Rome rose in might and co-opted the Greek Theatre as she co-opted Greek culture, she debased both. The Roman stage had actresses, mostly pantomimists or mimes, for the art of satiric mime was very popular in Rome and extremely obscene as well. These actresses—if they can be so called—were classed as prostitutes, and indeed it was that stratum of society from which they were drawn. True, the craze to act affected even women of rank. But it is hoped that they performed as amateurs—in every sense. The actresses or women performers of Rome were a debased lot, just as the rank of actor was of the lowest. One or two actors of supreme ability earned great wealth and were given status, but the standing of the actor was beneath the contempt of well-born and respectable people. Truly the ladies of the Roman stage were not ladies who came first, except for one of them, who became the Empress Theodora. Historians, contemporary and otherwise, have not dealt too kindly with this lady. None the less, she appears to have been a remarkable woman indeed, and, in the course of many good works, tried to improve the lot of the members of what had been her calling. She made it possible for a woman who had appeared on the stage to attain on marriage the standing of a legal wife—from which she had hitherto been barred.

The Christian Church was the open foe of the Roman Theatre. The Early Christians desired to see this sink of iniquity wiped off the face of the earth. In the end, the Theatre was closed down, and its performers scattered to the four points of the compass to earn their living as best they could, as strolling minstrels, musicians, mimes, mimics, acrobats and tumblers. The Romans did nothing to help them. But a large number of them rather remarkably embraced Christianity, which had ruined them, and the Church took them under its charitable cloak and did what it could for them, but not as actors and actresses.

The Theatre, with its players, went into eclipse. Except for the Greek period, the Theatre has always been the most persecuted of all the Arts. Nobody has done much in the way of persecution of singers, musicians, painters, poets, sculptors or even authors, except when they have been politically inclined. But it was anybody's and everybody's job to persecute or humiliate the players. Yet the Theatre, because of the strength latent within it, has steadfastly refused to die. Outcast, outlawed, harassed, tortured, starved, degraded, with no home and no standing, it has always managed to hold on. The deterrent has not yet been discovered which can stop an actor or an actress from acting. No other calling so completely absorbs its followers. Members of other trades and crafts can sometimes forget them, but the actor —never. On or off the stage, he is what he is. And that is how it should be. That is why the Theatre has survived.

It was a queer irony of fate that the Theatre was recalled from outlawry by the very force which had sent it there. The Church, dealing with mass illiteracy, had to appeal through the eye. It did so, indirectly, by ritual. It did so, directly, and after a considerable lapse of time, by plays. Thus the Miracle, Mystery and Morality plays were born. True, most of the actors were monks, but it is an amazing fact that a very early and most successful dramatist was a nun. She was, indeed, the first woman playwright and she was a German. Her name was Hrotsvitha, a Benedictine nun of Gandersheim. She lived in the middle of the tenth century. A woman of some breeding, she had entered the church to escape a distasteful marriage. She wrote several plays and they were successes. There has been much dispute as to whether they were actually her work or whether she was used as a cloak, but there seems a reasonable foundation for belief that she did write them. It appears she had an urge to write and it was a study of the works of Terence which put her mind to writing plays. She wrote several and they seem to have been not only good but funny and exciting. One of them even had a scene in a brothel. They were enacted by the nuns, and maybe Hrotsvitha played herself and probably produced them, so far as that sub-art of the Theatre was then understood. But she became famous and her plays endured. So over a thousand years ago there was a woman dramatist and nuns who acted. However, women did not appear in public for many years to come.

But the Church resurrected the Theatre. The first enclosed building in this country in which a play was performed, and to which the public was admitted on payment was—rather surprisingly—at Dunstable. There in 1119 a monk named Geoffrey presented a play based on the life of St. Katherine. The saint was played by a man. Details as to charges of admission are not available, but doubtless there was some such payment, or a collection, for the benefit of the Church, otherwise why was the performance not given in the open air? That small theatre with its monkish manager made history and also set a tradition which endured. For it was burned down as so many playhouses have been burned down since. Its manager retired to a cell of his own free will (there were members of the calling he founded who did the same later but not in a voluntary manner). His incursion into theatre management did him no harm; indeed it may have done him good and made him better known, for he became Abbot of St. Albans, and his name is writ large in the history of that lovely and ancient foundation.

In the public performances of the Mystery, Miracle and Morality plays the actors were either amateurs, or semi-professionals who received a payment for their acting and then resumed their normal business. There were no actresses. Naturally the vogue for the Theatre started by the Church encouraged secular plays, as was only to be expected. Let one management today score a success with a particular line of entertainment and its competitors will quickly join in the trend. So when the Church showed that crowds flocked to see their religious productions, which attracted as much for the acting and show value as for their message, private enterprise sprang up and plays were staged which frankly sought to amuse. This did not please the Church, which at once rounded on the young and growing Theatre and tried to destroy it again.

The priests gave the players a very bad time. Meanwhile, ladies did not come first; nor indeed anywhere at all. Women's parts were played by boys or by men. The players had no fixed abodes or playhouses. They were strollers with nearly every man's hand against them, for even those who flocked to see them perform treated them with the utmost suspicion. They were outlaws; they were denounced by the Church; they must be disreputable.

Strange how that belief lingered down to modern times. Its echo is faintly heard even today. Not so long ago a man had to see a company playing in a little town in South Wales. Arrived there he went to the so-called hotel, and asked for a room. He was so ill-advised as to say he was connected with the Theatre. There was no room vacant, he was told. He sought out the manager of the theatre, a small enough place, and asked what he was to do. "Go back to the hotel," he was told, "and wait until the person you saw is not at the desk and then say you are a commercial traveller." He did this and a room was forthcoming at once. That was in 1913. And everyone knows the story of a railway porter who in answer to an enquiry said the train in the station contained "Fish and actors," to which an old actor, putting his head out a window, rejoined "Laddies, you might have put the actors first." Typical too is the one about the child in a small Midland town who seeing a company arrive at the station rushed home to her mother, shouting "Ma, take the washing off the line—the actors are coming."

The early actors travelled in groups and no doubt their womenfolk went with them. They were persecuted by every authority. Only when they became part of the retinue of a great noble and wore his livery did they enjoy any sort of immunity. Even then, when outside his jurisdiction, they had a pretty rough time. It is commonly supposed that in those days all actors were classed as rogues and vagabonds. That is not quite the case. Directed specially against them were all sorts of byelaws which they had to obey. If they failed to do so in the smallest respect, then they could be, and were, dealt with as rogues and masterless men.

While civic authority hounded them physically, the Church fulminated against them spiritually. One divine at Paul's Cross, angry that the Theatre which Burbage erected in Shoreditch in 1576 drew greater crowds than did his sermons, openly told his congregation that the actors and their plays were the cause of the Plague. For, he argued, the cause of the plague was Sin. Plays and players were both sinful, so the cause of the Plague was the Theatre, its plays, and its players. The civic authorities everywhere—and nowhere worse than in London—chased and chivvied them from pillar to post and finally drove them to Southwark, beyond the City Council's jurisdiction.

But when so many hands and voices were against them, the Theatre and its people always had one friend. The Crown of this country always stood by them and encouraged them. Richard the Third was the first king to have his own company of players. Unfortunately, the Theatre reciprocated scurvily by making him the arch villain of drama for all time. No matter who assailed it, our monarchs were always staunch supporters of the Theatre. Henry VIII loved it and adored appearing in masques; he wrote good songs and sang them too. Elizabeth bestowed on every branch of the Theatre the greatest favour, and under her it blossomed like a rose. Never were greater days. That odd character James I, who had not much in his favour, nevertheless liked masques and witnessed the first performance in this country of what was to be the *Commedia dell'Arte*, which the English seized and turned into Pantomime. In his reign the blossom which Elizabeth had fostered grew stronger still. And a very notable event occurred although there were still no actresses. A Queen—James I's own wife, Anne of Denmark—appeared in a masque at the Palace of Whitehall. She played as an amateur of course, but she created a sensation by wearing a very short dress, or, at any rate, a dress much shorter than was customary and showed far more of her legs than was usual. This memorable event in the history of the Theatre is one all too seldom recorded and it is good to find it in A. Ll. Matthison's delightful book, *Bullocks at Stamford Fair*.

Under Elizabeth and James I our drama reached a height it has never achieved since, with Shakespeare, Ben Jonson, Marlowe, Kyd, Ford, Beaumont and Fletcher and so many more pouring out plays. Theatres were springing up like mushrooms and the populace adored to go to the play. Here were plays, here was great acting. Here were parts, monumental and classic as those by Sophocles, Euripides, Aeschylus, Aristophanes, treading on each other's heels. Yet there were no actresses, still none of those wonderful women whose magic and mystery have been for centuries now one of the most enticing and powerful elements of the Theatre. All the women's parts were still played by men or mostly by boys. It seems incredible in these times to imagine such a thing, yet so it was. It was not considered right and proper for women to appear: the Church forbade it, the civic authorities would have had them under lock and key in a jiffy. The Protestant Church, if not quite so bitter against the players as the Church of Rome, was still hard enough, and the rapidly growing Puritan element in the country went to lengths that the Roman Catholic Church never dreamed of. It was an offence against morality. Yet a Queen had appeared. In private, yes, but she had done it and crowds of courtiers had looked on and, of course, applauded. There is no record of them coming to any harm from this dreadful sight, although nobody knows what happened to them thereafter.

Then yet another Queen deigned to appear in a Masque. This time it was Henrietta Maria, the wife of Charles I. He, like all the Stuarts, loved the Theatre and it is more than possible that he played in masques as well, with his wife and family. There were constant performances at Court, and on Sunday nights too. Henrietta Maria's performance was on a Sunday night. And that had a great deal to do with the Civil War and the loss of the head of the poor little plucky but misguided King.

What seems so strange today is that the very critical playgoers of the Tudor and early Stuart days accepted and were delighted by the performances of the boys who played the heroines. This is the earliest evidence of that Illusion which the Theatre can create. They knew they were watching boys, they knew that "Juliet," "Rosalind," "Portia," "Hermione," "Desdemona"—all that frieze of wonderful women—were being played by members of the male sex, yet they took them to their hearts and believed in them. Sir Herbert Tree was right when he said that the whole business of the Theatre was Illusion, and the really successful men of the Theatre—Cibber, Garrick, Macready, Irving, George Edwardes, Ivor Novello—knew it and fostered it. Noël Coward's greatest success, *Bitter Sweet*, was pure Illusion. And that is to name a mere handful.

One of the main things today which is publicised as being possessed by the Theatre—and even more so of plays which are presented in shadow form on the screen—is that nebulous thing called Glamour. That comes from the actresses. In the mighty days of the Renaissance, when the surge and wonder of words held an audience entranced, there was no Glamour. But there may have been considerable art and an immense amount of talent to more than make up for it. Those boys held their audiences all right.

Choir boys had played in the religious plays, and the tradition went on. When the secular stage arose, commercialism came with it. The boys were apprenticed to adult actors who trained them and who made a profit out of them. Old Philip Henslowe, whose pious diary and account books (peppered with the exclamation "In the name of God, Amen" before so many items of profit and loss) are such a help to theatre historians, makes frequent references to these lads. He paid seven shillings to an actor who had trained a lad named James Bristow and he charged the boy's appearance against the company with which he performed—they worked on a kind of commonwealth basis then—at 3*s.* a day or, at least, 3*s.* for every time he acted. It would appear that a good boy actor playing women's parts could earn as much as 15*s.* a week, which was big money then. Edward Alleyn, the creator of Tamberlaine, had a boy actor in his company named Pig. That does not seem a good name for the bills—not that they had any—and little is otherwise known of him; perhaps it was a nickname. These boys were bound for seven years, beginning when they were ten years old, but the indentures were personal ones and not so tightly binding as those of their brother apprentices of the crafts and guilds. At seventeen they became their own masters.

The Puritans, who would never have allowed actresses and who were very prone to seek out evil, found plenty of that in the boy players. They made many insinuations and charges, some maybe well grounded. But their main complaint was that the tenets of Deuteronomy were being broken by these boys and their wearing of women's clothes: "The woman shall not wear that which pertaineth unto a man and neither shall a man put on woman's garments, for all that do so are abomination unto the Lord thy God." One wonders what chance Deuteronomy has today?

Anyway, the Puritans hated the Theatre with a deep loathing. Prynne in his *Histriomastix* (1634) charged Henrietta Maria and her court ladies with appearing in a pastoral masque. Disregarding the fact that the accusation was true, the Queen had him whisked into the Star Chamber, fined £5,000 and put into the public pillory with his ears cut off. That not being enough, he was thrown into prison for life. Such was the punishment for the vile offence of saying that a woman—royal at that—was an actress! But that episode did much to fan the smouldering fires of revolt. Prynne was released from durance as soon as Parliament could get him out. They could restore his freedom, but they could not give him back his ears. However, that ear-lopping was the prelude to the loss of a Royal head. . . .

It is a pity that the names of so few of the boys who created those wonderful classic roles are known. Some of them are remembered as full-fledged actors. There was James Nokes, whom old Downes, the famous prompter of Drury Lane and the Duke's Theatre, mentions together with a man called Angel, William Betterton (younger brother of Thomas Betterton, the great actor), Mosely and Floid. All these had been boy actors who had remained in the profession.

William Betterton was drowned whilst swimming in the Thames at Wallingford. He had played Aminta in *The Maid of the Mill* with success. Mosely was addicted to gagging, and Floid appeared to specialise in such characters as "bawds and whores." But of this quartet, James Nokes was the most famous. He became one of the leading comedians of the day. His elder brother, Robert, an excellent performer, also gained fame. James was a born actor. His facial expressions were marvellous, and when arousing the most laughter in his audience he always maintained a complete and utter solemnity. His appearance was greeted with loud applause and cheers which he appears to have entirely merited. He played all sorts of comedy parts—old fops, stupid old husbands, old widows and hags. One of his very biggest successes was Sir Martin Mar-all in Dryden's play of that name. In another play current French fashions were made fun of, and Nokes so far excelled himself that the Duke of Monmouth gave him his own sword and belt as a reward, buckling it on the actor personally. Nokes kept it until his dying day. His first entrance in this play threw the King and the Court into roars of laughter, but the French nobles present did not like it at all. This happened at a Royal Command Performance at Dover in 1670. Nokes continued to play women's parts from time to time. So good was he as Lavinia's Nurse in Otway's *Caius Marius*, a version of Romeo and Juliet set in Roman days, that he earned the nickname of "Nurse Nokes." His last appearance was as a woman, Gremia, in Shadwell's *The Amorous Bigotte* at Drury Lane in the Spring of 1689. He also ran a toy shop, which he called a "nick-nackatory." He died in 1696 leaving a good deal of money.

Samuel Pepys had the luck of being in at the transition stage of the Theatre when women were first appearing and men were still playing as women. He saw the most famous of all the boy actors in both kinds of roles. That was Edward Kynaston, a name immortal in Theatre history. Of him Downes says in his *Roscius Anglicanus*, "Mr. Kynaston acted Arthiope in *The Unfortunate Lover*; the Princess in *The Mad Lover*; Aglaura; Ismenia in *The Maid of the Mill* and several other women's parts; he then being very young made a complete female stage beauty, performing his parts so well, especially Arthiope and Aglaura, being parts greatly moving compassion and pity, that it has since been disputable among the judicious, whether any woman that succeeded him so sensibly touch'd the audience as he." That is high praise, coming as it does from so experienced a man of the Theatre. Downes evidently subscribed to the idea himself. He may have been a die-hard who resented the intrusion of women into the Theatre but his opinion is upheld by other excellent judges. That is where Sam Pepys came in. He records a visit to the old Cockpit in Drury Lane in 1660 to see *The Loyal Subject*, "where one Kinaston, a boy, acted the Duke's sister, but made the loveliest lady that ever I saw in my life" and nobody would accuse Samuel Pepys of being unobservant where female charms were concerned. In the same year Pepys saw Kynaston again (although he prefers to spell the name with an "i") in Ben Jonson's *Epicoene*: "Among other things here Kinaston, the boy, has the good turn to appear in three shapes, first as a poor woman in ordinary clothes, to please 'Morose'; then in fine clothes as a gallant and in them was clearly the prettiest woman in the whole house, and lastly as a man and then likewise did appear the handsomest man in the house."

Colley Cibber saw Kynaston play many parts but never in petticoats. He had the highest opinion of his acting powers. He records the story that Kynaston was so handsome that ladies of fashion and quality prided themselves on taking him with them in their coaches to Hyde Park, in his theatrical habit (presumably his women's clothes). It was Kynaston who all unknowingly was one of the means of opening the Theatrical Profession for women. He it was who kept Charles II waiting for the curtain to rise because, before he could play "The Queen" he must be shaved very close. This diverted the Merry Monarch, but also gave him furiously to think. Cibber gives Kynaston pages of praise in his *Apology*—the best theatrical autobiography ever written—and draws a very clear picture of him. He was a man of wit and intellect as well as being a good actor. He was instrumental in the merger between Drury Lane and the rival Duke's Theatre, to the benefit of Drury Lane, which he represented. His stage career stretched from 1659 to 1698 and to the last his good looks remained. Even when past sixty his teeth were as complete, as white and as even as when he played girls. He always had a rather measured, stately step, brought about by wearing long skirts. Cibber thought, however, that he lingered a bit too long when past his prime. And, of course, Kynaston who had been a "leading lady" lived to play opposite real leading ladies.

There is one point about the boy actors which seems to have escaped notice. Shakespeare had the habit of letting his heroines disguise themselves as boys. Portia, Rosalind, Viola and Imogen all do it. Was it just the need of the story and dramatic contrast? Was it just coincidence? Or was it Shakespeare's uncanny stage sense that made this the case? For they all have their best scenes and chances when wearing boy's clothes. Did he know and realise it gave the boys a better chance?

Be that as it may, the Ladies now wait in the wings, panting to strut and fret their hour, eager to break their bondage, and find their liberator in no less a person than King Charles II, that great lover of ladies himself.

CHAPTER ONE

The Ladies Arrive

IN the seventeenth century the English stage, although leading in everything else, still lagged behind the Continent in the matter of actresses. The English Theatre was pre-eminently a masculine affair whereas women had invaded that domain overseas. They had arrived in Rome as early as 1565. There were women in the *Commedia dell' Arte* and the first woman who could lay claim to being a great actress was an Italian, Isabella Andreini, who first appeared on the stage in Florence in 1578. France had an actress as early as 1545, but she was a rather isolated instance. Women first entered the genuine theatrical profession there about 1610.

But tradition-bound England still tarried. Travellers to France and Italy saw women on the stage and returned with various reports. Some liked them, some scoffed, some utterly condemned. It was largely a matter of personal taste and a regard for tradition.

One traveller from England, visiting Venice in 1608, commented disparagingly on the Venetian theatres as compared with those of London. But he put this on record: "Here I observed certain things that I never saw before, for I saw women act, a thing I never saw before, though I have heard that it hath sometimes been used in London and they performed it with as good grace, action, gesture and whatsoever convenient for a play as ever I saw a masculine actor." And why not, pray? But he had been misinformed about this thing having happened in London. If so, it had never been recorded, which, of course is inconceivable.

But the day was not far distant when a London audience was

to see the astonishing spectacle of women on the public stage, acting on equality with men. It was a memorable occasion in more ways than one. Nobody present was likely to have forgotten it, especially the players—and the feminine portion thereof.

It happened during the reign of the ill-fated Charles I, and was made possible because his wife was a Frenchwoman. A French company, complete with actresses, came to London. They appeared at the Blackfriars Theatre and London playgoers gazed with astonishment which turned to horror at the sight of women actually performing in public in plays, at women doing men's work. Evidently quite a shameless and immoral lot of hussies! The Puritan blood was strong and conservatism even stronger; this was not to be tolerated. It was not English, it was a foreign idea. No need for the watchful Prynne to rise in wrath: London audiences did it for him. A man named Brand, an eye-witness, reports "Glad am I to say that they were hissed, hooted, and pippin-pelted from the stage, so that I do not think they will soon be ready to try the same again." He hoped that the Lord Chamberlain had had his attention drawn to this disgraceful episode—by which he meant the actresses, not the hooting and apple-throwing—and that proper action would be taken. There was no need. The French company bundled off home, cursing the English barbarians. Prynne designated the actresses as "monsters, unwomanish and graceless." Yet there was growing up a section of society who really did not regard it as very wrong for a girl to play Juliet instead of a boy, and it is quite possible that girls were mixed with the boys on occasion, with few if any knowing the difference. So, though the Continent had actresses, when Cromwell closed down the Theatres it was only the actors who were out of work.

Though the playhouses were closed, theatregoing still held on surreptitiously and, most suitably, at one of these semi-private performances, given by the stalwart, indomitable and unconquerable champion of the Theatre Sir William Davenant, in his own private residence, Rutland House, there happened what might have been the first appearance of an English actress on the English stage. The woman broke two laws, that which forbade women from acting and that which forbade plays being given at all. She appeared in *The Siege of Rhodes*, a sort of dramatic opera which Davenant himself had written. It was an afternoon in September, 1656. Curious observers might have noticed that rather more people were passing down Aldersgate Street than usual and that they were rather more fashionably dressed than the customary passers-by of that neighbourhood. But those who did so would have needed very sharp eyes, for the ladies and gentlemen in their smart clothes who were making their way to Rutland House wore sombre black Puritan cloaks over their finery to allay suspicion. They were going to break the law and see a play. Maybe some of them did not know they were also going to see a woman appear in a play, but for those who did, it added to the excitement. Somebody might have let the cat out of the bag and there might be a clatter of hooves, a thump of marching feet and Cromwell's men might bang at the door and arrest them all. But nothing like that happened on this occasion. There, in the big room, was a small stage only about fifteen feet in depth and eleven in width on which this species of opera was to be performed. But there was another marvel. There was an innovation, a backcloth depicting the harbour at Rhodes painted in proper perspective and there were what we now call "wings." This was indeed a gala day and wonder piled on wonder.

The excitement in the front was as nothing to the excitement behind scenes. But the high point of the proceedings was the fact that a woman, instead of a man in woman's clothes, was actually going to be the leading lady. She was Mrs. Coleman, the wife of the man who had composed the songs and the music. She had found it quite impossible to learn either words or music, so she took the script with her. When the cue came—"This is Ianthe, the Sicilian flower"—on she went and history was made.

A woman had for the first time played a part before an audience which had paid to see her, in the very centre of the city of London. She did not give a very smooth performance, one imagines, but she got through and she read her recitatives and sang her songs from the music. Ianthe had opened the door—the women had received their first call—and the stage was set. But Mrs. Coleman, described as "fat and pleasant," cannot lay claim to the title of first English professional actress. She was an amateur. She played in a private house, albeit to a paying audience, and she did not really act, she sang. Queens had done almost as much before.

But Mrs. Coleman, a most respectable married woman, had acted and the heavens had not fallen. What obstacle now barred women from their first step towards equality and the freedom of the Profession? Only the little matter of the Commonwealth, it would seem.

There had been rumours of a woman appearing before at the Fortune Theatre in 1610, in a play by Middleton and Dekker called *The Roaring Girle—or Moll Cutpurse*. Presumably the character was drawn from life for the author in an epilogue promised that Moll herself should appear if the public wanted her to do so. There is no record that this ever took place. Had it happened, it would have justified the quip so beloved of the late lamented Sid Field "What a performance!" There is little doubt that a riot would have ensued. But the affair remains wrapped in mystery—and myth.

Despite the appearance of Ianthe—she told Mrs. Pepys afterwards that she could not have played the part without the book—four long years were to elapse before the Ladies tasted their first full draught of freedom and equality. Much had to happen first, and the most important—the thing which made it possible—was the restoration of King Charles II. The theatres reopened even before he resumed the throne—the moment weak-kneed Richard Cromwell, "Tumbledown Dick," took his final fall. But as yet there were still no actresses. The old order carried on.

Back with King Charles II came that merry gentleman, fitting friend and Groom of the Chambers to the Merry Monarch, Thomas Killigrew. He and his friend Sir William Davenant, who had so nobly supported the Theatre during Cromwell's time, soon got a document from Charles II which made them jointly the dictators of London's Theatreland. Joining hands, they presented a joint company, and then they parted, with a gentleman's agreement, strictly kept during the lifetime of each, not to tread on each other's toes nor to interfere in business with each other. Killigrew went to the King and got his famous Charter to raise a company of players. He was granted even more, a Charter which enabled him to erect the first Theatre Royal which the world had ever known—Drury Lane Theatre, and thus he stabilised the Theatre and ended its persecution for all time. This was a tremendous achievement.

Charles II loved the Theatre and was delighted to oblige his friend Tom Killigrew, one of the few men who had any influence with him. But he had also given the matter some thought, being a very astute and observant man. He did not want to upset the large portion of his subjects who were Puritan at heart, but he did very much want to be able to see good plays again, properly acted. He had been a great playgoer in his exile abroad. There he had seen actresses. Here in his own kingdom, there was none. The King proposed to redress the matter. His action might be illegal, but was he not the king riding on a wave of popularity and loyalty? He could make innovations. And he did. To Killigrew he granted a Charter—which still exists—in respect of his Company, which was to be the King's Own Company and which made Drury Lane the King's house, and in it he put two revolutionary provisions. Here is the actual extract in the spelling of the period, from that document which is now cherished at Old Drury. . . .

> And for as much as many playes formerly acted doe conteine severall prophane, obscene and scurrilous passages, and the women's part therein have byn acted by men in the habit of women, at which some have taken offence, for the preventing of these abuses for the future, wee doe hereby strictly commande and enjoyne, that from henceforth noe new play shall be acted by either of the said companies conteyning anie passages offensive to pietie or good manners, nor any old or revived play conteyning any such offensive passages as aforesaid, untill the same shall be corrected and purged by the said masters or governors of the said respective companies from all such offensive and scandalous passages as foresaid: And wee doe likewise permit and give leave that all the woemen's part to be acted in either of the said two companies for the time to come may be performed by woemen soe long as their recreacones, which by reason of the abuse aforesaid were scandalous and offensive, may by such reformation be esteemed not onely harmless delight, but useful and instructive representations of humane life, to such of our good subjects as shall resort to the same. . . .

So there it was in black and white, written by hand on parchment, bearing the King's own seal in green wax and signed by Howard, the Lord Chamberlain. Not only had women been invited into a profession hitherto barred to them, but they had been admitted at the command of His Majesty the King himself. . . . That was a triumph indeed.

The King had played his cards well. He made the whole thing look like a purification crusade. He forbade licence on the stage and he forbade the shaking of his subject's morals by seeing men dressed as women, pretending to be women. Old Rowley was no fool. He got his own way. He wanted the actresses and he was soon to show his deep and abiding interest in them. And, of course, according to the Charter, he did it for the sake of morality. He commanded and "enjoyned" that plays should not be licentious. Well, we know all about the Restoration comedies. Nevertheless it must be remembered that, in those plays, the Theatre fulfilled its task of holding a mirror up to nature and so reflected the life of its times, together with its customs and its morals. And that is still the fundamental job of the Theatre.

It must have been a strange place, that womanless Theatre, incredible to those who are part of the Theatre of today. No women there, no leading ladies—it would not be right to add no temperaments, for actors can "throw them" as well as actresses and often better. It must have been a place of strange Illusion. The actors must have been men of talent who could summon up their passions for the scenes with outpouring of love and undying affection for other men, some of whom were probably not shaved so well as Kynaston on the famous occasion when the King had to wait. It says a great deal for their talent and for the illusion which they created. It must have been necessary for them to lose themselves in their parts, otherwise they must have felt like a lot of Principal Boys in Pantomime, making love to Principal Girls, but in reverse. Yet the Theatre flourished and reached a very high point of artistic excellence so far as acting and plays were concerned. It was at its farthest point from Realism. It had no scenery as we know it. It had rudimentary lighting, it had no audience discipline. The public invaded the stage—as they did, even more so for that matter, when women joined "The Profession." There was noise, disorder, and always that tendency to pelt the players to register disapproval.

The Elizabethan Theatre was even cruder. Yet there are people today who want a return to it. These Elizabethans believe that plays should be staged and acted in the Elizabethan manner. But you do not find them advocating the abolition of actresses. They stop short there. What they really want is a semblance of the Elizabethan manner, with all the modern improvements as well, plus the actresses. So it comes to Illusion again, which of course is Theatre. Today the Theatre without actresses is quite inconceivable. Indeed a play with an all-male cast is a news story. Sometimes such shows succeed, which is yet another news story. The same applies to the all-women casts.

But let us return to good King Charles who was demanding actresses. Both Killigrew and his friend Davenant knew he must have his way. They probably wanted it too. Though there is no record of what the actors said about it. Things were in a turmoil anyway. A man called Sir Henry Herbert, Master of the King's Revels, claimed that what the King had granted to Killigrew and Davenant was really his perquisite. As soon as they ordered one thing, he ordered another. The poor actors were so harried that between the rivals they did not know how they stood. They petitioned the King. He handed them over to his Lord Chamberlain. Peace was restored at last and the egregious Herbert did pretty well out of the settlement. What was really hurting him was his loss of fees for licensing plays. So maybe all that trouble, coming so soon on top of the reopening of the Theatre and the terrible years of hardship preceding the Restoration, made the players ready for any surprises which came along.

They were so anxious to work that they would have swallowed anything. But one can imagine the amount of grumbling which went on in "The Cock and Pie," "The Black Bull" and other inns and taverns around the Theatres. Women to act? What next? Was it not hard enough to get a living without this fresh competition? One can imagine some outraged actor saying "The public won't stand for it, my boy, they won't stand for it. They never have and they never will. It's not—it's not English. Remember what happened to those French hussies? They pelted them off. They'll do it again—if the women dare. What? are we to rub shoulders and share our Art with a lot of raw amateurs who may be no better than they ought to be?" And one can conjecture some pretty lewd jokes.

There would also be another school of thought—the modern

school—and there is little doubt that Thomas Killigrew would be leading that. They would say that one must move with the times: France had actresses, Italy had them, even Holland and Germany, and no harm had come of it. They regarded the invasion of the women not merely as a novelty, but as an attractive novelty. They realised it would bring fresh patrons to the Theatre: the gallants would flock to see the girls, would pay them court, would run after them, would talk about them, would spend money on them, and thus it would all be good for the Box Office. They saw that more, and not less, employment was likely to accrue when women took the stage and that the Theatre would be a far more attractive place. And they also knew that women playgoers would crowd to see these most daring of their sisters who would thus flaunt themselves in the public eye—that they would appraise, condemn and concoct and impart much scandalous gossip. And gossip—the more scandalous the better—is good publicity. It would be good for the Box Office in every way, they reckoned; and, of course, they were right, for the Theatre, then as now, was commercial and may it always remain so.

It was Killigrew who engaged and presented the first actress to appear in public in this realm. How he found her, how he selected her, whether he had auditions from many eager women and girls who wanted to act and thus to become equals with men, nobody knows. It is almost certain that she was not brought to his notice by her agent, since that form of theatrical parasite (no offence is intended, but all agency is to some extent parasitic) had not yet come into being. There might have been influential recommendation. A great man might have whispered, a noble might have made a suggestion, or the lady herself may have made the direct approach. However, Thomas Killigrew, a Cornish gentleman of cockney birth, courtier, actor, man of the Theatre, playwright, soldier, Court Official and ex-Ambassador, took the plunge. He had not yet built Drury Lane. But he had his company of His Majesty's Comedians. Two years were to elapse before they entered their own Theatre Royal. Meanwhile they were quartered in an odd little place—a tennis court converted into a playhouse—Gibbons Tennis Court, in Vere Street, Clare Market, long since swept away by the construction of Kingsway and Aldwych. The massive structure of the Stoll Theatre now covers the site on which such vivid theatre history was made. But it was in that little place on Saturday, December 8, 1660, that the First Actress appeared.

The news had gone around, of course. The modish portion of the town was agog with it. The fops, the wits, the gallants in and around the eating houses and places of public resort were chattering about it. No doubt it was a matter for discussion in the brothels which abounded thereabouts, in Lewknor Lane (now Macklin Street, off Drury Lane) and in Whetstone Place, just behind what used to be the Holborn Empire. Doubtless, too, it was discussed by the more staid citizens of London, for the City folk were staunch playgoers. Killigrew was a good showman and would know what to do. The bills would go on the posts—just a few of them; some would be pushed under doors and fixed under knockers; and they would be handed around in the taverns.

And, of course, even the Court at Whitehall would be agog, for had not the King himself commanded that this step be taken? Swarthy Charles probably smiled to himself and had his anticipations. Doubtless Killigrew told him who was to be the daring female first to make her debut, though there is no record that he ever came to see her. But otherwise her name was kept a complete secret. If those bills were posted, her name was not on them—and not one bill has survived. So well kept was the secret of that first actress's name that even now there is no absolute proof of her identity. It is all based on hearsay.

Anyway, it was a terrific occasion and caused great excitement. The little place was thronged. Killigrew had selected *The Moor of Venice* as the vehicle, a version of Shakespeare's *Othello* with a good many liberties taken, the lady playing Desdemona. Maybe Killigrew knew it suited her; maybe she herself asked for this role.

Killigrew had commissioned Thomas Jordan, a popular and expert writer of such things, to prepare a prologue to be spoken before the play, to put it plainly before the audience—to warn, to admonish, and also to entreat. It is not known who spoke that prologue; it might have been Killigrew himself. Whoever did it doubtless had an excited, eager and attentive audience, which was not always the case.

The Prologue struck the right note. It gave a good reason for this astounding innovation in that most conservative place, the Theatre, and it drew attention to some of the anomalies which this new and revolutionary idea would banish. Fortunately that prologue has been preserved and here it is as spoken in Gibbons Tennis Court—the Vere Street Theatre—on December 8, 1660—two hundred and ninety-two years ago, as these words are written.

It was officially called "A Prologue, to introduce the first Woman that came to act on the Stage, in the Tragedy called *The Moor of Venice*":

I come unknown to any of the rest
To tell the news; I saw the lady drest
The woman plays today; mistake me not
No man in gown, or page in petticoat
A woman to my knowledge, yet I can't
If I should die, make affidavit on't
Do you not twitter, gentlemen? I know
You will be censuring; do it fairly though.
'Tis possible a virtuous woman may
Abhor all sorts of looseness, and yet play;
Play on the stage—where all eyes are upon her;
Shall we count that a crime France counts an honour?
In other kingdoms husbands safely trust 'em;
The difference lies only in the custom.
And let it be our custom, I advise
I'm sure this custom's better than Th'excise,
And may procure us custom; hearts of flint
Will melt in passion, when a woman's in't.
But, gentlemen, you that as judges sit
In the Star Chamber of the house—the pit
Have modest thoughts of her; pray do not run
To give her visits when the play is done,
With "Damn me, your most humble servant, lady"—
She knows those things as well as you, it may be
Not a bit there, dear gallants, she doth know
Her own deserts—and your temptations, too.
But to the point;—in this reforming age
We have intents to civilize the stage.
Our women are defective and so sized
You'd think they were some of the Guard disguised;
For to speak truth, men act, that are between
Forty and fifty, wenches of fifteen;
With bone so large and nerve so incompliant
When you call Desdemona, enter giant.

We shall purge everything that is unclean,
Lascivious, scurrilous, impious or obscene;
And when we've put all things in this fair way
Barebones himself may come to see a play. . . .

And so the play went on. The tension can be imagined by any playgoer who has been to a big first night just before the entrance of the leading player, or of a great visitor from overseas. This was a real theatrical sensation. There has probably been nothing comparable to it since, except that night at His Majesty's Theatre in April, 1914, when Mrs. Patrick Campbell uttered the hitherto unmentionable word "bloody" publicly on the stage. The word was never used in polite conversation then—nowadays it would appear to be seldom absent—but the sense of surprise and shock which ran through the theatre cannot have been less than that occasioned by the novelty of a woman appearing in a play for the first time.

It is interesting to conjecture what her own feelings must have been as she waited for her cue and made her entrance. The most experienced actresses dread first nights, fearing them mentally and physically. How, then, must this woman have felt, who was playing a part that would make theatrical history?

The Epilogue was a piece of extreme tact . . .

And how do you like her? Come, what is't ye drive at?
She's the same thing in public as in private,
As far from being what you call a whore
As Desdemona injured by the Moor;
Then he that censures her in such a case
Hath a soul blacker than Othello's face.
But, ladies, what think *you*? For if you tax
Her freedom with dishonour to your sex
She means to act no more, and this shall be
No other play, but her own tragedy.
She will submit to none but your commands
And takes commission only from your hands.

It must have been an anxious moment for everyone concerned when the end came to that play. Audiences then were far from well behaved. They would have been passing audible comments all the time, calling out to each other, quizzing the actress, and making a good deal of noise. No doubt at the end the daring lady had plenty of male visitors. On the whole, the women seem to have supported her, for playgoing ladies then had to be pretty broadminded and not squeamish.

It seems to have been a success all round, and the woman herself seems to have acquitted herself well. Whilst as has been said there is no positive identification there is practically no doubt, despite a few rival claimants, that she was Mistress Margaret Hughes.

Margaret Hughes can rest secure in her claim because old Downes, that famous prompter, was of the opinion that she was the Desdemona at the Vere Street Theatre. Margaret joined the company—the original company—at Theatre Royal, Drury Lane, played many good parts and played them well. If she was not the best actress of her time, at least she was the literal leading lady of the Stage. After a time at the Lane she went to its rival, the Duke's Theatre, which Davenant had founded. There she had a triumph, not so much of acting as of conquest. For she enslaved the fancy of no less a hero than Prince Rupert himself, the fierce, dashing Cavalier who led the charges of the Royalists against Cromwell's Ironsides, a man of great character and courage. In a time and a Court given to intrigue, amorous adventure and loose morals, he had always held aloof from such things, devoting himself, when peace deprived him of further martial glories, to the study of Chemistry. The eyes of Mistress Margaret Hughes shone more brightly and were not so elusive as the much sought philosopher's stone, and her neat, dainty figure had more charm than the shapes of the retorts and alembics. So the dashing Cavalier fell for her very heavily, to the great delight and astonishment of the entire Court and the open amusement of the King.

Rupert lavished gifts upon his charming actress. Amongst other trifles, he presented her with Brandenburgh House, a magnificent mansion in its own grounds at Hammersmith, which cost him £25,000, an immense sum then. She led him a fine dance; she tantalised him; she lured him and then refused him her favours, until he was well nigh frantic. Then, she named her price—and got it. In return, she gave him a daughter, who was named Ruperta. The daughter did well for herself and married Lieutenant-General

Howe whom she survived. Her descendants live today. Ruperta died at Somerset House in 1740 wealthy, happy and generally respected.

Mother Margaret, who was a dashing, flashing brunette, almost gypsy in her colouring, died in 1719. She had amassed a considerable fortune for she acquired all Rupert's wealth. He died a poor man, leaving only his jewels to pay his debts. Margaret proceeded to squander what she had received from her Princely lover and took to gambling. When Rupert's jewels were disposed of by lottery, Nell Gwynne bought a pearl necklace for £4,520, a proceeding which Margaret Hughes considered an insult . . . which it was probably meant to be. Before she met Prince Rupert, Margaret was said to have been Sir Charles Sedley's mistress and Pepys once had the pleasure of kissing her in the Green Room: "A mighty pretty woman, and seems—but is not—modest." Trust Samuel for summing them up. It is to be feared that Mistress Hughes hardly lived up to the character assigned to her in that famous Prologue.

There is no knowledge of how many women aspired to become actresses when this profession was first thrown open to them. But Pepys chronicles on January 3, 1661, "To The Theatre, where was acted *Beggar's Bush*, it being very well done; and here the first that ever I saw women come upon the stage." One could have expected more from such a lover of the Theatre and ardent admirer of the ladies. The Theatre was probably the Vere Street one, where Killigrew reigned. Naturally Sir William Davenant, Killigrew's partner-detached, followed suit at his theatre, in Lincoln's Inn Fields, another converted tennis court. And his ladies will very shortly come into the story. At that place, in April, 1662, Davenant revived his *Siege of Rhodes* which had so very nearly produced the first actress at the somewhat surreptitious performance under the Commonwealth. Another Prologue makes mention of the women on the stage:

> Hope little from our poet's withered wit
> From infant players scarce grown puppets yet
> Hope from our women less, whose bashful fear
> Wondered to see me dare to enter here
> Each took her leave and wished my danger past
> And though I came back safe and undisgraced

Yet when they spy the wits here, then I doubt
No amazon can make them venture out,
Though I advised them not to fear you much
For I presume not half of you are such.

That was obviously spoken by a woman and it was done before the second half of the play. The play—or opera, for it partook of the nature of both—was performed in two parts, on successive days.

There is little doubt that the lady who spoke that prologue was Mrs. Davenport. Pepys saw her although he does not mention her by name. There is a lot of confusion over this lady, both in dates and statements by various authorities, but there is no dispute about the eminence in theatrical annals of Mrs. Davenport who played Roxalana for Sir William Davenant. When Davenant opened his theatre in Lincoln's Inn Fields—no trace of it remains now—he lived in a house next door and he saw to it that the four leading ladies of his new chosen company lived there too, so that he and his wife could keep them under observation. According to the invaluable Downes, prompter (he would now be stage director) of that Theatre, and later of Theatre Royal, Drury Lane, those four leading ladies were Mrs. Davenport, Mrs. Saunderson, Mrs. Davies and Mrs. Long.

So in the Spring of 1662, Davenant had four leading ladies ready to take the stage, besides four of lesser rank, whose names were Mrs. Ann Gibbs, Mrs. Norris, Mrs. Holden and Mrs. Jennings. Here were eight actresses all considered worthy of public appearance by Davenant, a real man of the Theatre, a much more careful and painstaking manager than his friendly rival, gay Thomas Killigrew of Drury Lane, and a man who may have been an illegitimate son of Shakespeare himself, which would account for much.

Now those ladies deserve attention. Foremost amongst them must stand Mrs. Davenport, not because she was the best actress —Mrs. Saunderson was that—but because she caused the greatest excitement and stir.

When Davenant opened his theatre with a revival of a re-written version of his *Siege of Rhodes*—into which he had introduced Roxalana, a new character, Mrs. Saunderson (sometimes spelt Sanderson) played Ianthe. The new part was played by Mrs.

Davenport. She was a success. Pepys saw her and he ranks her as the best of the rest whom he saw later play the part. She was a very early star actress indeed and she has her own special niche in history because she was nearly the first actress to marry—or so she thought—into the Peerage.

Aubrey de Vere, bearer of an old name and title, the twentieth Earl of Oxford (he held the title himself for seventy years, too) fell in love with this charming and pretty actress. Ignoring the sage advice offered in that prologue by Jordan, that it was possible for a woman to be an actress and be virtuous too, he laid siege to her. He was not a nice character. He led a wild life, kept a house filled with brawling drunken companions, brawled himself and when in his cups, which was most of the time, was given to slashing about with his sword, irrespective of the safety of those around him. He pursued the fair Davenport relentlessly. But he found himself up against it. No amount of temptation would make that lady consent to be his mistress, or, as they said in those days, his Miss (hence the adoption of the married title by all actresses to prove their respectability). She was adamant. She spurned his protestations, his promises, his expressions of constancy. For her, it was marriage or nothing. How much of this was virtue and how much the desire to be Countess of Oxford must always be open to doubt. It is unlikely that she loved the man, but she may well have loved the title.

Anyway, so adamant was she that Aubrey de Vere realised that without marriage he could not possess her. He had not the slightest intention of making her his wife, but outwardly he surrendered. He offered marriage and was accepted. He took the precaution—or so it seemed—of swearing her to secrecy because there would be a terrific scandal over the marriage of an Earl to an actress. But it should be arranged, it could be arranged, he assured her. And arranged it was. She met the Earl, who had the parson handy, and the wedding ceremony took place in the lady's own lodgings. She had refused his written promise of marriage, by the way, being content with not less than the ceremony. The parson brought one witness, and the other was a friend of the bride's. It all seemed fair, square and above board. The happy couple went off for a honeymoon, the Earl delighted at having at last won his desire; his lady delighted that she was now a real

Countess. But after a short while the Earl's ardour cooled off. He laughed at his bride's demands that she should now be presented at Court and ride openly in the carriage bearing her arms. Then the truth came out. The "parson" was one of the Earl's trumpeters and the witness a drummer. Both had completely vanished. It had been no wedding at all: the "Countess" was still Mrs. Davenport.

Roxalana was thunderstruck. She stormed, she railed, she cajoled. The Earl laughed and went on drinking. She threatened suicide and he threw her out of the house. She took her claim to the highest Court; she appealed to the King. The King, to his credit, granted her an audience. She threw herself at his feet and poured out her tale. The King had her case adjudicated and gave judgment for her as to an income, to be paid by the wicked Earl, of £500 a year. With that she had to be content. It was a goodly sum. She gave birth to a boy who was christened Aubrey Vere, after its father, in 1664, and she never returned to the stage. Many lamented her. Downes has a characteristic reference: "About this time the Company was much recruited having lost by death Mr. Joseph Price, Mr. Lovell, Mr. Lillisdon, Mr. Robert Nokes, Mr. Mosely, Mr. Coggan, Mr. Floid, Mr. Gibbos; Mrs. Davenport, Mrs. Davies, Mrs. Kennings, etc. The last three were *by Force of Love erept the stage*." But apparently Mrs. Davenport bore up. Pepys who missed so little, reports that being at the play he "saw the old Roxalana in the chief box, in a velvet gown, as the fashion is, and very handsome, at which I was glad"! Pepys always held that she was the best Roxalana he ever saw.

Mrs. Davenport, who was born in 1642, had good looks, vivacity and talent. She certainly had an exciting, if short, career. Much of the confusion about her arose because there were other actresses of the same name at Drury Lane shortly after. But Roxalana, even if she never became a Countess, bore herself better than her blue-blooded seducer. He may have been Chief Justice in Eyre, Lord of the Bed-Chamber, Privy Councillor, Colonel of the Royal Regiment of Horse Guards, Lord Lieutenant of the County of Essex and, later under William III, Lieutenant-General of the Forces and a Knight of the Garter. He may have been buried in Westminster Abbey when turned eighty. But he was no gentleman.

CHAPTER TWO

Ladies of Lincoln's Inn

THE Ladies of the stage who pass in review across these pages will not only be those whose names are famous. There are, down the years, a host of women who brightened the stage and the lives of playgoers with their art, who have never had their full meed of recognition. Maybe they had it when they lived, but the career of the actress is ephemeral and all too often her name dies with her, or at most, with her generation. As the people who beheld her pass away one by one, the last flicker of her existence goes with them, and she ceases to be a name, save to those who delve into theatrical records, and such records are scanty enough.

All these women did something to build up their profession, even if they only had one moment of flashing triumph, even if they only added to the scandalous news of their day. Ask people which old-time actresses they can recall. The vast majority will mention Nell Gwynne, better remembered as an orange girl (which she may never have been) and as a King's mistress than as an actress; Mrs. Siddons, justly one of the great immortals; and Ellen Terry. That is about all the man in the street will know offhand. Some may recall Lady Bancroft, though one official of the B.B.C. had never heard of her or her illustrious husband, and just a few, Mrs. Kendal, though those who remember her grow fewer and fewer. More people will recall Sarah Bernhardt, who was French, but who really became a great star when she played at the Gaiety in London.

Yet there have been so many women who lit our stage, so many women who in their own way have helped to make our

Theatre the place of fascination and brilliance that it is and always has been. All too few have received their measure of remembrance and it is the purpose of this book to distribute a little Rosemary here and there.

With the advent of the professional actress, Killigrew started training the ladies who were to grace his Drury Lane Theatre. Easygoing and careless in many ways, he set great store by training. He it was who founded the first school for acting, which he called the Nursery and where he trained children for the stage. Not much came of it, for the method of making the poor little mites perform the current and classical plays in the manner of their grown-ups was not very commendable. Nevertheless, Killigrew, having selected his ladies, lost no time in grooming them.

Meanwhile, Davenant had opened his theatre in Lincoln's Inn. While he still had some men who played women's parts, he also had those actresses whose names have already been mentioned. It has been stated that he made the four leading ladies live in his own house; yet despite his care and his trouble, three of them were—by Love—"erept the stage."

Mrs. Davenport has made her bow. There remain Mrs. Saunderson, Mrs. Davies, Mrs. Long, Mrs. Ann Gibbs, Mrs. Norris, Mrs. Holden and Mrs. Jennings.

Let us take the least first. Little is known of Mrs. Long. She was the mistress of the Duke of Richmond, but she appears to have been a good actress as well. If she got her chance by influence, as is likely, she maintained it by talent. Downes gives her considerable praise, notably for her performance of Mrs. Brittle in *The Amorous Widow or the Wanton Wife* written by Betterton. He says "She performed it so well that none equalled her but Mrs. Bracegirdle." That is praise indeed. Mrs. Long had quite a list of parts to her credit, ranging from the comedy of the time, to classics and to Lady Macduff in *Macbeth*.

Another great accomplishment of Mrs. Long was that she broke new ground. Very soon after women were permitted to become actresses one of them donned male attire and appeared in it in public, on the stage. It was in a play of Shirley's called *Dulcino the Grateful Servant* and it was Mrs. Long who took the sensational step. The town rang with it. For years men had appeared in women's clothes; now women had dared to reverse the roles. It was all most intriguing to the gallants and not less so to the ladies. Mrs. Long, in her breeches, was a furore. Breeches were "box office" when worn by women and, curiously enough, have remained so ever since. Not so much today, perhaps, when familiarity has bred contempt. Nevertheless the legs of the Principal Boy were the main attraction in Pantomime for many years, to say nothing of those of the other female members of the company who appeared in symbolic male attire.

Downes has a comment on Mrs. Long's Dulcino: "being acted by Mrs. Long, and the first time she appeared in Man's habit, prov'd as Beneficial to the Company, as several succeeding new plays." Thus was woman's emancipation on the stage virtually sealed.

Thereafter, actresses loved to play what became known as "breeches parts" and instances will be met with frequently. It may be that Mrs. Long was not the first woman to wear breeches on the stage, since the confusion of dates in records carelessly kept, casts a doubt on the matter, but unquestionably she was the first to be successful in that attire, and so set the pace. There followed productions by all-women casts, women playing all the male parts in male attire. Pepys witnessed some. But Mrs. Long put the seal of attractiveness on it, and leading ladies down the ages followed her example. Good King Charles had allowed actresses to appear because, so he said, many deemed it immoral that men should appear in women's clothes. There was no outcry of horror when the boots—or rather the breeches—were on the other legs.

Mrs. Norris was an actress of a different type. She appears to have been thoroughly respectable, or, at least, a married woman, for she was the wife of an actor of the same company and a player of small parts. They lived in Salisbury Square, off Fleet Street, then part of London's Theatreland—and handy for the ill-famed Alsatia—and there a was child born to them. This boy also became an actor and did very well. In 1699 he played Dicky—Jubilee Dicky—in Farquhar's successful comedy *The Constant Couple*, and rose to be one of the leading comedians of his day. Mrs. Norris was a character actress. She was probably plain, which was another inducement to respectability in Restoration times. She played the characters of old gypsies and splenetic and awkward old Dowagers, and was very popular in them.

She provides an early example of back stage "temperament." She quarrelled with somebody over something—it may have been the management, it may have been a sister actress or brother actor —anyway, she flounced out and left the company. She was an established favourite at the time, but she had the worst of it because on May 7, 1681, a letter came to Betterton, the leading man and general manager of the company, which read "I did yesterday signify unto you that Mrs. Norris should be received into your Company againe And this is to explain that order; That it is His Mates (Majesty's) pleasure that shee reconcile her selfe unto her adversary, and submit herselfe to the rules and Government of the Company and upon this condition shee is to be admitted as formerly." And of course she was. The King took real interest in his theatrical servants, it appears. Or maybe, he took the shortest road to peace.

Mrs. Holden, not a remarkable actress, was the daughter of a publisher, John Holden, who issued Davenant's works. So her position is easily explained. Betterton, by the way, had been apprenticed to Holden in his youth. In the main she played very minor roles, but on one occasion she distinguished herself—unwittingly—and caused the loudest laughter ever heard in a playhouse up to that time. Downes says that "London Bridge at low-water was silence to it." The play was *Romeo and Juliet* and Mrs. Holden, playing Count Paris's wife, had the misfortune to drop, not an "h", but a vowel. The occurrence is described in *Roscius Anglicanus*. It is sufficient to give her immortality. The version was Howard's adaptation.

Mrs. Ann Gibbs was of surprisingly respectable parentage for the stage of that time. Her father, Thomas Gibbs, was a Proctor and Public Notary of Norwich. She married Thomas Gawdy of Claxton, Norfolk, in 1662, and, on his death, she became the wife of Thomas Shadwell, the dramatist and Poet Laureate. She was a good actress and a versatile one.

Miss Jennings did not aspire to much, playing minor parts and was not long before the public. She was one of the "erept."

There remain two of the best and most sparkling, the one a real actress, a woman of quality, and a claimant to be the first great actress this country produced, the other a piece of sparkling mischief, gay, unmoral, a flash of merry looseness and laughter. The first was Mistress Saunderson, the second Mary, or Moll Davies.

Mary Saunderson shone like a good deed in the naughty world of the Restoration stage. Why she decided to become one of the earliest of actresses, and where and how she got her preliminary training, if any, is not known. But there she was at Lincoln's Inn, one of Davenant's leading ladies. It is likely, indeed it is certain, that she was the first woman to play, with the exception of Desdemona, the great Shakespearean tragic roles. And she played them magnificently. Betterton was the star actor and indeed one of the finest this country ever had. So, of course, she played "opposite" to him. They fell in love and the news spread abroad like wildfire, adding piquancy to the situation and probably helping the box office. When Betterton played Hamlet she was the Ophelia.

Betterton's *Hamlet* is historically famous. He packed his theatre with the pushing, jostling mob of noisy playgoers common to that period. But Betterton held them; he compelled attention; he had that irreverent, usually inattentive mob in the hollow of his hand. Even the orange girls were still and listening. The whole audience stood—or sat—immovable. And then came the Ophelia. There was a stir, a thrill: here were a couple of lovers in real life to play unhappy lovers on the stage. Mistress Saunderson completed the spell. She had personal beauty, a lovely voice and perfect diction, she understood what she was about, and she was an actress. She had virtue and a character of sweet simplicity and honesty which shone through all she did. Those two, playing together, reacting to each other with perfect give and take, shed enchantment over the whole house. Samuel Pepys, hard to please but enthusiastic when satisfied, was of the opinion that Betterton was the best actor in the world, and he was probably right. His opinion of *Hamlet* on that occasion was that it was "the best acted part ever done by man." And Mrs. Saunderson was not far behind with her Ophelia. Downes's comment is "No succeeding Tragedy for several years got more Reputation, or Money, to the Company than this."

Mrs. Saunderson also played Juliet not to Betterton, but to Mr.

Harris, who had been the Horatio of the *Hamlet* production. He was young, handsome, debonair and a good actor, but as Romeo he had not the touch of greatness which belonged to Betterton. But the Juliet thrilled them and was enthusiastically acclaimed. Betterton played Mercutio and consolidated his claim to be the best ever. It was in this production that Mrs. Holden blotted her copybook so badly by a mispronunciation.

There were two versions of *Romeo and Juliet* then, the proper and tragical one, and another devised by James Howard, who kept the star-crossed lovers alive and provided a happy ending. In their desire to please the patrons, the company at Lincoln's Inn played the two versions on alternate days, and *Romeo and Juliet* held the stage for quite a while.

Betterton married Mary Saunderson on Christmas Eve, 1662. He was then about thirty and she about twenty-five. She is described as a Spinster of St. Giles, Cripplegate. Her mother, a widow, gave her consent to the wedding, and a witness was Enoch Darrick, a grocer of St. Pancras. Thus they became the very first married couple to play leading parts opposite each other on our stage, the first of a long line of distinguished husbands and wives who have done so since, which includes the Trees, the Kendals, the Wallers, Charles Wyndham and Mary Moore, the Bensons, the Martin-Harveys, Fred Terry and Julia Neilson and the Bancrofts.

Amongst the parts played by Mrs. Betterton, as she can now be called, were Portia in *The Adventure of Five Hours* by the Earl of Bristol and Sir Samuel Tuke, which was played for fifteen consecutive days, a very long run; Bellmont in *Maligni, the Villain*, which ran for ten days, "with full houses to the last," records Downes (Betterton himself was not in it, the leading role being played by Price); Queen Catherine in *Henry VIII*, which was another big hit, running for fifteen days; Graciana in Etherege's *Love in a Tub*; Aurelia in *The Cutter of Coleman Street*, which ran for a week of big business; the Duchess of Malfi in Webster's great play, which packed the theatre for eight days and became a most popular stock tragedy; Roxalana in the tragedy *Mustapha*, which received a Royal Command to Court; Mandana in the tragedy *Cambyses* which had six days of success; and amongst many other parts Lady Macbeth; a test part if ever there was one.

Here is what Colley Cibber says about that. She was "so great a mistress of nature that even Mrs. Barry [to be met later] who acted the Lady Macbeth after her, could not in that part, with all her superior strength and melody of voice, throw out those quick and careless strokes of terror, from the disorder of a guilty mind, which the other gave us with a facility in her manner that rendered them at once tremendous and delightful."

That description is an inspired bit of dramatic criticism which only an actor could have written. "Those quick and careless strokes of terror"—that is, of course, how Lady Macbeth should be played. She whose almost masculine mind was tortured beyond her woman's strength, whose woman's intuition saw always the threat of doom in the shadows beyond the door, in the darkness of the night, and who even in sleep could find no oblivion from the constant probing and stabbing of a mind diseased. To have seen Mrs. Betterton's Lady Macbeth must have been as thrilling as seeing her husband's Hamlet. Pepys records the sweetness of Mrs. Betterton's voice. The theatrestruck Sam saw her in *Henry the Fifth* and gives her full marks, but he did not like *Mustapha* very much and considered it beneath the talent of both the Bettertons.

For thirty years Mrs. Betterton shone on the stage, an example to those who came after her both in personal character and in her great and varied talents. Here was no one-line specialist; here was a woman who could play any sort of part that might come her way. The towering figures of tragedy were hers, and so were the gay rattling puppets of light comedy. She played so many parts, a large number in plays which were of the moment and long since forgotten but none the less acceptable at the time. She was an amazingly quick study; she could learn her lines with rapidity and accuracy and was never "out," as Pepys puts it, or in stage parlance, "dried up." And since play followed play with bewildering rapidity, that was an achievement. Whether in tragedy or comedy, she and her husband filled the house. She even played Greek tragedy, being very successful as Jocasta in *Oedipus*, a part in which many have failed. She sang in Opera with distinction—her Ianthe enchanted them all—and she could also dance divinely; every sort of dance from a stately measure to a rousing, speedy country jig. Truly, Mary Saunderson—Mary Betterton—has every claim to be considered our first Great Actress.

Not the least of the personal tributes to her was penned by Colley Cibber, who said "She Was a Woman of an unblemish'd and sober life, a faithful companion to her husband and his fellow labourer for five and forty years."

Mrs. Betterton was not overstrong and she left the stage, or gave up regular playing in 1694 or 1695. She was granted a pension of £2 10*s*. 0*d*. a week from the management, out of compliment to her great husband.

The couple were devoted all their life long. No scandal attaches to either of them. Their married life was a model, though they were opposites in outlook and characteristics. Betterton was energetic, optimistic and lighthearted, whereas Mary was thrifty, thoughtful and serious-minded. They adored each other but to their grief they had no children. When Betterton suffered his reverse of fortune, by entering into a disastrous speculation on the advice of a friend,what did this couple do? Upbraid, revile their well-meaning but unfortunate friend? Bemoan their fate? No, they took that friend's daughter to their home, adopted and made her their own. She was educated and trained for the stage, and finally happily married to a steady and good actor—one Bowman.

Betterton's loss was a staggering one. He had by his own exertions amassed quite a nice little fortune—as fortunes went in his day—which probably included his wife's savings. They accepted their reverse courageously despite Mrs. Betterton's slight tendency to melancholy. Mrs. Betterton never lost her beauty despite advancing years and her talent remained with her. It is a pity there is no portrait of her extant. She undertook the tuition of many of her husband's leading ladies-to-be and she trained them well. It was a signal honour for her when the Princess Anne, afterwards Queen of that name, elected to play the part of Semandra in *Mithridates* in some private theatricals at Court, for it was Mrs. Betterton who was asked to coach her.

Constantly by her husband's side, she must have been very proud of the amazing benefit Betterton had at Theatre Royal, Drury Lane, in 1709. Every player of note appeared. Mrs. Barry spoke a Prologue which Rowe had written, and the amazing sum of well over £500, was raised. His Profession gave him another benefit in 1710 on April 13. This was at the theatre in the Haymarket which Sir John Vanbrugh had built and which had not been a success. It was filled on this occasion to overflowing. But it was a very anxious day for both the Bettertons. He was the victim of a very violent attack of the gout. It was to be his Farewell to the stage: henceforth he and his wife were to live in retirement. That was more her wish than his. But she saw clearly his failing power, how he had surrendered so many of his star parts to younger actors, not because he could not play them with art, but because his infirmity and physical decay were creeping on him. It must have made her sad, for all her life she had loved and taken such pride in him and his work. Now she drew comfort that for a few years perhaps she would have him all to herself and could lavish care on him. He had played only fifteen or sixteen times in the preceding season and his salary had been £4 a week. But they lived in a good house in Russell Street, Covent Garden, well furnished and appointed and kept spotless by the wife. And it was from that house that the old actor must leave to make his farewell.

It seemed doubtful if he could do so. His foot was terribly painful, swollen and inflamed. She may have tried to persuade him not to go or simply to attend and say Farewell. But he would not have that. He must go in glory, he must play his last part as Betterton should play it. It was Melantius in *The Maid's Tragedy*, one of his great roles. So go he would. At last a coach was called and she helped him in. She could not bring herself to go with him, and he, too, preferred to face the ordeal alone. They kissed and she watched the coach drive off, her eyes misty with tears. When he got to the Theatre, he was carried to his dressing room where he put on his costume and managed to get on one buskin, but the other would not go over that swollen foot. His foot was swathed in bandages which he removed in order to wear the buskin, but it was impossible. So he called for a slipper—for play he would. Even the slipper could not fit on to that unhappy foot. He plunged the foot into a bowl of water to try and reduce the size of the swelling. He succeeded. He took the stage and triumphed. Never before in all his long career—he was seventy-five and had been on the stage for fifty-one years—had he won such a success. All his old vigour came back and he was once more the Great Betterton. To an audience which cheered him almost continuously he gave the performance of his life. And then it was over—the curtain fell.

PLATE I

MRS. JORDAN

MRS. YATES

HELEN FAUCIT

MISS FARREN

PLATE II

Top left: MRS. MATTOCKS

Above: MRS. OLDFIELD

MISS POPE

MRS. BRACEGIRDLE

Betterton had retired in such triumph as never an actor had received before and very few have achieved since. But he was ill —very ill—now that the strain was over.

They got him into his street clothes and home to his anxious wife. Perhaps he told her of his triumph and of the very welcome news that they would have Five Hundred Pounds. But she cared little for that. She saw the danger sign, she saw death in the face of her beloved. That immersion of his foot in the bowl of water was fatal. The gout had penetrated to his stomach. Mrs. Barry and Mrs. Bracegirdle, two great ladies of the stage, colleagues and friends of the Bettertons, helped the distracted wife, telling her not to worry and assuring her that health would return. She knew better. She knew her husband as she knew herself. She knew that having left the stage he must now leave her, a greater wrench by far for both of them. And she was right. She never left him day or night until April 28, 1710, the end came. Thomas Betterton, who had said farewell to the stage, said farewell to life and to his wife who had shared everything with him.

He was buried with great pomp and circumstance in Westminster Abbey. But it meant little to Mary Betterton. The shock of her husband's death unhinged her mind. Later she recovered, but for only a little while. The Princess she had coached was now Queen, and the Queen did not forget her. She bestowed on her a pension of £100 a year. But before the chariot of death came to convey her to those shades where her husband awaited her, she was able to make a Will. She left £20 to her sister Mary Head (née Saunderson), her husband's portrait to Mrs. Francis Williamson, and several other small legacies, such as twenty shillings each to Mrs. Bracegirdle, Wilks, Dogget and Mrs. Anne Betterton to buy rings wherewith to remember her. The bequests were to be paid "out of the arrears of that pension which Her Majesty had been graciously pleased to grant her," from such it may be gathered that the Royal payments were not notable for their regularity. But the Theatre rallied to her, of course, and on June 4, 1711, Drury Lane gave her a benefit, when *The Man of Mode* was played "at the particular Desire of several Ladies of Quality for the Benefit of the Widow of the late Famous Tragedian Mr. Betterton."

Her Will was dated March 10, 1712. She must have recovered

her sanity, but she lingered only a very little while. She was looking for her husband, it seemed to those around her, and on April 11, 1712, she slipped away to join him. On the 13th of that month, two years after Betterton had taken that benefit which killed him, their bodies were united in his grave in Westminster Abbey. They lie there yet. . . .

Thus departed the first great actress of the English stage, first of the line of Shakespearean tragediennes—a lovely woman with a lovely character, a devoted wife, and one who remained unstained in a period and a profession which was almost devoid of morals.

Her husband had written, or caused to be written, a History of the Stage. It is a rare book now. It contains one reference only to his wife: "Mr. Betterton, now making, among the men, the foremost figure in Sir William D'Avenant's Company, he cast his Eyes on Mrs. Saunderson, who was no less eminent among the Women, and married her. She was bred in the house of the Patentee, improved herself daily in her Profession, and having by Nature, all the accomplishments required to make a perfect Actress, she added to them the distinguishing Characteristick of a Virtuous Life." That is perhaps enough for the epitaph of Mary Saunderson—Mrs. Betterton.

And now from one extreme to the other, from the pattern of propriety to modish immorality, from faithful wife to wayward wanton. From Mary Betterton to Mary Davies, or Moll as she was universally called. Today, we know of the "Gangster's Moll." This one was a Monarch's Moll.

She was one of those four principal actresses whom Davenant kept under his own roof, or, so far as she was concerned, tried to do so. What a handful she must have been! For she was the incarnation of the spirit of the Restoration, an adept practitioner of "the oldest profession in the world." Probably she was more amoral than immoral. She was a Toast in her day, the idol of the gay sparks, resplendent in their silks, satins, bows, buckles and laces. No doubt she was much loved and gave her favours generously, if not too promiscuously. One of her special claims to fame was that she stood as a rival to Nell Gwynne. Yet Nelly has lived on through time, but who remembers pretty, gay, laughing Moll Davies today, except the historians?

The circumstances of her birth and parentage are not clear.

Pepys says, very bluntly: "It seems she is a bastard of Colonell Howard, My Lord Berkshire." Thomas Howard was the first Earl of Berkshire. But there is a claim that she was the daughter of a blacksmith at Charlton, Wiltshire. Nobody will ever know. She was very young when Davenant took her into his company and she does not appear to have been a good actress. That did not matter. She was a very attractive young lady, with a roguish way. It would seem that she had that extraordinary thing—star quality—about her. Stars are not always the best players, by any means, but they possess some sort of fascination which holds and binds an audience, and Moll Davies had it. She played quite a lot of parts, but Davenant carefully cast her within her limitations. And he always used her, at the end of the entertainment, to come on the stage to announce the play which was to be performed on the morrow. She pleased the audience, no matter what they thought of the entertainment; they always brisked up when she tripped on and she sent them away happy. Nell Gwynne had the same ability. But, also like Nelly, Moll Davies's chief accomplishments were her singing, and dancing. It was through these she rose to fame, notoriety, and a certain amount of fortune.

Her great day was the occasion of the production of *The Rivals*, a play written by Sir William Davenant himself and produced at his playhouse in Lincoln's Inn. According to Downes, it had a very fine Interlude of vocal and instrumental music, mixed with diverting dancing. Mr. Price, one of the players, introduced this and gained great applause. Harris, Betterton, and Underhill were in the cast, and the old prompter records "And all the women's parts admirably acted; chiefly Celia, a Shepherdess, being mad for love, especially in singing several Wild and Mad songs—'My lodging it is on the Cold Ground.' She perform'd it so charmingly that not long after, it rais'd her from her Bed on the Cold Ground, to a Bed Royal." Could anything be put with more tact and neatness? For that evening, or it may have been late afternoon, Moll Davies, in theatrical slang, really "knocked them."

In the audience was a tall, dark, swarthy man, with a rather melancholy face decked with a dark moustache and a sweeping black periwig. He had looked bored to begin with, but the antics of the girl, her grace, her exuberant vitality, her lithe and agile dancing, and her undisguised femininity made the rather sombre eyes smoulder. He joined in the applause with a courtly grace and flashed a smile at the little actress. The house clamoured, and he highly approved—the girl as much as her performance. He was none other than Old Rowley, His Majesty King Charles II, seeing a play and passing in review the ladies whom he had commanded and enjoined should appear thereon. It was an occupation he was finding much to his taste and satisfaction. Moll Davies had caught the fancy of the King. She had danced herself into popularity and sung herself into fame, and she was, although she did not know it then, on the way to her final exit.

And the song which so ensnared the Royal fancy—what was it like? Here it is:

My lodging it is on the cold ground
And very hard is my fare
But that which troubles me most is
The unkindness of my dear.
Yet still I cry "O turn, love,"
And I prythee, love, turn to me,
For thou art the man that I long for
And, alack, what remedy?

I'll crown thee with a garland of straw, then
And I'll marry thee with a rush ring
My frozen hopes shall thaw then,
And merrily we will sing.
O turn to me, my dear love
And prythee love, turn to me,
For thou art the man that alone canst
Procure my liberty.

But if thou wilt harden thy heart still,
And be deaf to my pitiful moan
Then I must endure the smart still,
And tumble in straw alone.
Yet still I cry, "O, turn, love,"
And I prythee, love, turn to me,
For thou art the man that alone art
The cause of my misery.

That was the song which captured the King. At any rate, her singing of the ditty was the cause of the "force of love" which was to "erept her from the stage." Did she sing that song directly at the susceptible Monarch? She would know he was there—all the house, back and front, knew that. Charles always moved about very much in public. There was little of the backstairs intrigue about him. No doubt, whenever he attended a play there was a flutter amongst the ladies just in case one of them might make a royal conquest, a thing to which few of them, except Mrs. Betterton, would have been averse. No doubt Miss Moll shot a glance or two at her king as she sang those most suggestive words, maybe with just a slight emphasis on the matter of tumbling alone in the hay. At any rate she won him.

Not at once was she "erept." She became the King's mistress or she joined the Royal Harem, some time before she left off acting and made a full-time job of it. She played on at Lincoln's Inn and she went with the players when they moved into the Duke's Theatre, which Davenant had founded but never lived to see opened. But she was a source of trouble. She sang her King-winning song in 1664, and she remained for three more years on the stage.

She was a centre of storm and of admiration. Others beside the king sought her favours and perhaps she was amenable. A poet moved to verse lyricised her as follows:

> Who would not think, to see thee dance so light
> Thou wert all air or else all soul and spirits?
> Or who'd not say, to see thee onely tread
> Thy feet were Feathers, others feet but Lead?
> Atalanta well could run and Hermes flee
> But none e'er moved more gracefully than thee:
> And Circe charm'd with wand and Majick Lore
> But none like thee e'er charmed with Feet before.
> Thou Miracle! whom all men must admire
> To see thee move like air and mount like fire
> Those who would follow thee, or come but nigh
> To thy perfection, must not dance, but Fly.

Samuel Pepys thought her wonderful. She even shook his avowed adoration for Nell Gwynne; indeed, of the two, he thought Moll the better dancer. He saw her on March 7, 1666, at the Duke's Playhouse when witnessing a performance of *The English Princess, or Richard III*, "a most sad melancholy play, and pretty good, but nothing eminent in it, as some tragedys are; only little

Miss Davies did dance a jigg after the end of the play, and there telling the next days play, so that it come in by force only to please the company to see her dance in boy's clothes; and the truth is, there is no comparison between Nell's dancing the other day at the King's House in boy's clothes and this, this being infinitely beyond the other." That, from Pepys, is a tribute, for he adored Nelly Gwynne.

It will be observed that both of them, to make effect, adopted male attire. There is a very pertinent note in that entry of Pepys which has a topical touch today: "This day was reckoned by all people the coldest day that ever was remembered in England, and God knows, coals at a very great price." The price of coal at that time was £4 per chaldron!

Pepys nosed out much scandalous gossip about Moll Davies and he gloated on it. His friend Knipp, the actress, told him that Moll was leaving the Duke's House because the King had taken a house for her and had already given her a ring worth £600. Pepys was sorry because he thought no good could come to a State whose King was so devoted to his pleasures. Nell was also in Royal favour at the same time and indeed, the two were desperate rivals, on and off the stage, for the favour of the public and the King. Nell won in the end, but she was not above artifice. On an occasion when she knew the King had sent for her, she invited her rival to tea. Moll, who should have known better, accepted the invitation and also ate largely of chocolates which Nell pressed upon her. She paid dearly for that: for those innocent looking sweets were filled with jalap. Thus was a glamorous night ruined. But maybe Nell reckoned all was fair in love and war.

The King's devotion to and extravagance over Moll Davies was common knowledge, known even to his Queen. Pepys reports on this. He picked up the story at the house of a friend of his wife who related that Miss Davies was the most impertinent slut in the world, and worse, since the King showed her such favour, that Lady Castlemaine was put right out of countenance, and that Moll had another ring, which was worth £700, which she showed everyone and told them all it was from the King.

When Moll left the Theatre the King set her up in a house in Suffolk Street, Haymarket, where she lived luxuriously and in great style. One night she was summoned to the Court to dance a jig at the end of a play. The Queen swept out of the room before the dancer appeared, and it may perhaps have embarrassed the King a little, and then again, perhaps not, because he had brought Moll there himself.

Moll Davies bore the King a daughter, who was called May or Mary Tudor. The girl grew up and married Francis, second Earl of Derwentwater. Their son was prime mover in the Rebellion of 1715, he being a Stuart by blood, and the Pretender being in some sort his cousin. He was condemned to be executed for high treason, as seemed just. The Duke of Richmond, another son of Charles II by Louise de Querouaille, was entreated to present a petition for Derwentwater's life to be spared. The Duke did so, adding a plea of his own to the effect that Their Lordships in Council assembled in the House of Lords would see their way to reject the Petition. Thus did the illegitimate offspring of Charles II treat each other. The House of Lords rejected the public petition but granted the Duke's. Derwentwater's head fell, and he went to his lodging in that cold cold ground of which his female progenitor had sung and perhaps because she had done so.

Moll Davies did not retain the royal favour very long. Perhaps Nell Gwynne's trick had something to do with it. But whilst she was in favour the King was not above making eyes at her in public for all to see. Pepys saw this himself at the Duke's Theatre whilst *Macbeth* was being performed. "It vexed me to see Moll Davies, in the box over the King's and Lady Castlemaine, look down upon the King, and he up at her, and so did my Lady Castlemaine once, to see who it was, but when she saw Moll Davies, she looked like fire, which troubled me." It probably troubled Lady Castlemaine more. That was in December, 1668. The girl who had sung and danced her way into royal favour lived in Suffolk Street from 1667 to 1676. She had lost her favour by then, but was in receipt of a pension of £1000 a year. She moved to St. James's Square where she remained until her death in 1687. She did not hold the King's love as did her one time rival Nell Gwynne. But she was a colourful woman, who played her part on and off the stage and so wrote a page in theatre history.

Such were the Ladies of Lincoln's Inn Theatre, the first troupe of actresses to gain the public favour. Of course they were a scandal, whether in breeches or skirts. It would seem the men preferred them in breeches. But they had their antagonists, too. Evelyn attacks them in his *Diary*, saying that he seldom now went to public theatres "as they are abused to an atheistical liberty, fowle and undecent women now (and never till now) permitted to appear and act, who inflaming several young noblemen and gallants, became their misses and some their wives, witness the Earl of Oxford, Sir R. Howard, Prince Rupert, the Earl of Dorset and another person greater than any of these, who fell into their snares to the reproach of their noble families and ruin of both body and soule." But it was not quite as bad as that. Those gentry would have acquired "misses" anyway, actresses or no. It is, however, significant of her standing that even Pepys always speaks of Moll Davies as "Miss."

That little theatre in Lincoln's Inn made history in many ways. Here the first great actress dominated the stage in the person of Mrs. Betterton, and here Mrs. Long in breeches set them in a furore. Here for the first time scenery was used in the presentation of plays in public. Sir William Davenant was a wonderful man. Not only was he the Theatre's saviour during the Commonwealth, going to prison for his pains, but he was a pioneer of the Drama and of Opera. Lincoln's Inn Theatre stood in Portugal Row, to the south of Lincoln's Inn Fields from 1660 to 1743, and no trace remains today. It had originally been Lisle's Tennis Court. According to Davenant's Charter it was the Duke's Theatre, a title later borne by the theatre he started but never lived to see finished elsewhere. It was a most popular house, but it caused a lot of trouble, too. The audiences were unruly, and duels often took place in the pit whilst the play was being performed. Men quarrelled and fought not only with swords but with fists. Yet it was the first theatre to have the honour of a Royal Visit, and the monarch so honouring it was of course Charles II. It has gone now without trace and all too few memories abide save to those whose business it is to recall them. Not the least of those memories must be vested in that first company of actresses of the English Theatre—the Ladies of Lincoln's Inn.

CHAPTER THREE

Ladies of the Lane

THOMAS KILLIGREW'S ladies have an outstanding place in the history of the Theatre for they were the first to adorn the stage of the Theatre Royal, Drury Lane. "The Lane," as it is affectionately called, was the world's first Theatre Royal; it was also the playhouse that was to give stability to the English Theatre. Some of them, among whom was Margaret Hughes, the first woman to take the stage in this country, had appeared for Killigrew at Gibbons' Tennis Court, the Vere Street Theatre, but they really entered history on that famous day —May 7, 1663—when Old Drury first opened its doors. The first of them were Mrs. Ann Marshall, Mrs. Corey, Mrs. Eastland, Mrs. Weaver, Mrs. Uphill, Mrs. Knip (or Knep), Mrs. Hughes, and a little later came Mrs. Boutel, Mrs. Nell Gwynne, Mrs. James, Mrs. Rebecca Marshall, Mrs. Rutter, Mrs. Verjuice and Mrs. Reeves. The Ladies of the Lane is sufficient title for them, but they were in fact the Members of His Majesty's Company of Comedians—as are all players at Drury Lane—and they had all taken an oath of allegiance to the king.

The first production at Drury Lane was *The Humorous Lieutenant*. Mrs. Ann Marshall, in the part of Celia, was the only woman in the play. In the next production, *Rule a Wife and Have a Wife*, Mrs. Marshall, playing Margaretta, was joined by Mrs. Boutel, in the character of Estifania. Then followed *Volpone*, with Mrs. Marshall as leading lady and Mrs. Corey in the cast, and *The Silent Woman*, with the female parts played this time by Mrs. Knip, Mrs. Rutter, and Mrs. Corey. Thereafter they rang the changes. Mrs. Marshall went on to play leads at Drury Lane for a matter of fourteen years, Mrs. Barry taking over her roles when she left.

Though little is known about her, Ann Marshall was a very beautiful woman and appears to have been a first-class actress. She possessed a fine voice, her diction was good, and she excelled in declamation, an art on which most of the plays of the age depended. Pepys leaves us a glimpse of her in *The Indian Queen*: "But above my expectations most, the eldest Marshall did do her part most excellent well, as I ever heard woman in my life, but her voice is not so sweet as Ianthe's (Mrs. Betterton)." Certainly her merit must have been considerable for Killigrew to make her his leading lady to such consummate actors as Hart and Mohun. She was the creator of many of the heroine's roles in Dryden's plays, and played also in classical dramas and comedies. Declamation, however, was her strong line.

We have told the story of Mrs. Davenport's betrayal by the scoundrelly Earl of Oxford. For a long time this story was wrongly attached to Mrs. Marshall and, indeed, old Betterton had given it so; but it seems likely that the Earl did importune her. After he had attempted to carry her off, she appealed to King Charles and was given a guard of soldiers, who soon put the Earl and his followers to flight when they appeared. Betterton says of her that she had a haughty and severe virtue, though he may still have been confusing her with Mrs. Davenport. She appears to have died unmarried in the end. In other respects she followed the prevailing mode of the actresses of her time, for in 1672 we find her speaking a prologue dressed in men's clothes. The actresses, it seems, could not leave the breeches alone.

Rebecca Marshall, Ann's sister, known chiefly as Becke or Becky, was a great friend of Pepys, so we are able to get a better picture of her. Like Ann she was a beautiful woman, though not so good an actress. But she seems to have been a better mixer and a good gossip, and knew how to look after herself, making use of a quick and a biting tongue. Though a friend of Nell Gwynne's, she often quarrelled with her. However, they seem to have been on good terms on April 3, 1665, for they both sat with Pepys at Drury Lane to watch a performance of *Mustapha*, which he says "pleased me mightily." It would have pleased most men to have been so honoured. On a later occasion he sat with her at the Duke's, and observed that she had a beautiful hand. Unhappily, the two women had a stand-up row later when Becky taunted Nell with being Lord Buckhurst's mistress (which she was). Nell flashed back her answer. "I was but one man's mistress, though I was brought up in a brothel to fill strong waters to the gentlemen, and you are a mistress to three or four, though a Presbyter's praying daughter." If Nell was right, there is nothing on record to confirm it; but who shall say in those times?

It is doubtful, too, whether she was right about the Marshalls' parentage. The Presbyterian divine referred to was Stephen Marshall, a great Cromwellian and incumbent of Finchingfield in Essex, whom posterity, largely on the strength of Nell Gwynne's report, has assumed as their father. He was regarded as a man of great piety and during the Commonwealth his advice on all matters was eagerly sought. He died full of years and honours, and was buried in Westminster Abbey, but his body was removed therefrom by the Royalists at the Restoration.

He seems, therefore, an unlikely father for two Restoration actresses, beautiful and—for their time—cultured though they may have been. Yet the legend may be true. For certain records show that he was chaplain, at one period in his life, to Lord Gerard of Bromley, a staunch Royalist, and whilst so employed married Elizabeth, the illegitimate daughter of one Dutton. The actresses, according to the same source, were the offspring of this marriage. They must have taken after their mother. This story was put down solemnly by Sir Peter Leicester, who was related not only to the Gerards but to the Duttons. Well, it is possible, for very many good actresses have come from vicarages and parsonages. Why not the Marshalls? We do not know anything about their mother, but she may have been more worldly than the reputed father.

Whether Rebecca had as many lovers as Nelly suggests, or even any at all, is not certain, but she could certainly look after herself, as the story of her brush with Orange Moll shows. Orange Moll, the first refreshment contractor to the Theatre Royal and consequently the first in history (ladies came first there) was a rough, unruly type who ran the orange girls and was always mixed in intrigue. She could curse and swear with the best of them. One day she gave Rebecca Marshall the rough side of her tongue. A day or two later, to her horror and dismay, she was served with a writ from the Lord Chamberlain "for abusing Mrs. Rebecca Marshall, one of His Majesty's Company of Comedians, to ye disturbance of His Majesty's Actors . . . and committing other misdemeanours." Orange Moll climbed down. She was in trouble enough, for she was behind with her rent, and certainly did not want to lose her concession for the sale of refreshments in the Theatre Royal. None the less, she was eventually ejected and the law-suit she laid was still unsettled when she died. But after Becky Marshall's action she left the actresses alone.

Modesty was at a discount in Restoration Days and even if it had not been, it would have been difficult for the Ladies of the Lane and their contemporaries at the Duke's Theatre to preserve this virtue, for their communal dressing-rooms were open to all. The gallants could stroll around and watch them while at their toilet or dressing and undressing for their stage roles, and they took the fullest advantage of the privilege. Their comments on what they saw—and sometimes on what they did not see—was of such a lewd nature that the actresses would often send their maids away. As it was part of their job, the actresses themselves had, of course, to put up with it.

There was a gentleman called Sir Hugh Middleton (nothing at all to do with the benefactor who brought the New River to London) who frequented the dressing-rooms of both Drury Lane and the Duke's. He was not a popular man, and on one occasion he was so very critical of the beauty displayed at Drury Lane that Becky Marshall rebelled. She bade him begone. If he did not like what he saw at the King's Theatre, well, let him betake himself to the Duke's and see if he could be better suited there. Sir Hugh was horrified that an actress had dared to answer him back. Being a perfect gentleman he told Becky that he would kick her or, rather, not to defile himself by so doing, would get his footman to do it for him. That was on a Saturday night in 1667. Becky was furious. After thinking it over, she went on Monday to Whitehall, besought an audience with His Majesty and laid her complaint before him. The great upholder of woman's virtue and preserver of chastity listened and, no doubt, thought it over, but he took no immediate action.

Tuesday night found the gallant Sir Hugh at Drury Lane again. He was by the stage door and he cast black and ugly looks at Becky as she left the theatre with a friend. Then she noticed a rough-looking man walking very closely behind her. Scenting trouble and even fearing that Middleton was going to have her stabbed by an assassin, she screamed. The desperado dropped back, but only for a few moments. Then he sprang upon her, rubbed a handful of ordure gathered from the gutter over her hair and face, and took to his heels.

The next morning, washed, scented, fresh and sweet, handsome Becky Marshall went to see the King again. She told her story, and he listened again. This time, however, he took action. There is no record of the punishment, if any, dealt out to Sir Hugh Middleton, but a fortnight later a Royal Decree was issued forbidding men from going backstage and into the dressing-rooms of the ladies. There was great indignation and resentment about this. No doubt Middleton bore the brunt of it, for Becky Marshall was never one to keep her tongue quiet, and he would be blamed for the loss of the most intriguing occupation in town. Business suffered, too; for many came to visit the dressing-rooms rather than to see the play. It seems, however, that when the anger over the assault on Becky had died down, the actresses themselves did not like their modest seclusion. It cramped their style considerably. So, after a little while, the Royal Decree was ignored and nobody took any notice. Least of all, the King.

Pepys saw Becky play in *The Virgin Martyr*, Massinger's tragedy, and, although he formed a poor opinion of the play, said that she acted finely in it. He was at Drury Lane shortly after to see *The English Monsieur*. He went backstage, for reasons we shall see later, and picked up a nice bit of juicy gossip. It appeared that Lady Castlemaine, the King's Mistress, was having an *affaire* with Charles Hart, the leading man at Drury Lane. Becky Marshall, he learned, was the go-between and the means of arranging their meetings, and believed that nobody else knew it. Fancy trying to keep that secret, or any other secret, in the Theatre! This shows a sidelight upon the fair Becky who had been very indignant when Nell Gwynne had accused her of having several lovers.

The reason given for Lady Castlemaine's action was that she

wished to get even with the King because of his infatuation for Moll Davies, of the rival theatre. Maybe Becky Marshall assisted out of loyalty to her own playhouse and its chief; maybe not. Lady Castlemaine probably needed little encouragement as Hart was a very handsome man and a fine actor.

When her elder sister left the stage, Rebecca became the leading tragedienne. Her best parts were Dorothea in *The Virgin Martyr* and the Queen of Sicily in Dryden's *Secret Love*. On at least one occasion the sisters appeared together, in *The Damoiselles à la Mode* by Flecknoe. Ann and Rebecca Marshall were amongst the first of the stars, so far as the women were concerned, and certainly at Drury Lane.

The incident of Rebecca turning on Sir Hugh Middleton in the dressing-rooms shows the condition of the Theatre and its people in Restoration times. The public were the masters and could do very much as they liked. The actors were still held in contempt, the status of the actresses being about that of a superior prostitute. It must be remembered that although Charles II had given Drury Lane its Charter, it was hard to break old custom and belief. The players had been treated as no more than servants for so long that a change in the attitude to their profession was unlikely to take place immediately. There had been no respect for the players before; why should there be now? Women on the stage did nothing to raise their position; indeed it must be admitted that most of the early actresses were a loose-moralled lot. They were of their time, and their position made them more than usually vulnerable. Their dressing-rooms were not their private sanctuaries as now, places difficult of access to any but close friends and completely inaccessible to strangers. Nor had they private dressing-rooms of their own. They shared a room or rooms between them, the first Drury Lane Theatre providing only one dressing-room for them. So let a woman be never so virtuous or modest, she must put up with the conduct of the majority. Yet Mrs. Betterton managed to keep herself inviolate as did Mrs. Bracegirdle, and, possibly, Anne Marshall. They were not all lights-o'-love.

Mistress Catherine Corey, a very talented actress, made a great claim later in her life to have been the first actress to appear on the stage. Indeed, so much was said and written about it that some authorities for years acknowledged her as such. But it would appear that her claim really rested on the fact that she was the first of the actresses selected by Killigrew to appear at Drury Lane who took the special oath of allegiance to the King, for which the Charter called. She was a character-actress and comedienne of the first rank, and in her time played many parts. She was a tower of strength, reliable, popular with the public, and possessed a gift of characterisation and comedy which never failed her. She had a very decided mind of her own and was in the forefront of any dispute which might be toward. When in 1678 the egregious Scum Goodman led a revolt of Drury Lane players and deserted along with Clarke, Hains and Gray the treasurer, Mrs. Corey, who often imagined grievances, went with them, though she returned to the fold later.

She excelled in certain parts: as Doll Common in *The Alchymist*, and as Abigail in *The Scornful Lady* she was without equal. Pepys was a fervent admirer of her art and always referred to her as "Doll Common." She was an immensely successful Mrs. Otter in *The Silent Woman*, and especially good as Lady Would-be in *Volpone*. Another of her successes was Sempronia in *Cataline* in which role she once caused a riot, though for reasons other than any inability to act the part. Her *tour de force* was her creation of the widow Blackacre in *The Plain Dealer*. This was regarded as the best piece of low-comedy acting ever done by a woman. Give her confidential maids, old ladies of character, elderly dames who were no better than they should be, stupid women, and low life characters, and she was the delight of the playgoers. She was also a superb mimic. That was what caused the riot in *Cataline*.

Mrs. Corey was a friend of Lady Castlemaine's. That personage had conceived a dislike for Lady Harvey, whose brother was Edward Montague, the Lord Chamberlain. Despite the eminence and power of this close relation, one evening Mrs. Corey, in the role of Sempronia, proceeded to give a marvellously life-like delineation of Lady Harvey. She made up like her, and imitated her dress, hair style, voice, walk, and mannerisms. Lady Harvey was in front at the show, and she soon realised what was afoot. So did her many friends, who were highly delighted, even if they pretended not to be. A whisper soon ran round the house and the audience joined in the laughter. Lady Harvey, justly incensed, rushed to her brother and demanded that the vile actress should be locked up. The Lord Chamberlain acted quickly on his sister's complaint, probably for peace and quiet, and Mrs. Corey was put in the Round House. But Lady Castlemaine, who had the ear of the King, acted too and the King had her released without loss of time. On her release she was also told "to act it again, worse than ever." She understood that the instructions to do so had come from the King, and had she not taken an oath of allegiance to him? Actually, of course, the orders were from Lady Castlemaine. Mrs. Corey, in her loyalty, obeyed. The play was repeated, and the imitation was more unmistakable than before. But Lady Harvey had expected this. She had a hired gang in the house, who hissed Mrs. Corey and then pelted her with fruit. It was a long battle between them, but the actress kept on to the end. In the Royal Box sat the King, who wondered what all the trouble was about—or so he said. It is possible he never knew anything about the original arrest or release, but that Lady Castlemaine was his understudy.

Mrs. Corey's name vanishes from the records after 1692; nor is there any record of where she died. But of the ladies who came first upon the stage, she was in her day one of the best comediennes of the low-comedy type if not, indeed, the best of all.

Next we come to Mrs. Eastland and Mrs. Weaver. The former was not an actress of much note and played few parts of any importance. Mrs. Elizabeth Weaver is more notorious though not because of her success as an actress for she was certainly not a star. Her name originally appears in the list of those entitled to wear the Royal Livery, but was omitted the following year. She appears to have been a lady of easy virtue and doubtful honesty, was obviously extremely extravagant and was in constant trouble. In 1662, one Henry Dobson appealed to the Lord Chamberlain about her. She had passed herself off as the wife of a gentleman of Gray's Inn, named Weaver, whereas, Dobson claimed her name was really Farley and not Weaver at all, though she had borne Weaver a child. It appeared that immediately she had been sworn in as a member of the Drury Lane company she had got credit and had run up bills amounting to £25 11*s*. 6*d*. After continual dunning she had paid £14, but Dobson could not get the balance; hence his appeal to the Lord Chamberlain. For it was one of the

PLATE III

NELL GWYNNE

The most romantic figure the British stage ever produced

PLATE IV

Above:
MRS. BOLTON

At right:
MRS. CENTLIVRE

privileges enjoyed by His Majesty's Company of Comedians that they were immune from arrest, except with the approval of the Lord Chamberlain. (One hastens to add that this privilege no longer exists.)

She was in the same sort of trouble again in 1663. This time she owed a man called Kerby money and he was allowed to proceed against her. In the following year she had a battle with Killigrew and the management, and walked out of the Theatre, handing back all the parts regularly allotted to her. She then went on to complain that she had been illegally dismissed. The management insisted that she had left of her own accord, despite their request that she should stay, adding as a rider that she was far advanced in pregnancy. But there seems to be another figure in the game, though he is shrouded in the background: the Merry Monarch. Mistress Knipp told Pepys that His Majesty had spoiled Mrs. Weaver, which Pepys thought "very mean in a prince." Whether Knipp meant that the King had seduced Mrs. Weaver, or had raised her expectations and then ignored her, is not clear. But poor Charles II, by his carelessness, laid himself open to much abuse.

Mrs. Uphill was also a member of the first company of Drury Lane actresses. Whatever her stage talents may have been, she ended up with a title. If not a peeress, she at least became a Lady. Her name was Susanna and she appears, like many of her sisters of the stage at the time, to have had the lightest regard for morals. There was a gentleman named Sir Robert Howard, the sixth son of the Earl of Berkshire, interested in the Theatre and in high favour at Court, who had found Killigrew a lot of the money needed for the building of Theatre Royal. He had nine shares in it, out of a total of thirty-six, so he was a man of power. More than that, he wrote plays and pretty good ones. He was in many respects a remarkable man, and a brave and gallant gentleman, for he had rescued Lord Wilmot at Cropready Bridge, for which action he was knighted on the battlefield. He had a post at Court, but he loved the Theatre and was perhaps interested in that most of all. What is more, he was remarkably interested in Susanna Uphill. Indeed, she was his mistress. She is reputed to have been a very beautiful woman, which would have given her her chance upon the stage, especially in Restoration times, even if her abilities, which were not considerable, had been less than they were. Howard's intrigue was well known, and as he was a public man it did not escape notice. Shadwell, the dramatist, based a character upon him in *The Sullen Lovers*, calling it "Sir Positive At-All" and he also drew a life-sized and lifelike character of Mrs. Uphill as Lady Vaine, described most politely as "a Whore that takes upon her the name of a lady." Those were the days of the pamphleteers, and those in politics, as Sir Robert was, could not escape them. One pilloried Howard in the following way: "Sir Robert Howard, Auditor of the Receipts of the Exchequer, with £3,000 per annum; many great places and boons he has had, but his whore Uphill spends all and now refuses to marry him." That was hardly true, for Howard was already married. On the death of his wife, however, he made Mrs. Uphill his legal lady and she died Lady Howard in 1691. Howard was a very important man in theatrical affairs during the Restoration years and Montague Summers, that master delver into the intricacies of theatrical pasts, gives a remarkably good picture and account of him in his book *The Playhouse of Pepys*, a treasure house of theatrical history. Sir Robert, the gallant Cavalier, was a man of parts, a true lover of the Theatre, even if this included the ladies thereof, and was no worse than his peers if not a great deal better than many.

And now the gay, dancing, singing Mary Knipp (or Knep) takes the limelight. She is much better known than most of the others we have mentioned because she was a friend of Samuel Pepys—a pretty near friend, one gathers—and she has appeared in plays, films and books right down to the present time. Pepys tells us much about his favourite. He does not enthuse on her beauty—"pretty enough" is his description—but saw her as "the most excellent, mad humoured thing," who "sings the noblest that ever I heard in my life." That was the key to Sam Pepys's affections; by mad humoured he means gay and mischievous. She was properly married, so far as ceremony and legality went, to Mr. Knipp (or Knep), of whom Pepys formed a low opinion: "a kind of jockey, an ill, melancholy, jealous looking fellow," he says. But there may be something to be said for Mr. Knipp. It cannot have been conducive to an easy mind in that immoral period to have had as one's wife an actress who was pretty and "mad humoured." Nor does it seem that Mistress Mary was over-faithful to him.

Killigrew reported that even in the early days she was likely to be the best actress that ever came upon the stage, because she had such intelligence, and that they were going to give her £30 a year more. Nobody knows what her salary was nor those of her colleagues; but it was pretty small, as they all were, if £30 a year was going to be a great advancement. Still, money went a long way and living was as cheap as were morals. Killigrew may have been partial, or not too explicit. As an actress she had her limitations. She was no tragedienne, but a bright comedienne of considerable range, and it was her singing which put the crown upon her. Give her a song or a dance in a show and she brought down the house. She played lead in Sedley's *Mulberry Garden*, named after that pleasure garden whereon Buckingham Palace now stands and, of course, she had a song. Wycherley gave her three big leading roles and she played them well. She was versatile, too, for in *Tyrannic Love* she doubled Nakar, an aerial spirit, with Felicia, the mother of St. Catherine. She does not appear to have caught the errant fancy of the King, but then Nell Gwynne overshadowed her and was her friend, so they played fair. But Pepys tells us much about her in few words. In one flash he shows her at home: "To Knipp's lodgings whom I find not ready to go home with me; and there staid reading of Waller's verses, whilst she finished dressing, her husband being by. Her lodging very mean and the condition she lives in, yet makes a show without doors, God bless us." Well, that was always true about the hard working "pros." One presumes that because the husband was "by" Pepys had to play propriety. Mrs. Pepys had something to put up with, for she had to receive Knipp whom she designated a "wench" and Pepys spent much time with Knipp.

There is no record in his diary as to how they first met. She comes suddenly into the pages on February 15, 1665, two years after the opening of Drury Lane. She is part of a domestic interior whilst the artist John Hales (or Hayls) is painting Mrs. Pepys's portait "in the posture we saw one of my Lady Peters, like a St. Katherine. While he painted Knipp, Mercer and I sang." One hopes Mrs. Pepys enjoyed the concert. Of course he must have known her long before or she would not have been at his house on this occasion. She appears to have been a friend of the Pierce family who were friends of the Pepys. Strange that Pepys, a man of such preciseness, should not have recorded his first meeting with his *inamorata*; or perhaps he thought better of it and let it all be taken for granted.

A few days later Mrs. Knipp called to see his wife, or so he says. Is it possible that Mrs. Pepys knew her first and introduced the two to each other? Anyway, of that occasion Pepys says "I spent all the night talking with this baggage and teaching her my song of 'Beauty Retire,' which she sings and makes go most rarely, and a very fine song it seems to be. She also entertained me with repeating many of her own and others' parts of the playhouse, which she do most excellently, and tells me the whole practices of the playhouse and players and is in every respect most excellent company." That does not look like long or intimate acquaintance. One marvels how, with his eye for beauty and a pretty wench, he had not spotted her before.

Not long after he went with her to their mutual friends Mrs. Pierce and her family in Chelsea thinking to refresh themselves at the "Swan" by the waterside, but a kindly passer-by warned them the sickness (the Plague) was there, so they turned tail for Kensington. Pepys admits his own fear "for my part in great disorder." Mrs. Knipp knew how to handle Pepys. She told him that his song "Beauty Retire" was "mightily cried up, which I am not a little proud of; and I do think I have done 'It Is Decreed' better, but I have not finished it."

Mrs. Knipp appears to have got about a bit for in 1666 she and Pepys met at Mrs. Williams's. There Knipp reported that both "houses" (Drury Lane and the Duke's) would shortly re-open after the Plague. Pepys thought they would get little good by it. Mrs. Williams, who appears to have been a knowledgeable person about the Theatre, gave it as her opinion that the Duke's would be the better of the two, "because of their women." Not very tactful before a lady of Drury Lane, but her remark shows the importance which actresses had already achieved. Pepys was glad to hear about the women. But he probably expressed no such opinion before Knipp. On October 29, Pepys went to what he called the new playhouse in Whitehall, which must have been the redecorated and newly appointed Cockpit in White Hall Palace, where plays were often given before the Court. He had not been there before and he was joined by Mr. and Mrs. Pierce, Knipp and his own wife. The play was *Love in a Tub*, which he records as being the first play he had seen since the Plague; but did not like it. The place was grand enough but bad for sound. He enjoyed seeing the King and Queen, the Duke and Duchess of York and all the noble ladies, especially Lady Castlemaine, and probably Mistress Knipp too. She was at a party at the Pierce's when the news came of the fire at Whitehall and the Horse Guards.

We get our first glimpse of Knipp the actress through the eyes of Pepys when he saw her at Drury Lane on December 27, 1666, in *The Scornful Lady*, in which Mrs. Corey did well as Abigail. He says "Knipp the widow very well, and will be an excellent actor, I think." He was right. And on January 2, 1667, he is there again, this time to see *The Custom of the Country*, which he thought about the worst play he had ever seen, though he thought Knipp played the Widow very well and sang a song admirably. So the evening was not wasted. Later the same month a great adventure befell him, for Mrs. Knipp introduced him to Nell Gwynne, whom his wife kissed—and so did he. "A most pretty woman," he writes, "who acted the great part of Celia today very fine and did it pretty well, and a mighty pretty soul she is." Knipp had further treats in store, for she let them see the dances being rehearsed for *The Goblins*, the next night's production, which Samuel enjoyed. She came to his house to a party the next night, wearing the costume in which she had appeared in *The Goblins* as a country lass in a straw hat. He did not know her at first but found her "a merry jade." He went to her rooms to hear an Italian called Baptista teach her a part in a new opera, "and there she did sing an Italian song or two very fine, while he played the bass upon a harpsichon there, and exceedingly taken I am with her singing and believe she will do miracles at that and acting."

Pepys had also gleaned some interesting theatrical details from Killigrew, who had imported this Italian and persuaded the King to support the efforts he was making for music. As to the state of theatrical affairs and house management, this expert had laid it down that things had changed since the Great Fire of London. Drury Lane, for one thing was not taking half as much money. Nevertheless he was making the Theatre greater and more glorious than it had ever been. In the post-Fire days, he boasted, he used only wax candles, whereas in pre-Fire days he had been content with tallow and only 3 lbs. of candles at that. Nowadays there was far more order in the house which previously had resembled a bear-garden (this must have been very relative, one fears, and a bit of wishful thinking). The rushes with which the floor had been spread were now swept away. The King, too, came far more frequently than heretofore. And instead of three fiddlers he now had nine or ten of the best. One very true thing he said was to the effect that City audiences were just as good as those from the Court.

Pepys never tired of singing Knipp's praises. If the play failed to please him, she made up for it. A play called *Queen Elizabeth's Troubles and the History of Eighty Eight* he dismissed as rubbish but he was delighted with Knipp's dancing as a milkmaid and with her singing, "to see her come out in her night-gowne with no lockes on, but her bare face and hair only tied up in a knot behind, which is the comeliest dress that ever I saw her in to her advantage."

On October 1, 1667, he went to Drury Lane. He met Knipp going in and she took him to the dressing-room called by him the "tireing rooms" and to "the women's shift," where he saw Nell Gwynne dressing. Apparently she had not got very far with it, for he remarks that she was "all unready and is very pretty, prettier than I had thought." He continues: "And into the scene room and there sat down and she gave us fruit and here I read the questions to Knipp, while she answered me, all her part of Flora's Figary's which was acted today. But Lord, to see how they were both painted would make a man mad and did make me loathe them, and what base company of men comes among them and how lewdly they talk." Well, he was there himself, anyway. That "scene room" is the Green Room. It had both titles in the seventeenth century but gradually the word Green Room ousted the older form, of which it was a corruption. The "scene room" was the original version, the room in which the players waited for their scenes on the stage and from whence they were "called." That entry of Pepys gives a light upon backstage life amongst the ladies of the profession of his time. His feeling of "loathing" did not last long. Pepys was no subscriber to the stage illusion—he liked reality. He did not like "make-up." He would have had a poor time today. It was Knipp who gave Pepys the gossip about the King and Moll Davies and also Nelly, about which he said he was sorry but which he duly chronicled.

He has something quite important to relate about his visit to Drury Lane on February 20, 1668. He went there at one o'clock and saw a play, called *The Duke of Lerma*, written by Sir Robert Howard, who himself married into the Theatre. The King and the Court were there. Pepys thought there would be a disturbance because the play satirised the King and his many mistresses, but it all passed off peacefully and well; Knipp and Nell Gwynne apparently made a duet of the Prologue, and Pepys thought Knipp spoke better than anyone he had ever heard. He was probably prejudiced. Later he was there again, and despite his remarks about the rude and lewd men who frequented the dressing-rooms, he made no bones about going into the room whilst Knipp undressed and stayed there whilst she changed. She told him the scandal about Lady Castlemaine and Charles Hart. And apparently Knipp had a turn for heavier stuff than the usual light-hearted role, for in *The Sea Voyage* the critical Samuel decided that she "did her part of sorrow very well." She had an eye to the main chance, had Mistress Knipp. She did not fail to send her maid to remind Pepys that a certain day was "woman's day" at the theatre and that he must be there. By "woman's day" she meant that it was for the benefit of the actresses. He went, too, and saw *The City Match*, which he dismissed as silly, but the King was there and all the Court and the house was crowded so the ladies of the stage had a bumper benefit.

He adored his Knipp and was delighted when she sang and the whole house clapped her. The only thing he did not like was her making up for the stage. In many ways Mistress Knipp is the most typical of them all. She was a cheerful soul, and she endured the hardships of home and a husband who occasionally beat her, though, perhaps, with good reason. As frail as she was fair, she kept gay and merry, dancing through life as she danced on the stage. She sang with charm and taste, she could play a part, grave or gay, and she could look enchanting and shed brightness round her. She could even keep mainly on the right side of the redoubtable Mrs. Pepys, and she was good-natured and friendly with it all. She vanishes from the records after 1678, when she had been an actress for fourteen years. What became of her nobody knows. But Pepys gave her immortality.

Some few remain before the greater and more renowned ladies take their place. Mrs. Boutell, a good actress, played young, innocent heroines beloved of young heroes who were not so innocent. She was short, which enabled her to play young girls; she was pretty; and she had the most amazing blue eyes with which she made great play. Her hair was lovely and of a rich chestnut hue. She was a great favourite, and, despite a rather weak voice, which was, however, of good tone, she played many important parts. When Drury Lane and the Duke's Theatre merged, she retired. But she came back some six years later, owing to popular demand and was as big a success as ever. In 1679 she left the stage for good. It was reported that she had saved money and had had generous gifts from her lovers which enabled her to live in comfort. There is no record of her age, or of her death.

Mrs. James played minor roles only; practically all that is known of her personally is that she had a good voice. And there trips on in the rear the graceful figure of Mrs. Rutter, player of small parts, but tall and fair and lovely.

Last in the cavalcade come two ladies, one Mrs. Verjuice, of whom hardly anything is known (she must have played the smallest of the bits and pieces and hardly ever got her name on the bills), and then Mistress Reeves, who is the right one to bring the list of ladies who first trod the stage to a close, for her own end was remarkable. She has little claim to be reckoned an actress, except that she was on the stage. But she was the mistress of the poet and dramatist Dryden and so she got parts in his plays, which is only natural and something not entirely unknown in the theatre history of later days. She played Amaryllis in the Duke of Buckingham's brilliant and cruel burlesque *The Rehearsal*, in which Dryden and others were so bitterly if wittily satirised and flayed. It was indeed a stroke of satiric genius to get Mistress Reeves to play therein, and one wonders how it came about that she did. For Dryden knew that he was the butt. Maybe he thought it would lessen the blow and deflect the public's interpretation.

Maybe he did not mind and wanted to see his *inamorata* get a good chance.

Mistress Reeves was another of the actresses who liked to appear in male attire and she was popular with audiences when she did so. She played the page Ascanio in *The Assignation* and charmed everyone by her appearance. She wore the breeches again when there was an all-woman cast in a performance of *The Mayden Queen*. It was her appearance rather than her talent which won her applause. And that has been known since, too. There is absolutely no doubt as to her relationship with Dryden. Many contemporary writings are very much to the point on this subject and as explicit as they are broad. She vanished from the stage in 1672; her career, and maybe her love affair, was over. What happened to many of these ladies in later life is not known, but what happened to Mistress Reeves is very well known indeed. To the astonishment of all, she went abroad, took the veil and vanished into a nunnery. Maybe she had much for which to atone. But in this she is unique of all that first company of the Ladies of the Stage.

These were the First Actresses, save one other who deserves more space and individual treatment. These were the women who brought a new and great interest in the Theatre, who created indeed a revolution, not only into the drama but in the status of women generally. They brought a romance to the Theatre which it had never known before and they gave it that valuable thing, the reality of illusion, by playing parts written for their sex instead of such parts being played by men. In that they obeyed the King's command. They opened up a new field for dramatists and there is not the slightest doubt that they added to the business at the box office. They added also to the publicity, which the Theatre obtained, in those days, by word of mouth. They were quizzed, they were the objects of scandal and of keen interest to their own as well as the male sex. Their temptations were many and, if few resisted, who shall blame them? They were the observed of all observers, they were courted, petted and spoiled. Except in the case of Mrs. Betterton and perhaps Ann Marshall, none of them was spotless or irreproachable, but it is likely that they were not without reproach before they took to the stage. They only did as others did, as their superiors in rank did openly. They merely followed a fashion of the times, and women were ever the slaves of fashion. They did not bring their profession down, it was pretty low already, but they set a mark upon their branch of the profession which was to last for centuries and which is only just fading away. They made the word "actress" a term of moral reproach. Not so long ago, in the West of England, that word and the term "prostitute" were synonymous. Tens of thousands of people came to regard the Theatre as an immoral place, with the result that they made every effort to keep their daughters out of it and their sons from marrying into it. How long is it since an officer of the Army, marrying an actress, had to send in his papers? The British are a tenacious race: once let them get an idea into their heads and it takes centuries to remove it. For the idea that all actresses are wantons and of no worth, we have to thank those ladies who came first in the Theatre, that gay band of light-hearted women with even lighter morals.

Let us, however, remember them kindly, for all their frailty. Let us remember they were pioneers and that, in morals, they were of their time, no better, and certainly no worse. Let us remember their impact, their talent, their gaiety and their contribution to the amusement of their day. Let us also remember that they opened the door to so much greatness which was to follow them in the Theatre and that they were the forerunners of so many great women who were to raise the status of their art with their shining talent.

CHAPTER FOUR

Nell-Never-to-be-Forgotten

NO English actress is better remembered than Mistress Nell Gwynne—Ellen Gwyn—Ellin-Gwin, spell it how you will. She is and she always will be Sweet Nell of Old Drury. Most people have very little idea who she was or what she did, except that she was mistress to King Charles II. They mistakenly believe that she was an orange girl when the King fell in love with her. Very, very few have any idea of what sort of an actress she was. But they all know that she appeared at Old Drury, and that she was fascinating and frail.

What sort of a woman was she? What sort of an actress was she? Who was she, this little creature who attained immortality for her immoral life, but against whom nobody harboured a hard thought? It is not easy to answer these questions. Some, indeed, are unanswerable, but there is enough to work on for us to make a pretty picture of this enchantress. For that is what she was. She put men under a spell, she even delighted the women; she could control an unruly house when others failed and could send a previously disappointed audience home happy and laughing. She was the very embodiment of feminine charm and also of that quality now known as sex-appeal.

Other actresses of far greater merit and ability have left hardly an imprint on peoples' minds; women who had claim to greatness are forgotten save by the scholar. Women of far greater beauty and brains have not left even a trace of the dust into which they dissolved to fleck the memory. Nell Gwynne, Sweet Nell, dances on down time, without any loss of brightness; of such queer things is immortality made.

An actress for a short time only, she was able to print her image so deeply on the great Theatre Royal that she and Drury Lane are always indissolubly linked. There is, underground in the present playhouse, one small portion of the first Theatre Royal which escaped the fire of 1672. Today it forms the walls of a store cupboard, but it is known as Nell Gwynne's dressing-room. Needless to say, it never was. Tradition will not be denied, however; there are the walls of the actual theatre in which she played, and so it is Nell Gwynne's dressing-room. Deep below the stage are a succession of tunnelled passages, known as the crypt, one of which is at present in use. There they stand, steadfast and strong, as firm and as fresh as the day on which Sir Christopher Wren put them there when he built the Second Theatre, opened in 1674. Beneath them runs a long passage of brick coming to a dead-end under Catherine Street, the street on to which Drury Lane faces (only the rear of the theatre is in Drury Lane proper). Again legend and tradition have taken hold. That passage had no apparent use, so legend found one for it. It was the secret entrance through which Charles II came to visit Mistress Nell. Once again a pretty idea must be debunked. That passage was not there at all when Nell used the theatre; she only appeared in the first theatre and this is part of the second. Nor would Charles II have condescended to such needless privacy. What he did, he did openly, for all to see. That stands to his credit.

One sees films and plays, and reads novels wherein Mistress Nell persuades her Monarch to grant the Charter which founded and still controls Drury Lane. Once again this is a legend. Killigrew got that Charter in 1663 and needed no help. Nell never appeared in the Theatre until 1665. Nor is there a vestige of evidence that she was ever an orange girl, although it would have been an occupation at which she, with her quick wit, understanding, and immense power of repartee, would have excelled. It is possible that she may have sold oranges for Mistress Mary Meggs—Orange Moll—the first theatre refreshment contractor, but if she did, it is quite certain that Charles II never noticed her whilst she was doing so. Thus is another romantic idea of a love affair between a Monarch and an orange girl blown quite away by the breath of truth. Had Nell worked for Moll, she would have said so; but she never made such a claim. She is also credited with having persuaded Charles to found Chelsea Hospital. This indeed she may have done, although here again no proof exists. It was exactly the warm-hearted thing she would have thought of and wanted to see carried through, for all her life she had a care for those in want or in trouble. She had known both herself, and she did not forget.

With all these pretty stories dispersed, there is still enough to make a great Romance. Even if some of it is sordid, it is transformed by the passage of time as well as by her amazing progress from the dirt of the gutter, the bestiality of the brothel, to the bed of a King and to semi-royal state. Nobody helped her much and nobody helped her without a return asked and taken. She achieved what she achieved by the fact of her undeniable womanhood, her courage and her charm, not to mention her honesty. For one can be immoral—or perhaps amoral is the better word—and yet be as honest as the day. So she gleams in gold, not only on the tapestry of our Theatre history but in the history of England itself. She stands on a par with the great French courtesans of the Louis régime; indeed, she stands higher for she was a much better and far more human soul than any of them, outshining her foreign competitors. Many of them caused the downfall of their Royal Masters, but she helped her King to keep his throne and, even more important, his head as well. "They'll never kill me, James, to make you king," said Charles to his brother, the Duke of York. And they did not. Yet there were times when the populace was furious with him, but a thought of Nell Gwynne gave them a smile. The thought of her may often have softened feelings of treason and rebellious desires. After all, Old Rowley couldn't be that bad when he loved Nelly, they thought. Nell Gwynne was something more than a popular actress and a favourite alike with King and People. She was a very remarkable woman and, in an odd sense, a great one too.

What was her origin? That will never be quite clear. Three towns contend for the honour of this so-called wicked woman's birth-place. Oxford has its say but it is not very convincing. Hereford points today to a tablet on a house in a lane leading down to the river which bears the legend that she was born there. The tablet is fact but the legend, legend. It is far more likely, it is indeed more than probable, that she was born just off that street from which the suffix to her name sprang, off Drury Lane itself. The actual spot was in what was then known as Coal Yard and is now called Goldsmith Street.

There are suggestions that her father, at least, was of gentle birth. But who was he? Even her mother must have had her doubts. About her mother there is no doubt at all. She was called, or called herself, Mistress Gwynne and she did indeed live in Coal Yard. Whether she could have been certain of the paternity of Nell, or of her other daughter Rose, is very open to doubt. For Mistress Gwynne, not to be delicate about it, was a common prostitute and not a prostitute of any standing in her ancient profession. She did not attract the gentry. She had no luxurious love nest at which the gay noblemen might call for dalliance; the streets were her market and a dirty attic her shop. She took her custom as it came and was not at all particular. There is some slight foundation for the view that the male progenitor of Nelly was a fruiterer in Covent Garden, and there is a blunt statement in a contemporary record that "a battalion of soldiers" was responsible. Well, who is to say? Either is equally likely. Anyway, Nellie was born in squalor and sin, and saw no other kind of life. Her mother was seldom sober and the children did the best they could. There was no comfort and little food, and as little motherly care or love. Both the girls were forced by one means or another to find a living for themselves when most children would still be in the nursery. Rose took after her mother. She was in trouble all her life and in later years Nell often came to her rescue and helped her, not only financially, but by saving her from prison when the gates were yawning wide. Nor did she forget her sister when she herself was living in splendour, guilty but gilded and full of comfort and fun. She even persuaded Charles II to grant her a pension. Rose married, in fact she married twice, although she is known to have followed her mother's trade. The first husband was Captain John Cassells, who was said to have been a man of some fortune who spent it in the service of the Crown. This could be construed as meaning that he had lent Charles I money during the Civil War, or Charles II when in exile, but he is far more likely to have been one of the swaggering roisterers, claiming to have been Cavaliers ruined in the cause, who got a living in odd ways by gaming and by bullying. He may even have been of a decent family which was really reduced during the Civil War, but he was certainly arrested for being concerned in a burglary. The second husband was one Foster. Little is known of him, nor did he live long. But Rose had this advantage socially over her more famous sister. She was twice a legally married woman, even if she could not claim to be a respectable one. There is hardly any doubt, however, that Rose Gwynne, using her maiden name, if the term be not inappropriate, was in Newgate for robbery in 1663 and that Killigrew got her out. She was also on extremely friendly terms with Browne, a high official of the Duke of York. Later she was in trouble again and this time Nell did the trick for her. She also left her £200 in the first codicil to her will, to be paid to her at any time within a year of her death; then in a second codicil she bequeathed another £200 on top of that. She calls her sister Rose Forster and she left £50 to the husband, too, to buy a ring. It seems doubtful if he was then alive.

The life of Mistress Gwynne senior and her elder daughter show what Nell's family history was like. Who then shall blame her for the life she herself was to lead? What other choice had she? Such a life was what she saw all around her; it seemed to be a normal method of existence. She was not a cultured person, and nobody ever gave her an education. Somehow or other she must have learned how to read, but otherwise she was almost illiterate, being able to do little more than scrawl something which passed for her signature. The streets were her books, the gutter her thoroughfare, the vice-ridden area of her birth her seminary. There she learned what she learned.

It is remarkable that the privations and bitterness of her youth left so little trace or that the filthy squalor surrounding her did not warp her character, except her sexual morals, which were no worse than the aristocracy with whom she later mingled and who indeed often had to court her for favours. She never lost a deep sense of fair play and justice; she never pretended to be other than what she was—and that is a great virtue. She once sent a message to a nobleman through another who was writing to him and said: "She presents you with her real acknowledgments of all your favours, and protests she would write in her own hand, but her wild characters would distract you." No getting someone to write and pretending she had done it, as a lesser character would probably have done.

She was born, as far as one can discover, on February 2, 1650. An old horoscope of hers discloses that date. It may not be accurate to a year or so, but it is near enough. There was no great fuss at her entry into life and doubtless she gave little delight to her mother, to whom she would be a hindrance, a drawback and another mouth to feed, another form to drape in rags. Old Mother Gwynne probably felt little of the pride and joy of motherhood and a worse mother could scarcely be imagined. Could Nell then have been blamed if, when she rose to fame, she had cast the dreadful old woman off? She did no such thing. She looked after her and gave her every comfort. For a time she even took her to live with her in Chelsea, where the old lady died. She was drunk at the time and she fell into a ditch face downwards, and was drowned. Some reports say she fell into a fishpond and a lampoon published at the time said:

> She that so oft had Powerful waters tried
> At last with silence in a fishpond died.
> Fate was unjust, for he proved but kind
> To make it Brandy, he had pleased her mind.

Another remarked:

> Yet brandy merchants sure have cause to grieve
> Because her fate admits of no reprieve.
> Die in their debts she could not, yet they'll find
> Their trade decay'd, for none is left behind
> That in one day could twenty quarts consume
> And bravely vaunt, she durst it twice presume.

Another was blunter still and came from the pen of Sir George Etherege:

> Maid, Punk and Bawd, full sixty years and more
> Died drunk with brandy in a common shore.

The brandy she was able to procure because of Nell's generosity, and that generosity killed her. Yet Nell Gwynne had her buried, in a handsome and ornate grave, in St. Martin in the Fields.

Nell was a pretty child. She was thrown early upon her own resources to get the barest necessities of life, food, clothing and probably even lodging. What was there for Nell to do? Born in what was really a brothel, she found employment in one. She was engaged by one of the most notorious brothel-keepers in London, Mother Ross, whose establishment was in the most notorious street for such places in town, Lewknor Lane, off Drury Lane. It is now called Macklin Street, named after one of Drury Lane Theatre's finest and most astonishing actors. There are rumours that earlier she had been in domestic service and was bundled out because the master of the house showed an amorous disposition towards her, but there is no real support for the story. Her career began as a hawker of herrings in the street. She cried her wares and she went into taverns to sell them as well. In those taverns she got her first taste of an audience, showing the first glimmering of the actress to be. As a mere child she sang songs therein, low, lewd songs at that, and gathered a small harvest of pence. Disreputable sentiments and questionable (or, rather, *un*questionable) "blue" jokes, sung by a child, had a piquancy for the vice which ruled the period. Then she had a lover when she had just passed into her 'teens. She always admitted it. He was a linkboy, a poor boy himself, but maybe between them they found some happiness in their precocious passion. He gave her a pair of worsted stockings, which she craved. She had nothing on her poor little feet. They were pretty feet, but she was much troubled by chilblains. So she lived, hawking fish, singing songs to the lowest form of drunken revellers, and running errands in a brothel. Perhaps she had observed the talent within herself. Her songs were popular and she was told on all sides she sang well.

She would see the fine ladies going to the play at the King's Theatre in Brydges Street, Drury Lane Theatre. And she would see, to her, equally fine ladies who played there, going in and out. She would observe the way in which the gallants courted them and thus no doubt her ambition was fired. That cute, observant cockney mind would miss nothing. It is very improbable that she was attracted to the stage by her "art"; rather would it be the firm belief that she could do as well as the ladies she had seen going in and out of the theatre—and reap as rich a reward. If she did serve Orange Moll as an orange girl, she would have had personal contact with these actresses. For not the least part of the girls' work was the taking of messages, verbal and written, from the gallants to the female players. The stage called her and she determined to answer that call. She managed to save up what was for her the immense sum of two guineas. That she carried to the great actor, Thomas Betterton, the leader of his profession, and asked to see him. He was then the chief actor and general manager of the Duke's Theatre, Drury Lane's rival founded by Davenant. He was a good and courteous man, and a kindly one. He listened to what the little ragged, red-haired girl had to say, and then gave her an audition. He did not think she was suitable for the stage and he told her so. He advised her to work hard and honestly for her living and was not at all tempted by the couple of guineas. Nor was he tempted by the bodily charms of the girl which, no doubt, she brought into full play. Betterton was a man of quality and an example in morals to those around him, without a blot on his character. As we have seen, he was happily married and devoted to his wife, as she was to him. Had he not been, had he succumbed to the easily gained prize, had he seen talent in what Nell did, then she would have gone to the Duke's Theatre in Dorset Gardens and never been Sweet Nell of Old Drury. That would have been a double loss, for "Sweet Nell of the Duke's" is not nearly so romantic as "Sweet Nell of Old Drury." Lovers of Drury Lane must be grateful for both Betterton's staunch morality and his momentary blindness to talent.

Nell, however, was not easily put off. She was a cockney, and she was tenacious. So she betook herself to handsome, debonair Charles Hart, great-nephew of Shakespeare himself, chief actor and manager for Killigrew of the King's Theatre, of Old Drury. Hart was at the opposite pole to Betterton. He saw the girl, heard her recite and was conquered by her charm and personality. He did not take the two guineas, either: he took her. She became his mistress and in return he trained her for the stage. Old Betterton himself has something to say on this subject in his book which was published in 1741 by one Curll at Pope's Head, in Rose Street, Covent Garden and was priced five shillings. How much was Betterton and how much Curll is doubtful. It is as outspoken as it is inaccurate, but it is intriguing all the same. Betterton says, or is made to say, "Nelly was eased of her virginity by Mr. Hart, at the same time that Lord Buckhurst sighed for it. But His Majesty carrying off the prize, we must leave her under the Royal Protection." Mr. Betterton gets his facts wrong: Lord Buckhurst had not seen Nelly at that time, nor had His Majesty. Much later Lord Buckhurst took her down to his house at Epsom, where she lived for some time before returning to Drury Lane. His Majesty, of the three gentlemen, was a bad third. Not that he cared much about that.

Hart gave Nelly two years' training and then, in 1665, he launched her on the stage. She played Cydaria in Dryden's *The Indian Emperor*. She was not very good for it was a tragedy and Nelly was no tragedienne, which was all the more reason why the Theatre should try to make her one, as is the usual custom of the Theatre. It persists even today. Nell herself did not want to play tragedy; she wanted to play comedy and to dance and sing. She got her own way.

The only person who can give evidence as to her talent is Samuel Pepys. He sat next to her at the Duke's Theatre on April 3, 1665, and Becky Marshall was with her. The play was *Mustapha* which he did not think gave Betterton and his wife a proper chance. But, writing of the occasion he calls Nelly, "Pretty, witty Nell" and was delighted with his luck at sitting with her and Becky. Evidently he missed her début, but he saw her in *The English Monsieur*, a comedy by James Howard, "which is a mighty pretty play, very witty, and pleasant. And the women do very well, but above all, little Nelly." Actresses were still at this time a bit of a novelty to Pepys. He saw *The Humorous Lieutenant* which he did not like but he was taken by Knipp to see Nell, "a most pretty woman, who acted the great part of Celia today very fine and did it pretty well. I kissed her and so did my wife and a mighty pretty soul she is." That was a thrill indeed. One is rather curious about his meaning. First he says that Nelly played Celia "very fine" and in the same breath that she did it "pretty well." But he is in no doubt on March 6, 1666. "After dinner with my wife to the King's House to see *The Mayden Queene* a new play by Dryden, mightily commended for the regularity of it and the strain and wit; and the truth is, there is a comical part done by Nell, which is Florimell that I can never hope ever to see the like done again by man or woman. The King and Duke of York were at the play. But so great performance of a comical part was never, I believe, in the world before, as Nell do this, both as a mad girle, then most and best of all when she comes in like a young gallant:

and hath the motions and carriage of a spark, the most that ever I saw any man have. It makes me, I confess, admire her." Nelly was wearing the breeches already. Shortly after, he saw Moll Davies dance at the Duke's house and this time commented to Nell's detriment: "and the truth is, there is no comparison between Nell's dancing the other day at the King's House in boy's clothes and this, this being infinitely beyond the other." At that time King Charles agreed with him, too. However, he returned to his allegiance when he saw *The Mayden Queene* again: "and so done by Nell her merry part, as cannot be done better in nature."

He gives us the most delightful glimpse of her on May Day, 1667, when on the way to Westminster he met milkmaids with garlands on their pails, dancing with a fiddler before them. He "saw pretty Nelly standing at her lodgings door in Drury Lane in her smock sleeves and bodice, looking upon one; she seemed a mighty pretty creature." No milkmaids dance in Drury Lane now on May Day with garlanded pails and to the music of a fiddle. The more's the pity. And there is no Nelly to stand half dressed at the lodgings, long swept away but which stood opposite the Winter Garden Theatre, to add enchantment to the scene. Those things have gone from a London which was far from picturesque. But, then, the Plague has gone too.

On July 14 of the same year Pepys was at Epsom. He set down the day before he went: "Mr. Pierce tells me what troubles me, that my Lord Buckhurst hath got Nell away from the King's House and gives her £100 a year, so as she has sent her parts to the house and will act no more." The next day found him at Epsom, ostensibly to visit the Well, where he reports much company. But the outstanding item of news is that Nell and Buckhurst are established next door to the King's Head and that Sir Charles Sedley is with them and what he calls a "merry House" is kept. No wonder, with three such people in it, for Buckhurst was a particularly bright spark and wrote, when he was serving with the Navy, a very good song "To all you Ladies now on Land," which still lives. And Sedley's gaiety was proverbial. But Pepys is worried about Nell. "Poor girl, I pity her, but more the loss to the King's House." Now what took him hot foot to Epsom? Curiosity?

Nell was not away long, as he might have known. He saw her act on August 22 and did not like her performance. The play was *The Indian Emperor* "where I find Nell come again, which I am glad of; but was most infinitely displeased with her being put to act the Emperor's daughter, which is a great and serious part, which she does most basely." Another unhappy failure in tragedy by a comedienne out of her line. She knew it, though. He finds the reason for her return a few days later and is full of it. His great friend Sir W. Penn is with him and they get the gossip from Orange Moll. She reports "that Nell is already left by Lord Buckhurst, and that he makes sport of her, and swears she has had all she could get of him; and Hart, her great admirer, now hates her; and that she is very poor, and hath lost my Lady Castlemaine, who was her great friend also; but she is come to the playhouse but is neglected by them all." So Nell's path was not the primrose one of dalliance at that time, anyway. Lady Castlemaine seems to have had much to do with the ladies of the Lane; but those whom she befriended could not rely on her. She would be a friend for a time only to turn to an enemy later, a change probably dictated by the way in which Charles II cast his roving eye. My Lady probably kept hers pretty wide open for possible rivals. She had plenty of brushes with Nell later and did not come off a winner.

Business was bad at the Lane and Pepys records how, in the dressing-room, he saw another side of Nell: "But to see how Nell cursed for having so few people in the pit, was strange"—he did not know professionals, evidently—"the other house carrying away all the people at the new play and is said nowadays to have generally most company, as being better players. By and by into the pit, and there saw the play, which is pretty good." This was the occasion when Knipp took him to the dressing-room where Nell "was all unready, and is very pretty, prettier than I thought." He was again upset when he saw Nell once more in tragedy. It was *The Surprisal.* He liked neither the play, nor the acting, "and especially Nell's acting of a serious part which she spoils," which is blunt enough for anybody. She was soon back in his books for he paid another visit to Drury Lane and saw Nell and Hart in *A Mad Couple*, "which is but an ordinary play, but only Nell and Hart's mad parts are most excellent done, but especially hers;

which makes it a miracle to me to think how ill she do any serious part, as the other day, just like a fool or a changeling and, in a mad part, do beyond all imitation almost." Pepys, for all his playgoing, knew little about actors and actresses and their limitations. It was on this same occasion that Hart, having occasion to use a baby for the business of the play, borrowed one from a woman in the audience. Unfortunately it howled when he brought it on the stage, and its anxious mother rushed on to the stage, snatched it away, and bore it off to deafening cheers from the audience. The "mad parts" to which Pepys refers were not those of lunatics, but of extremely fantastic and farcical characters.

If the gossip was right and Hart now hated Nelly, which is not likely, then there must have been some nice back-stage rows, albeit they played together so superbly. That has happened many times since. They don't seem, however, to have tried to queer each other's performances, unless Nell made the baby cry.

On one visit to the Lane, Pepys heard from Knipp that the King had set up Moll Davies in fine style, and that "the King did send several times for Nelly and she was with him"—which Pepys did not relish at all. He says it was the unreliability of the King in matters of State that worried him, but he probably disliked the idea of Nell being a Royal mistress, although she was as yet only one of the many "casuals." Mention has already been made of the time when Knipp and Nell Gwynne shared the speaking of a prologue to a play which twitted the King for having so many amours. It hardly became Nell to assist at that. Pepys had occasion to admire Nell in her boy's clothes again on May 7, 1668, when visiting Knipp, and of seeing Becky Marshall looking "mighty fine, pretty and noble." "But Lord," he cries, "their confidence! and how many men do hover about them as soon as they come off the stage and how confident they are in their talk!"

The last glimpse Pepys gives of Mistress Gwynne does not show her on the stage at all. He went to see *The Island Princess* by Beaumont and Fletcher, a play that was new to him. He liked it, found good in it, "and a good scene of a town on fire." There was Drury Lane being spectacular in 1668! "We sat in an upper box, and the jade Nell came and sat in the next box, a bold and merry slut who lay laughing there upon people and with a comrade of hers, of the Duke's house, that came in to see the play."

One thing about Nell: she knew her limitations and hated herself as a tragedienne as much as Pepys did. She was neither fitted for such roles temperamentally nor had she had the experience. To be pushed on the stage when about fifteen and to attempt to perform a great tragic role is asking a bit too much of anybody. She also believed that her taste for comedy was shared by the audience, which indeed it was, when she played it. There were authors, too, who thought the same. In the prologue she shared with Knipp she said:

> I know you in your hearts
> Hate serious plays, as I hate serious parts.

And she gave extra point to her lines in *Tyrannic Love*: "I die—out of my calling, in a tragedy." Give her a gay part, give her one of robust comedy, however highly spiced, and she not only loved it but she could put it over too. Give her a song and she was her own and the audience's delight. Give her a dance and all was right with the world. She proclaimed in *All Mistaken, or A Mad Couple*, "A fiddler, nay, then I am made again. I'd have a dance if I had nothing but my smock on." We may be sure she got applause for that.

Nell attracted the men, and the famous men of the time at that. The Duke of Buckingham and the rake Rochester were her suitors, and the former probably enjoyed her favours. Rochester, who made many vitriolic attacks on her, did not. It was a very coarse and outspoken age, and Rochester's attacks, which are extant, cannot be printed here. Lord Buckhurst was also a successful lover, as has been shown, but it did not last. No doubt Nell had her eye on the Throne for real and lasting business. There are stories that Buckhurst hung on to her—he had probably spent a lot on her—and that the King made him an earl to get him out of the way; but the story is unlikely for the *affaire* was short lived. It is possible that Orange Moll lied when she gave the news that Nell and Buckhurst had parted. Some credence is given to this by a nasty and very dirty little poem by Etherege, which drew the King's attention to Nell Gwynne in a most forthright manner, advising him to take her because she was better than all the women he had around him and telling him he would not find her nearly so expensive. He warned the King she was at present the property of Buckhurst. It is also suggested that the Duke of Buckingham urged her upon the King, being desirous of having someone who could counteract Lady Castlemaine, who had at least pretended to be a friend of Nell's. But why all this should have been necessary is obscure, for it is clearly on record (vide Knipp) that the Monarch and Nell were by no means strangers. It is most probable that she needed no recommendation, having sufficient of her own. The King had his eye upon her—this pretty, attractive, clever, honest wanton—and it only needed just some fillip to inflame this jaded passion. That fillip was duly administered.

The King went to his own Theatre, to Drury Lane. The play was *Tyrannic Love* again. This was a tragedy but Nell spoke the epilogue, which had been written specially for her. She died and a bearer came to carry her off. She sat up and said to him:

> Hold, are you mad, you damn'd confounded dog?
> I am to rise, and speak the Epilogue.

And a gay, sprightly epilogue it is:

> I come, kind gentlemen, strange news to tell ye
> I am the ghost of poor departed Nelly.
> Sweet ladies, be not frighted; I'll be civil
> I'm what I was, a harmless little devil.
> For after death we spirits have just such natures
> We had, for all the world, when human creatures
> And therefore I, that was an actress here,
> Play all my tricks in hell, a goblin there.
> Gallants, look to't, you say there are no sprites
> But I'll come dance about your bed at nights
> And faith, you'll be in a sweet kind of taking
> When I surprise you between sleep and waking.
> To tell you true, I walk because I die
> Out of my calling, in a tragedy.
>
> O poet, dam'd dull poet, who could prove
> So senseless, to make Nelly die for love!
> Nay, what's worse, to kill me in the prime
> Of Easter term, in tart and cheesecake time
> I'll fit the fop! for I'll not one word say
> To excuse his godly out of fashion play
> A play, which is you dare but twice sit out
> You'll all be slandered and be thought devout.

> But farewell, gentlemen, make haste to me,
> I'm sure, ere long, to have your company.
> As for my epitaph, when I am gone,
> I'll trust no poet but will write my own.
> Here Nelly lies, who tho' she lived a slattern
> Yet died a Princess acting in St. Catherine.

That epilogue is probably the best portrait of Mistress Nell Gwynne we have. It hits her off to a nicety. She spoke it magnificently, and she understood just how to "put it over." There was no doubt at all about her having the gentlemen's company. Did a sly glance go to the Royal Box when she spoke that line, and was there an answering smile from the King? For at the fall of the curtain Charles himself went backstage, and, so we read, "carried her off to an entertainment."

It was not, however, her final conquest. She was not yet fully installed on the left of, or behind, the Throne. That came shortly after.

The play was *Almanzor and Almahide, or The Conquest of Granada by the Spaniards*. She captured the King, not by an epilogue, but a prologue. Down at the Duke's Theatre, Nokes, a famous comedian, had made a great hit by appearing in an enormous hat, provoking tremendous laughter by it, and doing no good to the business at Drury Lane. Nokes and his hat were the talk of the town.

As the house hushed, as near as a Restoration Theatre audience ever could hush, to hear the prologue to *Almanzor and Almahide*, all eyes turned to the stage, including those of the King in his box. On walked Nell Gwynne, dressed in boy's clothes—gallant's clothes in fact—in the very height of the then extravagant fashion. She looked a dream. The applause broke out and was drowned in a roar of laughter. For on her head Nell wore—a hat. A hat beyond compare, a hat of such immense dimensions and absurdity, so wide of brim, so befeathered, that the headgear of Nokes was a bonnet beside it. Everybody realised the joke and relished it. She made a figure as entrancing as comic, and she knew how to exploit both moods to the full. She stood and smiled at them and this only served to accentuate her femininity. Then she spoke the prologue twitting the public for crowding in just to see a hat, twitting authors who wrote plays to exploit a hat, and saying:

This is that hat, whose very sight did win ye
To laugh and clap as though the devile were in ye
As then, for Nokes, so now I hope you'll be
So dull to laugh once more—this time for me.

Laugh and applaud they did; they raised the roof. She, and the hat, made the hit of her life. Indeed, it was her last and final success on the stage. Once more, at curtain fall, His Majesty was backstage, and this time Mistress Nell Gwynne, seller of herrings and tavern songster, spirit fetcher to a brothel and mistress to many, rode home with her King in his coach, never to return again to the playhouse as an actress. That was the end of her career on the stage, but five years in all. During that time there were breaks because of the Plague closing down the theatres and of her absence at Epsom. But she made such a mark that time has not effaced it, and is still known when so many others have sunk into oblivion.

With the end of her stage career, Nell Gwynne belongs no more to this story. As an actress she failed in tragedy, but shone in comedy. A play which might have died got another chance because she filled the audience with pleasure. She was not a beautiful woman; she was more than that. She possessed real charm, real fascination, what is now called Glamour. It was the real brand for it came from within her; it was not applied outside from bottles and sticks purchased from chemists and beauty parlours. She had red hair—and that tells its own story for there is an allure about redheads which draws most males. She was quite small, and had a neat, trim, shapely figure; she was not slim, but she had curves and softness—she was a woman. And she had the smallest, prettiest foot in town. Above all, she was full of spirit and gaiety, radiating life and activity. She also had that thing which always succeeds both on the stage and in life. Ivor Novello, who knew all about his calling, wrote a song about it called "Vitality." He said it was the most treasured possession of all. Nell Gwynne was Vitality Plus, every bit of her. She was alive and made her audiences come alive, too.

She was, despite her morals, a very honest woman and a very generous and kind-hearted one. She loved only one man at a time. It is certain that she really loved Charles II and that he loved her, so far as in him lay. She never robbed him and her demands were far more reasonable than any of his other favourites. And what she had, she shared with others. Nor was she ever afraid of him: she was never afraid of anyone. Let some Court favourite try a haughty sneer and out of Nell's mouth would come a reply which laid the opponent in the dust. It would be loaded with good oaths and so pointed in repartee that no answer could ever be found. Least of all did she put on airs when she rose to her Court favour, she just went on being Nell Gwynne. She was a true cockney, with all the virtue of the cockney. She remained one of the people from whom she had sprung, and for that the people always loved her. They were as loyal to her as she was to them. And she was loyal to the King—and it is certain she helped him. She bore him two sons. Her blood exists today. Much has been written about her extravagance and her love of diamonds, but she appears to have had a passion for silver plate which was greater than that. She was careless in her dress, but everything became her. In the old account books, there stands far less to her charge than to the others. But it appears that she persuaded Charles to give that good-for-nothing sister of hers a pension. One of her sons became a Duke—and she had a grandson who was a bishop. That was pretty good going from such a start in life. She became Charles's mistress when she was but nineteen, holding him to the end. His last whispered words were of her: "Don't let poor Nelly starve." And another King, James II, whose mistress she was not, kept his promise to his brother and paid her debts.

Hers was a short life and undoubtedly a gay one. She died of apoplexy at the age of thirty-eight. A bishop preached her funeral sermon. And true to herself at the end, by her own wish, she was buried in the same grave as that disgraceful old mother of hers, for whom she had so little to thank. But there they lay in St. Martin in the Fields, street walker and Royal mistress, mother and daughter mingling their common dust in the end.

CHAPTER FIVE

The Ladies are Established

SO far the ladies on the stage had been a novelty. Their acting had been judged tolerantly and their talent appraised according to their looks and attractiveness. It was not because of their greatness as actresses that some of them had become famous but because of their morals—or lack of them. Yet there had already emerged, in Mrs. Betterton, a woman who could be called a great actress; and a remarkably good one, if not a great one, in Ann Marshall. The stage had also produced several very good character actresses, a sparkling dancer and—Nell Gwynne.

More and more women were now taking to the stage, and from their ranks two certainly earned and deserved the title of "great." These two, whose stories we shall tell in this chapter, are Mrs. Barry and Mrs. Bracegirdle. The latter would probably be remembered if only because of her unusual name. Both of them began their career at the Duke's Theatre, founded by Davenant under his patent from Charles II. Davenant never lived to see the theatre completed, but his family carried it on until it was merged with Drury Lane, when they relinquished its stars to its senior rival. A blue plaque marked the spot where it stood in John Carpenter Street, and the boys of that fine school, the City of London, now use its site as a playground. But Drury Lane goes on.

Elizabeth Barry was a great actress. Born in 1658, she was the first woman of good family to take up acting as a profession. Her father, a barrister, had espoused the cause of Charles I, taken up arms and raised a regiment himself of which he became colonel.

But the King lost the war against Parliament and Barry lost all he had, save his life. He became one of that considerable army of broken Cavaliers, living as best they could, in constant fear of arrest and the block.

The prospects for his baby daughter Elizabeth were, accordingly, not very bright. When she was reckoned old enough, she tried for the stage. She had beauty, a handsome face, and a pair of lovely blue eyes which shone from beneath a mass of dark hair. She was also full of life and spirit, but it seemed that she could not act. Davenant, who tried to train her, could make nothing of her, and though she played for a whole year she got nowhere. Colley Cibber, who wrote such words of wisdom about the Theatre and the craft of acting that every young stage aspirant should read what he says, remarked of her: "The fame Mrs. Barry arrived to is a particular proof of the difficulty there is in judging with certainty, from their first trials, whether young people will ever make a great figure in a theatre. There was, it seems, so little hopes of Mrs. Barry at her first setting out, that she was at the end of the first year, discharged the company, among others that were thought to be a useless expense to it." Well, she was not the last to be a late starter; plenty more were to follow.

Cibber, who only saw her when her beauty had begun to fade but when her talent was at its height, thought there must have been a defective ear, a dissonance of some kind to explain it. It is more likely that the methods she had been taught by were too academic, for her next teacher made an actress of her. This was the disreputable, loose-living but brilliantly witty and accomplished Earl of Rochester, the arch rake of his time, the supreme lady-killer, but a man who knew all about the Theatre and what was required therein. Tradition has it that he undertook Elizabeth Barry's stage training, and it can be taken for granted that his training was pretty thorough and complete. He would show the clever managers who had rejected her, what was what! Davenant had tried for a year, had he? Well, he boasted he would make Elizabeth Barry an actress in six months. She would certainly know a great deal about the world and its ways, as well as what are now referred to as the facts of life, after a short course of lessons from My Lord of Rochester. Whatever means he employed, he succeeded in making an actress of her. Perhaps she was one of those people who must have first-hand experience before they can assume emotions convincingly. Maybe she was too calm, too placid and that he woke her up, as he was perfectly capable of doing. If he did instruct her in the arts of love, he did not neglect to impart the art of the Theatre.

He instructed her in parts, taking her through line by line and impressing on her what the author meant by the words she was saying. She was alert and alive now and desperately keen to learn her job; her intelligence was stimulated and she worked hard. Rochester took her, slowly and carefully, through the leading parts in several plays until she understood them all and could play them. Then he arranged an engagement for her. Leaving nothing to chance, he made her give thirty rehearsals of each character, twelve of which were done in costume. At length she made her début as his pupil. She played Isabella, Queen of Hungary in *Mustapha*. A little page bore her train—a boy's part played by a girl—and that little girl, also making her début, was the future Mrs. Bracegirdle. Thus two great actresses started on the same night in the same play.

Elizabeth Barry succeeded. She showed herself a sound, efficient actress, with complete mastery of her art, but no more than this. She got applause, she pleased, but she did not excite. Rochester worked on, fanning the flame he knew was there, until, one evening, he was sure. She played Isabella again. He had asked the King and the Duke of York to come and see her. The flame burst forth. Her talent, her art, suddenly flared up. She swept the audience with her and electrified the other players. At the end she was acclaimed, the storm of applause being led enthusiastically by Charles II and his Royal brother. Mistress Barry had triumphed. This must also have been one of the greatest moments in Rochester's life. Tired, vice-jaded, wicked to the core, he was still an artist to his finger-tips. He had been right, his judgment had been vindicated, and he had the satisfaction of having made this woman an actress. Up to that night, she had been approved, but little more. She had not had the sureness of touch, nor the audience control that an actress must have. She had been known to dry up, even to lose her place in the dance which so often ended the plays. That night, however, something happened: the force sprang to life, and what had been no more han exceptional competence was transformed into greatness. There were still "knockers," as there always are, still those who lecried her, who said she was no cavalier's daughter but a lady's naid. There were those who held that her performance in *Mustapha* was a fluke; the part was so good, they whispered, that nyone could play it. Why, she had not done it so well at first, she vould not do it so well again!

Every successful actress, right down to today, undergoes the ame thing from those immortals of the Theatre, the "knockers," vho grudge success to anyone, even their so-called dearest riends. They, and those who pour cold water on aspirations and mall successes which may lead to so much more, are two of the greatest curses of the Theatre. A word of praise in season, a kindly pat, a bit of encouragement, so often turns failure into uccess, so often opens a door which has seemed bolted and barred. Such things are all too seldom given. Maybe it was just hat timely word and praise which did the trick for Barry and set he smouldering ember into a blazing torch.

Anyway those who "knocked" had a day of awakening coming o them. She played on, gaining experience in touch-and-go omedies—parts of audacity with daring lines to speak. They kept the flame alive until it was to flare up once again one night in 680. She was twenty-two at the time and had been on the stage or seven years. The Duke's Theatre was crowded. There was a new play by Thomas Otway, a tragedy called *The Orphan, or the Unhappy Marriage*, and Mistress Elizabeth Barry was to play the eading woman's part, that of Monimia. The audience were not very excited over that, save those who remembered that flash of greatness she had shown once before. But Betterton himself was playing Castalio and that drew the crowd.

The play began, and Mrs. Barry entered. Once again she had a page holding her train and once again that page was small Bracegirdle, who had done the same six years before. Even as she entered omething crept over the audience and there was suddenly a eeling that this was going to be a great night in the Theatre. The part suited her as none had ever done before, and it gave scope for ll she could give. She had beauty, she had dignity and a wonderful carriage and grace of movement. She had a fine, clear, nelodious voice of perfect diction and she could do what she liked with that voice, given the chance. No emotion was beyond its range: it could soar like a bird, ring out like a trumpet, or send its softest whisper to the uttermost corners of the theatre. On top of that her face could mirror all her voice was saying.

This, then, was her great chance and she took it. Accept the evidence of a man who knew her and saw her act: "Mrs. Barry, in characters of greatness, had a presence of elevated dignity, her mein and motion superb and gracefully majestick, her voice, full clear and strong, so that no violence of passion could be too much for her; and when distress or tenderness possessed her she subsided into the most affecting melody and softness. In the art of exciting pity, she had a power beyond all the actresses I have yet seen, or what your imagination can contrive. In the former of these two great excellencies, she gave the most delightful proofs in almost all the heroick plays of Dryden and Lee; and of the latter in the softer passions of Otway's Monimia and Belvidera . . ." That is a tribute from Colley Cibber, a man who knew all about acting, who became one of the greatest figures in our Theatre history and in the history of Drury Lane, and who died Poet Laureate. As an actor-manager and a dramatist, he was, indeed, a great success himself. Much has been said to his detriment, but whatever his faults he knew greatness when he saw it and he always gave greatness its due. He remembered how an unexpected word of praise from a man who was as good an actor as he was bad a character—Scum Goodman—given to him when he was a starving, penniless young beginner, had put new heart into him and helped him in his own climb to greatness.

That night in March Mrs. Barry stepped into her own. She wrung the hearts of her audience with her performance of the sorrows of the heroine. The play itself became a classic for many years and Monimia a best part for aspiring actresses. Barry filled Betterton with joy: here was someone near his own stature, someone who could give him, on the stage, the same response, the same feeling as his wife had been wont to do. That was what he had wanted for a long time. A friendship grew up between Mrs. Barry and the Bettertons. Later, when Barry was to play Lady Macbeth, Mrs. Betterton, who as Mary Saunderson had been the finest Lady Macbeth and was the first woman to play it with success, coached her. She taught Mrs. Barry all she knew. In that most exacting role, however, the pupil, good as she was, never outshone the tutor.

Maybe the four greatest Lady Macbeth's of all time were Mrs. Betterton, Mrs. Pritchard, Mrs. Siddons and Ellen Terry. That does not mean that there have not been other excellent performances, and Mrs. Barry's is amongst them. But her Monimia placed her in the very front rank, making her, in fact, the leading actress of her day. She was much more than a pretty woman speaking lines intelligently; she was a real actress feeling, living all she said and did. When the curtain fell that night, Elizabeth Barry was the first actress on the English stage—the Leading Lady of the English Theatre.

If she had pleased before, she enchanted now. Already the great ones had appreciated her. The Duchess of York had, as a mark of esteem for her performance as Isabella in *Mustapha*, made her a present of her own treasured wedding dress to use as a stage costume. The Duchess also took lessons from her on how to speak. When she played Elizabeth in *The Earl of Essex*—not too good a play but she made a fine part of it—the Queen gave her the actual Coronation Robe she had worn when crowned. She appears to have brought the character to life and thrilled all beholders. *Alexander the Great*, a favourite play, she endowed with a new majesty by her performance of Roxana, in which she ran the whole gamut of emotions.

Dryden wrote of her, in his preface to the printed version of his play *Cleomenes*, in which Mrs. Barry played Cassandra, the following tribute: "Mrs. Barry, always excellent, has in this tragedy excelled herself, and gained a reputation beyond any woman I have ever seen in the Theatre." Although actresses had not been in the Theatre for long that, from such a man as Dryden, was a testimony worth having. Cibber, although he agreed as to quality, was of the opinion that she had been even better in other parts she played, and preferred her as Monimia, Cleopatra and Roxana.

She was indefatigable in her work, creating no less than one hundred and twelve new characters during her career of thirty-seven years. She stood as the foremost actress of her time, and as proof of that she was the first actress to be given an annual benefit. She was always willing to learn, never resting on her laurels, as witness her being coached by Mrs. Betterton as Lady Macbeth. This shows that she understood that great truth of the acting profession and of the Theatre, that nobody ever knows all about it, that there is always something new to be learned, some improvement to be made, perfection to seek. Not all the people of the Theatre are as aware of that as was Mrs. Barry. As Belvidera she held her audience in complete subjection; they came again and again to see her suffer and weep, to join in her tears and her tribulations. The part is in Otway's play *Venice Preserv'd* and was a favourite with Siddons. It was probably Otway's finest play and held the stage for many years, and has been revived as a museum piece in recent times. If a cast could be found who were able to play it as it should be played, it would in all likelihood draw the public still.

During her stage career, starting from the time when Rochester launched her, Mrs. Barry had no rival. A bad start was retrieved because that spark of genius, which only needs the right conditions, had flared out. Irving himself had only minor successes until *The Bells* gave him his real opportunity. Stage success, for real actors and actresses, is a matter of seizing the opportunity, of answering the call. Those who are not of the great never hear that call, even if it comes. No other actress ever tried to challenge Mrs. Barry's pre-eminence, and that says much. As we shall see, the only one who could have done so refused. So for thirty-seven years she was the first Lady of the Theatre and even advancing age did not dim her greatness of quality. But as the years went on and added their total to her burden, she played less and less. When Betterton took his famous benefit at Drury Lane, she came back to support her old friend and stage partner. At the end of the performance, she stood on one side of him, while Mrs. Bracegirdle, on whom her mantle had descended, stood on the other. Both had come from virtual retirement to pay tribute to this great actor whom they so admired. And Mrs. Barry spoke the very touching and beautiful Epilogue which Nicholas Rowe had written specially for the performance, which ended:

> Had you with-held your favours on this night
> Old Shakespeare's Ghost had ris'n to do him right,
> With indignation had you seen him frown
> Upon a worthless, witless, tasteless Town;

Griev'd and repining you had heard him say
Why are the Muses' labours cast away?
Why did I write what only he could play?
But since, like friends to wit, thus throng'd you meet
Go on, and make the generous work complete;
Be true to merit and still hold his cause,
Find something for him more than mere applause,
In just remembrance of your pleasures past
Be kind, and give him a discharge at last
In peace and ease life's remnant let him wear
And hang his consecrated buskin here. . . .

They did as she said, and no doubt she spoke it nobly. But that buskin, alas, killed poor Betterton the next year when he had his benefit again at the Haymarket. Barry was there again, doing her best.

Mrs. Barry made her last public appearance at the Haymarket on June 13, 1710. This was the theatre Vanbrugh founded, on the site of which Her Majesty's now stands, not the "little Theatre in the Hay," the progenitor of the present lovely Haymarket Theatre, which was not then built. She appeared as Mrs. Easy in Colley Cibber's *The Careless Husband.* After her retirement she did what she could to help Mrs. Betterton, for she was of a kind and generous nature, but she lived only three more years. In her last hours, when she was delirious she still acted in that misty world of unreality in which her mind floated. Snatches of words came from her lips, to which her friends listened. They were all declamations in blank verse, some recognisable from parts she had played, some without any clue. But just before her end, she roused herself and said, in her old ringing tones:

Ha, ha! And so they make us Lords, by dozens.

Those were her last words, a political tag popular then but lost now. She had played to the end.

She was the complete actress in many ways. Despite her generosity of nature and her warm heart, she could have temperaments and tantrums, and, indeed, had the temper of a fiend when roused. There was a scene in one performance of *Alexander the Great,* which was as real as stage realism could be. She elected to wear a very handsome veil from the theatre wardrobe. This led to a protest from another actress, named Mrs. Boutell, who claimed that she always wore that veil when appearing in *Alexander* as Statira. There was a wrangle and the Property Master was called upon to adjudicate between the two heated ladies. He awarded the veil to Mrs. Boutell on the grounds that she had worn it when playing the part at the original production, with Charles Hart as Alexander and Ann Marshall as Roxana. Mrs. Barry perforce gave way and the other lady appears to have made a good deal out of this, crowing over her and flaunting the veil before her. The play proceeded and the two women met for their big dramatic scene. All the scenes had been played at fever heat and no doubt the audience sensed that something unusual was afoot. When the big moment came, when Roxana played by Mrs. Barry, seized her rival-in-the-play and rival to the veil, in a desperate struggle, she had to declaim, "Die, sorceress, die. And all my wrongs die with thee." Then she had to stab Statira. And did Mrs. Barry stab Mrs. Boutell with a vengeance? She did indeed. She plunged that gleaming dagger forward as if she really meant it; the point pierced the stiff, strong stays of the actress Boutell and entered into the flesh beneath. There was a yell, a scream, and Mrs. Boutell fell to the boards. She was carried off, while Mrs. Barry stood panting, with gleaming eyes, the dagger clutched in her hand—and perhaps not a little terrified. However no great harm had been done, just a scratch—and a little, a very little blood. But it was quite enough for a good big backstage row, with recriminations filling the air like meteors and everybody taking sides. It was suggested that Mrs. Boutell had enticed a lover from Mrs. Barry, a suggestion which the latter scorned as a lie. Her version was that the whole thing was an accident; she had been carried away by the scene, had overacted, and she now apologised. Nothing more was said about the scarf which had caused the trouble. Mrs. Boutell's wound, slight enough, was patched up and the two ladies patched up their quarrel. Outwardly, at least.

Elizabeth Barry had no need to feel jealousy. She had her lovers, of course, but they were true to her, and, in her way, she was true to them. They included, naturally, the Earl of Rochester and later, Etherege the wit, poet and playwright. She bore each of them a daughter.

Mrs. Barry was no fool. Because she saved her money and never squandered it she was often taxed with parsimony, but she had the sense to remember that the time would come when her powers would fail and she had no desire to go down the hill and die in penury. She had seen too much of that. She went from the stage before she lost the slightest grip on her public.

She had the power of investing lines, which with a lesser actress would have meant little or nothing, with great power and reason. It was said of her that when she played Monimia and spoke the line "Ah, poor Castilio"—in that simple phrase was the whole pity of the world. Without being a raging beauty, she had fine features, fine eyes and hair, and great charm. She had that priceless gift—Personality. She had the equally priceless gift of Power. With her, the line of great actresses truly began, for as good as Mrs. Betterton had been, she had not the range of Mrs. Barry.

On her retirement and prior to her death, she went to live in what was then the country, at Acton Vale. She left her town house near the Savoy Palace for a nice cottage amidst the trees and fields. And she was laid to rest in the churchyard there, with a tablet on the church wall to mark her final bed: "Near this place lies the body of Elizabeth Barry, of the parish of St. Mary-le-Savoy, who departed this life on 7th November, 1713, aged 55 years."

And that little page, who bore the train of Mrs. Barry? She became as famous, if not more famous. Mrs. Anne Bracegirdle is one of the old time actresses far more often remembered than Mrs. Barry, perhaps, as suggested earlier, because of that somewhat extraordinary name. None the less she had talent and qualities which entitle her to a place in the great frieze of the immortals of our Theatre.

There is no certainty as to the actual year of her birth, but if she was indeed six when she appeared as a page to Mrs. Barry in 1680, the year would be 1674. She died in 1748 and was said to be turned eighty so maybe she was a little bit older than those six little years. She was of good birth, the daughter of a country gentleman, Justinian Bracegirdle of Northamptonshire, in which county she was born. Her father suffered very severe reverses in fortune; he appears to have gone surety for somebody, a friend whom he trusted, it is said, and found that his whole estate and money was lost. He must have been on friendly terms with those

good people, the Bettertons, for they took the child under their care and trained her for the stage. There is, however, another story, that she was the daughter of a man who made and let out coaches in Northampton and that he was actually a coachman himself. Betterton himself gives the former version and he ought to know, unless, of course, Justinian of the aristocratic name was a coachbuilder. However, Betterton claims she was born of gentlefolk of good extraction.

She certainly showed good breeding all her life, for in an age of unchastity she remained chaste, and was nicknamed the Diana of the Stage. Whether she was cold and distant by nature or whether she was indeed a very moral woman will never be known. She did not lack for suitors—of high rank, of every rank; but she showed them no favours save courtesy and friendship. She was most punctilious in her manners and always did the right thing, and said the right thing. The Earl of Burlington, thinking to please her, sent her a very handsome gift of china. It was delivered by his footman, together with a flowery, flattering letter, protesting his affection. Mrs. Bracegirdle read the letter. Indeed, she kept the letter. But she told the footman that a mistake had been made and that he should not have brought the china to her. It was, she said, intended for the Earl's wife and he had better take it back to her. Not doubting, the flunkey did as he was bid and the Countess received the unexpected gift of china from her husband. She was delighted at the surprise and profuse in her thanks. There is no record of what the Earl said or did. Doubtless he realised that he had escaped from a very difficult position.

Another great thing stands to her credit. She steadfastly refused to take over any of the parts which Mrs. Barry played regularly, even when that great actress was ageing and might have been expected to relinquish them to a younger woman, though few in her position would have done it willingly. When the proposal was made to Mrs. Bracegirdle by the management, she refused point blank. Not many actresses in her position and in her period would have done that. But she had no need to worry, for she had plenty of parts. She was Congreve's leading lady and she played his works to perfection. There is no doubt that Congreve was in love with her and would have given much to make her his mistress, but though she held him in the highest esteem and regarded him as a very dear friend, she refused any such relationship. She was in fact capable of true platonic friendship. A man named Curll, who published and wrote books, desired to issue a volume called "Memoirs of the Life, Writing and Amours of William Congreve Esq." He approached Mrs. Bracegirdle, asking her to give him facts and details of her friend the playwright. The actress sternly refused, telling him his book would not have "a new sheet in it," by which she meant he would have to "lift" everything from other people. She was right.

Despite her chastity, Mrs. Bracegirdle brought tragedy and death to an actor, although she was not to blame. He was Will Mountfort, one of the best performers of his day. He was handsome, debonair, and graceful, and the best stage lovemaker of his day. It is said that the actresses with whom he played love scenes were carried away by his pleadings, although they knew it was only part of the play. He was natural in his method when stylised and stilted acting was the vogue. He was also a wonderful mimic, and could sing and dance excellently. He won high commendation from Queen Mary (William of Orange's wife) who was, like all the Stuarts, a good playgoer. The Queen although shocked and disgusted at a play by Aphra Behn, the woman dramatist and first of her time, called *The Rover*, expressed delight at the performance given in it by Will Mountfort. He was the original Sir Courtly Nice. Mountfort could have reached the peak of his profession had it not been for his untimely death. The attraction exercised, quite unwittingly, by Mrs. Bracegirdle's restrained beauty and pure reputation on two of the worst scoundrels in Town, was unfortunately to be responsible for this.

The worst man in London was Charles, Lord Mohun, already tried for murder but acquitted by his Peers on a solemn promise never to brawl again. A friend of his, equally dissolute, one Captain Richard Hill, had fallen in love with Mrs. Bracegirdle. Her coldness fascinated him but he did not really believe in it. He thought she used it as a cloak and that underneath that appearance of virginity was a passionate woman. He had made approaches and been instantly repelled. So he decided to carry off the actress by force, if necessary. He had also made up his mind that Will Mountfort was Mrs. Bracegirdle's lover. He had seen them play scenes on the stage in so real and natural a manner that he believed their acting could only have sprung from real passion. So he decided it might be necessary to remove Mountfort. He spoke to Mohun, found him more than willing, and they laid a plot.

They learned that Mrs. Bracegirdle, on December 9, 1692, was going to sup with her friends, the Pages, in Princes Street, Drury Lane. They engaged six men who were to lie in wait near the Pages' house and to carry her off on her way home. The streets were dark, ill lit and unpoliced. They were to seize her, bundle her into a carriage stationed nearby and drive off.

Mrs. Bracegirdle duly left her friends and set off for home at ten. The men pounced on her. But they caught a tartar; not only did she resist most violently but she screamed with all her might. Her friend and his brother who were escorting her fought manfully. A crowd gathered and the paid abductors fled. Lord Mohun and Captain Richard Hill, who were present, came up and offered their escort. Maybe the Pages had had enough, maybe they were hurt, so the escort of the gallants was accepted. But Mrs. Bracegirdle had her suspicions and must have been relieved when her house in Howard Street, Strand, was reached. Perhaps she knew that neither of the men dared attempt abduction when it was known they were escorting her. Also, she was very popular and an outcry would have brought a quick rescue. Nevertheless when she got in, she kept the two men under observation. They remained outside her house and were drinking from a flask. They looked about them keenly. Mrs. Bracegirdle remembered that when Hill had been pestering her, he had often cursed Mountfort and uttered threats, saying that he knew the actor was his rival. Mrs. Bracegirdle, who was very shrewd, came to the conclusion that violence was intended against Mountfort who lived nearby in Norfolk Street. She managed to get a message to Mrs. Mountfort to tell her to warn her husband that danger threatened.

Will Mountfort was at home. He was no coward but a gallant gentleman. He was not afraid of either of the two rogues, but he thought his friend Bracegirdle might be in more danger than he, so out he went to see if he could be of help. He soon came upon Mohun and Hill together. He did not know they were both in this plot, and did not suspect Mohun. He went up to His Lordship, whom he knew, and greeted him. Mohun, as was then the fashion, threw his arms round him and embraced him. Mountfort whispered a few words of warning against Hill and little did he know how true his last words were, for whilst Mohun held him tight in that Judas-like embrace, Hill ran his sword through the actor's body and dropped him mortally wounded to the ground. The two assailants made off. Mountfort was carried home and in his dying breath asserted that Hill had pierced him in the manner described and that he had no chance to draw his sword. Hill fled the country but Mohun surrendered to arrest, was tried again by his peers and, although a minority declared him guilty of murder, a majority acquitted him. Appropriately, his own end was bloody; he and the Duke of Hamilton fought a savage duel in Hyde Park and hacked each other to death.

There were accounts which state that Mountfort was killed in fair fight. In view of the character of his assailants, it does not seem very likely. He was only thirty-three when he met his tragic end, a fine actor and a dramatist of promise.

Mrs. Bracegirdle, for all her purity, was on another occasion fined for obscenity on the stage. It happened at Lincoln's Inn Fields Theatre. Betterton, her patron and teacher, had revolted against the misrule of Rich at Drury Lane, and led a company of actors to Lincoln's Inn Fields Theatre, where he opened in opposition and did Rich no good. At this time, a man called Jeremy Collier made a violent attack on the morals and manners of the stage and the lewdness of the plays. Common informers went to the theatres, took notes of what they considered objectionable and laid information with the authorities. The consequence was that three of the chief performers at Lincoln's Inn, Betterton himself, Ben Johnson and Mrs. Bracegirdle were hauled before the Justices. Johnson got off but both Betterton and Bracegirdle, the two people whose lives were beyond reproach, were fined. Good Queen Anne soon stopped all that. She made many difficulties for the informers, who found it did not pay and gave it up.

Although she played many parts and played them all well, she must go down to fame as the creator and leading lady of those delicious roles written by Congreve. It is said he would sit for hours, his hat pulled down over his eyes, and watch her. In *The*

Old Bachelor, his first success, performed at Drury Lane in 1693, she spoke the prologue pretending to be frightened and finally running off the stage, and also played Araminta. It ran for 14 consecutive performances, a real wonder in those days. At Drury Lane in December of the same year she was Cynthia in his *Double Dealer*. The part, a pure woman amongst rakes, was obviously written for her. When Betterton, Mrs. Barry and she went to Lincoln's Inn and became joint patentees, she was Angelica in *Love for Love* and in 1696 Almeria in *The Mourning Bride*. She was also the creator of Millamant in *The Way of the World* and it must have been a remarkable performance. She spoke the epilogue, too. At the Dorset Gardens Theatre, when it was in decline and went in for Opera, she was Venus in Congreve's *Judgment of Paris*. His farce *Squire Treelooby* was played for her benefit and she was in it, too. When they tried to popularise the Vanbrugh Theatre in the Haymarket, then called the Queen's, she spoke the prologue to an Italian Pastoral. By this time she was getting near her retirement. But she came out of that retirement to support her friend and benefactor Betterton, in his wonderful benefit at Drury Lane, when she again played Angelica in *Love for Love*.

From time to time she wore the breeches, too, filling the house when she did so. She wore them to speak the prologue to D'Urfey's *Marriage Hater Matched* and feigned embarrassment. Part of the fun was the continued assurances from her brother and sister players that her mannish attire became her (undoubtedly it did), but, with a cry of "Lord, I'm so ashamed," she finally turned to the audience and spoke her prologue.

She lived in greater comfort and style than most actresses, always going to and from the theatre in her sedan chair. But she was very charitable and would go into Clare Market, then a rough slum filled with the poorest of the poor, and a notorious and noisome place, to give money to the most needy people she could find. She was beloved there, and woe betide anyone who had tried to molest her when any of her faithful Clare Marketers were in sight! They would cheer her in the street.

Although so many tried to make her their lover, she had admirers who respected her purity and her talent without lascivious thoughts. On one occasion my Lords of Devon, Dorset and Halifax, with other peers, were discussing her over their wine.

They agreed that she adorned the stage not only by her ability, but also by her virtue, a very rare a thing. Lord Halifax felt so strongly about it that he declared they ought to do something more to show their appreciation than merely to discuss and approve it. He slapped down two hundred guineas on the table as a token of his unselfish admiration. Not to be outdone, the others followed suit, and in all, eight hundred guineas was presented to Mrs. Bracegirdle as a result. The lady, assured there were no "strings" to it, accepted it graciously.

In appearance she was dark and dainty, with lovely hair and fine-arched eyebrows. Her eyes were large and sparkling and she had the gift of blushing—a warm roseate glow flushing over face and neck, which men found well-nigh irresistible. There was little blushing in those immodest and immoral days, so her gift was unique. It is Colley Cibber who draws the best picture of her. He wrote it when she was in retirement, saying he thought she would not be pleased at being once more dragged forth but asking her to excuse the liberty because of the delight she occasioned when she was an ornament to the Theatre. Her unblemished reputation, he writes, "contributed not a little to make her the Cara, the darling, of the Theatre; for it will be no extravagant thing to say, with scarce an audience saw her that were less than half of them lovers, without a suspected favourite amongst them. And though she might be said to have been the universal passion, and under the highest temptation, her constancy in resisting them served but to increase the numbers of her admirers; and thus perhaps you will more easily believe, when I extend not my encomiums on her person beyond a sincerity that can be suspected; for she had no greater claim to beauty than what the most desirable brunette might pretend to. But her youth and lively aspect threw out such a glow of health and cheerfulness that, on the stage, few spectators that were not past it could behold her without desire. It was even the fashion among the gay and young to have a taste or tendre for Mrs. Bracegirdle. She inspired the best authors to write for her and two of them, when they gave her a lover in a play, seemed palpably to plead their own passions and make their private court to her, in fictitious characters. In all the chief parts she acted, the desirable was so predominant that no judge could be cold enough to consider from what other particular excellence she became delightful." Cibber's particular favourites among her roles were Statira in Lee's *Alexander the Great* and Millamant in *The Way of the World*. And he noted that when singing was required, her voice gave the play an added charm.

There is a remarkable contemporary statement which confirms her complete hold and mastery of an audience. This is to the effect that when she made an exit the audiences suddenly found their faces relax and realised that the whole time she had been playing, they had been moulding their own faces to the expression she used. That is a tribute indeed.

She left the stage at the height of her popularity. She was never lured back, even by the most tempting offers, save by the desire to help Betterton at his benefits. She lived to be over eighty. That she was of a nice, generous nature is shown by the fact that when old Colley Cibber was disparaging the young Garrick, whom she had at that time never seen, she tapped him on the elbow and said "Come, come, Cibber, tell me if there is not something like envy in your character of this young gentleman. The actor who pleases everybody *must* be a man of merit." Old Colley stared, took snuff, laughed and said generously, "Faith, Bracey, I believe you are right. The young fellow *is* clever."

Congreve, despite his desire for her or perhaps because of it, wrote a poem obviously about her—addressing her as "Belinda," and one can understand from it the feelings which made him perhaps more than a little bitter:

Pious Belinda goes to prayers
Whene'er I ask the favour,
Yet the tender fool's in tears
When she thinks I'd leave her.
Would I were free from this restraint
Or else had power to win her,
Would she could make of me a saint
Or I of her a sinner.

This neatly sums up delicious Bracegirdle who created such widespread desire which, so far as is known, she never satisfied. . . . Bracegirdle the Desired but not the Desirous.

CHAPTER SIX

An Aureole of Actresses

BY the end of the seventeenth century actresses of quality were no longer rare. The ladies were beginning to make their mark not only by their personal charm, appearance and the influence of their lovers, but by their ability. Many of them have been forgotten, multitudes who now flock to the Theatre have never even heard their names, but they played an important part on the female side of their profession and are worthy of remembrance.

By 1682 the Duke's Theatre had finished its short, if glorious career, and its company had amalgamated with that of Drury Lane. One of that company was a very good actress indeed, and deserves to be remembered as much as Mrs. Barry or Mrs. Bracegirdle.

This lady did nothing by halves, and even had three names during her stage career. Her maiden name was Percival—Susanna Percival—but she adopted the prefix "Mrs." according to custom to show she was nobody's mistress, although it made little difference. She first married Mountford, that good actor and promising playwright who met such an unfortunate end at the sword of Captain Hill, whilst going to the defence of Mrs. Bracegirdle. Then she married an actor called Verbruggen. Her life was full of excitement and full of tragedy. Yet she was an actress of comedy without equal in her time. Perhaps her talent was inherited for she was the daughter of an actor named Percival.

She could play any form of comedy, from dainty, bepatched and bepowdered dames luring their lovers, swooning with emotion or counterfeit terror and shock to roles in the broadest of broad low comedy. She was not only a fine mimic but had every dialect at her tongue's command. She also possessed the rare gift of being able to transform herself into the character she played, of being able, so it seemed, to alter her very shape and face at will. She could look beautiful, gracious, queenly and she could be the broad, round-shouldered, labour-bent, vacant, grinning country bumpkin to the life. It was all the same to her if she had to imitate the airs and graces of a fine lady of fashion or the pinched, spinsterish character of an elderly lady's maid.

She had a laugh which sent the house into roars of sympathetic mirth, and she had a curious titter which made them roar the louder. Her timing was near perfection. She could change the mood at the correct split second and keep her audience sitting forward in delight. She knew all the tricks with a fan and with gesture. She wore the breeches, too, and she was most popular in such parts, and was one of the first women to play the character of Bayes in *The Rehearsal*, which for many years was a stock character for leading actors. It was said that at first she was not willing to play a part in *Oroonoko* because she would have to wear male attire. She considered it would not suit her, and it would appear that her legs were thick and not too shapely. But she played the part, and so much was she the gallant, so much did she assume the male air, that her public acclaimed her. Having succeeded, she went on and the public could not have enough. She seemed to transform herself into a gay, sprightly young fellow, still keeping her feminine allure.

She may or may not have been deeply in love with Verbruggen, but she was faithful to him. Verbruggen was a rugged actor, and a rugged character in real life, too, by no means as faithful to his wife as she was to him. Yet despite pretence to the contrary, he held her in great esteem. He would declare: "Damme, though I don't much value my wife, yet nobody shall affront her by God," and his ready sword would come whipping out. People hurried to reassure him, for he was no mean swordsman, and discreet, tactful Mrs. Verbruggen, as she had become, took good care to give him no cause for anger.

She was a fine woman, plump as the fashion then ran, full of feminine curves, fair of complexion and with a rather full oval face. It is said that she had moles on it, as well as on her neck and breast, and judging by the praise bestowed upon what might nowadays be regarded as blemishes, they were evidently considered to enhance her beauty. Other times, other tastes.

She was an actress of the natural school at a time when acting was mannered, and contemporary writers say that when she played a part, it hardly seemed that she was acting at all. Her masterpiece seems to have been Melantha in *Marriage à la Mode*. To her performance in this play Colley Cibber gives wonderful and well-considered praise and goes into the greatest technical detail and exactitude. She must have been very good to overcome the serious drawback of bad legs, especially at a time when more attention was paid to an actress's physical perfections than to her art. But the public loved her and respected her.

When she became Mrs. Verbruggen, tragedy visited her again. Her father, old Percival, got himself involved in a plot to assassinate King William III; he and others were arrested and thrown into jail, and he was amongst those condemned to death. His daughter, who loved her father, moved heaven and earth to save him, and, daring everything, she appealed to good Queen Mary. She got access to the Queen, presented her written petition and even pleaded her cause. Mary was a Stuart and she loved the Theatre. Moved by Mrs. Verbruggen's pleading, she got old Percival reprieved and the death sentence altered to one of transportation. Unfortunately, the old actor was so weak from privation, anxiety and jail fever that he died on the way to Portsmouth to the ship which was to take him overseas. But his daughter had, at least, saved him from the gallows.

It is only fair to record that there is a different version of the crime of Mrs. Mountford-Verbruggen's father. He was a useful if undistinguished actor, playing secondary or tertiary parts, such as Fortinbras in *Hamlet* and Artimedorus in *Julius Caesar*. It is stated on good authority that he was arrested in 1693 on a charge, not of conspiracy against the Crown, but of coin clipping. This annoying business was very prevalent and the Law, which sent people to death in those days on the slightest provocation, took a gloomy view of it, and Percival was sentenced to death. Whatever the real story, it is true that his daughter saved his life and that he died as chronicled.

Mrs. Mountford herself died in 1703. Cibber left a wonderful picture of her: "Mrs. Mountford was mistress of more variety of humour than I ever knew in any one actress. This variety too was attended with an equal vivacity, which made her excellent in character extremely different. . . . Nothing, though ever so barren, if within the bounds of nature, could be flat in her hands. She gave many heightening touches to characters but coldly written and often made an author vain of his work that in itself had but little merit." Could more be said of any actress?

The Percival family was destined to suffer disappointment and tragedy, even unto the third generation. Grandfather Percival had been condemned to death; though the sentence was commuted to transportation, he had died a convict. His daughter, as we have seen, was widowed by murder. But she gave the murdered man a daughter—a second Susanna, who also went on the stage. She did not adopt the name of her stepfather, but kept the more famous name of Mountford. Not her mother's equal as actress, she nevertheless had beauty, grace, and a certain wistful appeal, which made her a most successful Ophelia, a part destined to give her the speck of immortality she possesses in theatre history. She was dark, and the famous ballad by Gay, "Black Eyed Susan," was inspired by her.

Whilst her mother seems to have been discreet and to have preferred wedlock to irregular unions, she had not the same scruples. She captivated the heart of the rising actor Barton Booth, who was destined to become one of the immortals of our stage, and the two of them lived together very happily. Booth was at heart a very generous and good man; he looked after his mistress's affairs and took charge of the moderate fortune—it was a fortune in those days—of £3,200 which she had amassed. In case there may be wonder at an actress having got together, at so young an age, so much money out of the meagre salaries then paid, it has to be confessed that when Miss Susanna Mountford formed her attachment to Booth, she was no inexperienced girl. There had been Lord Berkeley, who was apparently quite infatuated with her. He gave her a landed estate, very considerable sums of money, and on his death left her £300 a year, on condition that she did not marry. It was after his death that she met Booth and fell in love with him. To judge the lady fairly, she might have married Booth, but then that very nice little income of £300 would have been lost. She had no lack of suitors—mistresses with money and settled incomes were rare in any walk of life—especially when the glamour of the stage was added. But she preferred Booth and so they set up house together. The fact that she had money did not weigh much with him. He looked after it very well for her, and in another way he gave convincing proof of his good nature and unselfishness. He and Susanna used to like a flutter in the State lotteries which, in those dark, benighted times were used to raise money for the country and were the immoral substitute for that beneficent institution now so approved and well beloved by the people of this realm, the Income Tax. They bought some tickets and agreed that they should pool whatever they got, no matter whose ticket was the lucky one. The luck fell to Susanna, one of her numbers turning up trumps to the extent of £5,000. Booth refused to press his claim for half, and let her keep the entire amount. Again, in fairness, it must be stated that she made him the offer but he refused. It may well be that the sum of £3,200—her money—which is currently reported as being in his care, was lent to him by his mistress.

Unhappily the course of their love did not run smoothly. For some time they were very happy, but then a serpent appeared in Eden. It led to rows and disagreements, to reproaches and recriminations. It is probable that the fault was with the lady, for in the main Booth was a good fellow and no libertine. Probably Susanna was conscious that no bond of wedlock existed and knowing too well the laxness of the times, feared the approach of any charming lady to her lover. It so happened that Booth was appearing in several plays with a delightful young lady, an actress and dancer, whose name was Hester Santlow. She had begun as a ballet dancer and as such had won fame. But she graduated to be an actress and a pretty good actress, too. She first played opposite to Booth in *The Fair Quaker of Deal*. He had admired her before that, in her dancing days, and, no mean poet, he had written an ode to her long before they became attached so closely. It is worth quoting:

Whether her easy body blend
Or her fair bosom heave with sighs,
Whether her graceful arms extend
Or gently fall, or gently rise,

Or returning, or advancing
Swimming round or sidelong glancing
Gods, how divine an air
Harmonious gestures gives the fair.

and again:

Such Daphne was—
Such were her lovely limbs, so flushed her charming face!
So round her neck! her eyes so fair!
So rose her swelling chest! so flowed her amber hair!
While her swift feet outstript the wind
And left the God of Day behind.

Booth fared better than the God of Day; he was the better Apollo of the two, for he caught his Daphne all right. With his fame, his good looks, and his ability to string verses, no wonder he succeeded!

No doubt there were reasons for Susanna's suspicions; no doubt she had cause to be jealous; and no doubt at all that she told Booth a few home truths about his Daphne. For this nymph was not pure and chaste; she was the mistress of one Craggs, a Secretary of State, who was so generous to her that she could, if she so wished, have lived without acting at all. Probably those jibes did not affect Booth, for Susanna's own past would not bear much examination. Some historians have been hard upon the dainty Santlow; she is set down as a strumpet and other terms of reproach are levelled at her. But she was no better and no worse than the rest of her profession at that time.

In the end Booth and Susanna Mountford broke off their affair. He returned to her the £3,200, which he had either borrowed or taken care of for her, and he was given a receipt in full, dated January 21, 1718, which was witnessed by no less than six people, so that there should be no doubt about it. Thus ended the love of Booth and Mountford. Susanna then took another lover, one Mishull, who spent all her money as fast as he could. Barton Booth married his Santlow and the two spent a happily married life together. It was unluckily not a long life, for Booth died all too young, but the pair were an ideal couple and divinely happy.

Against all precedent for actors of his time, Booth was a man of education and cultured tastes. His leisure he spent in writing and in translating Greek and Latin verse into English. He wrote about the joys of married life—and wrote well:

> Happy the hour when first our souls were joined
> The social virtues and the cheerful mind
> Have ever crowned our days, beguiled our pain;
> Strangers to discord and her clamorous train.

It is worth reminding ourselves that there are very many happy stage marriages. Because actors and actresses are in the limelight and are "news," whenever there is marital strife it gets publicity out of all measure to its importance. For one stage divorce or scandal, there are tens of thousands of others never heard of at all. So do people form their judgment of the morals of the Stage. Nobody will defend the morals of the late seventeenth century, but they were no worse in the Theatre than elsewhere.

When poor Booth died, somewhat suddenly and mysteriously, at once the evil tongued tried to traduce his wife with accusations of poisoning. But the members of his profession soon scotched that rumour. Hester Santlow was his beloved. His will testified to it and is worthy of reproduction as an example of the fact that even in the looseness of the eighteenth century, married bliss was possible. Leaving everything he had possessed to his wife, and nothing to his relations, his will said:

> "As I have been a man much known and talked of, my not leaving legacies to my relations may give occasion to censorious people to reflect upon my conduct in this latter part of my life; therefore I think it necessary to declare that I have considered my circumstances, and finding on strict examination that all I am now possessed of does not amount to two-thirds of the fortune my wife brought me on the day of our marriage, together with the yearly additions and advantages since arising from her laborious employment on the stage during twelve years past, I thought myself bound by honesty, honour and gratitude, due to her constant affection, not to give away any part of the remainder of her fortune on my death, having already bestowed, in free gifts, upon my sister Barbara Rogers, upwards of thirteen hundred pounds, *out of my wife's substance*, and full

> four hundred pounds *of her money* on my undeserving brother George Booth (besides the gifts they received before my marriage) and all those benefits were conferred on my said brother and sister, from time to time, *at the earnest solicitation of my wife*, who was perpetually entreating me to continue the allowance I gave my relations before my marriage. The inhuman return that has been made my wife for these obligations, by my sister, I forbear to mention.

That was the feeling which Hester Santlow inspired in her husband; Barton Booth took his love for her to his grave and she remained constant to his memory. It was doubtless from the disgruntled brother and sister that the whispers about poison originated.

Truly, she must have been a lovely woman. No wonder she had captivated the men before Booth caught and kept her heart. Booth was not the only poet inspired to draw her image in words, and many great people had courted her. The great Duke of Marlborough forgot his Duchess and gave her not only his favour, but something with which he could far less bear to part—money. Secretary of State, Master Craggs, who had started as a barber's son and risen to high office, also poured treasure upon her, giving her everything but his name. In return, she gave him a daughter. That daughter achieved something her mother did not, although the mother achieved great happiness. The daughter was mother of a Lord—Lord St. Germans—and by a second marriage, of another peer, the first Marquis of St. Albans.

Hester Santlow gave up dancing for acting just when Old Drury wanted a new and attractive leading lady. She stepped into the breach and filled it in *The Fair Quaker of Deal*. The simple Quaker dress suited her graceful figure and piquant face; her eyes which could glance sidelong did so with deadly effect from under the Quaker bonnet. Her voice was gentle and soft, and she played naturally, never overacting. But good as she was as an actress, many regretted her retirement from dancing. For then her full grace was disclosed. She had a trick which never failed to send her audience—or the male portion of it—into ecstasies of delight. When she danced her beautiful auburn hair came loose and fell about her perfectly modelled neck and shoulders. Then, with hair flying and limbs twinkling, she danced and danced, and the hearts of her male audience danced with her on the end of those flying auburn tresses. . . .

Such was Hester Santlow, who succeeded with Booth where Susanna Mountford failed. Mountford took her defeat very much to heart. She is supposed to have been a friend of Santlow's and to have been thrown in an agony of rage and grief when the Booth marriage took place. It is more than likely that she was a very jealous woman and, having lost her man, could not endure the sight of his happiness with another. She took another lover, maybe for affection, maybe for spite. And that lover robbed her. She was not happy and she continued to brood over her unhappiness, the inroads on her money made by her lover probably contributing to her agonised state of mind. She went into the country, locked herself away, and eventually became insane. Her friends brought her to London to see doctors, but the medical profession knew little or nothing about insanity and its treatment, and could do nothing for her. Lunatics had a dreadful time in those days, and their hospital, Bedlam, was a free and public show. Mercifully Susanna Mountford did not go there. Hers was no raging mania, but a gentle mourning, wandering loss of balance. Sometimes, indeed, she seemed quite sane and conversed normally. She was not kept closely watched or confined, and was given the freedom of the house.

One day, when she seemed most lucid, she asked what play was being given at Drury Lane. When she was told that it was to be *Hamlet*, she became quiet and thoughtful. She had often played in *Hamlet* at Drury Lane, and had been a very good Ophelia indeed. The cunning of her madness came to her aid and she formed a plan. She managed to escape from her watchful attendant and she sped through the streets to the great theatre she knew so well. Somehow she got backstage; she probably had little difficulty in doing so, for they knew her there and could have had no suspicion of what her warped mind was holding in its dark and wayward depth. Standing in the wings, she was probably unnoticed, for those were the days when the public wandered all over the stage. When the scene came where Ophelia enters insane, the audience sat up and drew its breath. For just before the cue, on walked, not the Ophelia of the evening, but another—

another whom some of them had seen but had never expected to see that evening—an Ophelia who played that scene of tragic tenderness, of deep, deep sorrow, so perfectly portraying the distraught mind of a gentle girl, driven mad by love, in a manner in which it had never been played before, with such depth, such infinite pathos, such perfect understanding of the unhinged senses as no actress had hitherto accomplished. There is no record of what happened off stage, but at least no attempt was made to restrain this sudden and unlooked for Ophelia. The actors and actresses, astounded as they must have been, nevertheless played on without showing their sense of anything unusual.

The scene was played right through without a hitch. It might have been carefully rehearsed, such was its perfection, from that first sudden and arresting entrance of this strange, distraught Ophelia with her query, "Where is the beauteous majesty of Denmark?" and her sad, moaning little ditty, half uttered, half crooned "How should I your true love know," right down to the last exit "And of all Christian souls I pray God, God be with you" . . . That line said, Susanna Mountford walked from the stage into the shadows of the wings, back into the shadows which encompassed her. It was all over with her, and her mind was clear enough to know it. She, mad, had nevertheless once more played her part. The blood in her veins had conquered. Grand-daughter of an actor, daughter of an actor and actress, she had made her last bid for self-expression in the manner best suited to her, playing the part which she had always played best and never before so well. Then she tottered and fell, exclaiming "It is all over." She was carried to her home and put to bed. She drooped and the waters of death carried her along with them as the waters of the brook had carried poor Ophelia. Surely in all the long and eventful history of Theatre Royal, Drury Lane, there was never such a page as when a mad woman, mad for love, played so superbly the poor mad girl whom Shakespeare drew.

Before we move on to the greater days of the actresses, when the names of famous and remembered women take the stage, when it will become so crowded that only a few of the women who made their mark and delighted playgoers can possibly be mentioned, there still remain some of the ladies who came first who deserve a place in this record of their calling. If some of them had little talent, if few of them led lives free from blame, it should be remembered that as pioneers they made history.

Among them there was a Mrs. Jennings, who made no great impact but who yet played some good parts at Lincoln's Inn Theatre, and a Mrs. Wiseman whose name occasionally appears but of whom nothing is now known. She may have married and left the stage, she may have played on under another name and by so doing lost her identity. Mary Aldridge, who was for some fifteen or sixteen years leading lady at the Duke's Theatre, Drury Lane's rival, before Mrs. Barry came to take that eminent position, claims more of our attention. She was to become Mrs. Lee and to play with great distinction with Betterton himself. She made her début in a play by Aphra Behn in 1670. She played leads in many plays of Otway. In the very front rank of actresses, she also attained high social rank, becoming Lady Slingsby. She was buried as "Dame Mary Slingsby" in the graveyard of St. Pancras Church in 1694. It is said she was of a good Yorkshire family, named Scriven, who were of the baronetcy. Here would seem to have been another virtuous woman of the stage. Her first husband, Lee, was an actor, her second a baronet, of Bifrons, Kent.

Another actress of quality was Elinor Leigh, the wife of a very good actor. Altogether she had a stage career of some forty years. She had a sense of characterisation not possessed by many actresses of her time. Her line was comedy and she excelled in ageing beauties who still believed, or affected to believe, that they remained in possession of all their old charms, matchmaking mothers of affected manners trying to find suitable husbands for their daughters, and old maids whose tragedy was that they had missed the market, but still hoped. Colley Cibber gives her high praise, especially for her performance in *The Way of the World*, of Lady Wishfort, whose languishing manner she played to perfection. Round about 1707 her name drops out of the casts, but she was alive in 1709 for she was signatory to a petition to Queen Anne.

Also worthy of mention was Mrs. Butler, a goddaughter of Charles II, who saw to it that she became an actress. She was, it would seem, the daughter of a knight who had ruined himself in the service of Charles I. His son made this restitution to her, and at the same time did something to compensate the Theatre from which he had taken, or "erepted" such people as Nell Gwynne, Moll Davies and others. For Charlotte Butler was a good actress and an even better singer and dancer. She shone in the operas of the day, in such works as *Dioclesian* and *King Arthur*. Her excellent speaking voice, clear diction and good bearing made her also a good player of more serious parts. She could play comedy, too, and was of a gay, lively nature, with a charming personality and her full share of good looks. Cibber states that in certain parts nobody, save Nance Oldfield who played them later, excelled her, and that is praise indeed. But she was a poorly paid actress, earning only £2 a week. Very naturally, she wanted more, and asked for an additional ten shillings; but the rascally Christopher Rich refused. Mrs. Butler then got a chance of going to Dublin, where a manager named Ashbury was busy forming a company to resuscitate the old theatrical fame of that city. He offered her, within reason, her own terms. She accepted and Dublin's gain was Drury Lane's loss.

The ladies who came first upon the stage had need of good looks as well as talent; indeed, they did better if the looks outweighed the talent, for the gentlemen preferred the former to the latter. But some of the ladies had both. Such a one was Mrs. Johnson. She was of the Duke's Theatre company around the year 1670. Her beauty is remembered because it was enshrined by no less a judge of femininity than Etherege himself, who, when wishing to proclaim an actress beautiful, compared her with Mrs. Johnson. Otherwise little is known about her. She played some good parts, notably in *Woman's Conquest*, *The Reformation* and *The Empress of Morocco*. Of her talent or the details of her beauty there is no record. It would seem, however, that she was a very lovely lady, this fair unknown.

Mrs. Elizabeth Currer was another very beautiful actress of this period. She was Irish and came from Dublin. She appears to have played there first, later joining the company at the Duke's Theatre. Lively and spirited, she had that vivacity which is the source of stage success and she had vitality brimful and running over. So London took her to its heart and audiences applauded her to the echo. Current reports say that she was as popular as she was beautiful, and she was certainly very popular indeed. In 1678 she was Lady Fancy in Aphra Behn's *Sir Patient's Fancy*. She also played in D'Urfey's *Squire Oldsapp* and in *The London Cuckolds.* When the merger of the Duke's and Drury Lane took place, she joined the Drury Lane company, playing in it from 1689 onwards. Her best part was Aquilina in *Venice Preserv'd.* This is the part of a bold, flashing courtesan and, when partnered by Leigh, the comedian, as the stupid old man who is her doting slave, her performance never failed to draw forth immense applause. There is no trace of when she left the stage or when she died.

At the Duke's House also was Mrs. Slaughter, who about 1671 appears as the performer of some leading roles. Then her name vanishes. It is thought that she married and became Mrs. Osborne, for a Mrs. Osborne appears from then on, playing the sort of roles previously undertaken by Mrs. Slaughter. It is all too seldom that players of small parts get any recognition in their time, or remembrance afterwards, so the name of Mrs. Knapper should also be recalled. Records of this actress are few, but she did her job well in and about the year 1676 and onwards.

Mrs. Twilford, also of the Duke's Theatre, was a more distinguished actress. She had a long service and she played excellent parts. She was popular with playgoers and had the power of evoking applause directly she appeared. What is more important, she got applause again when she went off. She was a leading lady of the second rank, maybe, but a good actress and a reliable one all the same.

There is also a special claim to fame to be put forward in respect of Mrs. Sarah Cook. It will be observed that few of the ladies who came first on the stage adopted any high-sounding names which would "look well on the bills": Barry, Cook, Marshall, Gwynne, Davies, Saunders, Knipp, Aldridge, Currer, Johnson, Lee, Percival, Rogers; only the Bracegirdle smacks of the unusual. But it is not the actress or the actor with the unusual name, adopted for stage purposes, who achieves greatness. Angelica Montmorency may never get above the lines devoted to "friends and guests" but Sarah Siddons and Ellen Terry blaze like jewels. Mrs. Cook was the daughter of a woman who kept a small toy shop. There may have been an affinity between toyshops and the stage for the great comedian Nokes had one too. This small retailer had ambitions for her daughter and she sent her to Killigrew's Nursery, the first academy of acting. And Sarah Cook graduated from there to some position, though it is hardly possible to be sure of the names of any others who did so. She made her début at Drury Lane in 1677, playing Gillian in *Country Innocence*. She played quite a few good parts before the union of the theatres and she specialised in the speaking of prologues and epilogues. This would indicate that she had a good voice, diction and a personality, and was on good terms with the audiences. A well-spoken prologue could help a play by putting the audience in a good humour, and a cleverly delivered epilogue might avert a bad reception. It had been shown that both Nell Gwynne and Moll Davies were in great request for these delicate and difficult jobs of the Theatre. To Mrs. Cook was entrusted the speaking of the prologue, which had been specially written by Aphra Behn for Rochester's play *Valentinian*. She also spoke the epilogue for *The Duke of Guise* by Dryden and also his epilogue to Lee's tragedy *Constantine the Great*, in which she also appeared as Serena. She played many roles and it would seem that she was a serious actress, for amongst them are Edith in *Rollo, Duke of Normandy* and Portia in *Julius Caesar*. She does not appear to have been either flighty or good looking, for Etherege (he had something pointed to say about most of the women on the stage in his time) wrote about her: "Sarah Cooke was always fitter for a player than a mistress." He adds a final "e" to her name to which she has no claim. She died in April, 1688, when she cannot have been more than thirty, if as much. She is presumed to have died of consumption.

Mrs. Rogers, another actress with a commonplace if honourable name, used to play big and important leading parts before the rise of Barry and Bracegirdle. She went on the stage about 1692 and she died about 1719. She is credited with a long list of leading roles and she has a certain claim to fame. It is not often that an actor or actress displays such power as to astonish their fellow players, or even to inspire fear in them. Garrick did this when playing *King Lear*, his curses terrifying the company. Kean did it, too, especially when playing Sir Giles Overreach, when he made his leading lady faint and paralysed old Munden, so that the comedian had to be dragged off the stage. But Mrs. Rogers once had fear put into her by the performance of the man she was playing opposite. This was when she was playing Amanda in *The Relapse*. The leading man was an actor named George Powell, who was the son of an actor and therefore should have behaved better than he did. Powell liked good company, loved laughter, and loved that easy means of promoting temporary jollity, the bottle. Often drunk, he always put off learning his parts until the very last thing and, consequently, he was all too often unreliable. Yet for all this he was a very good actor and he could put fire and spirit into his performance, often providing a double dose of these to cover up his scanty knowledge of his lines. So it was when he played Worthy to Mrs. Rogers's heroine. He put so much ardour and tempestuous passion into his love scenes that he frightened her out of her wits, and it took her all her time not to rush off the stage screaming. What she said to him when both of them were off stage after the scene had been played is, unfortunately, not on record.

To this company of ladies, must finally be added two more names, not of actresses but of singers—the first of their kind in the country. They were Margarita Delpine, wife of Giacomo Greber, a famous German musician, who was one of the very first vocalists—if not the first—to sing Italian opera in this country, and Maria Gallia, another singer in Italian opera. Two home-bred operatic stars were Mrs. Lindsey and Mrs. Hudson.

These were the ladies who graced the stage at this time. Now what of the audiences they charmed, delighted or displeased? What was the playgoing public like in those days when the Theatre had shaken off oppression and taken on stability? It was noisy, ill-behaved and made up of as mixed a bunch of people as could possibly be imagined. Royalty was constantly at the play, but its presence made little difference. Although the public loved him, it held Old Rowley in little awe. Nor did he set too good an example. He took his mistresses along with him, openly and unashamed, though his wife to be, Katherine of Braganza, had been first shown to the London public in a box at the old Cockpit Theatre. Pepys gives wonderful pictures of what the audiences were like, revealing delightful snobbishness on occasions, as when he was horrified at finding the house "full of citizens," and deplored the fact that not a single gallant person was present.

There was a pleasant little occurrence at the Duke's Theatre in 1679 when the Duchess of Portsmouth visited it, ablaze with finery and diamonds. Some gentlemen, whose high morale had been brought about largely by liquor, decided to protest and created a diversion by rushing into the pit with drawn swords in their right hands and flaming torches in their left hands, laying about them and then throwing their torches at the actors on the stage. The outcome was unfortunately hard on the actors as the King closed the theatre to show his displeasure. Two young gallants, on another occasion, quarrelled in the pit. The house being crowded, they had no room to fight it out, and consequently they climbed upon the stage. The audience highly approved of this extra bit of free entertainment. Finally, one of the fighters, named Dering, was thrust through the body. He was not mortally hurt, it is pleasant to record.

The fops and smart young gallants walked about all over the place, crying out comments on the play and players, shouting jests to their companions and cracking jokes with the orange girls who, although "no better than they should be," usually gave better than they got. There was a constant coming and going, there were disputes with the money takers, and very audible criticism of the talents and appearances of the players, especially the women players. Members of the audience even walked all over the stage. There were no stalls and no reserved seats, though the King could have some privacy if he desired it. The stalls' space of today was all pit. Running footmen, rough, tough fellows whose job was to run beside their employers' carriages to protect them from crowds and footpads, were sent to keep seats until their masters and mistresses arrived. They were then allowed to sit in the upper gallery where they fought amongst themselves and made themselves a general nuisance. No apples or oranges were sold up there as audiences were very prone to throw things as well as to shout, bellow, bawl, hiss and hoot.

How the players managed to make the impression they did and hold their audiences is almost inconceivable to us today, when the slightest noise is considered enough to spoil a scene or put an actor or actress off his or her stride. These women and men, especially the women of the early days, had difficulties to contend with which would make the present-day players leave their profession.

They were actors, they were actresses, and the Theatre came first. They played because they had to. This is the hall mark of the professional and explains why, for years, the bogus manager was able to get away with the takings, leaving his company, already several weeks in arrear, without a copper but still full of hope and courage, ready to start again with another company just as likely to meet the same fate.

The ladies who came first in the Theatrical Profession may have been lights of love, they may have taken advantage of their public appearances to line their pockets and obtain rich lovers, they may have been wantons and hussies, but they were real professionals, carrying on under conditions which to our way of thinking seem absolutely astounding. They could have got lovers elsewhere, but then they could not have satisfied that most vital of all urges, the urge to act, which produced, as we have shown, some very, very good actresses and a few who were really great.

CHAPTER SEVEN

First Ladies of the Pen

WITH the acting profession open to them women naturally turned to the other branch of the theatre related to it, that of writing plays. Controversy will always exist as to which is the more important, the dramatist or the actor; but as the two are so entirely dependent on one another, no complete and conclusive judgment can ever be passed. Without a play, the actor or actress is a mere personal entertainer; without the players a play is a mere string of words on paper, lacking life. Some plays are better read than performed, but plays which belong to the library are not plays but literature. A real play is a thing of the Theatre, and the living art of the Theatre is the art of the actor. It can best be left at that. Plays are like those slot machines which, in happier and more plenteous days, used to yield chocolate, confectionery and all sorts of good things on the insertion of a penny. They will not work until the actors put in the penny.

The controversy as to who was the first woman to turn her thoughts to writing for the stage has also raged for a long time. It was undoubtedly Hrotsvitha, the tenth-century German nun. But she is so much hidden in the mists of time, and belongs so definitely to a religious phase of the drama, that we must look nearer to our own time and turn to the secular drama. There had no doubt been many women down the centuries who, having seen plays and being inspired by them, had toyed with the idea of expressing themselves in this form. It is said, and it is quite possible, that Queen Elizabeth I was so tempted and did, in fact, do some work in translating the plays of Seneca. That wonderful woman with the feminine form and the masculine mind was capable of anything; if she did employ herself in that way, she may have been more interested in perfecting her Latin—a necessary accomplishment then for one in her or any distinguished position—than in having her version produced on the stage. Though had she had it performed, she would have seen to it that it was a success.

The ill-fated Lady Jane Grey, who translated the classics, was no mean writer, and there have been many other noble ladies who have done the same. One of them, Lady Elizabeth Carew, actually got a play published, probably at her own expense, called *Miriam, the Fair Queen of Jewry*. The Marchioness of Newcastle also published plays of her own, though they never achieved stage production. The critics were kind to her—it was probably politic so to be—and said that the plays were of her own invention, original in plot and story, and not adaptations or borrowed from elsewhere.

So far as can be ascertained the first woman to get a play of her own writing or adaptation produced was a poetess who was married to a Welshman. Her name was Mrs. Philips and her pseudonym was "Orinda." She fostered a love of poetry in her time and even formed a Society for that purpose. Her essay into the drama was a translation into English rhymed couplets of Corneille's *Pompée*. She called it, simply, *Pompey*, following her distinguished original, and it was produced, not in London but in Dublin, at the celebrated Smock Alley Theatre in 1662, before Theatre Royal, Drury Lane was even built. It may have come to London in 1663 and some authorities say it was a success and received a Royal visit and approbation.

Evelyn reports that he saw the tragedy of *Horace* (also written by the virtuous Mrs. Philips) acted before their Majesties. Between each act was a masque and an antique dance. Pepys, too, went to see it at Drury Lane on the third day of its acting, but denounced it as silly, though approving of the interpolated dances by Lacy and Nell Gwynne. It would appear that Mrs. Philips wrote two plays, or one and a bit, and that *Horace* was the one performed in London and not *Pompey*. She did not complete it herself and it was finished by Denham, her work not extending beyond Act IV, Scene VI.

Of *Pompey* it is not possible to trace a London production, but a play of the same name and from the same source "translated out of the French by Certain Persons of Honour," was announced in 1663. The translators were indeed a team, for it took no less than five brains, all of them belonging to persons of distinction —Filmer, Godolphin, Sackville, Sedley and Waller—to produce this tragedy called *Pompey the Great*. But it did not please Mrs. Philips, who said her heart was not at ease for the "confederated" translators had not made a good job of it. In a letter to a friend she wrote: "I wonder much what preparations for it would prejudice Will D'avenant when I hear they acted in English habits etc yet so a propos yet Caesar was sent in with a feather and a staff till he was hissed off ye stage." It would not have been the "feather and the staff" which got the unfortunate actor of the mighty Roman the unwelcome "bird." It was customary then, and for many years afterwards, for the hero of a tragedy to wear a big plumed and feathered headdress and to carry a staff, truncheon or baton, to show he was the hero and leading character. The great feathered headdress of the tragedians was a proudly worn and closely cherished tradition of the British stage. Maybe, in this case, the gentleman playing Caesar was just a bad actor.

Mrs. Philips's name was Catherine. She was the daughter of a Mr. Fowler, a merchant of London, in which city she was born, on January 1, 1631. She married James Philips, a gentleman of Cardigan. After his death she went to Ireland, where she was attached to the retinue of Viscountess Duncannon and had her play produced. She did not long survive the event, or the production of the other version of her *Pompey*, for she died in London of small-pox in 1664. Doubtless that was why her second play *Horace* was finished by another hand. The poet Cowley held her and her work in high esteem and wrote an ode to her memory.

In many books on the drama, the name of Mrs. Manley as a dramatist is dismissed in a few lines, but she deserves better than that. Her name was Mary de la Rivière Manley and she was the daughter of a knight, Sir Roger Manley, who also had a turn for writing for there is reason to believe that he wrote a portion, almost certainly the first volume, of a book, entitled *The Turkish Spy*, which caused no little sensation when it first appeared. He gave his daughter a good education, and she showed early signs

PLATE V

Above:

MRS. PRITCHARD who knew nothing about any play except her part in it

Below:

GEORGE ANNE BELLAMY—she had a weakness for trousers

PLATE VI

Above:
MRS. GLOVE

At left:
MISS STEPHE
who once fled fron
altar, but later beca
Countess

of intelligence of a very high order and of abilities above the average for the women of her period. It was a severe blow when she lost her mother while she was still young. This was not the family's only misfortune, for her father, through supporting the cause of Charles I, lost everything. Then Mary was decoyed into a bigamous marriage. A relation, charged with the girl's care, took her to London, vowed the deepest love and affection for her, seduced her, and married her. He had a wife living and he soon deserted his victim, leaving her to shift for herself.

A young girl, deserted, almost penniless and alone in the London of that time had a pretty grim time of it. But the notorious Barbara Villiers, Duchess of Cleveland, one of Charles II's mistresses, showed a better heart than might have been expected, took compassion on her and took her under her wing. They had met by chance and the Duchess had been attracted by the girl's looks, intelligence and generally distinguished air. But the Royal mistress was fickle and, soon tiring of her *protégée*, who probably showed no desire to live according to her surroundings, trumped up a charge that Mistress Manley was intriguing with her son. A general, one Tidcombe, with whom the young woman had made friends, offered her his "protection," which, however, she declined. She then retired into a seclusion of poverty.

It was then that she started writing and achieved literary fame. She first wrote a tragedy entitled *Royal Mischief* and it was done by Betterton at Lincoln's Inn Fields in 1696. She followed it up with *The Lost Lover, or the Jealous Husband*, a comedy, which was produced at Drury Lane in the same year, two months before her tragedy *Royal Mischief*. Both plays were moderate successes. She soon became a social pet, the wits rallied round her, and admirers flattered her and thronged her lodgings. It was not long before she began to indulge in amorous intrigues and her success proved fatal to the virtue she had so far possessed. There is a line in an old book which states that "she was taken into keeping." But, if she fell into disreputable ways, it did not stop her from writing. She turned out four volumes called *Memoirs of the New Atlantis*. Written with great frankness, even for the time in which she lived, the memoirs gave intimate descriptions of amorous dallyings and exposed the frailty of her sex. The book sold like hot cakes.

In the same book she also went into politics. Her father was a determined Royalist and she was a confirmed hater of the Whigs. She drew character studies in her book which scarified the Very Important Personages of that political persuasion, especially of those who had done anything to bring about the downfall of Charles I. So pointed were these allusions, so direct, that action had to be taken. As the book appeared anonymously, the Secretary of State gave orders for the arrest of the printer and publisher, who were hauled off to prison. Then Mary Manley showed her true colours. Refusing to let innocent people suffer, she came forward and publicly acknowledged that she was the author. She was taken before the Secretary of State and closely cross-questioned. Maybe her knowledge and ability to present it gave the authorities pause, and though kept under arrest for a time, she was never brought to trial. When the Whig Government fell to be replaced by a Tory one, she became a person in high favour. She was employed to write in support of the new Government's measures, especially when these were of a controversial nature, and as a pamphleteer, a very important calling in those days, she soon had no equal. Indeed, when the celebrated Dean Swift gave up his journal, *The Examiner*, she carried it on with success. She had often finished works begun by the eminent Doctor, and nobody could distinguish their contributions. She found time to write two more plays, *Almyna or the Arabian Vow* (1707) and *Lucius, the First Christian King of Britain* (1717).

She remained a staunch Tory, she even went under the protection (or into the keeping of) the chief printer of that party, one Alderman Barber, with whom she seemed very happy, for she lived with him up to her death on July 11, 1724. Mary de la Rivière Manley deserves her niche in the story of professional womanhood, especially of those connected with the Theatre.

Contemporary with her are two other women dramatists, Mrs. Pix and Mrs. Trotter. The former of the two, Mrs. Mary Pix, was born at Nettlebed, in Oxfordshire, a place beloved today by theatrical folk and others in search of a charming village not too far from civilisation. How many of them know that a dramatist was born there? Between 1696 and 1705, Mrs. Pix wrote nine plays, displaying no little versatility, for she varied from farce to tragedy. She was a very fat woman, but a living example that fatness and stupidity do not go together. Her plays were well done, the plots being carefully conceived and worked out with ingenuity, but their dialogue was weak. However, she had success.

The case of Catharine Trotter, the daughter of Captain David Trotter, a Scottish gentleman, is a very different matter. Born in London in 1679, the true desire for learning possessed by all good Scots was hers in full measure. Apparently self-educated, she taught herself Greek and Latin and French. When she was only seventeen her tragedy entitled *Agnes de Castro* was produced at Drury Lane, and she was acclaimed. She revelled in pure sentiment and romance and there was nothing in her plays of the ferocity which marked those of Mrs. Manley, in which everything was carnal love and desperation, sudden and remorseless murder. (Mrs. Manley showed great ingenuity in devising methods of extermination. In one of her plays an unfortunate man was put in a cannon and fired off like a shell. Immediately afterwards his wife, according to the authoress's stage direction, "gathered up the smoking pieces of her lord.") There was nothing like that about the plays of Mrs. Trotter, which, whether comedies or tragedies, were sentimental and full of high thought. Altogether she wrote six plays, four tragedies and two comedies. She also wrote verses in praise of Congreve. These came to the latter's attention, and a friendship as platonic as that between Congreve and Mrs. Bracegirdle grew between them. Then she wrote a defence of Locke's *Essay on the Human Understanding*, remarkable for its clarity and grip of the subject. She was a very learned young person indeed, with a most enquiring mind that led her into the Roman Catholic Church, and out again. She finally married an English clergyman (or he might have been a Scot), the Rev. Mr. Cockburn, curate of St. Dunstan's in Fleet Street. They had tastes in common, even if he was not of the Theatre. For he wrote an account of the Great Flood, which was highly approved by the learned of his day, and several other works of scholarship. Not to be outdone, Mrs. Trotter, having read some articles by eminent writers on the foundation of moral duty and obligation, wrote a most arresting series in *The Literary Journal* called "The History of the Works of the Learned." She had no limit to her thirst for knowledge and to her powers in absorbing it, for when a book called *Essays on the Nature and Obligations of Virtue* by

Dr. Rutherford appeared, she read it at once, mastered it and went on from where the Doctor had left off, her work gaining the highest commendation from the Bishop of Gloucester, Dr. Warburton, who had it published as a supplement to the original book. How this lady managed with the people of the Theatre cannot be told, but she must have had great understanding and adaptability. Maybe she just wrote her plays and then let the theatre folk get on with it. She was devoted to her husband and they had a long and happy married life. Her husband died in 1748, at the age of seventy-one and she was stricken down with grief. She mourned him deeply and she did not want to live. Indeed, she followed him very quickly in the following year. She was of quite a different type from either Mrs. Pix or Mrs. Manley, but all three were satirised together in a farce called *The Female Wits*, in which their abilities and weaknesses were held up to ridicule. But that is as great a compliment as can be paid to workers in the Theatre. Mrs. Trotter and Mrs. Pix both had connections with the Church, for Mrs. Trotter married a clergyman and Mrs. Pix was the daughter of one. Thus again did the closeness of Church and Stage demonstrate itself, and is it not reported that Ann and Rebecca Marshall's father was a Presbyterian minister?

There was also a Mrs. Boothby whose name is spelt variously Francis or Frances, who wrote one tragedy, *Marcella* (1670), but left no other mark on the annals at all. Among this first detachment of the ever-growing army of women who have written for the Theatre are two names, however, which tower above those already mentioned, two women of greater gifts and of immeasurably greater theatrical stature—Mrs. Centlivre and Mrs. Aphra Behn, the last named being the greatest and most extraordinary of them all.

Whereas most of the ladies of the stage had been of Royal loyalty and sympathy, Mrs. Centlivre belonged by birth to the other side. She was born Susanna Freeman, daughter of a Dissenter and staunch Parliament man, who, when Charles II came into his own again, was very greatly persecuted. Her mother had died young. But Susanna spent a very busy life. While so many of the ladies of the stage had indulged in irregular unions —in that delightful old phrase, had been "in keeping"—Mrs. Centlivre was apparently a glutton for wedlock. Whether she was a dragon of virtue and would only give her favours when the Church had given its blessing, or whether she had a way with her which compelled her admirers to marry her, is not known. But the fact is that she was a widow three times before she was out of her 'teens, a sufficiently surprising thing in any age. One would have thought the men would have been wary before undertaking such a *femme fatale*. But there it is.

First, a gentleman named Anthony Hammond made her his wife. He did not live long, and then she married a nephew of a knight, Sir Stephen Fox. This second husband lived only a short while to enjoy his bliss. The widow, apparently not inconsolable, and evidently ardently wooed, then married a Captain Carroll. And he died too. But the men of those days either had pluck or there were violent exceptions to the notoriously lax morals which obtained, for there was almost immediately a fourth husband presenting himself. He was named Centlivre and he was a cook—a chef—yes, but he was chef to no less a person than good Queen Anne, of blessed memory, and he operated at her castle of Windsor. There must have been a short interval of single estate before this marriage because Susanna Carroll, as she then was, decided to become an actress. In 1706 she even appeared at Windsor before the Royal mistress of her husband-to-be in *Alexander the Great*. Perhaps that was when the couple met, who knows? Susanna was not, however, a good actress at all; indeed, she was a pretty bad one. She none the less gained some stage experience, and with a trio of husbands behind her, she had had a good deal of experience of life.

She decided to remain a dramatist. She had written a play called *The Perjured Husband, or the Adventures of Berenice*, a tragi-comedy, which was produced at Drury Lane in 1700. (Some authorities give the sub-title as "The Adventures of Venice.") It was not very good but there were some amusing comedy scenes in it. She followed this up, after an interval of three years, with a comedy, entitled *Love's Contrivances*, which did much better. In the same year she had another comedy on the stage, *The Beau's Duel—or a Soldier for the Ladies*, and this was quite a success. Realising that she had a gift for comedy, she pursued that vein, and in 1704 came *The Stolen Heiress, or, Salamanca Doctor Outwitted*, which did pretty well. *The Gamester* followed in 1705,

The Bassett-Table and *Love at a Venture* in 1706—all comedies. She did *The Platonic Young Lady*, another piece designed for laughter, in 1707.

By this time she was well known. Then in 1708 she wrote a comedy called *The Busybody*, of which she sent the manuscript to Drury Lane Theatre. It was read to the company, and one and all the players denounced it. It was no good at all, they said, and they would have nothing to do with it. This shows how bad as judges of plays are the people who have to play in them. For *The Busybody* was eventually a great and lasting success, though it took the persistent Mrs. Centlivre a year to persuade them into that play. It went on, to the discontent of all who appeared in it. But the audience begged to differ. They loved it. It was a great, roaring success. It held the stage for years. It became one of the most popular of all stock pieces, challenged only by others from the same pen.

She went on, flushed with triumph. She was a celebrity now, an established dramatist of the front rank. *The Man Bewitched, or the Devile to Do about Her*, a farce in 1710, had nothing like the same success and *Marplot*, a continuation or sequel to *The Busybody* (1711) shared the fate usual to such things. *The Perplexed Lovers* (1711) was a bit better but nothing like so good as *The Busybody*. Had she shot her bolt, this woman writer of comedy? She showed them whether she had or not the following year when she wrote *The Wonder; a Woman Keeps a Secret*. This was an enormous success, perhaps her greatest. The town rang with it; Robert Wilks, who played the hero Don Felix, was fitted to perfection, and Drury Lane audiences applauded him to the echo. It brought much gold into the treasury of the famous triumvirate, Colley Cibber, Wilks and Doggett. That play and that part were destined to be vehicles for all the great actors down the years, right into Victorian times. Don Felix was a favourite part with David Garrick. He chose it for his farewell performance on the stage. Mrs. Centlivre was by no means defeated or written out; maybe her husband prepared a special feast for the celebration. But then, in 1717, she deserted comedy, her real line and essayed a tragedy called *The Cruel Gift*. Nobody wanted that. What they wanted from Mrs. Centlivre was comedy. So she gave in to popular demand. She went back to the laughter business and she wrote *A Bold Stroke for a Wife*, which was produced in 1718. This was her zenith, the success of her life. It was even bigger than *The Wonder*, for it held the stage for upwards of two centuries. It amused our grandfathers and even our fathers saw it, if we are advanced in middle age. It outshone in reputation and lasting power many a play produced with greater flourish and applause at the beginning. It was really humorous, it held real characters and it put a phrase into the language: "The real Simon Pure." That was coined by Mrs. Centlivre—and an actor called Griffin first used it. This was the triumph of Centlivre. She wrote one more play, *Artifice*, a farce in five acts, which has not lived. There were two other farces by her which were never acted. In all she wrote nineteen plays and of that number she had three big successes, not at all a bad average.

Her strength was her comedy, which was never blatant nor forced, but skilful, quiet and natural. Her wit did not sparkle, but her characters said and did the right things at the right moment. *A Bold Stroke for a Wife* grew in success with the years. It had not the immediate success of *The Wonder* or *The Busybody*, but it was real and it mellowed and stood the test of time. If she did not deal in epigrams, she at least dealt in sayings or remarks which were so much to the point that people repeated them and they became like proverbs. It was mainly her sense of the Theatre and of the public mind which made her fame. Not all of her plays, by any means, were original; some were adaptations, and, like most of her period, she borrowed heavily from Molière. There were no rapier flashes of deadly wit, no great scenes to arrest and linger in the memory but there were complete pictures, all in the right mood and tense, all pieced together so that no join showed. If she never wrote a great glowing speech which rang out like a trumpet, if she never constructed a tremendous scene which gripped in its intensity, there was yet a complete whole which made a real, satisfying entertainment and sent people away feeling that they had spent an evening, not with a set of stage characters, but with folk who acted as they might have done themselves in similar circumstances and had said things which they themselves had often thought but never known how to utter. It is most probable that Mrs. Centlivre understood life and understood audiences. She had had experience enough, at any rate, and evidently she had not wasted it. Utterly unlike in the main treatment though they were, her plays had the same quality as those which made the success of Ivor Novello, that sense of completeness and harmony and balance between stage and public throughout the whole thing.

Perhaps they were very like herself. She has often been decried, but she was a mistress of her craft and she knew her job. She failed when she left her most expert line, but she succeeded when she stuck to it. She has often been sneered at by learned historians who judge merely academically and not by the effect of work on an audience—and on audiences down the years—which is the real test of a dramatist and the real test of the Theatre. She had enemies in her own time—like all successful people. She incurred the wrath of Pope and that wasp could sting. He called her "a cook's wife" with a sneer at such a status. She did not mind. She was a cook's wife—and he was cook to his Monarch. In his line he was as eminent as she. And they appear to have been very happy together. She died on December 1, 1723, at the age of forty-five, young in years but rich in experience for she had lived every day of those years. She was buried in St. Paul's, Covent Garden, the actors' church.

The first woman writer for the stage to show genius and really to establish the fact that women could write as good plays as men, the first eminent woman dramatist of our stage, was Mrs. Aphra Behn.

Arresting and extraordinary as that name is, it is no more so than the name which was hers by birth: Afara Amis. Despite her name, she was English to the core. She was moreover a gentlewoman by birth and her birthplace was the little town of Wye, not far from Canterbury, in the year 1640. A child with such a name is surely destined to go far. It was from Afara that probably her own childish lisping produced the name Aphra which stuck to her all her life. The name of Amis is also very unusual. But those were her baptismal names—the family name was plain Johnson. Later she took a sort of nom-de-plume—"Astrea"—but she will always be Aphra Behn.

Her father seems to have been a connection of Lord Willoughby. His Lordship got Mr. Johnson a job as Governor of Surinam. His title was to be Lieutenant-General and according to his daughter's account he was not only Lieutenant-General of Surinam but of thirty-six islands besides. Anyway, it was a good enough job for a moderately placed Kentish gentleman, and he lost no time in sailing for the colony with his family. Unhappily, he never saw the realm he was to govern for he died on the voyage out, but the family, naturally, went on and were very well received. They lived there for some years. It was a new, wild and wide life after Wye, in Kent. Young Afara—now become Aphra—took the fullest advantage of it. She was gifted with great intelligence, great courage, a spirit of adventure, and she had the mind and determination of a man in her attractive woman's body. She went everywhere and saw everything. Venturing with parties into the jungle, she met bands of Indians who had never before seen white people. They were duly awe-inspired and impressed, and by nobody more so than handsome Aphra herself, in her brilliant clothes, her close-cropped curly head (she had her hair cut because of the climate and the adventuring), and they gazed at her in wonder and even ventured to touch her to see if she were real. She wore a feathered headdress too, which the simple savages thought very fine. They had seen nothing like this striking, well-proportioned girl, with her brown hair and rather prominent eyes, her fair complexion and her flashing smile.

Those were the days of slavery and there was a slave serving the family who had known better days. He had been a prince in his own country and his name was said to be Oroonoko; probably he tried to explain that he had come from the land near the river Orinoco and the name got attached to him. He could speak some English, and Aphra would talk to him and listen to his disjointed tales, never forgetting a thing and fixing the whole picture in her mind. The result was that Oroonoko became very famous, although he never knew it. For Aphra Behn, before she turned playwright, wrote a novel the title of which was the slave's name, which the dramatist Sothern made into a play. It endured for years and the character of Oroonoko was played by all the great actors for centuries.

The novel itself made a great impact, for up to that time novels had been written in the manner of the French writers—long, wandering tales of infinite complexity and twists and turns. *Oroonoko*, on the other hand, was direct and downright, a forceful, sharp, swiftly told story of tragedy, thrill and grief, of souls harrowed, of tropical savagery, noble Indians and all the colour of the Western Isles. If the story bore a resemblance to Othello, it was none the worse for that. Nobody before Aphra Behn had ennobled the savage, had shown that the coloured people had souls and feelings akin to their European conquerors and masters. *Oroonoko*, a national success, was a landmark in literature from which much was to spring.

Aphra Behn and her family (she was not Aphra Behn then, but Afara Amis Johnson, of course) remained in Surinam all through the Commonwealth period, but when Charles II returned to England, they did the same, and the charming, handsome Aphra was soon enjoying herself in London as much as she had done in the more primitive and maybe purer jungle of Surinam. She went about, she met people, amongst them a Dutch merchant of some standing whose name was Behn. She married him, became Aphra Behn, and went to Holland with him. Little is known about him. Though reputed to be wealthy, he left her very little when he died, save some good connections in Holland, especially in Amsterdam and Antwerp, and it was not long before his widow found herself short of money.

She had been to Court either before leaving with her husband for the Continent or on her visits home, and had been well received. King Charles had taken notice of her and there may very likely have been an intrigue between them. Anyway, she made an impression, as she was accustomed to doing. Now, her husband dead and her means straitened, she wanted something which would earn her money. She was chosen to play her part in the English Secret Service. The two countries were maritime and trade rivals all the world over, and were frequently at war. The Dutch were bold and resourceful enemies, and were good seamen with good ships. Very efficient intelligence would therefore be of inestimable value. Here was a woman who would fill the bill. So Aphra Behn became in reality that figure so well beloved by dramatists and novelists down the years, the beautiful spy.

She was in touch with a master spy, one William Scott, based on Antwerp, a city she knew well and where she had friends. So she went there, and began doing her job with that complete thoroughness which marked her whole passage through life. There have been attempts to whiten her methods, to apologise for her life, to try and explain away, quite needlessly, the extreme licence which marked the plays which were to follow. There is no need. She was a self-reliant woman with a strong will. She felt no moral trammels and conscience was never her master. She kept up a whirl of gaiety, got to know the right people, and did whatever was needed to further her ends. Her *amours* were as wholehearted as they were numerous. She was soon sending full and detailed accounts of it all back to headquarters. Eventually she established a complete influence over Mynheer van der Albert, a very important personage in Dutch affairs, who knew everything that was going on. He could deny her nothing, as she apparently denied him nothing. From him she learned the details of a scheme whereby Admiral de Ruyter was to lead a dash up the Thames itself and burn the British Fleet at its anchorage. She sent this terrific piece of information home and she awaited her reward with confidence. But all she got was laughter and ridicule. The English simply would not believe it. As it happened, the Dutch later did exactly as she had said they would. But she was, at the time, derided. Returning to London, she was, if not openly laughed at, treated with a rather pitying politeness. She gave up her profession as spy. As she had no means, she had now a new living to find, but what could she turn to?

She had had plenty of love affairs, so the idea of settling down to idleness under a man's protection did not appeal to her. She was too vital, too alive for that. She knew she could write, as she had proved, so she turned to the Theatre. She did not make the mistake of trying to become an actress, as Mrs. Centlivre did later on, but turned directly to play-writing. And she did so with prodigious success. The plays she wrote were amongst the most full-blooded of their full-blooded period, and not believing that the public would accept them as a woman's work, she passed them off as written by a man.

She had great capabilities and might have written really great plays. But would there have been any money in them if she had? She was probably swayed, as have been so many gifted people, by the necessity of writing "down" for immediate success rather than "up" for glory and posterity. So she wrote plays she knew would please, and the public certainly lapped them up. Her first play was begun in 1671 and altogether she wrote eighteen. Although she adapted and altered more often than she invented, she brought a touch to the versions she pirated which made them all her own. She might not be original in conception but she was never the least bit dull.

She even succeeded in shocking, not to say horrifying, the none too squeamish public of her day. She was death to delicacy, merciless to morality. Tearing aside the veil she showed lustful, desirous humanity in all its nakedness. Perhaps only Wycherly could be nastier than she, but he had a salty wit which she lacked. She laid it on with a trowel whereas he redeemed it with a wicked laugh. She led the way in licentiousness and wantonness. In the world of her plays, only sensuality, lust, and unchastity mattered. She was attacked, of course, but she did not care. She wrote her plays, she wrote her novels, she "dropped into poetry," and she made money. She had been, just before turning to the Theatre, in a debtors' prison, which was her reward for attempting to serve her country and doing her job well. No wonder she thought little of the better side of life; she had seen little of it.

Her first play, *The Forc'd Marriage, or the Jealous Bridegroom* was produced by Davenant at the Lincoln's Inn Theatre in 1670. It could not have had a better chance, for Betterton himself and his dear and gifted wife played the leads, and it ran for six nights. But it spelt a form of disaster for one young actor who was on probation. He was cast for "the King," but failed miserably and he acted no more. But he made his mark on the Theatre all the same, for he was Otway, the future dramatist. Thus a woman dramatist made a successful début on this occasion and a man destined to be a far greater dramatist than she failed as an actor. It was a beginning for both. Otway's *The Orphan* and *Venice Preserv'd* have greater claims than any of Mrs. Behn's eighteen pieces of salacity.

She soon mastered all the tricks of the Theatre. She tried her hand at tragedy, as was the vogue, but it was in comedy, in comedy which was as topical as the minute it was uttered, in form, in thought and in dirtiness, that she excelled. *The Forc'd Marriage*, *The Amorous Prince*, *The Dutch Lover*, *Abdelazar* (tragedy), *The Town Fop*, *The Rover* (in two parts), *Sir Patient's Fancy*, *The Feigned*

Courtezans, *The City Heiress*, *The False Count*, *The Roundheads*, *The Young King* (tragi-comedy), *The Lucky Chance*, *The Emperor of the Moon* (which was almost the first real pantomime, with Harlequin as its hero), *The Widow Ranter*, and *The Younger Brother*: those were her plays, stretching from 1670 down to 1696.

It was the first production of *The Rover* which put the crown of success on her head, and established her securely. And the first play of that name was better than the second. She became a Queen of the Theatre, and she grew in influence and power. The great people of the Theatre—Killigrew, Davenant, Waller, Betterton, Otway—were her close friends. Poets acclaimed her:

> Oh, wonder of thy sex, where can we see
> Beauty and Knowledge joined, except in thee?

Beauty, yes, but not of thought and words; knowledge, yes, but of the seamy side. Yet, in herself, except when in the secret service, she does not appear to have been wanton. There might have been a lover to whom she wrote the letters published after her death, and, if so, he was John Hoyle, a lawyer and a rake but a clever and witty man. Despite her ingenuity on the stage, she frequently fell into traps herself, letting her heart rule her head in money matters. She was generous to a fault, she was open in manner and passionate by nature. She would sooner forgive than injure and she was a good conversationalist and the best of good company. So her contemporaries assessed her and they should have known her, for it was an age which did not too often speak well of anyone.

How does she stand with posterity, this pioneer amongst women, the first of her sex to be a real commercial playwright and make a good living by it? It must be confessed that with her the dramatist is greater than the dramas; she herself is more immortal than her plays. Her tragedy was that she never wrote her best play—*Oroonoko*—using it only as a novel and leaving it to another to reap the theatrical reward. But she was a woman who was never afraid, a woman of power and courage, who had a man's mind and who saw clearly. She overcame the debtors' prison, and she broke down the walls of the Theatre with her gall-like pen. She was vivid and was alive. She was perhaps an incarnation of all those virtues and all those failings which go to make up the last thing she served—and from her point of view, served so well—the Theatre.

Aphra Behn, at all times, was pure Theatre. That would have been a better epitaph than the one on her grave. She died on April 16, 1689. She lies in the cloisters of Westminster Abbey—and this is what they wrote on her grave:

> Here lies a proof that wit can never be
> Defence enough against mortality
> Great poetess, oh thy stupendous lays
> The world admires and the Muses praise.

She deserved a better and truer epitaph than that. That halting verse is unworthy of her for, despite her failings, she achieved so much. It would have been far better to record the fact that she introduced Milk Punch into this country.

CHAPTER EIGHT

From Bar Parlour to Abbey

SO far almost every actress who appeared on the English stage has had her mention, but now they come thronging fast and only the outstanding ones can claim our attention. But before we tell the story of the next really great lady of the stage, let us turn for a moment to look at the ladies in the audience.

Colley Cibber says they did not dare venture to a new play until they had heard whether they could do so without offence to their morals. But it appears that their desire to go to the theatre, or their curiosity to see for themselves, outweighed their moral scruples, so they took precautions to hide their blushes by means of masks or vizards. It is not likely there were many blushes, although some masked ladies were seen to be red in the face. This was usually because they were trying to contain roars of laughter; laughing outright would have conveyed that they understood and appreciated the dirt being purveyed, which, of course, they did perfectly well.

Farquhar the dramatist tilts at them. One of his characters says to another: "Didn't you chide me for not putting a stronger lace in your stays, when you had broke one as strong as a hempen cord with containing a violent ti-hee at a bawdy jest in the last play?"

These ladies of the vizards were also well described by the Marquis of Halifax in his advice to his daughter. Perhaps he did not attack women of his time as a whole, but what he said had obvious relevance to a good cross section: "Some ladies are bespoke for merry meetings, as Bessus was for duels. They are engaged in a circle of idleness, where they turn round, for the whole year, without the interruption of a serious hour. They know all the players' names, and are intimately acquainted with the booths at Bartholomew Fair. The spring, that bringeth out Flies and Fools, maketh them inhabitants of Hyde Park. In the winter, they are an encumbrance to the play-house, and the ballast of the drawing room."

That is true, however, of almost any time. One wonders what view the good Marquis would have taken of the film-fan clubs and the mobbing of the stars by excited, screaming teen-agers? At least he was spared that.

The vizards, unfortunately, led to confusion and embarrassing mistakes: a man might find himself in great trouble when attempting to get familiar with a masked lady who caught his attention, only to discover it was his own wife, and women of ill-repute flaunted in the masks and, so disguised, mingled with the "quality." So, eventually, masks died.

Politics flourished in the theatre when William and Mary reigned. Any allusion in a play bearing remotely upon State matters was cheered by the side in favour and hooted by the other. The play was very seldom the real centre of attraction, unless some of the very great ones held the stage, and not always then. The character of Lord Foppington had a clever hit at his audience's behaviour: "A man must endeavour to look wholesome lest he makes so nauseous a figure in the side box that ladies should be compelled to turn their eyes upon the play."

One often hears complaints that audiences today laugh in the wrong places and snigger at tragic scenes, but this is nothing new. Dryden declared that "In all our tragedies the audience cannot forbear laughing when the actors are about to die; this is the most comic part of the play." They never laughed, however, when such men as Betterton played tragedy. People who laugh in the wrong place still abound. There are always those who go to the theatre with the sole idea of laughing, and will roar and chuckle at a serious play: the more tragic the straits of the characters the more it amuses them. Some of this is pure nervousness, but far more is sheer stupidity. To be sure, in the early days

PLATE VII

At left:
LAVINIA FENTON
(later Duchess of Bolton)

Above:
MRS. ABINGTON

At left:
MRS. BRACEGIRDLE

PLATE VIII

KITTY CLIVE

it must have been hard, at times, to have one's imagination kept in thrall when stage hands came on with a roll of green baize, spread it before the players, who solemnly stepped on it in order that, when they expired, their costumes should get as little dirt as possible. . . .

Despite the licentiousness of this period, there was no lack of objectors who raised their voices against the Theatre and the women thereof. Among them were Collier, who really made a stir and got something done to lessen the lewdness, and South, who in a sermon preached to the Merchant Taylors, called theatres "spiritual pest-houses, where scarce anything is to be heard or seen but what tends to the corruption of good manners and from whence not one in a thousand returns but infected with the love of vice, or at least with the hatred of it very much abated from what it was before. "And that, I assure you," he went on, "is no inconsiderable point gained by the tempter, as those who have any experience of their own hearts sufficiently know. He who has no mind to trade with the devil, should be so wise as to keep away from his shop." In all justice to the worthy divine, it is only fair to state that he made it clear it was not a well-conducted and clean theatre to which he attached the label of the devil's shop, but the type then prevalent.

Waiting in the wings now for her entrance is a very great lady of the stage, Anne Oldfield, a woman of beauty, talent and brains, of great determination, with a mind of her own and a wit which stabbed like a stiletto, and whose story is as romantic as that of any play in which she appeared. She was born low down the social scale, and the stage raised her status until she found her last resting-place in Westminster Abbey. Second to none in the annals of Old Drury, to which her story like her career belongs almost entirely, she is also one of the immortals of the English Theatre.

There were rumours that Anne Oldfield was of gentle birth. She had, indeed, a natural air of quality about her, a lack of self-consciousness, a gift of calm self-reliance which usually comes of breeding, so perhaps it may be true. There is reason, at any rate, to believe that she had good blood on her mother's side, and it certainly showed.

Her opportunity came by a chance: if a man of the Theatre

had not gone into a tavern for a drink at a particular time, there might never have been that name which glows in the history of our Theatre. It is true that the young lady showed such determination to be an actress that she would probably have got there in the end. But the Theatre is a chancy place, and chance proved her friend.

One afternoon a man was walking through St. James's Market, which stood where Piccadilly Circus is now situated. He was a handsome man, but his face had a ruddiness not altogether occasioned by exposure to the weather or by rude health, and his good clothes had seen better days. There was a soldierly air about him and he walked with a swagger, yet he seemed rather ill at ease, taking quick glances at people approaching him, sometimes looking over his shoulder to see if he was followed. No stranger to debt, he knew what it was to watch for bailiffs and tipstaffs; indeed, he and impecuniosity were like brothers. Yet he was clever—nay, brilliant—and had made quite a name—and that name was George Farquhar.

Farquhar, the son of a gentleman of landed estate in Ireland, had been a Captain in the Army. He was a rolling stone, full of wit and talent, but entirely without ballast, although he could be true to those he loved. Things came too easily to him, and he took the easy road. He went on the stage, but was unsuccessful. Before he came to Town, he nearly killed a brother actor, by carelessly using a real sword instead of a "property" one, and that drove him from the stage. He became a playwright and a brilliant one. But he was always in debt, often penniless (he sold one of his best plays for £15), always dodging his creditors and seeking solace in the wine bottle. But he loved and was true to his wife, although the lady, who was violently in love with him, had tricked him into marriage by a pretence of means. He never held it against her; he loved her too much, and they were happy, bound together also by their two daughters, his great care in life being to try to provide for them all. Next to his family, he loved the Theatre, though his plays brought him more praise than money. He was a gallant gentleman, even though a debtor by nature and destiny, and he would always do a good turn. He was to do one during the walk he was taking when he enters this story.

Finding the coast clear, he stopped at the door of the Mitre

Tavern, which stood where the Criterion Theatre now stands, and walked in. The parlour was empty. Nobody was there to serve him, but from a room behind the bar he heard a woman's voice reciting. It was a lovely voice, declaiming lines from a play with full understanding, phrasing and timing. He listened in amazement. She was reciting from the plays of Beaumont and Fletcher. As the voice went on, he became more and more curious, and, at last, he could wait no longer. He knocked and called out. The voice stopped, there was a pause, and then a girl came in, a pretty girl, moving with grace. Farquhar gazed at her. She met his glance and asked him what she could serve him with. He gave his order and then asked if it was she whom he had heard reciting. When she told him that it was, he asked her if this was a hobby, if she did it often? She quickly told him of her love for the stage, of her desire to be an actress, how she knew so many passages by heart and how she just longed for the chance to show what she could do.

All Farquhar's theatre instincts were alight. Here was a find, a real find. He asked her name and she told him, Anne Oldfield, but said she was usually called Nance. He told her who he was, and then asked to see her people, for she had told him she was not the lady nor yet the daughter of the house, but merely helping there.

Anne, he learned from her employers, was the daughter of a soldier in the Guards, and grand-daughter of a vintner. The Guardsman was said to be a captain, which may or may not have been true. His wife was one Elizabeth Blanchard, and there was talk of a fortune which should have been Anne's but which her father had squandered. When her father died, she and her widowed mother had been left in poor circumstances, so she had while still a child gone to work for a dressmaker. The mother, for economy, went to live with her married sister, a Mrs. Foss or Voss, who kept the Mitre Tavern. In return for her keep, she made herself generally useful and so did Nance when she had time. Historians disagree about this Mrs. Foss, or Voss. Some say she was Nance's aunt, some her elder sister. There seems more proof that the former was the case. But there was Nance, working with her hands at sewing and serving wine, while her mind was away at Drury Lane, holding audiences enthralled. She recited again and once more Farquhar was certain he had made a discovery. He took his leave, promising to speak to the manager of Drury Lane, whose ear he had, and also to Captain Vanbrugh, a man of growing importance in the Theatre and the world in general.

The family were flattered, and Nance, outwardly calm, was starry-eyed. Here seemed to be a chance opening before her. She was too sensible to build castles in the air, but if she had impressed a man like Farquhar, whose fame she knew so well, it seemed to her she must be good and just in case the captain kept his word, she began to make plans for her future. There was nothing impulsive about her, and she decided that she must play her cards well. It would never do to be too anxious to please, nor to show her light before an audience which did not matter. She, an opportunist, must wait her opportunity. But meanwhile, and she admitted it later, she was just burning to be an actress.

Eventually Sir John Vanbrugh came, admired and was much impressed by what he saw and heard. He and Farquhar told the slippery, slimy Christopher Rich, then patentee of Drury Lane, that in this girl there was a prize. Rich did not want to disoblige these two men, but by making what he was going to do seem a favour, he might put them under an obligation to him, he thought. If she was as good as they said, it was what he wanted. Being a beginner she would be cheap, and, in any case, if he, in his delightfully forgetful way, let her salary get into arrears, she could do little about it. So he agreed to give this unknown girl a start.

Anne Oldfield joined the company at Drury Lane in 1699, but she made no sort of impact at all, none of that talent which her two sponsors had observed being visible. Sir John Vanbrugh gave her the part of Alinda in *The Pilgrim*, a part which suited her because, in itself, it contained all the hesitancy and insecurity of touch, the shyness, and lack of confidence of the beginner. She was unable to do anything with it. Even old Cibber, a shrewd judge of talent and with a great knowledge of the stage, formed a low opinion of her, regarding her as just another small-part actress. He gave her full marks for a lovely voice and fine appearance, but even then he had to get used to them. He said also that she muttered, and that everything about her performances was misty. A more trenchant critic, Charles Gildon, said that she was amongst the mere rubbish which ought to be swept off the stage with the "filth and the dust." But she hung on; she was useful, perhaps; and she was at least good to look at and, when she chose, good to listen to. So she escaped the sweeping out up to the year 1703.

In the summer of that year, Her Majesty's Company of Comedians from Theatre Royal, Drury Lane, followed Her Majesty Queen Anne to Bath, and performed at the theatre there. Mrs. Verbruggen, whom we have met earlier, had fallen ill, and most of the parts she played were immediately snapped up by the other ladies of the company. One, however, fell to the share of the quiet, misty Mistress Oldfield, that of Leonora in the play *Sir Courtly Nice*, a good part but one which might have been better written. It was to be performed at Bath before Her Majesty and her fat, somnolent easy going consort, Prince George of Denmark. Cibber himself played the lead and Oldfield opposite to him. He was scared by her methods and feared for the show, and he decided it was no good trying to give her any "production" for that mistiness was upon her.

On the evening of the performance the Queen was in her box, with her Consort behind her, preparing, as was his wont when visiting the play, for a good, sound, comfortable sleep, with snores audible all over the theatre. The curtain went up and Cibber was probably more nervous than usual, expecting to have to "carry" his leading lady. But, as happens in the Theatre, a miracle occurred. Anne Oldfield, playing before her Royal namesake, had decided this was the occasion for which she had waited, the occasion when she would show them what she could do and what sort of an actress she really was. Letting herself go, she electrified the house. The Queen woke up the Consort and had him wide awake and staring, like any Joey Bagstock. Cibber himself could scarcely believe his eyes and ears. For he admitted that she showed such power, and had made such a sudden step forward in her art, that it astounded him. What surprised him even more was that she had done it herself; nobody had taught her; she had not been "produced." His own words are: "She had a just occasion to triumph over the error of my judgment, by the amazement that her unexpected performance awakened me to; so forward and sudden a step into nature I had never seen; and what made her performance more valuable was that I knew it all proceeded from her own understanding, untaught and unassisted by any one more experienced actor."

Yet it was not a very wonderful part. She, by her art, had made it remarkable, and it is important to note that when she became established she handed it over to less eminent actresses. However, she had done enough to show Cibber, a man of the Theatre, that here was the great actress of the immediate future. Losing no time, he turned to an unfinished play, *The Careless Husband*, which he had laid aside because he could think of no actress who could possibly play its leading lady, Lady Betty Modish, and set about finishing it. Anne Oldfield was Lady Betty Modish to the life, the young woman who such a short time ago had been amongst the rubbish. He worked quickly on the play, and soon had it on the stage, with Anne in the role of the leading lady. Both play and actress triumphed. Cibber, author and actor-manager though he was, freely admitted that much of that success was due to her. Not only was this because of her splendid performance, but also because in writing the part for her to play, he had even used phrases and turns of speech which she had used, polishing them for dramatic use. She was the smart society lady to the life, and he considered that had she been better born, she would have been what she played so very naturally. For she had a poise and ease which were remarkable. When she later went into society, though she was an actress (then a calling despised by many), she conducted herself better than most of her social superiors—and that without acting at all.

Lady Betty Modish stamped her as the leading actress of her day. She brought more to the part than any author had dreamed was in it, astonishing them with the knowledge of human nature she displayed, and her ability to transmit it. She was versatile, but it was in high comedy and as the creator of ladies of fashion—smart, resourceful, witty and women of the world—that she excelled. She also played in tragedy, though she professed not to like it as she found the conventions of the tragic queens and distressed ladies irked her. They invariably had long trains and pages to carry them—it will be remembered how Bracegirdle as a child had done this for Mrs. Barry—and that was not to her liking. She said "I hate to have a page dragging my tail about. Why do they not give Porter these parts? She can put on a better tragedy face than I can." Porter was another Drury Lane actress of her time. When they revived *Mithridates* Anne made great demur about playing it, though she did so and to perfection. She was a magnificent Cleopatra, and in *The Fair Penitent* her performance of Calista, dwarfing that of the rest of the company, moved her audiences to tears and acclamation. Her voice thrilled with passion, her stature seemed to grow and pulsate, her eyes flashed, and the other players were filled with awe.

She challenged the great Mrs. Bracegirdle, but there was no direct contest for the Queenship of the Stage. Mrs. Bracegirdle was twenty years older than Mrs. Oldfield at the time. She was a sensible woman, had kept her head and her money, and was not going to be defeated in public in a contest for popular favour. Nor was she going to see parts which had for so long been her own given over to a younger rival, whilst she stood down or played inferior roles. So she retired gracefully in 1709 when the Oldfield tide was in full strength. There are stories that the two fought it out, each playing the same role on successive nights, but no evidence of this can be found in reliable sources and it does not sound a bit like either of them.

Anne, always called Nance Oldfield, was a woman of cool, clear judgment though an opportunist who did not betray her loyalties and always sided with her fellow players. When they revolted against the chicanery of Rich and went (for the most part) to Vanbrugh's new theatre in the Haymarket where Her Majesty's now stands, she went with them. Colley Cibber, another opportunist, stood by Rich. If he had been mistaken in his early judgment of her, she was never for a moment mistaken in him. She always kept her eye on him, and when he came to power, and with his partners Robert Wilks and Thomas Doggett, formed the famous Triumvirate which ran Theatre Royal, Drury Lane, with such glory and integrity, it was Nance Oldfield who was their supreme leading lady. She could, indeed, have been their partner, but she weighed up this opportunity and decided there was a better one, electing to be the leading lady at Old Drury. She knew that old, stubborn, prejudiced Doggett, masculine to the core, was against any petticoat influence in the government of the Theatre, though he would have acquiesced in her case but with a grievance. She did not want to be involved in managerial disputes and the cares attendant thereon. So she became the permanent leading lady, on her own terms. She knew they must make her a first-class offer, just as she knew that Wilks and Cibber wanted her as partner, whilst Doggett wanted her as actress only. She named her terms: two hundred pounds a year certain, and a clear annual benefit. By a "clear benefit" was meant that she received the entire proceeds of the benefit performance. Not only were her terms accepted, but as soon as the management settled down, they advanced the two hundred pounds to three hundred guineas per annum, the highest salary paid then to any actress, while it was estimated that her benefit doubled that sum. It should be added that there was no written contract between them at any time: simply a verbal one, which was scrupulously observed by both parties. It was more than observed, for when she made a tremendous success in *The Provok'd Husband* the management gave her a bonus of fifty guineas. They knew she was as honest as the day and would stand by them; she knew they would never, in their own interest, give her cause for complaint.

At the very end, during the last two months of her final painful illness, when she could act no more, they sent her salary just the same, and she, not to be outdone, and in all sincerity, returned it.

For the most part she played opposite to Robert Wilks, one of the greatest comedians, in the highest sense of the word, our stage ever knew. She also partnered Cibber; and in both cases the stage sparkled with brilliance. The latter, who mistakenly fancied himself as a tragedian, was a polished character comedian and found the ideal foil in the clear-cut and understanding comedy of Nance Oldfield. She never overplayed, she never forced, and could create a character of humanity out of the most unpromising material.

Her benefits were astounding affairs. All the rank and fashion attended and the ordinary playgoers thronged the cheaper parts. All wanted to benefit Nance. At one of them there was a strange extra attraction. Those were the days when the audience not only roamed about the stage at will, but on special occasions seats were placed thereon and sold at a high price. Two gallants quarrelled. They fought it out on the stage actually during the play, to the immense delight of everyone save the performers.

Much blood was shed which only added to the general joy.

Even then, Nance Oldfield kept her head. She was never at a loss, never flustered. On one solitary occasion, a single man in the pit saw fit to hiss her. She stopped dead, gazed at him with a look of infinite pity and said, very audibly, "Poor creature." The house roared approval, the would-be "birder" collapsed, and slunk away. Nance Oldfield was a very good study. She seldom "dried up," and had a short sharp way of dealing with those who did. Let an actor or actress do so when playing with her, and she promptly came right down to the front of the stage and said to the audience "Ladies and Gentlemen: it is not *my* turn to speak"—and then fixed her large, lustrous eyes on the offender. . . .

It is said that Farquhar was an early lover of hers and it may be true. Certain it is that, in his last desperate straits, when he was practically penniless before his early and painful death, she came to his rescue generously. She was always ready to help those in trouble. She was not the cold, dispassionate woman that her early rival Mrs. Bracegirdle had been, so she may well have been Farquhar's lover. She chose her lovers as she ordered her career, making no mistakes. Nor did the public ever fall foul of her on that account as often happened to her sister actresses. She was never known to encourage the advances of a married man. She liked her men all to herself, and during the progress of a particular *affaire*, she was faithful. There was Arthur Mainwaring, author, pamphleteer, man of learning and taste, and a clever politician. The two loved each other to distraction; it was as if both of them had fallen in love for the first time, not only with each other, but with Love itself. He became a Commissioner of Customs and held other Governmental jobs with good salaries. But he was careless with money and when he died in 1712, left only a small sum. He made Nance his executrix and left his money to his sister, Nance and Arthur the son she had borne him.

Her next lover was no less a person than General Charles Churchill who was the son of Sir Winston Churchill, a brother of the great Duke of Marlborough. The two were devoted, and there were strong rumours of a wedding between them. Nance Oldfield was much at Court, and would read plays to the Queen, who loved her beautiful voice and perfect diction. One day the

Queen snapped a question at her: "I hear, Mrs. Oldfield, that you and the General are married!" Nance turned her eyes on her sovereign. "So 'tis said, Ma'am," she replied quietly, "but the General keeps his own secrets." No further questions were asked. The remark is sometimes attributed to Princess Charlotte, but whatever the case it is the kind of answer Nance, always mistress of the situation, would have given. Her irregular unions were never a bar to her reception in Society. She went everywhere, an honoured guest and her manners were impeccable. Colley Cibber, her manager and oft-times acting partner, enjoyed the same privilege and an even greater one, for he was the first actor ever to be a member of the most exclusive White's Club. Nor was there another until Arthur Bourchier was admitted in modern times.

She gave the General a son, Charles, who entered the Army and became a Colonel. He saved Sir Robert Walpole, that famous and most persistent Prime Minister, from assassination by scenting a plot and sending the Prime Minister home in his own carriage instead of that which the politician owned. He had a daughter who married Charles Sloane, later Earl of Cadogan who left his name firmly implanted on London. Irregular unions and irregular births mattered little. The cream of Society, as it then was, not only received General Churchill and his actress-mistress, but delighted to be entertained by them at their own home, too, considering it an honour to be invited.

Nance Oldfield's taste in dress was faultless, everything she wore becoming her perfectly. It was said that her clothes seemed to grow on her, rather than be worn by her. Christopher Rich once fell foul of her over one of her dresses, and put a bitter complaint into his accounts: "In January, she required and was paid, ten guineas to wear on the stage in some plays during the whole season a mantua petticoat that was given for the stage and though she left off three months before she should, yet she has not returned any part of the ten guineas." One would like to hear Nance's version of that, for faith in Rich is not possible, especially as he carries out into his figure column, the said sum of ten guineas as £10 15*s.* 0*d.* In the same statement he goes on: "And she had, for wearing in some plays a suit of boy's clothes on the stage, paid £2 10*s.* 9*d.*" So Nance wore the breeches too! He gives his own case away: he discloses the figures for her benefit under his control as £69 7*s.* 8*d.*, when we have Cibber's word that when the Triumvirate were in charge, these performances often produced £600. . . .

At her house in Grosvenor Street she kept considerable estate. She did not mix very much in the theatre with the other players, holding herself somewhat regally aloof, going to and from the playhouse in her own sedan chair, attended by two footmen. Disdaining the theatre wardrobe, she chose her clothes herself, being allowed a sum of money to dress her parts.

All her contemporaries eulogised her. Here is a typical pen picture of her:

> She was in stature just rising to that height where the graceful can only begin to show itself; of lively aspect and a command in her mien, that like the principal figure in the finest painting, first seizes and longest delights the eye of the spectators. Her voice was sweet, strong, piercing and melodious, her pronunciation voluble, distinct and musical; and her emphasis was always placed where the spirit of the scene, in her periods, only demanded it. . . . The spectator was always as much informed by her eyes as by her elocution; for the look is the only proof that an actor rightly conceives what he utters, there being scarce an instance, where the eyes do their part, that the elocution is known to be faulty.

Another eminent authority said she was the most beautiful woman who ever trod the English stage. Steele, who could slash when he liked, could not be enthusiastic enough about her, holding that she was always well-dressed and always the genteelest woman to meet "but the make of her mind very much contributes to the ornament of her body. She has the greatest simplicity of many of any of her sex . . . everyone that sees her knows her to be of quality, but this distinction is owing to her manner and not to her habit. Her beauty is full of attraction but not allurement."

It would appear that her beauty of face and figure grew with the years and that when she died, all too soon, she was in the full flush of both. There was another characteristic of hers worthy of attention. It is Cibber again, and he knew her the best:

> She had one mark of good sense, rarely known in any actor of

> either sex but herself. I have observed several, with promising dispositions, very desirous of instruction at their first setting out; but no sooner had they found their least account in it, than they were desirous of being left to their own capacity, which they then thought would be disgraced by their seeming to want further assistance. But this was not Mrs. Oldfield's way of thinking, for to the last year of her life, she never undertook any part she liked without being importunately desirous of giving all the helps on it that another could possibly give her. By knowing so much herself, she found how much more there was of Nature yet to be known. Yet it was a hard matter to give her any hint that she was not able to take and improve. With all this merit, she was tractable and less presuming in her station that several that had not half her pretentions to be troublesome; but she lost nothing by her easy conduct: she had everything she asked, which she took care should be always reasonable, because she hated so much to be grudged as denied a civility.

Those words ought to be written or painted up in every dressing-room which any actress is ever likely to use. They are words of wisdom as between management and performer; moreover they are true. And Nance Oldfield knew it, which is one of the reasons why she was so great.

The parts she played were many, and, having once made her mark, she not only played them all with excellence, but she always brought something fresh and amazingly vital to them. The last part she created was that of Sophonisba, in Thomson's play of that name. Her last benefit was on March 19, 1730, when she played Calista in *The Fair Penitent*, which she chose herself. Her last stage appearance, which was for the benefit of an actor, Clarke, was as Lady Brute in *The Provok'd Wife*. Her career on the stage since that memorable occasion at Bath had been one of unchecked triumph. Only once did she suffer a combined attack from the public and this was organized by another actress, not an uncommon thing in those days. Mrs. Rogers took exception to Nance being given parts which she considered were due to her. She was a good actress but Nance was better. So she got friends and supporters to hiss Mrs. Oldfield. After this had gone on for a number of performances it was arranged that both actresses should play the same part to test their capabilities and the audience should acclaim the winner. Nance, electing to play Lady Lurewell in *The Trip to the Jubilee*, had a walk-over: Mrs. Rogers withdrew from the contest and was well advised so to do.

Nance Oldfield, the victim of cancer, suffered terribly, but played on, tears of pain in her eyes when she acknowledged the loud plaudits. At last, however, she had to give up. Tended by her friend Mrs. Saunders, another actress, whom she had introduced to the stage, she waited for the end. A touching testimony of the great actress's last weeks in this world is left by Mrs. Saunders: "Her funeral I never heard her once mention, but Christian fortitude she had sufficient; for though she had no priest she did the offices of one to the last. When her dissolution drew nigh and the lamp of life waxed dim, she then expressed herself in broken words and pious meditations in the most moving and strong manner you can imagine. It can be justly said that she prayed without ceasing. She was all goodness; the best of daughters, the best of mothers and the best of friends. Oh, that I had words to sound forth her praises. . . ."

Born in 1683, Anne Oldfield died on October 23, 1730, still a graceful, lovely woman in full bloom of beauty, save that at the end the ravages of pain had marked her. Of her courage there is no doubt. She asked her doctors to tell her frankly if her case was hopeless and when she heard the worst she made no outcry nor showed sorrow but met her fate bravely. She left the world in as remarkable manner as that in which she had lived in it. Always beautifully dressed and careful of person, she demanded that her corpse should be dressed in her best and that her face should be made up. There was a law which required that all corpses had to be wrapped in woollen sheets, which she abhorred, but she had her way. Mrs. Saunders attired her in her best underclothing, a fine Brussels lace headdress, a holland shift with a tucker and double ruffles of the same lace, and a pair of new kid gloves. She left a considerable fortune and a wonderful will.

She had a signal honour to mark her end, too. She lay in state in the Jerusalem Chamber of Westminster Abbey, the only actress ever to do so. The senior Prebendary of the Abbey conducted her funeral, her son Arthur Mainwaring was chief mourner, and Lord de la Warr, Lord Hervey of Ickworth, the Right Honourable George Bubb Doddington, Charles Hodges Esq., Walter Carey Esq., and Captain Elliott were her pall bearers. General Churchill asked to be allowed to raise a monument to her, but this was refused.

The beautiful body of that beautiful woman and great actress went to its rest in the royal and ancient Abbey of Westminster by Congreve's monument, and there she lies—Anne Oldfield, affectionately known as Nance, who always did her best, gave of her best and looked her best, to the very end.

CHAPTER NINE

Enter the Peeresses

AN epoch ended with the untimely death of the beautiful and talented Anne Oldfield and it was to be some time before a figure of similar eminence graced the English stage. That is not to say that in the meantime there were not other actresses of considerable attainments. There was, for example, the Mrs. Porter whom Anne Oldfield said should have the tragic parts "with the page to carry the tail." She had been given a start by Betterton in 1699 and she had played "seconds" to Mrs. Barry. When that lady died, Mrs. Porter was the chief tragedienne until Mrs. Oldfield arose. She was the original creator of Alicia in *Jane Shore* and many other good parts.

She came, it appears, of quite a good family, but was left an orphan at a very early age and thrown on her own resources. Having plenty of pluck she answered the challenge and got work as an actress in a booth at Bartholomew Fair, a great stage nursery then. It was there that Betterton saw her. But he had been taken there by two great actresses, who had seen her first, Bracegirdle and Barry. Little Miss Porter was playing the Fairy Queen and must have been good. It got her the chance she needed. Her career ran parallel with that of Oldfield's, and the two were great friends. Oldfield, poised and balanced, liked laughter; Porter, the tragic queen, was serious, determined and dignified, and always rather grim. Nance Oldfield in joke would call her "Mother."

She was at her best in regal characters, especially as Queen Catherine and as Elizabeth in *The Unhappy Favourite*. One night at Drury Lane she was playing the latter role. Good Queen Anne, who was following the play with keen interest and leaning over the edge of her box, let fall her fan with a resounding whack on the stage. Mrs. Porter stopped and, more queenly than the queen she played, and certainly more queenly than the fan-dropper, pointed to the object and said to a stage attendant "Take up our sister's fan." This was getting into the skin of a part with a vengeance! The Queen in the box, however, smiled good-humouredly, there was a burst of applause from the audience, and Mrs. Porter, coming to herself, realized what she had done in her excitement—and nearly died of shame.

Mrs. Porter was a woman of courage whose quickness of thought was equalled only by her quickness of action. She had a house at Heywood Hill near Hendon, Middlesex, which was then right in the country and every night after the show, she drove herself home, accompanied only by a brace of horse pistols! One summer night in 1731, she was suddenly confronted by a highwayman, who made the customary demand of his profession. Instead of a lady, alone and unprotected, screaming with fear and parting with all her valuables, the highwayman found himself staring down the barrel of a large and businesslike looking horse-pistol. Either he was not a very good highwayman or had not thought it worth while to draw his own pistol, for not only was he nonplussed but beaten. He begged for mercy. He assured Mrs. Porter he was no common thief, no ordinary follower of the High Toby. He had been driven to do this by distress, his family was in desperate straits. Indeed he told her such a pitiful story and told it so well that his tongue achieved what his threats had failed to do. She asked him to come into the carriage and she gave him all the money she had in her purse—ten guineas. Thanking and blessing her, the man stepped out and she, in the excitement of emotion, gave her horse a sharp flick with the whip. The horse reared, upset the chaise, and bolted. Mrs. Porter was thrown out and a dislocated hip was the result. It was a handicap to her ever after. But she did not hold it against the would-be robber. She had inquiries made and found that his story was true. She started a collection amongst her friends, raising £60 which was sent to relieve him and his family, who never ceased to bless her.

In her old age Mrs. Porter was visited by no less a person than Dr. Johnson himself. He said that she appeared to him so wrinkled that a picture of old age in the abstract might be taken from her countenance. She died in 1762.

There was also Mrs. Horton, who succeeded to many of the parts created and played by Nance Oldfield. Her strongest claim to fame, however, was her very great beauty. Her name was Christina and she said she came from a good family in Warwickshire. Barton Booth discovered her as a strolling player at Southwark Fair in 1714, when she was playing Cupid in a droll called *Cupid and Psyche*, the company being that of one Booker. Barton Booth took her to Drury Lane, where she made her début as Melinda in *The Recruiting Sergeant*. She remained there until 1734 when she went to Covent Garden. She took over the Oldfield parts, but, of course, she never played them as did Nance. She was at best a copy of the original. She had started with a voice sweet-toned but of no power, which she trained into a clarion call. Her private life remained spotless throughout her career. She retired in 1750.

Margaret Saunders, the faithful friend of Nance Oldfield, who stood by her and aided her last hours and passing, was born in Weymouth, where her father Jonathan Saunders was a wine cooper. She was sent to a boarding school at Steeple Ashton, in Wiltshire, and later was apprenticed to a milliner, Mrs. Fane, of Catherine Street, Strand. Mrs. Fane was well-known amongst the ladies of the profession and it was in that way that Mrs. Oldfield met young Margaret Saunders, liked her and, at the age of sixteen, introduced her to the stage at Drury Lane. Mrs. Saunders had the makings of a good actress but she developed asthma and had to give up the stage, so Nance took her under her wing as companion, and she served her, with love, the rest of Nance's life, receiving from her an annuity of ten pounds a year, quite a useful sum in those days.

Mrs. Younger, another actress of the period, was of Scottish birth. Her father, James Younger, was in the Guards and served in Flanders. Her mother was a Keith, and related to the nobility. She was born on September 2, 1702 and went to Drury Lane when she was seven years old, probably as a page, playing her first part, Princess Elizabeth in *Virtue Betrayed*. She became a good actress and one of her big successes was Emilia, the leading part in *The Dissembled Wanton*. The good blood inherited from Keith, Earl

M

Marshal of Scotland, must have stood Mrs. Younger in good stead for, as a middle-aged woman, she married the brother of the seventh Earl of Winchelsea and left the stage. She had a sister, also at Drury Lane, which was always a family house. This was Mrs. Bicknell, a lady of very lively disposition who was a good comedienne, excelling in rustic parts. It is possible that her father, when a soldier, was a comrade of Richard Steele's, for that man gave Mrs. Bicknell great praise in his *Tatler* and *Spectator*.

There was a Miss Evans who danced, to the town's delight, at Lincoln's Inn in Betterton's time. Her death was particularly regretted by Vanbrugh. He said in a letter to a friend: "Miss Evans, a dancer at the new playhouse, is dead. A fever slew her in eight and forty hours. She's much lamented by the town, as well as by the house who can't bear her loss; matters running very low with them this winter. If Congreve's play don't help 'em, they are undone. Tis a comedy and will be played about six weeks hence. Nobody has seen it yet." The play was all right. It was *The Way of the World* and although it had an indifferent first night, it succeeded and is a classic today.

Mrs. Bullock was another actress of the period, but of whom little is known save that in *Capricious Lovers*, a farce by Odingsell, she created a character called Mrs. Mincemode who, it was said, "grows sick at the sight of a man, and refines upon the significancy of phrases, till she resolves common observations into indecency."

Mrs. Seymour was an actress at the Lincoln's Inn Theatre, who was a very good performer, but did not remain long on the stage. She married an actor, Boheme, and apparently one in the family on the stage was enough. Another favourite at the same theatre who has left little mark on theatrical annals, except that she was very pretty, was Miss Stone.

And there was one more woman dramatist at this time to add to the list—Mrs. Jane Wiseman, at one time a domestic servant in the service of a Mr. Wright, of Oxford. She became stage struck, got her head full of romantic ideas, and wrote them into a play. She met and married a wealthy vintner of Westminster named Holt who got her play, a tragedy called *Antiochus the Great* produced. It failed miserably.

And there is just a little more to be said of that Mrs. Rogers, who tried to get Nance Oldfield hooted off the stage. She was a very handsome woman but she was a great prude at a time when such a thing was a rarity. Robert Wilks, with whom she appeared at Drury Lane, fell deeply in love with her. Carried away by passion, he laid close siege to her and swore that if she did not return his love he would kill himself! She yielded but whether through a desire to stop his self-immolation or whether by this time she really had some feeling for him, is not known. When they quarrelled later—partly because of her attempt to wreck Mrs. Oldfield—she hurled reproaches at him for what he had done to her and as a last barbed dart, exclaimed, "Ah, villain, did I not save your life?"

So many people are apt to regard the history of the Theatre as being entirely concerned with the dramatic stage paying very scant attention to the musical stage. That is a great mistake. The legitimate drama, in the days of the Greeks, arose out of the rhythmic singing and dancing rites in worship of Dionysos, thus the musical side of the stage is really the oldest. It had always been there, and at the period this chronicle now deals with it was very much in existence. Shakespeare never disregarded the claims of music in plays, popping in a song whenever he got a chance, to help the play along. So did many others. The drolls and jigs of the Elizabethan era, the masques of the Jacobean and Early Stuart period had music and when the Duke's Theatre opened there was a large amount of what was then regarded as opera. Shakespeare's plays were so adapted with considerable success. Pepys bears witness to the frequency with which songs were interlarded into the comedies of his day. Italian opera became the rage when Vanbrugh's Theatre in the Haymarket failed as a playhouse, and it was Opera that provided the stage with its first peeress. She was Anastasia Robinson, a woman of elegance and culture, who did not want to go on the stage at all. She had a lovely voice but never intended to use it professionally. Her father a portrait painter and musician of repute lived in Italy, so Anastasia's voice was trained by experts and was regarded as superb. When the father's eyes began to fail and he could no longer paint, he brought Anastasia and her half-sister (he had married twice) back to his native land. Much against her will Anastasia sang at concerts to provide for the family and received much sympathetic publicity, and she was acclaimed when she sang opera at Vanbrugh's Theatre in the Haymarket, where Her Majesty's now stands. Pretty, sweet-voiced Anastasia did not lack wooers. Her father favoured a certain General Hamilton, but his daughter would have nothing to do with him and astonished her family by falling in love with the father of the rejected suitor! He was the Earl of Peterborough, a remarkable man, whose adventurous life would have fascinated even Dumas. Now a widower of sixty he had at one time been a professional soldier whose services had gone to the highest bidder, and although he had helped to relieve besieged cities, and had heard himself hailed as a liberator, he was in fact a typical mercenary of his time and had been known to desert to the other side in the midst of battle. Kings had ascended to thrones with his help and the great Marlborough regarded him as a military genius. On one occasion, when the Earl was imprisoned in a fortress by a Papal Government, England had sent a fleet to his rescue.

The Earl's life was full of vicissitudes. He had been tried by his peers for a grave misdemeanour and clapped into the Tower, which would have been the end of him had he been less resourceful. But he survived to become the first nobleman ever to propose marriage to a woman of the stage. Despite his years Anastasia must have found him fascinating, virile and, of course, persuasive. She married him in 1722 at a secret ceremony and agreed that not until the Earl himself saw fit to proclaim it should it be known that she had become his wife. Anastasia set up a separate establishment at Fulham, not far from her husband's great mansion at Parson's Green and for thirteen years was regarded as the Earl's mistress. She continued to sing in opera, and at Bath was involved in an incident which the Earl brought to a summary close when he thrashed in public an Italian singer who had been rash enough to insult her.

In 1735 the Earl became seriously ill, and since an operation was unavoidable, it was arranged to send him abroad afterwards to recuperate. He wanted Anastasia to accompany him but while his operation was pending he borrowed a room in St. James's Palace and invited his friends to come and see him there. In the presence of a distinguished assembly the Earl turned to Anastasia and declared that she was his wife. In fashionable Bath the Earl made a second avowal of his marriage, and knowing that he was a dying man, he put his affairs in order so that Anastasia might be provided for properly. One of his gifts to her was Bevis Mount, his favourite country house near Southampton. After the operation the Earl and Anastasia sailed for Lisbon and the sun, but death broke their strange union six days after their arrival in Portugal and Anastasia brought her husband's body back to England to be buried in the vault of the Mordaunt family, whose dead had been interred there since the days of the Plantagenet kings.

Anastasia spent her widowhood in the country house the Earl had bequeathed her, and one of her closest friends was the Duchess of Portland. She was revered and respected and when she died at the age of eighty-eight it was said that her loyalty to her husband and his memory marked her as a lady of surpassing grace.

Although Lavinia Fenton, a pretty and enchanting creature, stepped from a musical show into high society—an achievement as satisfying as a well told fairy story—she had to wait twenty-three years before she became the stage's first Duchess. But to begin with let us take a look at an event that was memorable in the history of English music and, of course, of especial import to Lavinia, to whom it brought romance and fame.

In 1728, six years after Anastasia Robinson had secretly married her Earl, there was produced at Lincoln's Inn Theatre *The Beggar's Opera*—that light and comic masterpiece which, in the old catch-phrase, "Made Gay rich and Rich gay," for it was written by John Gay and produced by John Rich, with music by Linley. London had never seen the like of this tale of a dashing highwayman and his many loves. It involved, too, the rout of criminals and their doxies, showed up the seamy side of life and, greatly to the delight of all but its victims, mercilessly caricatured statesmen and celebrities of the day. It ran for sixty-two nights, a record then, and packed the tiny theatre to suffocation. The Prime Minister, Sir Robert Walpole and Townshend, another great figure in political life, went to see it and found themselves satirised in the characters of Peachum and Lockit, two of the thieves in the story.

The Beggar's Opera was really the first smash-hit of the musical stage and Gay's sensational success brought immediate fame to two members of the cast. They were the actor-singer Walker, who played Macheath, and a little lady named Lavinia Fenton, who played the beguiling Polly Peachum and became everybody's darling. Audiences acclaimed her and a select company of gentlemen formed a bodyguard to see her home nightly—and considered it a privilege. This gay, dazzling piece of femininity was born with the name of Beswick, but without any legal right to it. Her mother, it appears, fell in love with a naval officer of that name and did not wait to be married. The result was a little girl—and before there could be a wedding, if, indeed, the gallant sailor ever intended one, he was called to his ship and sailed for the wars. He appears to have been still in love with his inamorata and sent her a letter full of excellent advice, telling her to retire to the country and resist all temptations. The baby was not then born, but he indicated that if he became the father of a son he wanted it called Porteus and Lavinia if it was a girl. Having fulfilled his first duty to his expected offspring, he vanished for good, probably killed in action.

Lavinia's mother was a lively, attractive woman and she had no difficulty in finding a husband. A man named Fenton made an "honest woman" of her and also gave his name to her child who became Lavinia Fenton. Legally, it wasn't her name but it served. Mrs. Fenton was a woman of ideas and enterprising, and her spouse must have had some money, for she opened a coffee house in Charing Cross when such places were fashionable and much frequented by the quality. Gentlemen came to drink coffee and talk to the charming landlady. The little girl running about the place must have attracted attention too, for the fops and fine gentry made a pet of her and spoiled her completely. Or perhaps they did not. They certainly sharpened her wits, and even at that early age she appears to have had more than an inkling of the potency of feminine charm. She was a clever child and would sing, in a pretty little voice, the songs she heard others humming. Among the customers was an actor from Drury Lane who was so delighted with her that he gave her instruction in singing. But her mother decided that the time had come for education and packed Lavinia off to boarding school. Accustomed to the gaiety and freedom of the coffee house, school did not appeal to her—nor did the little ladies who were her school mates. They probably snubbed her badly. One of them received a letter from a young swain but she was careless enough to lose it and Lavinia found it. It is regrettable but it must be recorded that she told the headmistress that the recipient of the letter was going to meet a man at the garden gate that evening. The headmistress acted with promptitude. She sent all the girls to bed—except Lavinia. That young lady, who apparently had a grudge against the girl she had sneaked upon, kept the appointment with the ardent beau and told him that the object of his passion despised him! But, full of mischief, she bade him be of good heart, complimented him on his good looks and urged him to try again. Let him write another letter, slip it to her on the way to church next Sunday and she would see that his beloved received it. The young man did so and Lavinia so contrived the exchange that the lady he adored saw *her* receive the note from the admirer. Shortly after she had so neatly spiked Cupid's gun it became Lavinia's turn to become romantically involved with a young gentleman from the Inner Temple who saw her at a ball and promptly fell in love with her. She had reached the ripe age of thirteen, and when she received an ardent note from her admirer, she bribed a servant to allow her would-be lover into the garden for a meeting. She fell in love with him as deeply as he avowed he had with her, but appears to have acted with admirable circumspection (despite the fact that her knowledge was in advance of her years and the ardent wooing of the suitor was to her deep delight), for she kept it platonic. He appears to have had the makings of a very cautious lawyer, for having made enquiries about her, he found out the story of her birth and her position, and faded away. The pretty, vivacious girl took this desertion to heart. She moped and fretted, and the upshot was that her mother brought her home.

Mrs. Fenton had now moved her coffee house from Charing Cross to the Old Bailey and, away from school, Lavinia soon revived. Her mother noticed how she attracted men, and thought she could do something about her daughter's beauty and allure. She was herself a widow and not particularly moral, but before she could find a suitable "party," either as husband or protector, young Lavinia, who did nothing by halves, found a Portuguese nobleman and went off with him in his coach and four for what would now be called a "week-end." She returned home in pomp and guilty splendour, confident in her conquest. The nobleman was in love with her all right, lavished gifts on her and spoke impressively of settlements he intended to make. Probably he overdid it, for ultimately he found himself heavily in debt and lodged in Fleet Prison. This gave Lavinia a chance to show what she was made of and instead of casting off her ruined lover, as many another would have done, she visited him in prison and asked how she could help him. He seems to have been a gentleman, for he told her not to concern herself about him, to find her pleasure and fortune where she could and he would be content if she could spare the time for an occasional visit. Lavinia did much more than that. She sold all her jewellery and treasures, much of which he had given her, and raised enough not only to free him but to pay his passage back to his native land. That is an everlasting good mark in her favour.

Another lover soon appeared, a draper's apprentice who saw her at the theatre watching a play and at once lost his heart to her. He got up behind her coach and followed her home, determined to declare his love, became tongue tied, and instead wrote to her begging for a meeting. Lavinia agreed and received him as if he were a person of distinction. She was rather impressed and they went for walks together until one day his passion overcame him. He was quickly sent about his business and, although he wrote a humble apology, Lavinia ended the friendship kindly but firmly.

The year was now 1726 and Lavinia eighteen. She had to think of a career and it was the stage that called her. She was very pretty, very graceful, with a good voice and a ready wit. One of the many men who hung around hoping for her favours introduced her to the management of the Haymarket Theatre—not the Vanbrugh house but the "Little Theatre in the Hay," then in a precarious way indeed and the resort of adventurers and out-of-work actors trying to get a living. One of the latter named Huddy, who had been dismissed from the playhouse in Lincoln's Inn Fields, was given a benefit there. The play was *The Orphan, or The Unhappy Marriage*, in which Lavinia made her début in the leading role. It was a heavy, straight part with no singing, but she made a big hit, and followed this up with a brilliant success as Cherry in Farquhar's famous comedy *The Beaux's Stratagem*. It was a benefit performance and she shared it with an actor named Gilbert, and it led directly to the Lincoln's Inn Theatre itself, where Lavinia was accepted for the junior company —they had such things then—which played twice a week. But the manager, John Rich, had his eye on her as a potential star. This son of a crafty father, rough, uncouth and seemingly illiterate, knew all about theatre business. Under the name of Lun, he had proved a superb Harlequin when that character was highly regarded, and he eventually built Covent Garden Theatre itself. He paid young Lavinia the princely sum of 15*s*. a week, having obviously inherited his father's thrifty ways with actor's salaries. To this man came John Gay, a son of Devon, poet, playwright, and man of letters. He brought a light opera, which until then had been scorned and rejected by managements and actors alike. Colley Cibber had refused it for august Drury Lane, and James Quin, the leader of the stage, scornfully turned down the part of Macheath. But Rich was willing to take a gamble—a double chance—with the play and with a sparkling young girl. When he produced *The Beggar's Opera* he took Lavinia out of the junior company and gave her the leading part of Polly Peachum. The double came off, for Gay's opera became history and Polly the idol of the town. People raved about her, portraits of her filled the shops, and poets and writers everywhere acclaimed her charm and grace. Gay was not at all sure if her popularity did not exceed that of the opera itself . . . an instance of the part being greater than the whole. Her salary was thirty shillings a week. The opera ran for sixty-two consecutive performances and Lavinia was never without her retinue of admirers who made all sorts of offers to her. But she had eyes for one man only, a forty-three-year-old nobleman, rich and distinguished. He was the Duke of Bolton who had held appointments at Court, had sat in the House of Commons and was a colonel in the Guards.

Fifteen years before he had married Lady Anne Vaughan, the only daughter of the Earl of Carbery. The Duchess was a pious woman whose mind was filled with thoughts of the next world and she had displeased her imperious and unpredictable husband by failing to produce an heir. The marriage was never, in fact, particularly happy and it was doomed the moment the Duke caught a glimpse of Lavinia. Nightly he came to see her play Polly Peachum and tongues wagged even more furiously when the opera was withdrawn and Lavinia went off with her new lover, who gave her a tidy settlement of £400 a year, to be increased by a further £200 should they separate through displeasure. It was the end of Lavinia's short career and the beginning of a long association that endured the scandal that raged when the Duke left his wife for good. The Duchess of course could not compete with a rival who had charm and beauty and knew the ways of men. The Duke promised Lavinia that in the event of his wife's death he would marry her and thus make her his Duchess. Lavinia for her part produced three sons, all of them, of course, illegitimate. The abandoned wife, who was really a most worthy woman, is entitled to every sympathy and her only possible means of revenging herself was to live as long as possible and thus prevent her husband's wicked and scheming mistress (as she no doubt regarded Lavinia) from succeeding to the title.

The Duke took his Lavinia abroad and they travelled all over Europe. With them went a clergyman, so that if news of the death of the Duchess should arrive they could be married without delay. Twenty-three years were to elapse however before messengers arrived to inform the Duke of what he had waited so long to hear and on that same day, October 21, 1751, Lavinia Fenton became in truth the Duchess of Bolton—the first Duchess who had ever come from the Theatre. It was also the first name to which she had any legal right. Ladies of very doubtful reputation—or rather those of whose reputation there was no doubt at all—had become Duchesses by grace of King Charles II but Lavinia was the first actress to achieve such exalted social rank. One may not admire His Grace of Bolton but there is no doubt that on the day when his private chaplain pronounced him and his Lavinia man and wife he was a very happy man. He adored his little charmer and had kept his word. She had been scrupulously faithful to him and one likes to believe that, despite his dazzling rank, she loved him. It would indeed seem that she did.

The marriage was a happy one, but lasted only three years. From contemporary writings it would appear that the Duke's passion for Lavinia—and it was a passion—never cooled throughout their association and he was still greatly in love with her when he died in this country on August 26, 1754. He left everything he possibly could, everything which was not entailed, to his Lavinia, referring to her in his will as his "dear and well beloved wife." He made no mention of anyone else and nominated her his sole executrix, having already generously provided for her three sons during his lifetime. They, being illegitimate, had no chance with the family name and rank, so the title passed to his brother.

Lavinia survived him by six years. She became a very popular figure. Her performance in the role of Duchess was one of the best she ever gave. She died at West Combe Park, Greenwich, on January 24, 1760, and was buried in St. Alphege Church. There are many descriptions of the actress-duchess. They differ sometimes regarding her beauty but the testimony of the clergyman who married them should be of value. He had many opportunities of observing her before that day when he married her to her ducal lover at Aix-en-Provence, where they were staying when the news reached them which made the ceremony possible. He was the Reverend Dr. Joseph Wharton, a man of esteem and a friend of Dr. Johnson. In his testimony he paid tribute to Lavinia as a most agreeable companion, possessing much wit and a good taste in polite literature. He also added that she was well made (she had a good figure, in other words), though she could not be called a beauty. Who is to judge beauty? Is it not simply a question of personal taste? Even if Lavinia lacked classical perfection she had personality and sex appeal. She had the great gift of making those with her feel happy and gay. That matters much in this world. And according to her own lights, her upbringing and her times, she was by no means a "bad" woman. She was faithful to those she loved. She charmed, and the charm endured. A ballad does her credit—as actress and as woman:

> Since Poll has gained applause
> All vindicate her cause
> And prodigious crowds she draws
>   All conspire to clap her.
>   The house rings
>   When she sings
>   Must such thanks
>   Vanish in vapour?
> No, she outshines them all
> No, she outshines them all
> Pretty, pretty Polly.

CHAPTER TEN

Tempests and Temperaments

IT has been stated earlier that "temperament" is not the prerogative of actresses. Many actors can "throw a temperament" with equal ease, if not perhaps with as much hope of success, for when the manager is a man he is not likely to put up with so much from one of his own sex. It is probable that the members of the male sex who, before the arrival of the actresses, portrayed the roles of women, were prone to "temperaments," through enforced, habitual and, in some cases, inherent effeminacy. But temperament among actors has a harder and much plainer name, whereas in leading ladies it is something which is regarded as part of the game.

This business of temperament—in the sense of bad temper, deplorable manners and the general desire to be a confounded nuisance—has nothing to do with the art of acting at all. True, one must have the temperament to be an actor or an actress, but that is not what is meant when "temperaments" are spoken of. These "temperaments" are part of a person's character, and arise for all sorts of reasons—the type in which their names are billed, precedence, choice of clothes, dressmakers and costumiers, the question of dressing-rooms, salary, and the very great desire to crush and oppress rival players, whether equals or rising stars. Some, and there are many such, indulge in them for publicity, of which they can never get enough. Their constant demand is to see their names in print, their pictures in the papers, for any and every reason, good, bad or indifferent. They will make everyone's life a burden if there is the shortest interval between such bursts.

The man—or woman—who suffers most is the unfortunate individual who has been so misguided as to become a publicity "expert" for the theatre. They have only themselves to blame. They are scum and slaves, underpaid and overworked, ostracised and persecuted.

The actress with the publicity complex, and there are far more actresses afflicted in this way than actors, can be a fiend. They think everything printed in the papers about them is good for them—although much of it is really damaging. The worst kind of feminine publicity-hound is the actress passing or just past her prime—who either does not or will not realise it, who finds the play in which she is appearing is going down hill and imagines success can be coaxed by publicity. Ninety-nine and a half times out of a hundred publicity can neither make nor save a show—and the odd half is one when a really good show has by some mischance had a bad break—and that can happen. But the publicity-hound would never know that. It is not the show which matters—it is her. It never dawns on her that if she was half as good as she thinks, or wishes the public to think, that publicity would not be needed. Few, pitifully few, actors and actresses know anything about publicity at all and much the same applies to managers. The majority who do, become great. The best publicity is a good show, and a good performance.

These observations on the idiosyncrasies of players does not imply that ladies of the stage who were "headaches" have as a consequence failed to achieve greatness. Many of them have—but the greatness was bigger than the temperament. And such a one who possessed both was very great indeed, and owed her first big break to a coincidence concerning the very play, or comic opera, which gave the stage its first Duchess. This lady was not a member of the cast of *The Beggar's Opera*. She happened to be in a rival show which "got the bird"—but made the actress. That in itself is a claim to eminence, too. Her name was Catherine Raftor and she was the daughter of Kilkenny-born William Raftor, who, until attaching himself to the cause of James II, was a gentleman of considerable position and wealth. He was one of many to whom the Battle of the Boyne brought ruin and destitution, but he still remained loyal to the man he firmly believed was his King. He followed his leader into exile and secured a commission in the army of Louis XIV—for all the Irish gentlemen were, and are, gallant fighters.

Later Raftor gained a pardon in England and returned home. A handsome man of considerable charm, his tongue achieved what his sword had failed to do, for he married a Miss Daniel, daughter of a merchant who lived in Fish Street Hill, in the City of London. She brought him a considerable dowry and a considerable family arrived to spend it. One of the offspring, a daughter born in 1711, left an indelible mark on the patina of theatrical time. One fact emerges, she had the poorest of educations. She was very nearly illiterate when it came to writing—it was so bad that it seemed she must have been entirely self-taught and her spelling was atrocious. Yet her thoughts were well and clearly expressed and could be very pointed on occasion. Women generally were not well educated in the early eighteenth century—but they could nearly all write and spell better than this Catherine Raftor. From a host of conflicting statements it is apparent that she was stage struck very early and, in fact, had shown unmistakable signs of histrionic gifts as a child. She must have had a voice too, because Henry Carey of "Sally in Our Alley" fame took a hand in her training. The early history of the Raftor family is misty and inconclusive but it appears that Catherine used to hang around the theatres to watch the actors and follow her favourites about, particularly Robert Wilks, at whom she would gaze in open-mouthed wonder, which the actor no doubt enjoyed.

There being so many mouths to fill in the Raftor *ménage* it is pretty certain that Catherine was put to domestic service when little more than a child, for she was employed by a Miss Eleanor Knowles of Church Row, Houndsditch. Opposite was a tavern called The Bell whose proprietor used to cater for an organisation known as the Beef Steak Club. Many actors patronised it and one morning, when the tavern was at its busiest, its patrons heard a young voice, fresh and clear singing with all the truth and simplicity of youth. They listened and then went to the window to discover the young nightingale, who turned out to be a young girl trilling away as she washed the steps of the house opposite, where lived Miss Knowles. So charming and graceful did she look on that bright morning that everybody was enchanted, especially three leading members of the club who were present, Beard, Dunstall and Woodward, all men of rank in the Theatre. They went across to the girl, enquired her name, which was "Kitty Raftor." And so impressed were they that Beard and Dunstall agreed to sponsor her theatrical career. It is a pretty story and one hopes it is true.

There is another version, to the effect that it was Chetwood, for many years prompter at Drury Lane, when prompters were really stage managers, and Theophilus Cibber (of disgraceful memory) who first recognised the girl's talent and recommended her to Colley Cibber, Theophilus's father. Chetwood, always anxious to please, says of Cibber, "his infallible judgment soon found out her excellencies and the moment he heard her sing, put her down in the list of performers at Twenty Shillings a Week." Now Cibber's judgment was not always infallible, as is proved by his inability to recognise for so long the talent in Nance Oldfield. Anyhow, there Kitty was at Drury Lane in 1728, and earning at the age of seventeen a pound a week, a very good salary indeed, especially for a beginner. The mystery of the whereabouts of her family all this time will probably never be solved. Rumours that they returned to Ireland become less understandable in view of the fact that Kitty must have been in London when she was twelve, which she admitted was the age at which she used to gape at Wilks. Maybe there is a bit of truth in the step-washing story and that Miss Knowles was a friend of the family, who brought the girl over to London—there being so little money, and employed her. And maybe it was Beard and Dunstall who brought her to Chetwood and Cibber—who would have to be consulted in any case.

Kitty Raftor, as she was then rightly called, was one of those very rare and precious creatures, a natural actress—by which is implied that she had a natural gift for the stage. Garrick too was a natural actor and needed no preliminary training, gaining his technique by experience. It was also the case with Kitty Raftor.

At Drury Lane in 1728 she found herself among very distinguished company—Colley Cibber himself, Anne Oldfield, Mrs. Porter and her adored Wilks in person, actually a colleague now.

Like so many others Kitty began by playing a page, but this page was not confined to the mere carrying of "tails," but had lines to speak, and had a name, Ismenes, page to Ziphares in Lee's play, *Mithridates, King of Pontius.* Dressed as a boy Kitty wore breeches and of course she had a song to sing, which was interpolated. She was an instant success. Later she played Bianca in *Othello* and in the November of that year she had a busy time, playing in the same evening *Aesop* with Colley Cibber in the title role and in a pantomime entitled *Perseus and Andromeda, with the Rape of Columbine, or The Flying Lovers.* She did it all very well indeed.

But that year saw the production of *The Beggar's Opera* and Colley Cibber—Chetwood's infallible—having turned down that delightful work was very bitter about it when he saw the success it was achieving at the rival house. Not to be outdone he said, as managers still say to this day: "Oh, so they want this sort of thing, do they? Well, we'll give it to them." He set to work. *The Beggar's Opera* finished its run and was promptly provided with a sequel by Gay and Rich called *Polly.* But the magic was gone. Those who had been flayed alive with satire in *The Beggar's Opera* took action. *Polly* was not a success: it was banned and persecuted. Not without a fight, for the public took sides. Colley Cibber, a great man of the Theatre came in for his share of the blame. There were those who held that his spite in losing *The Beggar's Opera* made him "pull strings" which made the trouble for *Polly.* There was little foundation for this. The real culprit was Sir Robert Walpole, who was still smarting from the satire of *The Beggar's Opera.* That piece had annoyed King George II and had even divided the Court, the Duchess of Queensberry having been forbidden to appear there because of her championing of John Gay. A scapegoat had to be found during this controversy and Cibber was the recipient of this unenviable distinction. He was an easy target, for he was never popular and being sure of himself had created his own world at Drury Lane. He despised his rivals, ignored his critics and went his own way.

The hounds were baying when he decided upon a fresh venture in the light-operatic field, for although he had earned early fame by writing a clean play when the public was sated of unrelieved dirt, he still had his eye on the crime-filled atmosphere of *The Beggar's Opera.* He determined to follow the vogue for opera, but with a clean one. In an atmosphere of acrimony and at a time when a campaign was being waged against him over the banning of *Polly* he presented a light, pastoral ballad opera called *Love in a Riddle*.

The opening night turned out to be one of those hostile occasions which were once so frequent in the theatre and which sometimes occur even now. Noise and disorder was to be expected but there was a deep and sinister note in the angry murmur which filled every part of the house. Theatrical managers always profess great friendship, one with the other, and are ready with their sympathy and condolence over a failure. But there is, all too often, a gleam in the eye and a slight contraction of the lips if the sympathetic one happens to have notched a success himself and that recently. So far as *Love in a Riddle* is concerned there is no doubt that Gay and Rich set out to destroy the work and rivalry of Colley Cibber. They had succeeded in inflaming public opinion and the hostility was there at Drury Lane, seething and needing little to boil over. Cibber knew all about it but had no fear. He was used to trouble—it hit him most when he had to lose money, as on the occasion when Mrs. Rogers provoked a demonstration, with a paid claque, against Mrs. Oldfield. The disturbance there was so great that Cibber had to stop the show and—in his own words—"dismiss an audience of £150," who got their money back.

As soon as the curtain went up it was at once apparent that the play was not to have a hearing. Jeers, catcalls, howls of derision and clamour of all kinds broke out. Gentlemen in the boxes were as active as the malcontents in the pit and in the top gallery. There was, of course, a counter demonstration by the pro-Cibbers, and throughout the tumult the players battled. They acted and sang, and would not be denied although hardly able to hear each other, let alone the strains of the small orchestra below them. The din grew prodigious, but those players were tough folk and endured far more than any modern cast could put up with. Mad, as are all the real people of the Theatre, they reckoned that it was their job and being paid to act they carried on.

The noise and uproar grew worse, the "house" began to move, to sway, there were private fights in progress—until leaders of the anti-Cibbers saw that the moment for complete victory had come. Two such gentry were in private boxes, adjoining each other, from whence they could see the house, exchange comments and issue instructions to the demonstrators. Then, all at once, and unbelievably, the uproar lessened and silence descended on the theatre. A young girl had run upon the stage, all smiles, grace and vitality, and had begun to sing. By sheer force of personality, she made contact with the audience and arrested its frenzy. They knew her and liked her for her charm and courage. She sang and played on—and for a moment it seemed that the tide had turned, that Cibber had snatched victory out of the very jaws of defeat. The girl on the stage, it was none other than young Kitty Raftor, had the house bewitched and she had done it alone. Malcontents who had opened their mouths to roar rude epithets, relaxed into smiles. Those vile instruments from which the "cat call" was produced were withdrawn and there was even a scatter of applause until one of the leaders fearing that the plan to ruin the play had failed called loudly to his associate: "Zounds, Tom! Take care! or this charming little devil will save all." Then he began to bellow once more and uproar was again provoked but it had passed the zenith of its fury and could not be whipped into fever heat again. *Love in a Riddle* was played through to its end, but it would never have done so except for that "charming little devil," Kitty Raftor. Cibber, plucky and not a little obstinate, put it on again the next night and the Heir Apparent was in the Royal Box. The uproar broke loose once more, and appearing before his yelling subjects, dressed in his splendid best and aglitter with diamonds, calm Colley Cibber assured them—after a polite reminder of the august company in which they found themselves—that if they would let the play go on to its close they would never see it again. He won and kept his word for nobody saw *Love in a Riddle* after that. But they did see another ballad opera called *Damon and Phillida* produced remarkably soon after, which strangely enough had the identical characters, music, words and cast, although the author's name was suppressed. And playing Phillida was that young person of charm and devilry named Kitty Raftor. The public liked *Damon and Phillida*, and the fact that it bore such a marked resemblance to the damned *Love in a Riddle* escaped notice. Master Colley Cibber, one thinks, had won. . . .

A woman who could do what Kitty Raftor had done on such an occasion was obviously marked for greatness. She put the seal on her success as well in *The Devil to Pay*. The public now took her to their hearts and she became a real leading lady, even to getting a good rise in salary. Things were indeed happening to her rapidly. And to make her life complete, or so she thought, romance came into her life and she married one George Clive, a brother of Sir Edward Clive and a relation of Robert, Lord Clive. Her husband was a barrister but never appeared to have any briefs and how he lived was a mystery. He was some sort of assistant to a man of letters and he seems to have been a learned man himself. Perhaps he was carried away by Kitty's charm, or saw her as a useful wage-earner—maybe both. But Mistress Kitty Clive as she now became—and that is the name which has come down the centuries—was not cut out to be a wife. She possessed a strong personality, a sharp tongue and being a star, even in the days when stars were not so courted as they are now, was definitely "somebody" and considered herself better than most. She discovered that her husband was an idle man and that he proposed to live on her. The marriage had taken place some time in 1733 and did not last long—three years at the outside. There was a separation by mutual consent, so far as can be discovered, and Kitty's only link with her husband was his name. She certainly added lustre to it and disregarded his family and their accusations of a mesalliance. Mistress Kitty had ever a good opinion of herself and though she may have been a virago with a tempest of a temperament she was, nevertheless, a virtuous woman and of stainless character. She did not care for the company of high society and chose her friends from among the people she liked, rather than on account of their social position. Asked why she did not visit certain great families, as she could have done, she said, "Because my dear, I choose my company as I do my fruit; therefore I am not for damaged quality."

During Kitty Clive's long reign at Drury Lane, that theatre had its ups and downs. She came in almost at the end of the brilliant period of the triumvirate of Cibber, Wilks and Barton Booth. She was there when amateurs like Highmore, stage struck without having stage ability, took over. But she was, despite her temperament and difficult behaviour, a very loyal person, standing by her management when trouble came, taking the bad times with the good.

Highmore had trouble with his actors. Theophilus Cibber, old Colley's rascally son, led a revolt against him, with good reason, but the cause was worthy of a better and more disinterested leader. Kitty Clive stuck to her management, along with Bridgewater, a good actor, and Mrs. Horton. Highmore eventually won.

When Macklin, that tempestuous and commanding man who was such a superb actor, came upon the scene Kitty Clive was the leading lady. On that momentous occasion when he played Shylock and lifted that character from the buffoon and butt it had become and made it indeed "the Jew that Shakespeare drew," Kitty Clive played Portia. She was not a very good Shakespearean actress, but she was too good an actress to be bad in anything. Her loyalty on the occasion of the actors' strike drew a testimony from Fielding, then a playwright and destined to be a famous novelist. She created the part of Lettice in his play *The Designing Chambermaid*. He wrote a preface to the published work and said of her: "The part you have maintained in this dispute between the players and the patentees, of 1733, is so full of honour that had it been in higher life it would have given you the reputation of the greatest heroine of the age. You looked upon the cases with compassion, nor could any promises or views of interest sway you to desert them; nor have you scrupled any fatigue (particularly in the part at so short a warning you undertook in this farce) to support the cause of those you imagined injured; and for this you have been so far from endeavouring to exact an exorbitant reward from persons little able to afford it, that I have known you offer to act for nothing, rather than the patentees should be injured by the dissensions of the audience."

That was the sort of woman Kitty Clive was. But there was another side, too—the leading lady's side. Let her imagine herself slighted or put upon and the sparks flew at once. There was an arrangement to revive *The Beggar's Opera*. By this time Susanna Maria Cibber, the second and ill-used wife of Theophilus Cibber, was upon the scene, and she was a wonderful singer and actress. The two women, one supreme in tragedy and the other in comedy, watched each other like two sparring cats. Both claimed the part of Polly. By right it should have been Kitty Clive's, since she was the leading comedienne, but Susanna Maria wanted it badly—her idea being that Kitty should play Lucy. Now, that was indeed the right casting, for Susanna might have easily eclipsed Lavinia

Fenton in a part she had created and there could not have been a finer Lucy than Kitty Clive would have made. But both wanted the so-called "lead." Intrigue started, both lobbied the theatre and their friends for support and feeling ran very high. These two stars hated each other with a rich, red hatred, neither made any secret of what was going on—and the town rang with it. At length the part was cast—and Susanna got it. There was as near murder as made no difference, and it was fortunate for Susanna that Kitty was not able to lay hands on her. Each had a bodyguard, Kitty's for restraint, Susanna's for protection. The upshot was that the revival was shelved, and both claimed the victory, which was Pyrrhic indeed.

Kitty Clive's great art lay in comedy. All comedies, farces and light plays then had the part of a chambermaid, who carried the plot, arranged lovers' meetings, frustrated the unwanted suitors, and misled parents or guardians, and these were the roles in which Kitty Clive excelled—these and any low comedy. Naturally, being a great comedienne, she also wanted to play tragedy and blank verse, and being Kitty Clive, a tempest in the Theatre, with a way of overriding authority and taking charge, she did indeed play such parts. Of her Portia, one critic wrote, "Disgraceful both to herself and the audience." In the light scenes she shone, but delivery of blank verse and such speeches as "the quality of mercy" were beyond her. She was not too good in the higher characters either—her Lady Townly lacked polish, her Cordelia (to the Lear of Quin) had no depth. But on her own ground she stood supreme and was able to hold her audiences in the hollow of her hand with a gift of merriment, mischief, gesture and expression, that was matchless.

As the years went on, her popularity increased rather than waned. She held her place midst the best of them alongside Garrick, Mrs. Pritchard, Macklin in his prime, Quin, Susanna Maria Cibber—all the great ones. She earned big money, as things were then. During Fleetwood's unfortunate management at Drury Lane, she was paid £15 15*s.* 0*d.* a week and a guaranteed annual income of £525—a handsome sum. Her benefits averaged over £700 which was real wealth, but Fleetwood probably paid well over the odds and it broke him. There was a strike, too, in his time, just after Garrick had joined the company. This time

Kitty Clive stood by her fellow players—Garrick, Macklin, Barry, Mills and Mrs. Pritchard. No need to go into that unfortunate affair and recall how Fleetwood won, assisted by the Lord Chamberlain, when he should have been soundly beaten, but from that time on, Kitty Clive was always "agin the management." She was not always for the players, but on that occasion when Garrick and the others went back and Macklin, as instigator of the plot was excluded, Kitty Clive left Drury Lane as a protest and went to Covent Garden. They had been offering her big money for some time but when they knew she had indeed burnt her boats at the "Lane," they offered her only her old salary. That probably embittered her against managements for all time.

She quarrelled with the powers of Covent Garden and, being an impetuous woman, was always rushing into print and publishing her grievances for the public to read. Her literary style was, to say the least, curious but full of meat and invective and the broadsides she delivered gave the public a good laugh, for she was a comedienne anyway.

When David Garrick took over Drury Lane, the undisputed leader and King of the stage, Kitty Clive the Queen of Comedy, went back under his banner. It was during this period that she rose to her greatest heights. She played a vast number of parts in such comedies as *The Devil to Pay*, *The Miser*, *High Life Above Stairs*, *The Way to Keep Him*, and the public could not have enough.

She led David Garrick a dog's life but he adored her and did everything he could to keep her sweet. He was probably more than a little afraid of her, but he was a man of the theatre who knew her worth and admired her art.

Kitty Clive specialised in grievances and bombarded Garrick not only with verbal abuse but with long letters, full of meticulous detail, pointing out where she had been misused, swindled (according to her), slighted and underpaid. Garrick indeed needed all his diplomacy and patience. Yet, when they acted together, they were an ideal pair, providing no trace of rancour or disagreement, but offering just the perfection of art.

Garrick was not the only one who felt her lash. She was the terror of the Green Room, and scared every player, save only her friend Mrs. Pritchard. They never knew what she would do or say. If anything went amiss when she was on the stage, the heavens fell and the offender imagined it would be better to be dead. Woodward himself, a leading actor, made a slip in a scene with her once. She had used far too much make-up, having laid the rouge on with a trowel. His line should have been "Your coachman has a red face," instead of which he said, "Your Ladyship has a red face." The house rocked with laughter and the actress paled beneath her thick rouge, while Woodward went white with terror. For open hostility existed between them and she was the plague of his life. He had got something of his own back for what had happened once before—playing Petruchio to her *Shrew*. He had thrown her down very heavily and her angry looks, hiss of rage, and crooked talons made everyone fear for the actor's eyes. But on this occasion Woodward had no excuse. The play was not over, he had to meet her again, and when he came face to face with her in the Green Room there was real terror in his soul. But all that Kitty said was: "Come, Mr. Woodward, let us rehearse the next scene, lest more blunders should fall out." He breathed a sigh of relief while others perhaps were disappointed, for a backstage scene has its savour.

As the years increased, so did Kitty Clive's girth, yet she insisted on playing the parts she had made her own when a young and sprightly girl. Garrick was most concerned about this but could rarely persuade her otherwise. It made little difference to the public, as long as it was Kitty Clive they saw they were content.

She stood no nonsense, and she brooked no insolence. Ned Shuter, a good actor, raised her wrath over a benefit performance she was to give in a French farce. A rather scathing comment appeared in *The Daily Gazeteer* and in this Kitty thought she detected the hand of Shuter, whom she hated. So she wrote him the following letter which shows how little educated she was.

"Sir,—I much Desire you would do me the Favour to let me know if you was the author of a letter in 'The Dayle Gazeteers' relating to the News Piece I had for my benefet; as it was intended to hurt my benefet and serve yours, everybody will naturally conclude you was the author if you are not ashamed of being so I suppose you will own it; if you really was not concerned in wrighting it I shall be very glad; for I should be extremely shocked that an actor could be guilty of so base an action. I dont often take the liberty of wrighting to the Publick, but am Now under a Necessity of Doing it—therefore Desire your answer."

The malicious Shuter saw to it that the letter was printed exactly as written and then, in self-defence against the ensuing storm, had to swear an affidavit before a magistrate that he was not guilty of the first offence.

Kitty Clive retired in 1769, at the age of fifty-eight, having been on the stage forty-one years, and for most of that time she was Queen of Comedy. When she approached Garrick about it he placed himself and all his resources at her command for her farewell. She took it at Drury Lane on April 24, 1769. The plays were *The Wonder* and *Lethe*. She played Flora, one of her great successes, and Garrick himself, with King, Mrs. Barry and the strongest company, supported her. She spoke an epilogue written for her by Horace Walpole and she deserved something better.

She went to live in a villa at Strawberry Hill, Twickenham, which it is said Walpole gave her, but she probably paid him rent. There she lived in happiness and peace, being visited by her friends, notably Jane Pope, whom she had always liked and befriended and whom she was pleased to know had become her successor. She enjoyed giving card parties and although she became very stout and heavy, she retained her high spirits and also much of her truculence. She had her brother Jimmy with her, whom she had cherished and protected. He was ugly and uncouth and she had tried to make him an actor, without success, but loved him. His saving grace was a great sense of humour and an ability to tell a good story. Walpole found him entertaining and just adored the stout old lady who was Kitty Clive. It did not prevent him from poking fun, however, for when the powder mills at Hounslow blew up, he described the force of the explosion as having been almost enough to shake Kitty Clive.

She had never been handsome, but she was magnetic. Dr. Johnson himself wrote: "Mrs. Porter, in the vehemence of rage, and Mrs. Clive, in the sprightliness of Humour, I have never seen equalled. What Clive did best, she did better than Garrick, but could not do half so many things. She was a better romp than any I ever saw in nature." These two people, the ill-educated stage genius and the great scholar, liked each other and got on well together.

From her charming home, which Walpole suggested she should call "Drury Lane," but which she named "Cliveden," she kept in touch with those she liked. And she wrote very many letters to Garrick, couched in the friendliest of terms. Now she was no longer in his employ, she could let her appreciation of him show itself, and he always replied to his "Pivey" most affectionately. She addressed him as "Dear Sir" and on one occasion as "Wonderful Sir," but to him she was always "My Dear Pivey." They were the best of friends—enquiring after each other's health, sending news, and she always sending her love and respect to Mrs. Garrick, for whom she had affection.

Kitty's health began to fail in 1782, for she had jaundice, and she, who had been so mountainous, began to shrink. She would not give up, kept abreast of events and was gay to the last. The end came on December 6, 1785, and she was buried in Twickenham Churchyard. Walpole put an urn, after the fashion of the time, in the shrubbery of her villa and on it inscribed lines of his own:

> Ye smiles and jests, still hover round,
> This is mirth's consecrated ground.
> Here lived the laughter loving dame,
> A matchless actress, Clive her name.
> The comic Muse with her retired
> And shed a tear when she expired.

Not very inspired, but very true. Kitty Clive was one of the great ones of our Theatre, a wonderful comedienne, a tenacious fighter and a good woman. Her great love was Drury Lane, that majestic theatre in which she spent most of her life, and her memory will survive as long as that revered and much beloved fabric stands.

CHAPTER ELEVEN

Peg the Improper

TEMPERAMENT and temper were by no means exclusive to Kitty Clive. All the ladies who led the stage with David Garrick were so gifted, if that be the right word; some to a greater degree but, by and large, they all led him a pretty dance, one way and another. Susanna Maria Cibber and Jane Pope may be placed in the gentler class, but the rest were, to say the least, troublesome.

They each contributed something of worth to theatre history, and one of the most notable of them all, Peg Woffington, lived a life which was indeed itself a drama.

If ever a person filled "the unforgiving minute" that person was Margaret Woffington from Dublin, who bewitched so many and whose short gay life was so colourful and eventful.

She was born either in 1714 or 1715 in Dublin where her father was a bricklayer and her mother a washerwoman. From that humble and unromantic origin sprang one who was to become a beacon in the highly lit world of the Theatre, a strange creature who was a mass of contradictions, to whom morals mattered little and yet who could love and give—and live and die bravely. In other words, she was a Woman.

This child of the Dublin streets did not cry "Cockles and mussels," but at the age of eight she hawked fruit for her mother when that good soul, left a widow, opened a little general shop. Whether or not Nell Gwynne sold oranges is still open to question, but there is no doubt that Peg Woffington, as a barefoot child, sold them in the streets of Dublin. Ragged and unkempt, she did a fine trade with the students on College Green, for her quick repartee amused them.

One wild and stormy night in October somewhere around 1720-21 this little girl was staggering homewards, bearing on her head a pitcher of water. It had been a bad day for her since the unfavourable weather was against her open-air trade. Now, tired, hungry and pinched with cold she struggled towards the hovel which she probably never thought of as home, exhausted by the weight of the pitcher. Several times she stumbled and nearly fell, and unable to go any further she crept into a nearby doorway and burst into a storm of sobs. Then she heard a voice speak, a foreign voice, with a queer but kindly accent asking her what was the matter. Looking up, the child beheld a handsome lady magnificently dressed, gazing down on her. Between her sobs the rain-soaked urchin told the lady she was carrying the pitcher of water for her washer-woman mother. To little Peg's amazement the lady said she would come with her and side by side they walked along. The child, happy in the company of her strange companion, strode gracefully with her pitcher poised on her head, her dark hair tossed in the wind, her dark eyes shining with excitement. The youthful, lissom grace of the child impressed the fine lady.

"Do you know who I am?" she asked the child. "I am Madame Violante," she continued. "Not the wonderful lady who dances on the rope high up in the air?" gasped the astonished Peg. All Dublin was talking about Madame Violante's performance, and it seemed incredible to the little waif that she should be walking through the wild Dublin night with so famous a person. "Yes," she replied to Peg's question, and added: "How would you like to do it, too?" "Oh, Ma'am," stammered the girl, breathless with wonder. "Do what you do? Wear lovely clothes, be rich and famous. . . ?"

"I do not know about the riches," said the lady with a smile, "but these things might be. Come, we go to see madame your mother." They hurried along through the dark wet streets until they reached the dirty little court in which was the Woffington abode. Mrs. Woffington was busy at her wash tub as Peg announced the visitor. The mother looked up. If this was a new client who wanted to have washing done, she was indeed a promising looking customer. Peg gasped out the lady's name and the astonished widow asked Madame Violante to sit down. Briefly and clearly that good lady stated the reason for her visit. She wanted to take little Peg away with her, for she sensed that here was a girl she was sure she could train. She would, if the mother agreed, take over the child, be entirely responsible for her and probably make a name and a fortune for her. The mother was almost dumbfounded and little Peg, attending to her tiny sister, glanced at the pair with an agonised expression wondering what the outcome would be.

Widow Woffington poured out her tale of woe, laying great stress upon her respectability and the respectability of both sides of the family. Of course she loved Peg dearly, but she must not stand in the child's way, and the bargain being struck, Peg went off with her new protectress. A new show was to be produced almost at once, in which Violante was to walk the tight rope, with a basket on each foot and in each basket a baby. Peg was to be one of the "babies." The show opened but not even the babies brought it luck for it soon closed down and little Peg, who had had her first taste of the Theatre, was returned to her Mother. But the tight-rope walker assured her it would not be for long; she would send for her again and she was as good as her word. Madame Violante started a children's company, and she sent for Peg. It was soon evident that Peg had a natural aptitude for the stage and she quietly took on good parts, like Polly in *The Beggar's Opera*, and Nell in *The Devil to Pay*. Madame Violante liked her, she took pains over her, fed and dressed her well, taught her to speak properly and saw to it that her elocution became perfect. Natural grace the child had, but Violante's care added excellent deportment and poise thereto. She also taught Peg to speak French and although the curriculum remained purely theatrical, Peg managed to teach herself the rudiments of reading, writing and arithmetic.

Thomas Elrington, a well-known London actor, came to Dublin, then the most important theatrical city outside of the metropolis itself, and took over the theatre in Smock Alley, where much brilliance was hatched. His eyes always open for talent, he noticed little Peg and promptly engaged her. She was still very young, perhaps just over seventeen, but very experienced. Elrington gave her all sorts of parts and Peg played and enjoyed them.

This incidentally is the way to get on in the Theatre. She never minded making up and disguising her good looks, playing elderly dowagers and ugly old cronies, and even at the height of her fame and beauty, she would appear as wrinkled, shrivelled old women, with immense success. So long as she was acting, she was happy. Peg continued to play at the Smock Alley theatre, and at the opposition place, too, scoring many notable successes, and in 1740 she became the sensation of the town. This she achieved by following the example of the first ladies of the stage and donning breeches. She appeared as Sir Harry Wildair in *The Constant Couple*—and her reputation as an actress was made. Ever after, this was her famous part, and once, when she had become the great Mistress Woffington, with lovers by the score, she boasted "I've played this part so often that half London thinks I'm a man." To which James Quin, a famous actor-wit, rejoined drily: "And the other half knows you are a woman."

Quin was always tilting at her. Once, at Covent Garden, she was missing without warning from the cast, and on her return she said she had been to Bath. "What took you there?" queried Quin. "Oh, pure wantonness," replied flirtatious Peg. "And were you cured?" enquired Quin gravely.

The Dublin audiences knew all about Peg, that she came from the slums, what her antecedents were, and it endeared her to them. Her brogue did not matter, it was their brogue too, and they took the view that things would have been less rotten in the State of Denmark had all the people at Elsinore spoken as Peg did.

Peg Woffington was a beauty in a City proverbial for the loveliness of its ladies. She was small, but perfectly formed, with large liquid black eyes, amazingly long eyelashes which she knew how to use and eyebrows that seemed to have been placed in position by a consummate artist. She never powdered her raven black hair, when it was the mode so to do, and she never worried about her looks at all. She was the toast of the town, her dresses were daring but she possessed impeccable taste and though the Dublin ladies sneered they nevertheless followed.

In the theatre, Peg was goodness itself. She played for other people when they were ill, and everyone loved her.

Peg had plenty of suitors but she seems to have kept immune from their temptations until at last came Romance in the form of a younger son of a peer. He had birth and breeding, but no money. Handsome blue-eyed Taafe had a tongue which was honeyed and a gift of pretty phrases that could turn any girl's head. He turned Peg's. She fell madly in love with him and he persuaded her to leave Dublin, where she was a great figure, and go with him to London, to be his wife. Without more ado she threw up her career, and together they went to London, taking lodgings in York Street, Covent Garden, the heart of Theatreland. And there for a while they loved with passion. Gradually Taafe developed a habit of absenting himself for periods which seemed to grow lengthier, and one day he announced he must go back to Dublin. He was "broke," and while the "honeymoon" had been pleasant he had to think of his future. Actually the debonair young Irishman was paying court to a rich heiress. Peg found it all out for it is not easy to hoodwink a girl of her upbringing, and she planned a revenge on her faithless lover that was subtle and original. Only an actress could have done it. Peg dressed herself up as a young gallant, in the height of male fashion and she looked the most dashing blade about town, which wasn't difficult since she was used to wearing such attire on the stage.

Calling herself "Mr. Adair," she went to all places of public resort, to balls, ridottos, to the play and everywhere she made the heiress aware of her presence by respectful but ardent glances of admiration. It was not long before she got an introduction and she made overtures in the most genteel and refined manner to the impressionable young heiress who was greatly intrigued. The acquaintance ripened and then, at what Peg judged was the right moment, she confided to the unsuspecting heiress Taafe's perfidy and his fortune-hunting proclivities. The heiress promptly sent the Irishman about his business in no uncertain terms and he returned to Peg quite unaware that it was she who had cooked his goose with the heiress. Gleefully she told him of her ruse and revenge. He cursed her and cast her off, which was a lucky escape for her, for he soon fell into disgrace and came to a bad end.

Peg's wounded heart rapidly healed. She had to live. She was in London, she could conquer that capital as she had conquered Dublin. She went to Bloomsbury Square to see John Rich, the rough and ready founder and manager of Covent Garden Theatre, who could not speak the King's English and who was as blunt and coarse as his father, the wicked Christopher, had been cunning. She declined to give her name and Rich refused to see her. After twenty attempts to see him she sent in her name and was admitted at once. There was Rich, lounging on a settee with a dozen of his cats around him, all sharing his meal and he engaged her at once, at £9 a week, a wonderful salary for her.

She made her début at Covent Garden on November 6, 1740, as Sylvia in *The Recruiting Sergeant*. Dressed as a boy, she was an immense success, being acclaimed by the fashionable audience which included royalty. The play continued for three nights and Peg became the new sensation of London. And when she played Sir Harry Wildair for the first time in London, she made a bigger hit than she had in Dublin. The Town went wild about her and it was publicly proclaimed that after her wonderful performance no man would ever dare play the part again. Then she quarrelled with Rich—not at all a difficult thing to do—and she went over to Drury Lane, being welcomed with open arms. Here she met Garrick and also Macklin, playing Cordelia to Garrick's first performance of Lear.

Now the most popular actress in London, she went to Dublin to revisit the scenes of her early triumphs and accompanying her was David Garrick, not then the master of the stage but already famous.

The pair came back as lovers and set up house at No. 6 Bow Street. It was virtually a *ménage à trois*, for Peg the passionate shared her favours between Garrick and Charles Macklin—that fierce but forceful actor who had recreated Shylock and killed a man in the Drury Lane Green Room. It would appear that the trio did not complete the love nest for it is on record that once when Peg and Garrick were closeted in her bedroom, a Lord with whom Peg had "made a date" was announced downstairs. Garrick had to beat a hasty retreat leaving some of his clothing behind, which His Lordship inconveniently spotted. Peg calmly explained that they were clothes she wore on the stage—and the titled visitor was placated.

But that "three way" attempt at housekeeping, with apparently numerous interpolations, did not last. Macklin was cut out, and Peg and Garrick moved into Southampton Street where they

lived together, both being apparently deeply in love with each other. Impulsive Peg lavished all her affection on little David, and the question of marriage was raised and nearly arranged. She gave him many costly gifts, including a remarkable pair of diamond shoe buckles, and Garrick, who was a thrifty soul to whom waste or extravagance was abhorrent, presented Peg with presents of a more modest nature. They shared expenses.

Once, during a month when the housekeeping was not David's financial responsibility, Dr. Johnson came to tea. This was an occasion, for Garrick and the Doctor were the closest of friends. Peg made the tea and the thrifty David watching carefully, saw it was a very rich deep colour, several spoonfuls of tea at 12*s.* a lb. having evidently gone into the pot. It was too much for Garrick. He spluttered his protests in his staccato manner despite the presence of his guest. Peg looked at him coolly and remarked, "It is no stronger than I usually make it." Garrick was furious. "Hey—hey—no stronger than usual," he roared. "Why, damme —hey—all last month it would have harmed nobody's stomach. Now—hey—this tea, madam, is as red as blood!!"

Garrick who had been reared in very poor but genteel circumstances never lost his meanness over money. At the time of the tea party he and his inamorata had plenty of cash. She earned £7 10*s.* 0*d.* a week, had a good allowance for stage clothes and got about £200 a year out of her benefits. Garrick's income must have exceeded £1,000, a princely sum then. But he could not bear waste and those extra spoonfuls of tea were enough to snap the fetters which bound him to this lovely woman. Jealousy did the rest. Why Garrick should have imagined that Peg, who not long before had shared her bed with Macklin and himself and others, should suddenly become faithful, is difficult to understand. Nevertheless he was mortally offended by the ardent and public admiration of his Peg by Sir Charles Hanbury Williams—a gay, brilliant man about town and notorious rake. In his devotion to Woffington, he wrote verses about her which were repeated by everyone. Peg Woffington assured Garrick that between her and Sir Charles there was only platonic friendship. He did not believe her, and they agreed to part. The tea probably played a greater part than Sir Charles. Their establishment was broken up, they returned each other's gifts—except one, which Garrick said he would keep to remind him of a "happy time." That present happened to be the valuable diamond shoe buckles.

Peg Woffington may have been promiscuous, she may have had lovers by the score, but she was in many ways a very good woman. She rescued her old mother from the Dublin slums, set her up in comfort, with a home and an annuity of £40 a year, and she gave her little sister Polly the education which she herself had been denied. She sent her to France. And when she returned home, a demure and well read young miss, Mistress Woffington bought a house near Teddington wherein to shield the girl from the world and its wickedness. But there was wildness in the Woffington blood and it showed itself even in the placid Polly, who yearned to become an actress. Peg taught her and though the stage spurned her it found her a husband. He was then the Honourable Captain Cholmondeley, second son of the Earl of Cholmondeley. It was a wonderful match for the little girl from Dublin but it did not please the Earl, who rushed round to the house of the great actress to induce her to urge Polly to break it off. Peg put forth all her charm, which was considerable, and the Earl softened, admiring not only her beauty and sound common sense, when she gently argued with him, but eventually consented to his son's choice, adding that at first he had been deeply offended. That aroused Woffington. "You offended, my Lord? I think I am the person to be offended!" she exclaimed. The Earl opened his eyes. "You, offended, my dear lady. Might I ask why?" "Because," retorted Peg with some heat, "whereas I had just one beggar to support, now I have two."

The marriage turned out well and produced nine children, all the female progeny marrying into high rank.

Woffington's gifts as actress were many sided. She was at her best in comedy, though she played most things competently and her great charm captured her audiences. She played most of the Oldfield roles most delightfully but when it came to playing male parts in male attire, she had no rival. Her Sir Harry Wildair eclipsed that of Wilks, the gifted creator of the part.

Peg knew her job; she was not conceited, and never quibbled about playing a minor part where necessary. She would step into a breach when need be and help in moments of crisis. Susanna Maria Cibber, who towards the end of her career suffered from a fatal complaint, sometimes could not go on at the last moment, and time and again Peg stepped forward and saved the day, although she hated Susanna. Once Mrs. Woffington was advertised to play one of her own favourite parts, because Mrs. Cibber was ill and it so happened that Peg herself went down ill at the last moment and could not appear. When she returned the next night to play Lady Jane Grey, the audience, believing she had stayed off the night before just for a whim, hissed her loudly. They demanded she should apologise, an indignity often imposed by playgoers on players whom they considered had erred. Peg, whose conscience was clear, was at first taken aback by the bad reception, but her Irish temper boiled up and she stopped, glared at the audience with haughty disdain—then walked off the stage. In the wings an agonised management tried to placate her and the audience having quietened down she was prevailed upon to make her entrance. With regal dignity, she went right down to the front of the stage and with a glacier-like look in her eye addressed the house. It was her duty to play, she coldly informed the audience, but if they did not want her to, well and good, it was for them to decide. "On or off," she told them, "it shall be as you please. To me, it is a matter of perfect indifference." Peg Woffington won: they cheered her. She played and never again did her followers fall foul of her—nor she of them.

This generous minded and affectionate woman had one or two "hates." She and Kitty Clive could never agree—loud and long were their battles at Drury Lane—and she disliked Susanna Maria Cibber, although she often deputised for her. Her chief aversion was Tate Wilkinson, an odd character, a mixture of talent and tomfoolery, of curious simplicity and great cunning, who nevertheless rose to considerable heights in his profession and left the theatre literature of his period enriched by two most illuminating books. A great mimic, Wilkinson was a protégé of Samuel Foote, himself one of the greatest mimics of all time, and nobody was safe from his shafts of caricature, though he had not Foote's wicked satire, nor his force of character. Now Tate Wilkinson began to imitate Peg Woffington, and he hit her off to the life, especially her harsh and sometimes squeaky voice, which was Peg's one handicap. She was a gift for mimic Wilkinson, who won much applause by his impersonation. The only person not at all amused was Peg, for this caricature touched her sensitive spot. Tate wanted to work at Covent Garden, where Peg was appearing and in vain he hung around the theatre trying to get Rich, its manager, to give him a chance. One night a friend of his, a Captain Forbes, took him to dinner at the Bedford Coffee House and then proposed a visit to the play at Covent Garden. They had dined and wined very well, and though the liquor filled Wilkinson with happiness it made his military friend a bit obstinate. Nothing would suit him but the Royal Box itself right on the stage. The players, attracted by the magnificent military figure of the Captain in his full regimentals, were astonished to see Wilkinson, not even a member of the company but an actor looking for a job, sitting beside him. Mistress Woffington, who knew that Tate mocked her, as she called it, considered this invasion of the stage box an affront to herself, and she and other members of the Company promptly complained to the manager, who sent the box-keeper post haste to turn the Captain and his companion out. But the Captain would not move; he had paid his money for himself and his friend and nothing would induce him to leave. The play—it was *The Confederacy*—proceeded and Mrs. Woffington, who played Clarissa, was furious. It so happened that one of her speeches admirably fitted the situation as regards her and the offending Wilkinson so she came right down stage, delivered the lines directly at him, with all the venom she possessed; the audience quickly sensed this obvious attack and Tate was overwhelmed with horror and embarrassment. But the extra force which Peg injected into her speech caused the well-known squeak to come into the voice, and a "lady of the town," sitting in the circle just over the box, derisively echoed the famous Woffington's squeak. Naturally, Woffington thought the gibe came from Wilkinson, to whom she flashed a look of searing hatred. Fuming with anger she rushed to the Green Room where she denounced Wilkinson in the presence of the players, who gave her sympathy and support. Altogether it was a bad evening for Tate Wilkinson but worse was to follow.

John Rich, that curious man, held high state as master of Covent Garden. Each day, like a great noble or monarch he held a levee which all his cats and all his company attended and to his presence the next morning was summoned Tate Wilkinson.

In swept Peg Woffington. All her kindliness and charm were gone, there was only anger as she confronted the mortified Wilkinson and addressed him thus: "Mr. Wilkinson, I have made a visit this morning to Mr. Rich, to command and to insist on his not giving you any employment whatever, no, not of the most menial kind, in the theatre. Merit you have none, charity you deserve not, for if you did, my purse should give you a dinner. Your impudence to me last night, where you had with such assurance placed yourself, is one proof of your ignorance; added to that I heard you echo my voice when I was acting and I sincerely hope that in whatever barn you are suffered as an unworthy stroller, that you will suffer the same contempt you dared last night to offer me." Then withering him with a look of studied hatred and contempt she swept away, leaving the crest-fallen actor speechless.

Peg queened it mostly at Drury Lane, but after the difference with Garrick and his marriage, she graced Covent Garden. Often she went back to Dublin, where she was a queen indeed, and earned very big money. Strangely enough, it was on one of her visits to Ireland that Peg, who was born a Roman Catholic, embraced the Protestant Faith. There has been much controversy as to this apostasy, but it is probable that she did it to obtain legal possession of an estate which an admirer had left her, for despite her wantonness Peg was no mean business-woman.

Back to Covent Garden for the season of 1754-5, she played a big round of parts with immense success, her reputation, and her popularity, reaching their apex. She was rich as well as popular, but she had no intention of resting on her laurels. "When I can no longer bound on the stage with elastic step and when the enthusiasm of the public begins to show symptoms of change," she declared, "that will be the last appearance of Margaret Woffington." But that was not to be the manner of her exit.

During the particularly brilliant season of 1757, Peg Woffington was playing Rosalind, and as she went to make her entrance she passed a man standing in the wings. It was none other than her old enemy, Tate Wilkinson, now at last received into the Theatre. She glanced at him and sardonically congratulated him on being a beginner at the Garden at last. He watched her as she played four acts in her usually accomplished style, but when she came off the stage during the fifth act, she complained of feeling ill and Wilkinson, rather fearfully, offered her his arm which, to his astonishment, she accepted, and he half led, half supported her into the Green Room. She thanked him graciously, seemed to get better and after a quick change of costume went on the stage again. She was about to speak the Epilogue, having reached the line, "If I were among you I would kiss as many of you as had beards that pleased me . . ." when she stopped, swayed and faltered. She tried to go on, but could not. Screaming, she stumbled to the wings and into the arms of those standing by amongst whom was her old enemy, Tate Wilkinson. She was carried to her room—but her career was over. Paralysis had struck her down.

She lingered for some time, helpless in her villa at Twickenham, all the beauty gone, all the saucy charm and glitter faded—a woman young in years, wide in experience of life, accustomed to triumph and adulation, waiting resignedly for the end. If she had sinned, this was indeed an awful retribution. Her most faithful admirer to the last was a Colonel Cæsar, a very rich man, and it had been a jest between them that whichever died first would leave the other as heir. But it was really a jest, for Peg left the bulk of her money to her sister and the rest went to found a row of almshouses for the poor of the district. She had not forgotten the days when she herself lived in poverty.

Tate Wilkinson left a very true picture of her, and all through his books he praises her beauty and her talents. Despite her hatred of him, his last tribute to her was sincere: "I have not been sparing of her good qualities, either as an actress or a woman; what I have mentioned as to myself is only what belongs to my history, but no pique from what had long ago passed; and hope that when she died, if she favoured me with a thought, she forgave me as I now do her. For had I been in her place, I think I might and should, too probably, have acted the same as she did."

No doubt all her sins were forgiven her as freely as Wilkinson forgave the trouble she had caused him. Hers were very human sins—accounted as of little consequence in her day. She had been wanton, she had taken her pleasure where and when she found it but nobody was the worse for it. Lover she had been times out of number, but wife—never. Her stage talent was great, she was a joy to her audiences for most of the brief period of the forty-six years of her life. All men loved her—some women, especially of her own profession, hated her, yet she harboured no malice and tried to do no harm.

During the last sad years of her life, she was cared for by her dresser. She gave her thoughts to kindly deeds, helping those in need and finding much consolation in religion. She knew she was regarded as a sinner but she knew also that in Heaven there is more joy over one sinner who repents. . . . One of the last things she did was to ask to see George Anne Bellamy, with whom she had always been at war.

Mistress Bellamy, to her credit, came to see her—and at the end they were reconciled.

Margaret Woffington was laid to rest in the quiet churchyard of St. Mary, Twickenham, in 1760. She had actually died at the Westminster home of her sister Polly, whence she had been carried in order to see once again her little nephews and nieces, whom she so adored.

Peg Woffington, the poor little ragged girl in a Dublin slum, died a rich woman and a public idol. Throughout her life she had a motto, "Always do your best."

She obeyed it to the very end.

CHAPTER TWELVE

When Stars Collide

SOMETIMES leading ladies working in the same theatre get on well together, and sometimes they do not. In the eighteenth century, when theatres were few and actresses not so scarce, there were several eminent performers always to be found in the same playhouse, sharing the plays and the honours. Each had her own parts reserved for her, but now and again there was a bit of poaching and that nearly always led to trouble. Each of the truly great companies at either Drury Lane or Covent Garden, when those two Patent Theatres dominated London, had their own stars and in turn these stars had their own rivals. Theatre fought theatre and inside, such players as Kitty Clive, Peg Woffington, Nance Oldfield, fought each other.

One of the actresses who always disliked Peg Woffington was Mrs. Pritchard. *Per contra*, she was one of the few to remain on good terms with Kitty Clive. An actress of eminence and a character in her own right, Mrs. Pritchard was the absolute opposite of her life-long friend, Kitty Clive, in temperament and the antithesis of her opponent, Peg Woffington, in character. She was a woman of stainless virtue and reputation. Her birthplace and parentage are not known, but she was born Hannah Vaughan, or, rather, that was what she called herself on her first appearance.

She claimed to have been born in 1711, and first came under notice by singing at fairs, and she made quite a stir at Bartholomew Fair, where many prominent managers had booths, as well as at Southwark Fair and, of course, they kept their eyes open for talent. The critics, mostly self-appointed, attended these entertainments and were proud if they could get their remarks and discoveries into the public prints. One of them saw Hannah Vaughan singing in Fielding's booth, and said she was worthy of better things, having appeared at Goodman's Fields in *Anne Boleyn*. Worthier things came to Hannah as predicted, for Theophilus Cibber after leading a revolt of the players at Drury Lane took over the almost derelict "Little Theatre in the Hay" (now the Haymarket), and set up what he called The Company of the Revels—rebels would have been a better word. Miss Hannah Vaughan applied for a job and got it, for Cibber was glad of her; he wanted talent and especially players who did not expect much money. At the Haymarket Hannah was an immediate success in an astonishingly wide range of parts from low comedy to Ophelia, and when peace was made between them and the Drury Lane management, she went to Drury Lane. By now she was Mrs. Pritchard, having married an actor of that name, an insignificant performer about whom almost nothing is known save that he had a benefit at Drury Lane in 1747, probably through his wife's influence. But whoever he was, she was a good and faithful wife to him, for she must have been beset by the temptations of an actress of the time. Whether because she returned with the rebels, or because she was virtuous, it was nevertheless some time before she got her real chance. At first she played small parts and, being a kind of "general utility," as the old theatrical phrase went, had little chance of making her mark.

At that time Kitty Clive was ascending, Miss Horton was in her glory, and Mrs. Cibber was getting the leads. Mrs. Pritchard, in her quiet way, swam with the tide, and although the talent which she possessed had not been recognised, it was noticeable that the public liked her. She had no great beauty or persuasive charm, and lacked both inches and education, but she had the gift of charging a character with emotion, and although normally her speech was vulgar and her pronunciation unrefined, when she appeared on the stage she seemed to be inspired by gentility and understanding. On stage her voice and her enunciation was perfect; every word she spoke, every syllable, even when she whispered, was heard by the whole house. And that is the way to please the public. Many young modern actors imagine that it is not their job to worry about the audience; rather that it is up to those in front to come to them, to strain ears and imagination. Any old-timer will tell them they are wrong, but they will not believe it, and only in the end, when audiences have ceased to trouble about them, will they learn. Mrs. Pritchard knew that her job was to make her audience sit up and take notice and to let them hear what she said.

She got her long-deferred chance in 1735, coming, as it always must, as a reward for hard work and perseverance. She was given the part of Rosalind, not because Fleetwood had any great belief in her talent, but rather that he knew she was completely reliable and would do her best. Mrs. Pritchard realised her chance had come and that if she failed to take it she would be doomed to a round of inferior roles for ever. She gave a superb performance, for, still young and slight, she had the enthusiasm of youth and the ability to make an audience see through her eyes. She breathed in the charm of a part and exhaled it as her own. She was a wonderful Rosalind, her fine voice conquering the lines, so that every word told and the part was realised to perfection.

Having achieved success, Mrs. Pritchard was kept to comedy. Not yet had her gift for tragedy been recognised. She was not so impressive in some of the more sophisticated parts, like Lady Townly or Lady Betty Modish, for she was not up to that kind of playing and lacked the polish and education it demanded. But in Shakespeare she scintillated. Her Beatrice was a classic, perhaps the best ever until the advent of Ellen Terry. She would play this opposite the Benedick of Garrick, and each would try to outdo the other in artistry; which must have been a feast for the play-goers. Garrick had to pull out every stop to hold his own with her. One claim Mrs. Pritchard has to fame, if it can be called that, is that she created the part of "Irene" in Dr. Johnson's play of that name. It was an ill-starred venture, and Garrick, who loved Johnson, had his doubts about it from the start. The Doctor was a monument of obstinacy at all times, and displayed temper when Garrick suggested that the public would not stand for the heroine being strangled by a bowstring in full sight of them. Johnson retorted that they put up with the sight of Othello suffocating Desdemona and would not have it altered. The audience duly revolted and screamed, "Murder!" So great was the uproar that Mrs. Pritchard had to leave the stage. The next night the scene was altered, but the play was never a success, although Garrick, out of friendship, kept it on for nine performances.

Thanks to Garrick, Mrs. Pritchard was given the opportunity to show how superb a tragedienne she was, for in due course she played Queen Gertrude in *Hamlet* and won golden opinions, especially in the Closet scene, which became a pattern for subsequent players. Her Hermione was another well-remembered performance, and Queen Katherine in *Henry VIII* moved the beholders to tears. There were those who thought she was a little too strident and vehement as Volumnia, but in all other classic roles they gave her the palm.

She had plenty of opposition—Susanna Maria Cibber, whom Garrick much preferred to her, and Mrs. Yates. She never played Ophelia; that belonged to Mrs. Cibber, who had also made the role of Juliet her own. But Mrs. Cibber never played Gertrude, and could not have come within striking distance of Mrs. Pritchard in her greatest character of all, Lady Macbeth. Even Garrick, who once confided to Tate Wilkinson that she was apt to "blubber in her grief," had to admit it, and confessed that she put him as much on his mettle as Macbeth as she had done with Benedick. Perhaps he played these two parts so superbly because of this spur. As Lady Macbeth, Mrs. Pritchard held the house spellbound, and her performance set the standard for every Lady Macbeth that followed, for even when Sarah Siddons played it there were those who held that she was inferior to Mrs. Pritchard.

Yet, despite her brilliance, it is unlikely that Mrs. Pritchard knew more about *Macbeth*, the play, than what lay in her own part and what came to her as cues from the other players. She would have been the despair of the modern producer, or director, for she was above all an individualist. People went to the theatre not so much to see *Macbeth* as to see Mrs. Pritchard as Lady Macbeth. She never read any play in which she appeared, only her own part.

Eventually, after thirty-five years of active and hard life in the Theatre, Mrs. Pritchard took her increasing bulk and her money—she had a good legacy left her and, despite family expense, had saved on her salary and benefits—into retirement at Bath. Her son, it is believed, became Treasurer at Drury Lane, and, with her daughter becoming an actress, that kept the theatre in the family. She bade farewell in her fifty-eighth year and it was a grand occasion. The year was 1767, and she was given a season, during which she repeated all her favourite and most popular roles before her last appearance on April 24, 1768, in *Macbeth*. She was in the full glory of black satin and feathered headdress and the long black gloves so essential to tragedy then. Garrick wore a new brown court suit, laced with gold. Never had she played better, for once more she thrilled the house with an unforgettable performance. And when the play was over, she spoke an address which Garrick had written especially for her and which drew further applause. Mrs. Pritchard left a band of numerous sincere admirers of her art, who never forgot her. She had lived decently, brought up her family, kept herself respectable in an age when most women of the Theatre were soon tarnished.

At Bath, where she went to live she had only one worry, her brother Henry Vaughan, who often pestered her for money. She did not enjoy her well-earned rest for long, for an unfortunate accident to her foot, not thought to be serious at the time, proved fatal. Almost before anyone knew it, she became ill and died. And a host of playgoers mourned her, as did most of her colleagues. She had few enemies, but she had never liked Peg Woffington; they were poles apart.

Another great anti-Woffingtonian was a lady with the unusual name of George Anne Bellamy. She was herself remarkable inasmuch as it is doubtful if anybody ever had a more complicated entry into life. She was at one and the same time an illegitimate daughter of an Irish Peer and yet born in lawful wedlock.

It came about this way. An impoverished Irish nobleman named Lord Tyrawley fell in love with a young girl named Seal, who returned his passion, ran away from school and lived with him in London, where a son was born. But His Lordship was pressed for money and therefore cast about for a rich wife until he found a certain Lady Mary Stewart, reputed to be of great wealth and expectations. He married her, only to discover, as many had done before and since, that the biter is often bitten. The wealth of his bride was non-existent and so too were her expectations, and she was sent packing back to her people.

Miss Seal, having broken the convention which demands

marriage lines, and needing money, joined the only profession in which references are neither asked nor given. She went on the stage. She was not much good as an actress, but somehow she struggled along and meantime Tyrawley got a job at the British Embassy in Lisbon. He wanted his Miss Seal and wrote impassioned letters begging her to come to him. For some time she demurred, but at last undertook the journey and was received with joy by her lover, who lodged her at the house of a London merchant in the Portuguese capital. Whether he really wanted her at all or just wrote not expecting her to answer is a matter of conjecture, for he was, when she arrived, laying successful siege to the heart of a Portuguese lady of some wealth.

So his connection with Miss Seal was kept quiet; it was easy to persuade her, for she had no friends likely to chatter, even if she could have spoken Portuguese. But the merchant with whom she stayed had visitors, many of them sailors, who are notoriously impressionable men, and one of them, a Captain Bellamy, met and fell in love with Miss Seal on the spot. He wooed her with all his seafaring ardour, although she persistently refused his genuine offers of marriage. He suspected a rival, and made it his business to find out who was the man who stood in the path of his true love. It did not take him long to discover all about the nobleman and his liaison with the Portuguese heiress. He promptly put Miss Seal in possession of the true facts, and she was horrified beyond measure, for this was the second occasion that her lover, noble in name but not in nature, had cruelly deceived her. Thus caught by the Captain on the rebound she fell into his arms and married him in secret. They left as secretly for Ireland, but soon the Captain was to have his eyes opened, for in all too short a time for an honest married woman she brought a baby girl into the world. That was more than he could stand, and he upped and went, never to be heard of again. And that was how it came about that George Anne Bellamy was born in wedlock at Fingal on April 23, 1731, the illegitimate daughter of an Irish peer!

His Lordship returned to Ireland, acknowledged the child as his own, but, although she was duly christened, she could not bear his name. Her baptismal name was Georgiana, having been born on St. George's Day, but by some mistake it was entered in the register as George Anne and so George Anne she became.

Her real father took over, having lost his affection for the mother, if ever he really had any, and sent George Anne, at the extremely tender age of four years, to a convent school at Boulogne. She stayed there until she was eleven, when her father brought her home and put her in a house near Bushey Park, where he had installed his Portuguese heiress and his other children by different mothers. It was a strange household in a day of strange family affairs, but he liked this daughter of his and lavished affection on her. This paternal regard, not unnaturally, upset the Portuguese lady, but she got one back at His Lordship by having herself announced as Lady Tyrawley at a party she attended. This so infuriated the nobleman that he bundled her and the other two children out of the house, but he kept little George Anne.

Despite his irregular mode of life, George Anne's father had many influential friends, and she received a good education. For some reason that is not obvious, the Irish peer was made Ambassador to Russia. He placed George Anne under the care of a lady of his acquaintance with strict instruction that she was to have no dealings with his daughter's mother. For Mrs. Bellamy was becoming a headache. She had made a hash of her life from the start, and then contracted a foolish marriage, which soon went wrong and left her in poverty and despair. She appealed to her daughter for help, and the girl, who had a double inheritance of recklessness from both parents, gathered together the little money she had, together with her small and not very valuable collection of jewellery, and rushed to her mother's side. The money was soon spent and the father, furious on hearing of the deception, cast the daughter off. They were in a desperate plight, and might have starved but for a friend, a Mrs. Jackson, who took them to live with her at Twickenham. There they happened to meet no less a person than Peg Woffington, who, on hearing their story, took compassion on them and had them to stay with her. A performance had been arranged at her house, so that she could see if her sister Polly was likely to be of any use as an actress.

The play was *The Distressed Mother*. It was given in Peg's garden and George Anne asked for a part in it. She had never acted before, but she was game for anything and was given the role of Andromache. She stole the show and even Peg Woffington was impressed. Everyone who saw it foretold a brilliant stage career if she ever chose to follow it. Mrs. Bellamy and her daughter then went to London and, lodging near Covent Garden, became acquainted with the daughters of John Rich, the Manager of Covent Garden Theatre. The young people got very friendly and decided to get up a performance of *Othello* among themselves and their friends. George Anne Bellamy was chosen as the Moor, and rehearsals started. Father Rich happened to be present, and he was very much struck by the manner in which George Anne delivered her speeches. He told her that if she cared to study seriously for the stage, he would give her a job. She made her choice immediately and set to work. In a remarkably short space of time, she was at Covent Garden Theatre, engaged to play Monimia in *The Orphan*. She was then fourteen years of age and was to play a part which was a test piece for mature actresses. Quin, the great actor, was to play opposite her, but when he saw her and heard her age, he was outraged. He, the leader of the stage, to play with a child? Not in a thousand years! He refused point-blank. And the rest of the company, taking their cue from him, struck too. But Rich, obstinate and rugged, had made up his mind and would not give way. He fined his recalcitrant company heavily, and they had to surrender. And so too did Quin. Rehearsals proceeded, and on the night of George Anne's début, although she was not even billed a story about her had got around and a large and fashionable audience attended to see this extraordinary theatrical occasion. Little George Anne was in her dressing-room, almost petrified by fear, and it was of little use for Manager Rich to tell her all was well. Child as she was, she knew the hostility which the players, led by Quin, felt towards her. She knew, too, the importance of the occasion and that her future career depended on her performance. Children, under encouraging conditions, are apt to lack any feeling of fear of self-consciousness on such occasions, but George Anne realised that nothing could be done to help her. Her cue came, and in a daze she stepped on the stage, into the glare of the lights and a new world, and felt at once the power which surged from the crowded audience towards her, focused through hundreds of eyes. Every player knows that feeling and moment, so often expressed as the "You've got to show me" feeling from an audience. It smashed against little George Anne and stage fright, as some call it, held her in its deadly grip. She just stood, mute and very pitiful, staring before her. The audience relented and gave her a round of applause, but it had no effect; she still could not move, and the curtain had to ring down. Quin and his fellow players were triumphant. But Rich was a determined man. He went to the child, told her not to fear and that she must try again. She knew her part? She nodded; then all she had to do was to say it. The play began once more, and Rich took her right to the wings of the stage, consoling, entreating, praising. Her cue came and he pushed her on. There was a moment of terrible suspense, but this time the young girl spoke. Nobody could hear what she said because terror still muted her voice. But it was a kindly audience, luckily for her, and it kept on applauding her. The others played up. Quin, by virtue of his great position, gave of his best and, relenting, helped the little actress. Then, suddenly, when the fourth act began, something happened. The chains of fear fell from the child. She came to herself, opened out and she began to act. She seemed inspired and to the astonishment of everybody, took the stage and held it. The audience applause changed from kindliness to genuine approval, and even Old Quin was won over. He was then turned sixty, knew his theatre and real talent when he saw it. The evening finished in triumph for George Anne.

At the fall of the curtain, Quin, a good fellow at heart, seized her, lifted her high in the air for all to see and exclaimed, "You are a divine creature. The true spirit is in you." He became her friend from that moment, ready to help and counsel her and it is a pity she did not pay more attention to him. One day, after a rehearsal in which they had both been working, she received a summons to go to his dressing-room. This was unusual, and nearly always meant trouble and the rough side of Quin's tongue, for his sarcasm was like a whiplash. She went with trepidation, but Quin beamed upon her and was fatherly. "My dear child, I hear you have many followers," he said. "Now, don't let love of finery or any other temptation make you indiscreet. You are young and engaging and ought to be very cautious. Naturally, you desire nice things. So, if you want anything which it is in my power to give you come to me, and say, 'James Quin, I want such a thing,' and my purse is at your service." He meant it too; he was a very generous man and loathed being thanked.

George Anne played all that season at Covent Garden and had a "full benefit"—all the money which came in, with no deductions, a privilege awarded as a rule only to the great players. But she was proving a major attraction, not only on account of her youth, but also her undoubted talent. Admirers thrust themselves upon her and lavished gifts. George Anne, without doubt, did nothing to discourage them. She was a perfect young minx. The money pleased her mother, with whom she lived. That lady had now repented her sins and taken to religion, spending so much time over her devotions that she had none to spare to watch over her daughter, although she did not mind sharing in the purse. George Anne was sweetly pretty, fair, with blue eyes, and petite. Gentlemen liked blondes even in those days, and many sought her favours. Society smiled upon her and great ladies invited her to their homes, their routs and ridottos. It was Lord Byron, a great-uncle of the poet, who carried the young lady off. She swore it was not her fault and that she gave him no encouragement, but her mother, forgetful of her own youth, turned her back on her and shut her door against her daughter. George Anne, who had been leading a pretty hectic life, had what would now be called a nervous breakdown. Some distant relations of her mother's, now living at Braintree, in Essex, right in the heart of the country, asked her to stay with them to help recover her health. They knew little about her, as they were Quakers, but were horrified when they discovered that their pretty young relative was an actress—and the famous and somewhat notorious George Anne Bellamy at that. It was as if they had nurtured a snake in their bosom. George Anne returned to Town, and she and her mother became friends again.

An invitation came from Sheridan, who was running the Aungier Street Theatre in Dublin, to visit him, and was accepted with alacrity. Mrs. Bellamy, who had accompanied her daughter, began to look up relations of Lord Tyrawley, and found one in a blind old lady named O'Hara. She could do little to help, but managed an introduction to the leader of Dublin society, the Hon. Mrs. Butler. And the great lady took a fancy to the pretty, if pert, little actress, promised her support—and gave it, too. Her friends—in fact, all Dublin society—flocked to hear George Anne at the theatre. But backstage she had trouble. Garrick had come

PLATE IX

MRS. DAVENPORT

MRS. MARDYN

MRS. ORGER

MISS KELLY

PEG WOFFINGTON
the girl from the slums of Dublin who became a Queen of Drury Lane

over, and was naturally deferred to. He was arranging a round of plays in which to appear, and knew all about this girl. He watched her carefully, this tremendously live, exciting and vivacious young person whom Dublin now called "Blue Eye'd Bellamy," who had gratifying success in many parts. Garrick proposed to play *King John*, and George Anne, as leading lady, wanted and expected the role of Constance. But Garrick considered her too young and gave the part to an older actress, one Mrs. Furnival. George Anne, in temper and tears, flew to Mrs. Butler and poured out her fancied wrongs. Mrs. Butler supported her. She sent to all her friends and asked them not to support Garrick's venture and, since she was social queen of Dublin, such a request was a command. Her subjects obeyed. Garrick and Mrs. Furnival played to a house which did not contain £40 in money. This was a facer for Garrick, who, being a good business man, surrendered, and George Anne got the part she wanted. The embargo came off and the house was packed to the doors, but although the blue-eyed one had conquered she bore malice. Garrick's benefit came round, and he asked her to play with him in *Jane Shore*. She sent back the answer that if she was too young for Constance she was too young for that too. This scared David, and he wrote a humble reply, telling her he would write her an epilogue which she, by her manner and her eyes, would make most effective to the gentlemen in the house, let alone the ladies. He laid on flattery with a trowel, and then addressed the letter to make sure of it being opened, to "My Soul's Idol, the beautiful Ophelia." A careless messenger gave it into the wrong hands, and it got into print. Dublin roared, but David Garrick was not amused.

In 1748 George Anne went back to Covent Garden. She was now at the height of her powers and more than held her own with the other big star there, Susanna Maria Cibber. In some parts maybe she excelled Susanna, but she never concentrated and was inclined to be careless and lazy in direct contrast to Mrs. Cibber, who was the better actress of the two, without doubt. George Anne was never reliable.

Her father, Lord Tyrawley, turned up again. He was proud of this daughter of his, but was concerned with the life she was leading. She had lovers by the score and went from one to another like a butterfly from flower to flower. And these *affaires* were nearly all unhappy to her and nearly always disastrous. She was abducted again, this time by a Mr. Metham, who was really in love with her. He was well connected and there was a lot of money in the family. George Anne told him that nothing but a legal marriage and a carriage of her own would satisfy her. The lover pleaded that he could not get his father's consent and was dependent upon him, since he had no means of his own to uphold either a wife of whom his father disapproved or the upkeep of a carriage. She pouted, she cried, but she did not turn him away. She kept him dangling. One night, when she was playing Lady Fanciful in *The Provok'd Wife* to the Sir John Brute of Quin, Metham came up to her at the back of the stage and begged for a few words. Before she knew what was happening, he had gripped her in his arms, put a hand over her mouth, carried her from the theatre, put her into a waiting coach and carried her off. It is doubtful if she struggled very hard, and Quin had the worst of it. He had to go on and announce to the audience that they would see her no more that evening, and one can imagine the sensation caused when he told them the reason why! But George Anne did not mind the abduction in the least. She lived with Metham at a house near Leicester Square, as it is now, and then went with him to York, where she bore him a son. She kept on pressing, however, for a wedding, but he had taken fright over her extravagance and refused, and there was a violent quarrel and she left him. Her father tried to reason with her. He wanted her, despite all that had happened, to marry a man he knew, one Crump, who was very willing. But George Anne said she detested him. She went to Ireland, where she played for Calcraft, the Dublin manager, with whom she lived openly. Most people believed they were married, an idea they fostered. She bore him children and Calcraft provided for them in his will, but there was no marriage. She did actually go through a ceremony of marriage with Digges, an actor, but was not destined to be a wife, as Digges was already married, but she made a big mistake over Metham however. After their quarrel he came to her again, and this time proposed marriage, but she turned him down, and thus missed her chance. He became a man of wealth and title, and George Anne could have been My Lady, with several carriages. She was in and out of love affairs and in and out of debt, and always provided the gossips with something to talk about.

She went to Drury Lane and played Juliet to Garrick's Romeo at the time that Spranger Barry was challenging Garrick's supremacy at Covent Garden where Susanna Maria Cibber was Juliet. Garrick, with George Anne, won the battle and completed the rout of Barry when that rather foolish man challenged him as Lear. There Garrick had no rival within living sight.

George Anne got up against Peg Woffington, and the two disliked each other intensely and there were many clashes. Once Woffington, jealous of the blue-eyed one's finery and jewels, taunted her with having had them provided for her by one lover. "And you," replied Bellamy, "have half the town—who do not." But it was much more bitter when they played opposite each other in *The Rival Queens*, a most appropriate play for them. Woffington played Roxana and Bellamy played Statira, and it led to a terrible row about the dresses. Bellamy saw to it that she outshone her rival, and she presented a sight so provoking that Woffington, in a blind fury, tried to knife her. Thus did history repeat itself, for this situation had happened before between two other rival actresses. The play should have been blacklisted.

A point had now been reached when George Anne's constant love affairs and immense extravagance could not go on, and, becoming afraid of being arrested for debt, she fled to Dublin once more. There an actor named Mossop was establishing himself as Manager of the Smock Alley Theatre. He was an extraordinary man, but somewhat erratic, and he rarely had any money, so that his companies frequently starved. But on this occasion—the year was 1760—he was really making a serious attempt. He engaged George Anne Bellamy at a salary of £1,000 for the season and two clear benefits, and she was glad to accept. Dublin was agog to see her, for she had been away a long time, and she was as anxious to play to them as they were to applaud her. But, alas, the charm had gone. She had worn herself out. This tired, fading woman with the croaking voice was not the blue-eyed Bellamy whose silvery tones and immense vitality had previously electrified them. She failed, and so did Mossop. She never got her salary in full, and left Dublin heavily in debt. Thereafter she went steadily downwards, for nobody wanted her, and when poverty claimed her she could see only one end—death. One day she sat on Westminster Bridge watching the river and contemplating suicide, but it is said that the sight of a woman even more wretched than herself still carrying on saved her from the fatal plunge. It is far more likely that so long as she could dun her friends and borrow she did not *want* to take the last leap.

George Anne became reconciled to Peg Woffington just before that actress died, so that Peg triumphed in the end. At length George Anne's few remaining friends in the "profession," ever ready to help, arranged a benefit for her. And her few remaining friends elsewhere bought tickets, hoping thereby to save themselves from further importunities. The benefit was held at Drury Lane on May 24, 1785, and the play was *Braganza*. She was to have played the Duchess, but could not do it, and Mrs. Yates played it for her. Bellamy was not quite fifty, but life had brought her low. Her courage had gone, and so had the will to face an audience. It was almost a replica of her first appearance, when fear made her speechless. But this time she failed, and though besought to go before the curtain and say a few words of thanks, she could not. So Miss Farren did it for her, although there were calls for George Anne from people who remembered her and had paid their money to see her farewell appearance. Something had to be done, and at last they got her on the stage, urging her to make an effort. At a signal, the curtain went up and the audience perceived, not the lovely, shining, golden-haired, blue-eyed woman who had so often delighted them, not that alluring piece of femininity who had seemed so full of the joy and strength of youth, but an old shrunken, wrinkled woman, her face cast down, who could not rise to her feet to say "Thank you," but who sat crouched in an armchair. . . .

Yet she had not lacked pluck or impertinence once, and had challenged the highest in the land. Some may have recalled the time she was playing Alicia in *Jane Shore* and King George II was in the Royal Box, but had fallen asleep. This did not suit the quick-tempered, mercurial Bellamy. She was used to gentlemen, kings or no, watching her every movement and not nodding off. Going as close to the box as she could and raising her voice, she shouted her next line, which happened to be "Oh! Thou false lord," right at the sleeping King. He woke with a start and kept awake afterwards, for Bellamy sent him a flashing smile. . . .

She left the stage in 1770, and had that last benefit in 1785. The whole intervening period had been one of disaster. She had charmed so many, had lived with so many men—even Woodward, that fine actor, who had left her a gold watch, plate, jewels, household fixtures and furniture and an annuity. She squandered it all.

There is little to record of her last years. She died penniless in 1788, having wasted her chances and great talent. She who had so much beauty and charm, whose eyes were the despair of lovers, died unhonoured and unsung—a crone before her time. She had drawn too much out of the Bank of Life and paid in too little. Yet Woffington forgave her, and it is charitable to do likewise, forgetting the ill use she made of her chances, but remembering only that flashing loveliness which ensnared so many—not the least of whom was herself.

CHAPTER THIRTEEN

Ladies of Contrast

THE name of Anne Catley is not so well remembered as it deserves to be. Her genius lay mostly in singing, but she has every claim to be an actress of top rank, and since her story is a highly colourful one, let her take the stage.

She was born in 1745, a notable year in English history. Her father was a hackney coachman and her mother a washerwoman, who laundered for the officers stationed in the Tower of London; for it was on Tower Hill that the family lived. Little Anne's early social status was therefore not very dissimilar to that of Peg Woffington. She was a very pretty child and attracted attention in the streets, being very fair, with a skin like alabaster and eyes that sparkled. Her education was as rudimentary as was that of most children of her time, and she liked to play with her little friends on Tower Hill. She was a bit of a tomboy, could spin tops, play marbles and liked to leapfrog over posts. There was no child welfare in those days and Anne knew only too well what the inside of a tavern looked like.

One day, when she was fourteen, she was in one of these rough places when she was asked to sing a song; which she did on being treated to a beer. Fate, or whatever you care to call it, was hanging around in the person of a man well known in the musical world. He heard her, and was so impressed that he went into the tavern, gave Anne a few coppers and asked her to sing again, after which he thanked her and departed. He found out where she lived, called on her parents and told them she had a future with her voice. He offered to take her under his care and to give her proper tuition. Her parents jumped at the chance. And that was how Anne entered the home of a Mr. Bates and began her education. Here she lived under very different surroundings from those to which she had been accustomed. In the first place, she was sent to school and she had to study music under Mr. Bates, who later allowed her to return home on her promising to continue with her singing. Anne found that her parents were proud of her. She was now a lovely girl, and they showed her off by taking her to the taverns, where they made her sing. She was much admired, and the military gentry of all ranks soon had designs upon her, but she was still very young, though wise to the world. Yet it was not the redcoats who first conquered her virginity, but a young linen draper whose business was in the Minories. This love affair seemed to improve her voice and increase her charm, and Mr. Bates now had her bound apprentice to him, her father agreeing to indemnify that individual to the tune of £200 should Anne break her indentures. He took a risk, but her training proceeded, and in the summer of 1762 she had made her début at Vauxhall Gardens as a singer, and on the October 8 of the same year at Covent Garden as an actress. On both occasions she scored immense successes.

Anne felt the power of success. She had never liked Mr. Bates, and now she began to torment him, and although he argued and pleaded it was to no avail. He threatened to sue her father for that £200, and he in turn entreated her to save him from ruin. Finally, there was a compromise. Bates agreed to let her lodge somewhere else and to allow her £25 a year for expenses and board and lodging, and in return keep all the money she earned.

That situation did not last long for Sir Francis Blake Delavel, renowned as a rake even in an era of rakes, cast an eye on Anne Catley and desired her. Knowing that Anne was willing to live with him, he agreed to pay Bates the penalty of £200 and a further £200 in virtue of contracts made for her at Covent Garden Theatre and Marylebone Gardens, then a famous pleasure resort. An attorney drew up an agreement, and Anne, accompanied by her mother, went to live in lodgings under the protection of Sir Francis. She lived with him quite openly; his servants waited on her, and she drove about with him every day in his carriage.

But, by virtue of the first agreement, the father's signature was necessary for the transfer and that worthy man was now in private service as coachman to a wealthy merchant in Cheapside, a Mr.

Barclay. Mr. Catley had the documents read to him and did not like the sound of them. He confided in his master, who was a Quaker and was horrified, as well he might be. Off he went to his lawyer, and two motions were made in the King's Bench, one a writ of *habeas corpus* directing Sir Francis to deliver the person of Anne Catley into the custody of the court, and the other to show cause why he should not be proceeded against for a conspiracy to prostitute that young lady.

Sir Francis brought Anne into court and she was legally taken out of his custody, but when the girl was released her father lost his temper, grabbed hold of her and attempted to drag her away. Counsel for Sir Francis drew the attention of the Lord Chief Justice, the famous Lord Mansfield, to this and Mr. Catley was severely reprimanded. The Judge then ruled that although the girl was a minor, she had reached years of discretion, and asked her whether she desired to go with her father or remain with Sir Francis. Immediately she went back to Sir Francis and put her hand through his arm, made a curtsy to the court and, with her protector, swept out of Westminster Hall into the waiting carriage and home to guilty splendour once more.

The law, though, had the best of it in the end, for in the second motion, heard later, Lord Mansfield held Sir Francis guilty of attempted prostitution, and ordered a trial, in which Sir Francis was fined very heavily indeed. Nevertheless, he set Anne up in good lodgings, paid two guineas a week rent, and gave her a weekly allowance of five guineas. But she does not appear to have been faithful to him, for although she was very passionate, she was also mercenary. There were quite a few lovers, and from them she assembled a goodly collection of jewellery.

Anne attracted the attention of Macklin, the great actor, and he gave her very valuable tuition in dramatic art, so that she became a good actress, both on and off the stage. One night, while returning home in her sedan chair a footpad stopped her, presented a pistol and demanded her money or her life. Before he could seize her purse or jewels, a rescuer appeared, a gentleman very richly dressed, who put the footpad to flight. He was, of course, thanked very sweetly and given permission to escort the distressed damsel to her home. Whether or not the footpad was the paid servant of the gentleman who happened so luckily to be passing at the time does not transpire, but the rescuer certainly fell deeply in love with the enchanting little lady he had protected. He was a very rich Portuguese merchant, who proceeded to set siege to her. Anne kept him dangling just to kindle the flames even more, and then told him a remarkable story about being the widow of a rich Irishman and the mother of a daughter. She even produced a child which she said was her own and the Portuguese was much impressed. He begged to be allowed to express his adoration of Anne, in earnest of which he gave her a valuable pearl necklace and gold and diamond ear-rings, which she condescended to accept. Apparently the only dividend she generously paid was a single night with his charmer and even then he gave her a bank-note for £100.

And all this was happening while Sir Francis was still paying the bills, but nevertheless Anne bore him two children, and there was yet another, the paternity of which she placed upon no less a person than the Duke of York. This rather cooled Sir Francis's ardour, and he went to Ireland, leaving Anne to her own devices. She had always been fired by the determination to get as much out of men as she could, and she had been very successful, but the double life could not go on for ever. One night she was in a most questionable resort in company with a lover who was a mere attorney's clerk, and it so happened that Sir Francis, returning home unexpectedly, dropped in and caught them. This was too much! Next day he had what is now known as a "show-down," gave the lady £50 and told her to take herself off. Miss Catley was in no way abashed, and remained for a few moments to sneer at her cuckolded lover before departing.

All this time she had been singing and acting, and her talent stood high in public esteem. Nobody in those days bothered much over the morals of actresses, and today she would have been what is called a star, and a big one. As leading lady in a musical, she would have commanded a tremendous salary, because she could sing divinely, act well and was really beautiful. Also, she was constantly in the "news."

Having now lost her protector and the provider of an unfailing meal-ticket, Anne had to find another to augment her casual earnings, and she went to lodge in Covent Garden, over a milliner's establishment. It was a good pitch for her, right in the fashionable district. Although careless, Anne was far from foolish, and was not disposed to spend her stage earnings on the finery and display she loved. She felt these should be provided from the ample purses of others, and began to look round for likely prospects. She was playing at Covent Garden Theatre, and her looks and popularity ensured no lack of lovers. "The more the merrier" must have been her motto. What with her salary, not large, but adequate, her summer engagement at Marylebone Gardens, and the many private concerts for which her charming voice was in great demand—it was a concert-loving age (or, at least appeared to be)—Anne found herself doing very well indeed.

An offer from Ireland came along, from that same unreliable Mossop who had engaged George Anne Bellamy and failed to pay her. But he had better luck with Anne, for her appearance caused a great stir. She had taken two of her children with her and also her sister Mary, for whom she did not care much, but who came in useful. Miss Anne was hot-tempered, and when things went wrong, poor Mary became the victim of her violence, even to receiving a black eye. Mary, a trim little person who might have been pretty had not the smallpox marred her face, got tired of that and ran away. She could sing a little and got a stage job, and was able to hide her blemishes with make-up. Anne took it as a mortal affront when she ran off with a lover and, finding out where she was living, stormed into the house and threw everything she could lay her hands on, including the crockery, at poor Mary. Anne left vowing never to see or speak to her sister again, and kept her word. But the family blood seemed to run to passion, and a little later, Mary's lover found her in a compromising situation with a student from Dublin College, and very naturally threw her out. So far as can be ascertained, she ended up as a strolling player.

Anne, however, was never abashed by her own conduct and in Dublin she had an extraordinary number of *affaires*, all of cash value, so what with this source of income and the crowded benefit she enjoyed from an adoring theatre public, her bank balance grew. It would seem, in her case, the wages of sin were all profit. Although her mode of life was known to all, she was received everywhere for her talent and beauty appeared to have made even the most respectable among Dublin's society decide that she was just an eccentric. It suited her all right. She had an impish sense of humour that was well illustrated when a Dublin divine, Dean Bailey, who was the moving spirit in many charities and particularly interested in the welfare of a lying-in hospital, got up a concert on its behalf, and decided to secure the co-operation of Miss Catley. In all innocence, he wrote her the following note: "Dean Bailey's Compliments to Miss Catley and requests to know when she can give him a night at the lying-in hospital and her terms." The actress saw the humour of it and sent this naughty reply: "Miss Catley presents her compliments to the Reverend Dean Bailey; for three nights to come she is engaged to particular friends, but on the fourth will be at his service." It took the Dean a little time to get round the implication, but it all ended well. Anne sang without fee for the lying-in hospital and drew a bumper house.

One of Anne's many conquests involved an Irish nobleman of queer habits and known to be antipathetic to women. But Anne was a great player of breeches parts, as were all actresses of shapely figure, and he fell under her spell and called upon her. She professed to be charmed, and explained she was giving a party to theatrical friends and was in some confusion, as she was actually cooking a duck. Would his lordship be so good as to help? His Lordship was enchanted, and she led him to the fire, where the duck hung on a string, to be turned and basted. That was what he was found doing when Anne's high-spirited theatrical friends arrived, and she introduced him as her cook! For his pains with the ladle, Anne's admirer was lampooned from one end of Dublin to the other.

She numbered all sorts of odd people among her Dublin victims, but she collected money from them all. One of them, a lecherous old merchant, sent her a large basket of wine, which she promptly forwarded to his wife, with a note of explanation very much in the manner that Mrs. Bracegirdle had sent the china. The worn-out old rake gave Anne no more trouble; he had enough of his own at home.

Despite the fact that she was avaricious, not all her *affaires* were with men of means and she appears to have had a real liking for a major who was poor but handsome and attractive. She not only gave him her favours, but made him free of her purse. Another admirer who caught her fancy was a man of some means, but miserly. He used to hide his money all over his rooms, and had the utmost aversion to changing his shirt. She made him part with his money, but she could not get him to improve his linen. The *affaire* did not last long, and soon a rich lord became her devoted slave. He gave her a fine home, a handsome chariot and spent money on her lavishly.

She spent three profitable years in Dublin, and before returning to England met a man destined to play a large part in what remained of her life. He was a dashing dragoon named Lascelles, who saw her play Rosetta in *Love in a Village* and fell head over heels in love with her. She returned his passion, for she had always been over-sexed. Nevertheless, the *affaire* came to a temporary halt when she left Dublin.

Back to England, she found she was still the rage in the playhouses, and pursued her singing and acting and, of course, her very successful career as a professional love-maker. She was very much attracted by a young man from Oxford University who came up for a holiday in Town, when he should have been pursuing his studies. Under this able instructress, however, he studied the art of love for about a fortnight and then had to leave, giving her a handsome purse of gold.

Shortly afterwards Anne went down to Epsom and was introduced to an elderly man of considerable fortune. Her beauty made a deep impression on him, and she began to visualise marriage to the old man and a free and careless widowhood on his fortune. So when he called next, he found her playing the harpsichord and singing very sweetly, and he was enchanted. He asked her if she would consent to teach his fourteen-year-old daughter singing, and Anne leapt at the chance of getting into the family circle. She promised she would come down and give the girl lessons whenever she could, and she was as good as her word. The old man became her slave, and at last he made her a formal proposal of marriage. With joy in her heart, she accepted, although her business sense was well to the fore. Knowing the old man was wax in her hands, she demanded £1,000 to be paid within a month of his death, and also £100 a year in addition. Secondly, he was to settle annuities on any children she might have by him, such annuities to be paid throughout their lives. A third stipulation was that the old man should, prior to the marriage, set aside and invest the requisite sum of money to cover all these clauses in gilt-edged securities. Lastly Anne inserted that failure to conform to the agreement would render the marriage null and void and restore her liberty to marry again.

The foolish old man agreed, and, the documents being signed and witnessed, the prospective bridegroom pushed ahead with preparations for the wedding. A new carriage was bought, the house redecorated and refurnished, and lots of clothes for the bride were provided, together with the ring and the licence. The old gentleman then wrote to his son asking him to be present at the wedding, and he duly arrived; proudly his father presented him to his stepmother-to-be. Both the son and the prospective stepmother were dumb-founded, for the young gentleman was none other than the student with whom the bride-to-be had enjoyed such a passionate and profitable honeymoon not long before. The son recovered first, and, taking his father out of the room, told him the whole sordid and unvarnished truth. The old man took the crushing news quietly and recognised at once what a lucky escape he had had. He coolly informed Miss Anne Catley that there was nothing to prevent her leaving the house, and without more ado she left.

But for Anne there still remained the gallant dragoon, who was now in London. He had looks and a way with him that could sweep even this expert in promiscuousness right off her feet. They lived together, but there were plenty of rows and trouble. Anne had engaged a singularly handsome footman, who certainly had more to do than just answer the door and wait at table, and it wasn't long before Colonel Lascelles discovered what was going on and the footman quit hurriedly. In turn, Anne found the Colonel paying rather too much attention to a pretty shop-girl, and at one period, although they ate at the same table, they never exchanged a word for months. But they always made it up, despite Anne's amorous adventures, which never lessened over the years. In the end they decided to get married and come to terms about it, because the Colonel had never had any money. Anne's fortune after death was to go to her children—there had been several of which the dragoon was the putative father. Also, she insisted that the wedding was to be kept secret until such time as she decided to retire from the stage and public life. She evidently did not want to be denied what was left of her "fling." But it does seem that there was some kind of real affection between them, however odd the life they led, with its quarrels and mutual unfaithfulness. They were married in 1780.

The next season Anne reappeared at Covent Garden. But life and love had taken toll of her. She was no longer the ravishing Catley with the silver voice and the sparkling beauty. Her vivacity had gone and she had worn herself out just as George Anne Bellamy had done before her. Her voice was harsh, and even the figure, amply displayed in the breeches of Captain Macheath, had lost its allure. There was no applause for her, but the audience regretted her decline, and after another performance as Fanny in *The Maid of the Mill* she faded from the stage. She came back once only, in 1782, to Covent Garden for the benefit of Miss Yonge.

Anne went to live at Ealing, then a country district. She became a most respected figure in the neighbourhood, and was Lady Bountiful to the poor, but she developed consumption, brought on by her excesses. She struggled against her illness with fortitude, and her husband, now promoted a General, was her constant companion and consolation. She was forty-four when she died quite peacefully in 1789, and her husband buried her with all possible pomp in Ealing Churchyard and deeply mourned his loss.

Thus passed Anne Catley, one of the finest singers of her day and not at all a bad actress. Never once did she miss a performance or fail to give of her best. For an actress, it is a splendid epitaph. . . .

It may be remembered that among those who assisted at the last appearance of George Anne Bellamy was Mrs. Yates. She was in every way different from that poor soul whom she helped at the end, and was a tragedienne of the very front rank. A contemporary of Mrs. Pritchard and Susanna Maria Cibber, it was Mrs. Yates's misfortune to be overshadowed by both, for had her career not clashed with her formidable rivals, she might have ranked with Sarah Siddons herself. Indeed, she was the Queen of Tragedy after their retirement, and held sway until the might and power of Siddons arose and brooked no denial.

Doubt exists as to where and when she was born. According to some, she was a cockney; others say she was a Birmingham girl.

Certain records give the year of her birth as 1737, but even this is disputed. There is no doubt, however, that her maiden name was Graham and that she was called "Moll." She began her stage career under the elder Sheridan in Dublin in 1752, but was a failure and was dismissed, with a small solatium in lieu of salary. Miss Graham did not shriek about injustice, professional jealousy or a wicked management. She thought she deserved the sack, and knew her limitations. Her voice had no strength, and she was too fat. She therefore took herself to task and tried to improve, but without success, and decided to give up the stage. For the life of her, however, she could find no other employment, and came to London, where she tried again. David Garrick listened to her desperate plea for work and decided to give her the role of Julia in a new tragedy called *Virginia*. He mentioned her in his prologue and craved indulgence for her as a newcomer. It would be nice to say she triumphed, but she did not, and was coolly received. Garrick persevered with her, but although she worked hard she had no luck, and at the end of the season was again out of work.

But if she had not found favour with the public, she had done so with a sterling actor named Yates. He appreciated her good qualities by marrying her, and then set about coaching her for the stage. So well did he instruct and so hard did she try that Yates asked Garrick to give her another chance. Garrick engaged them both. This time Mrs. Yates did much better but she was up against Mrs. Cibber, and that was unfortunate. Mrs. Yates's luck seemed dead out until Mrs. Cibber went down in 1753 with a serious illness. A new play called *Orphan of China* was in rehearsal which Mrs. Cibber was to have appeared in with Garrick, Mossop and Holland. Garrick proposed a postponement until she was well enough to play. But Murphy, the author, would not agree, and wanted Mrs. Yates to do it. He told her that if she would follow his instructions, he believed he could get Garrick to consent to her taking the part. She worked with concentration and gave herself no rest until Murphy expressed his delighted satisfaction. He then persuaded Garrick, against that actor's will, to give her an audition. It seemed to him that she was worse than usual. She stumbled over the lines, was hesitant and unimpressive, and yet now and then appeared to promise something so much better.

Garrick was completely unaware that all this was a ruse between Murphy and the actress in order to astonish him "on the night." It nearly defeated its purpose, but Murphy seemed so pleased and expressed his complete faith in Mrs. Yates that Garrick, sick of the whole thing, gave her the part.

When they went into rehearsal with Garrick standing by, Mrs. Yates awaited her cue. It came and she began her opening speech, which left Garrick gasping. Was this the fumbling woman who had been so bad at the audition? He could hardly believe it. He knew at once he had been listening to a great actress. He whispered delightedly to Murphy that nothing better could have happened. Here was a novelty that he felt was wanted, and he could not restrain from rubbing his hands in glee. It turned out exactly as everybody had hoped, for at that first performance Mrs. Yates, as Mandane, swept to triumph. From a poor, unregarded actress she had achieved fame in a night—fame that had been earned by hard, unremitting toil.

From then on Mrs. Yates became one of the great tragediennes, even if her range of roles was limited. She was at her best in parts in which she could tear passion to tatters, where rage and storm predominated. She could be imperious, she could make the blood run cold, but in the more tender scenes she was less convincing. Nevertheless, she was capable of very great things, given the opportunity, and her Medea was so colossal that Mrs. Siddons never challenged comparison.

When she rose to eminence she attained a certain beauty of face and figure, and her carriage and bearing were those of a stage empress. She was a good wife and a virtuous woman, but the hauteur of the parts she played also became part of her own character and she was a considerable "headache" to people in the Theatre. Woe betide anyone, player or manager, who upset her. They got a real performance from her, without payment. All the same, she was one of the leading tragediennes of our stage and deserved to be remembered.

Mrs. Yates did not hold her crown without a rival, and she was a Mrs. Barry. She was a much more colourful person, but certainly lacked the virtue which Mrs. Yates possessed.

Mrs. Barry was a redhead, and she lived a life which matched the colour of her hair. She was born at Bath in 1734, the daughter

PLATE XI

At top: MRS. COUTTS
At left: MISS O'NEILL. *At right:* MISS ANNE CATLEY

PLATE XII

Above:

MRS. ANASTASIA ROBINSON, who became Countess of Peterborough

At left:

MRS. BEHN, one of the first women playwrights

of an apothecary named Street. He was a gay, lively man, happy in a gay, lively city. He liked going to parties and balls and would take his young red-headed daughter with him. Although little more than a child, her beauty was quite startling and everywhere attracted attention. She had a fair skin which so often accompanies hair of her colour, and a lovely figure, and had inherited her father's liveliness so that she soon became the belle of Bath. When she was seventeen she fell deeply in love with a man of good family, who proposed and was accepted. He went to London on business, which was apparently so absorbing that he forgot his Bath belle and never returned.

Miss Street was broken-hearted. She showed signs of passing into what was then known as a decline, and her parents sent her to relations in Yorkshire. They thought the change would do her good, and it succeeded rather more than they anticipated. Perhaps the strong air of the North woke her up, for she took the bit between her teeth and married an actor named Dancer, who was running a travelling company of his own. The family made a terrible fuss about it, but she took not the slightest notice, and decided to follow her husband's profession by becoming an actress. As in everything she did, she entered into the new career with zest, and her beauty and talent soon won recognition.

It appears that the couple left Yorkshire as soon as they were married and that Mrs. Dancer made her stage début at Portsmouth in 1756. Afterwards they went north again and played in and around York, probably to the extreme annoyance of the young wife's Yorkshire relatives. She did not care two straws about that. But Dublin, the cradle of so many stars, claimed her first appearance of importance. Woodward and Spranger Barry, two good actors, were in management at the Crow Street Theatre, and they engaged Mrs. Dancer to play Cordelia to Barry's Lear. Mrs. Dancer scored a nice little success and followed it with a round of the usual leading parts in the stock plays, including Juliet. She worked hard for nine years, for she loved her profession and never ceased trying to improve herself. From the first the public liked this very pretty girl, and now she had added good acting to her physical attractions. She had got rid of her first husband and had fallen deeply in love with Spranger Barry, but knew she was not alone. This tall, handsome man with the silver voice was the idol of the ladies. They threw themselves at him and his conquests were innumerable. But there was something about this fascinating little red-head which captivated him, and he fell in love with her. In 1767 they went to London as man and wife to put their fortune to the test. They were not, of course, married, for Mr. Dancer was still alive, but they secured an engagement at the Haymarket Theatre and registered a big success in *Othello*. The following year they were entrenched in Drury Lane, each earning a good salary. With the death of Dancer, Spranger married his actress love, and she became legally entitled to call herself Mrs. Barry. As time went on, Spranger became well-to-do and his wife, too, was enjoying success. She could play comedy as well as tragedy and she had charm and beauty. She was a wonderful Rosalind and an equally good performer in tragic parts, such as Belvidera and Mrs. Randolph. Just as Mrs. Siddons, when she arrived, had left Medea alone because of Mrs. Yates, so she feared Mrs. Randolph because of Mrs. Barry's performance in that role. The mighty Siddons was a bit afraid of this pretty, enchanting person and admitted it. She said she wished Mrs. Barry would retire, seeing that she was so rich. Now Mrs. Siddons was by far the better actress of the two, but she lacked the humanity of the red-head, who knew exactly how to handle an audience, who played to them, and was never so aloof that she could not make them feel that she was their friend as much as they were her friends. That was her great secret—the personal touch. She gave them all a run for their money—Woffington, Yates, Cibber and the rest. She always had an audience at her feet from her first entrance and had she been a lesser actress than she was, she could still have done it.

She outlived her husband who died in 1777, and after his death, that red-headed impetuosity reasserted itself. She had money and an assured position, and should have been content. But she took a third husband, an Irish barrister named Crawford. She was a woman who, when she loved, did so without reserve and she lavished affection on this man, who was younger than herself. He just wanted her money, and got it, for her fortune melted away. It became necessary for him to work, but he did not return to the Bar; instead he took his wife to Dublin (where she had been so successful) and went into theatre management. He "presented" his wife, as it would be said today. He was no more successful as a manager than he had been as a barrister, and there were constant rows. Mrs. Barry's business instincts were undimmed and she would not go on the stage until her salary was paid. Often her husband would be forced to collect money from the pit to pay her before the curtain went up. Her ardent nature was cut to the quick and she began to pine as she had done when she was jilted in her youth. Little wonder then that her sparkle began to desert her and her performances began to suffer.

From London came the news of the triumph of Mrs. Siddons. This aroused the Barry as nothing else could have done, for it brought back memories of the time when she too had had London at her feet. Here was a foe arisen whose challenge was very, very serious. She left her husband in Dublin to do the best he could, and she hastened back to London to give battle. Mrs. Siddons was at Drury Lane, sweeping all before her, and this was a new Siddons of increased power, experience and, what was more important, of better health. She packed Drury Lane; where people fought at the doors to get in and where there were many casualties. Covent Garden consequently was playing to very poor business and Mrs. Barry went there and was welcomed. Here was a favourite returned; here was someone who might stem the Siddons flood. She knew what kind of competition she was up against, did Mrs. Barry, for all her rashness. She was tired and unhappy, and much older, but red-heads are fighters. She revived one of her great roles, the part of Mrs. Randolph, and she triumphed. Press and public acclaimed her.

The fight was long and grim, but youth told. Step by step Barry declined; step by step Siddons advanced. Siddons dictated the fight by donning the Mask of Tragedy and Barry knew that in this field she could not match her rival. Her *métier* was comedy. She held on as long as she could in comedy, supported by her faithful followers, who could still recall her resounding successes.

Barry lost the unequal struggle and bade farewell to the stage at Covent Garden on April 16, 1798, when she was sixty-four years of age. She had been on the stage for forty-two years, and had been supreme in London since 1768. For thirty years she had reigned as a queen, undisputed since the death of Susanna Maria Cibber in 1766.

After her retirement she lingered on for three years, and died in 1801. She was buried in the same grave as her second husband, Spranger Barry, in the cloisters of Westminster Abbey, where there is a great deal of theatrical dust. They had loved each other and they were together at the last.

Mrs. Barry—the red-head from Bath—rightly takes her place in the cavalcade of the women of our stage. Few ever excelled her in that ability to enchant and charm an audience. There was no limelight in the theatre of her day, and she acted by candle light, but her gifts made those candles seem like suns.

CHAPTER FOURTEEN

More Sinned Against . . .

IN King Street, Covent Garden, in the early eighteenth century, stood a shop occupied by an upholsterer, a craftsman of skill and respectability. He did a thriving trade and his living quarters, above the shop, must have been very choice, for they were once the lodgings of some Red Indian chiefs on a visit to Queen Anne. The upholsterer's name was Arne. Nobody remembers his work today, and his claim to fame rests on his being the sire of two children, both of whom are among the immortals of the Theatre. Both were born in King Street, within the shadows of the great theatres of Drury Lane and Covent Garden and it is not surprising that they distinguished themselves in the world of entertainment, for they were set down, so to speak, in the very heart of it.

Arne the upholsterer is forgotten; the names of his children still live. They are Thomas Augustine Arne, a great composer whose fame would have shone the brighter had it not been for Handel's genius, and Susanna Maria Arne, whose married name was Cibber. The son was a King of English Music and the daughter a Queen of English Tragedy. The son composed, not only many operas, but the song which every Briton knows, be they never so unmusical, as "God Save the King." His sister Susanna Maria gave it the first public rendering at Drury Lane Theatre on September 28, 1745.

True, there had been previous versions of this anthem, already an old English tune, but Arne rearranged it, providing the version sung ever since, and to be sung, one hopes, as long as this realm exists. Not only that, he also gave us our second national anthem, "Rule Britannia."

Thomas Arne was born about 1710, so was five years older than his sister. He was christened in the Church of St. Paul, Covent Garden, the actors' church, and was buried there, too. The house in which these two stage geniuses came into the world became No. 10 King Street, but in their time was known as "The Crown and Cushion." It is worthy of note that the father, whose name was also Thomas, not only upholstered but made coffins as well. From such unlikely surroundings came so much glory that perhaps the coffins symbolised Susanna's gift of Tragedy.

Young Thomas Arne must have been fond of his sister, for he taught her to sing. He had fought his own fight to be allowed to make music rather than upholstery and coffins, and his victory was complete. Susanna was acting when she was fourteen, in little plays for which her brother composed the music. But he wanted her to sing in opera, and she did so, in *Amelia* at the old Haymarket in 1732, when she was about seventeen or eighteen. Her voice was sweet and low, but not very strong, but she was well received. The following year she sang at Lincoln's Inn Fields between the acts (they gave full value for money in the Theatre then), and had to give repeated encores. Opera, though, was really much too strenuous for her, despite her brother's enthusiastic prompting; yet, she might have continued to sing her way through life had she not fallen deeply in love. It was at once her stepping-stone to fame and her descent to disaster and unhappiness, for the man of her choice was none other than Theophilus, the unsavoury offspring of brilliant Colley Cibber. Theophilus was a competent actor of somewhat florid style and he had been married before. He saw something in this pretty and charming girl with the sweet voice, maybe a hint of the great future that was in store for her.

When Colley Cibber became aware of his son's intentions, he expressed his disapproval, for Susanna had no dowry to commend her, and Colley, always the hard-headed man of business, had little faith in his son's ability to make money or carve out his own career. The father felt that Theophilus should marry a rich woman, and Susanna was anything but that. But parental objections or not, the marriage took place in 1734, and the upholsterer's daughter found herself related to a family in control of Drury

Lane. Her powerful father-in-law was not one to cry over spilt milk—it was one of his abiding virtues—and he took a second glance at Susanna. What he saw was not altogether unpromising and he enquired if she could act. Theophilus said he thought she could, and his father gave her a try-out and then decided to make her training in dramatic art his own especial task. He found Susanna intelligent, conscientious and possessing initiative and of this early phase of her career paid a sincere tribute to her in giving evidence in a court action that Theophilus brought against her years later. "In the forty years that I have known the stage," he said, "I never knew a woman at the beginning so capable of the business, or improve so fast."

Notwithstanding this subsequent encomium, Susanna was still a very young and inexperienced actress when her chance came in January, 1736, with the first production at Drury Lane of *Zara*, a tragedy in which she had been rehearsed, line for line, by the author. The role called for resources of power that would have tested an established player, but there were other and more disturbing factors to be taken into account, of concern not only to Susanna but to Theophilus and his father. Fleetwood, the amateur who imagined he "knew it all," was then in charge of Drury Lane, and he had not the slightest appreciation of Susanna's potentialities.

The real peril to Susanna, however, lay in the fact that she had to play opposite a leading man who had been given the role because he happened to be the nephew of the author. Poor Susanna must have been in a dreadful state of nerves before the curtain went up, knowing that the play carried a passenger who was really lethal. She realised, too, that an audience, roused to an ugly mood, could kill without mercy. It was thus in fear and trembling that she stepped on to the stage that night immediately after Theophilus had spoken the following prologue that old Cibber had written to smooth her entrance and whip up sympathy. It is a fair specimen of the sort of appeal that it was customary to make in those far-off times and it must be said that it is much less blatant than the technique of publicity today.

Thus far the Author speaks—but now the Player
With trembling heart prefers his humble prayer.

Tonight the greatest venture of my life
Is lost or saved, as you receive—a wife
If time you think may ripen her to merit
With gentle smiles support her wav'ring spirit;
Zara in France at once an actress rais'd
Warm'd into skill by being kindly prais'd
Oh! could such wonders here from favour flow
How would our Zara's heart with transport glow.
But she alas, by juster fears oppressed
Begs but your bare endurance at the best.
Her unskill'd tongue would simple nature speak
Nor dare her bounds, for false applauses, break.
Amidst a thousand faults, her best pretence
To please—is unpresuming innocence.
When a chaste heart's distress your grief demands
One silent tear outweighs a thousand hands
If she conveys the pleasing passions right
Guard and support her this decisive night.
If she mistakes, or finds her strength too small
Let interposing pity break her fall.
In you it rests, to save her or destroy
If she draws tears from you—I weep with joy.

As events turned out, Susanna could have dispensed with the support of this heart-throb for that night, for despite a wretched display by her co-player, who, as expected, made a hash of his part, she revealed herself as an actress and won unqualified praise. A new leading man was introduced at the next performance and although he had the clock to beat in taking the part over, he proved a success, so that the play ran for fourteen nights, an excellent run for those days. *Zara* took its place in the repertoire and the part first played by Susanna Maria Cibber became a role for every aspiring tragedienne.

Having stepped into the front rank, Susanna soon consolidated her position. As one role followed another in quick succession she was able to garner the experience a flowering artist of her calibre needed. Roles such as Indiana, Isabella in *Measure for Measure*, Endocia, Belvidera, Desdemona, Amana in *The Relapse* and Cassandra in *Agamemnon* were all part of her education in dramatic skill. She was a superb Ophelia, perhaps unequalled until the appearance of Ellen Terry and, in our own time, Fay

Compton. Dense as he was, Fleetwood realised that when it came to tragedy Susanna Cibber was the greatest draw of the day. She was paid £100 and a benefit (worth about the same) during her first season and her salary was doubled later on, when she also enjoyed a most lucrative benefit. By then, and it is not surprising, she was feeling her feet and, no doubt prompted by her husband, she next demanded the largest salary paid to anyone in the house and the first choice of benefit. These terms were rejected and she left Drury Lane.

The Cibbers lived together at first in perfect amity, and in three years two children were born to them. Both died in early infancy and soon Susanna began to see Theophilus in his true colours. He was a bad lot, faithless, intemperate, extravagant and not a little cruel. Head over heels in debt, he lost all affection for his wife, and with a vile purpose in mind had introduced her to an acquaintance of his named Sloper. This young man was deeply in love with Susanna, who was indeed a pretty woman, with clear-cut features, lovely eyes and a gentleness which only turned to storm when she was crossed or considered herself insulted by another actress. In private life she was an extremely nice person indeed, and it is not to be wondered at that she found solace in the tenderness of young Sloper, who paid her assiduous court. Nor is it surprising that at length she yielded to him, perhaps finding happiness in her sin? And there is not the slightest doubt at all that Theophilus had intended her to do just this, for he threw the two together on all occasions and borrowed money from Sloper. But in 1738, despite his pimping, he was in such fear of arrest for debt that he had to skip to France to avoid the bailiffs. His wife, now completely estranged, left the Theatre and went off with Sloper to a retreat in the country. But Theophilus now judged the time ripe for a big kill and, returning from France, found Susanna and her lover in hiding at Burnham in Bucks. He had her seized and taken away, but she was rescued by her brothers. This act put paid to any further borrowing from Mr. Sloper and the scandal became the talk of the town. Spicy details were added and the story did not redound to the credit of Master Theophilus in his role of outraged and deceived husband. So he decided to play a new card by invoking the law and commenced an action against Mr. Sloper for "Criminal Conversation." Sloper stood charged with Assaulting, Ravishing and Carnally Knowing Susanna Maria Cibber, the Plaintiff's Wife. The damages claimed were £5,000.

The case was tried on December 5, 1738, in the King's Bench before the Lord Chief Justice and a special jury. All sorts of people gave evidence, among them one Stint, who was a candle-snuffer at Drury Lane, and whom Theophilus had laid on as a spy and guardian for his wife. He gave the following highly coloured account of the rescue by Susanna's brothers, led by Thomas, the great composer: "Mr. Thomas Arne, her brother, came there and he begged and prayed that I would let her go along with him, but I would not break my trust; I could not do it. He came several times, and finding I would not do it began to break open the house and at the same time bid her cry 'Murder.' She cried out 'Murder' and I believe there was a hundred of a mob, assisting him to break open the house. I had a case of pistols and laid my back against the door, but they were too strong for me and took my pistols out of each hand and held me fast by each arm and beat me severely and tore all the clothes off my back and took Mrs. Cibber away with them."

What a story for the front pages today! One wonders if Stint ever got any of the money which Theophilus must have promised him for the job. As to the action itself, the facts could not be disputed and the jury retired for half an hour. The verdict was for Theophilus Cibber, the outraged husband, but it is doubtful if the result pleased him. He claimed £5,000 damages and got £10, which showed what was thought of him! From then on he was a discredited man, ever sinking lower, but still able to sneak out of a hole and bite like a rat, as will be shown.

There was never any question of a reconciliation, even though Cibber declared that he was willing to forget and forgive. Susanna went into hiding once more, this time to have a baby. Sloper supported her and visited her with such discretion that nobody could produce evidence of their meetings.

Theophilus, having driven his wife out of his life and from the stage, still lusted for revenge, and once more he discovered where Susanna was living. He burst into her house in Kennington Lane, caused a terrible scene and laid hands, not only on her, but on everything of value he could discover.

Again he appealed to the law. This time the accusation was different. He charged Sloper, who was paying pretty heavily for his infatuation for an actress, with "Trespass and Assault, in taking, leading away and detaining the Plaintiff's wife," and further for "Assaulting, Beating, etc., the Plaintiff's wife whereby he lost her Assistance, to his Damage of Ten Thousand Pounds."

There was a good deal of hard lying on the part of Theophilus's witnesses. One of them, a cobbler named Walton who had accompanied Theophilus, stated: "I went along with Mr. Cibber. He went upstairs directly. He said he came to demand his wife. She promised to go. He took some linen and apparel. She was in bed, but we went out of the room till she was dressed. He said he was to dine at the Runner Tavern at two o'clock and desired her to come to him there and said she should never want a shilling whilst he had it. She promised so to do. He took her purse, in which there was eighteenpence and a pocket piece, but he threw it back. He had her watch; 'twas a silver watch."

Sloper's counsel said, with much justification, that the plaintiff did not come for his wife, but to strip her of what he could find. He asked, "Why did he not take her along with him?" The jury retired for half an hour and again returned a verdict for the Plaintiff. But although they refused to award his damages of £10,000, they did with unwarranted generosity allow him £500. That taste of the law sickened Cibber. He did not try again.

Mrs. Cibber remained in retirement for two years under the protection of Sloper. Theophilus was still her husband and she did not dare to act in a theatre for fear of what he might do, and eventually left England and went to Dublin. There on December 21, 1741, she played Indiana in *The Conscious Lovers* to the Young Bevil of Quin. Her engagement was for £300 for the season, and although the first night of her appearance only netted £40, it did not take theatregoers long to realise that an actress of superb gifts had come among them. It was a case of "house full" after that.

It was in Dublin that Susanna achieved her greatest triumph as a singer in a way that must have brought back memories of those days when she was just an unknown young girl with a sweet voice. Dispirited by the ill-luck he had experienced in London, Handel decided that his great new oratorio *The Messiah* should receive its first performance in the city that stands on the Liffey, and he evidently knew that Susanna Maria Cibber was the sister of Thomas Arne and could sing. Handel went to infinite pains to show her how to perform the arias, and consequently she was one of the outstanding successes of that memorable evening which gave the world a work of sublime beauty. Susanna's small but melting voice rang out that night, and so transported was a famous Irishman named Dr. Delany that after one of her solos he sprang to his feet and cried: "Woman, for this be all thy sins forgiven." Poor Susanna, she was more sinned against than sinning, heaven knows!

Susanna returned to London in the summer of 1742 and had apparently come to some arrangement with Theophilus, who was down and out. He realised that public opinion was dead against him and dare not interfere with her career. The scandal he had provoked was still a choice morsel of gossip, which was perhaps why Susanna's appearance at Covent Garden in the following September was regarded as "an occasion." She played Desdemona, and so much emotional intensity was invested in that poor creature's declaration of innocence that the audience realised it was a cry from the heart of the actress herself. It brought the house to its feet. In Quin, Susanna not only had her Othello but a doughty champion in every way. When Garrick over coffee at the Bedford Coffee House one day discussed the possibility of getting Susanna Maria to Drury Lane, but expressed doubts as to her suitability for certain parts, particularly the role of Constance in *King John*, Quin became quite angry. "I am amazed at you, Mr. Garrick," he thundered. "That woman has a heart: she can lay anything where passion is needed." And he was right, as Garrick was to discover. Perhaps David was just seeking a second opinion in his own cautious way.

In 1745 Susanna found herself once again at Drury Lane, and one of her early roles was that of Constance. It was a great favourite with all tragediennes, but critics of the day avowed that for real art the palm went to Susanna Maria Cibber. Certainly no one was her peer in the scene where she entered grief-stricken over the loss of her son, "her pretty Arthur." Others try to comfort her, but she sinks to the ground gripped by horror and madness and says:

> Here I and Sorrow sit! This is my throne.
> Let Kings come bow to it.

So magnificently did Susanna sustain this part that Garrick was hard put to keep up his end. Having suffered herself, Susanna could call forth suffering and she had a ready sympathy for those who met misfortune in real life. When a certain Samuel Smith, merchant, founded the Veterans' Scheme, to assist old soldiers, who, in those days lacked a pension, subscriptions were opened among the gentry, whose generosity was further enriched by gifts from the Society of Friends of 20,000 waistcoats and 400 great-coats as worn by watchmen of the period by the Vestry of St. James's, Westminster. Susanna offered to play the part of Polly in *The Beggar's Opera* for three nights, if the management agreed to donate the profits to the scheme, but there was some delay and John Rich at Covent Garden stepped in and asked Susanna to play Polly there. She agreed and the effort realised £602 7*s*., an enormous sum for those days. Everybody gave their services without fee and even the tallow-chandlers made a present of the candles required for lighting the theatre—no mean item.

Susanna commuted between the two great theatres. As soon as Garrick took over Drury Lane, with Lacy as actor-manager, she was there playing Aspasia in Dr. Johnson's *Irene* and Fidelia in *The Foundling*, but in 1750-1 she was back once more at Covent Garden in the company of Peg Woffington, Quin, Charles Macklin and Spranger Barry. She was Juliet to Barry's Romeo in that celebrated theatrical duel between Barry and Garrick. Macklin, who was the Mercutio, said of Susanna in that role that no other actress could excel her in the expression of love, grief, tenderness or jealous rage. That wag of the Theatre, Tate Wilkinson, paid his own especial tribute to Susanna by declaring: "She was the best Ophelia that there ever was, either before or since." Wilkinson knew what he was talking about for he was a great mimic and admitted that when he tried to take Susanna off her excellence defeated him. She was certainly a matchless Ophelia and no eloquence can describe the distracted manner and pathos she brought to the scene in which she had to say "Lord, we know what we are, but not what we may be."

Susanna found an ideal partner in Spranger Barry and together they drew the Town and were the ideal stage lovers of their generation. It was at that time that Susanna's health began to fail, and whenever she was unable to appear Barry was off, too, if Romeo and Juliet was on the bill. He would play it with nobody but her. The public keenly regretted their eventual separation, but Garrick wanted Susanna and, since it was a question of terms, Drury Lane won. When she went there in 1754 she never played anywhere else for the rest of her life.

Barry's loss was Garrick's gain, for David, with Susanna, made an incomparable pair and when they played Romeo and Juliet the theatre was overflowing and one occasion over 200 people stood close by them during the Tomb scene. In her first season Susanna went from one role to another, Venusia in *Boadicea*, the title role in *Virginia*, while one of her outstanding successes the following season was Perdita in *A Winter's Tale*. In the autumn of that year she suffered a grievous blow by the death of her daughter, of whom Sloper was the father. She hid her sorrow from the world, but returned to the stage in 1758, which was the year she became a widow by the death of Theophilus Cibber, who was drowned while crossing to Dublin. Apart from her regular roles, she scored two big successes in Garrick's version of *The Fatal Marriage* and as Mrs. Wilding in *The Gamester*, but in 1760 one of her rare failures was as Lady Sadlife in *The Double Gallant*.

The time came when she began to insist on playing comedy, and it must be admitted that she strained the loyalty of her admirers by her attempts. In the season 1761-2 there came into Garrick's hands a play called *The School for Lovers* and he and the company went down to the home of the author to have a reading of the play. Susanna had apparently set her heart on playing Celia in it, and when she expressed this wish the author gave her an anxious glance. She was fifty years old and had her spectacles on. The script placed Celia's age at fifteen and the author, humming and hawing, asked if it would not be advisable to add a few years to the girl's life. Susanna pondered, then looked up and said, "No; not at all. I'll play her as she is." And carrying her years like a feather, Susanna played the part with consummate grace, for she had never lost the slim figure of her youth and was in every way physically able to impersonate a young girl.

When he retired, Garrick liked to talk about his leading ladies and said that although he could cope successfully with most of them, Susanna Maria Cibber defeated him by her gentle persistence that would not be denied. She argued with intelligence and always won.

The illness which had come upon her some years before began to take an increasing toll, and audiences applauding her at her infrequent appearances little knew that the smiles she rewarded them with came from a woman racked with fearful pain. The last new character she created was Elvira, in a tragedy by Mallet that was performed in 1763.

She was living in Scotland Yard, Westminster, with her ever-faithful Sloper, through even when she was widowed they never married. Perhaps Susanna had not the heart for it, after her wedded experiences with Cibber. Nobody seemed to care and as they entertained in style people esteemed it a favour to be invited to their home. Susanna was nearly at the end of her tether, for her doctors appeared not to understand her malady and one eminent physician advised sea-water baths, to which she had a terrible aversion. She underwent this ordeal, and who knows but that it really killed her? King George III was blamed for her death. He commanded a performance of *The Provok'd Wife*, a play he greatly admired, and he asked that Susanna should play Lady Brute.

Although terribly ill, she consented, for she felt that as a loyal subject she should obey the command of her King. It was her last appearance and the day was December 13, 1765. She returned home never to leave it, and her end came on January 31, 1766, and almost certainly from cancer. When Garrick heard of it he exclaimed, "Mrs. Cibber dead? The Tragedy has died with her, on the female side." It was both a tribute and a reservation, for *he* was still alive!

Susanna left her property to Sloper in trust for her two children, and there has been a great deal of speculation about this, for it has been suggested that perhaps the young Cibbers did not die after all. Perhaps the truth is that Susanna had two more children by Sloper whose births were kept secret, so that their illegitimacy should not be a reproach upon them.

Her friends greatly missed Susanna, for, with Sloper, she had maintained a country house at Woodhays, where she entertained, among others, Garrick and his charming wife. An amusing diversion there was a parrot which Susanna had taught to speak lines from the great tragedies. Susanna had much more than physical attractiveness even then, though her nose was a little long and rather pinched. If her eyes were glorious pools, it was really her voice—that beautiful, gentle river of sound—that so moved everyone who heard it. In her quiet, passive way, she was an excellent conversationalist with a lively and intelligent mind, and she was as popular with women as she was with men, and that was something quite unusual in those days of temptation. She was sensitive and suffered mentally as well as physically for she would cry out when the audience roared for yet another curtsy from her, "Oh, that my nerves were made of cart-ropes." She endured a lot of sorrow in her life and was mortified when her daughter's presence at a ball at Bath was objected to and old Beau Nash, then being wheeled about, requested the girl to withdraw.

Susanna was buried in the cloisters of Westminster Abbey within a stone's-throw of regal company. Posted on the Roman Catholic Chapel in Lincoln's Inn Fields was a notice at the time of her death, "Of your charity, pray for the soul of Mrs. Susanna Maria Cibber." Let us say amen.

CHAPTER FIFTEEN

Masculine Femininity

ONE of Colley Cibber's unfailing witticisms in the days of his penury was to get up from a card table having lost his last few shillings and declare: "Now I must go home and eat a child!" Colley could have taken his pick of a large and troublesome brood, for, like King Lear, he was unlucky with his children, particularly with his daughter Charlotte, who, among other pursuits, grew up to become an actress. In her day the wearing of breeches had become a vogue with actresses architecturally suited to them but nobody wore them more often, or more defiantly, than Charlotte whose tragedy was that she had failed to be born a man.

She made her entry into the world in 1710 and was just four years old when she astounded the rustics of Twickenham, where the family lived, by parading in her father's clothes, which included a hat perched atop an enormous wig, an ornate waistcoat and a sword trailing from her tiny waist. She couldn't don the breeches because they were too long for her tiny legs. This display was Charlotte's first revolt against femininity and petticoats, but Colley was too busy with his affairs to realise that he had sired a misfit. In fact he seems to have displayed very little affection, if any, for Charlotte who, on another occasion, disturbed the family peace by mounting a baby donkey whose brays roused the neighbourhood. "Gad damme!" roared Colley when he saw her. "An ass upon an ass."

When her mother became an invalid and retired to Uxbridge, Charlotte went with her, but she was little use as a nurse and preferred to run wild in the country. She liked shooting, gardening, and riding and grooming horses. It so happened that there was an old woman in the village who suffered from some internal disorder, and one day Charlotte felt that she should do something about it. She filched some hartshorn and sal volatile from home, to which she added syrup, snails and gooseberry leaves before stirring well. The old woman, instead of dying, responded to this treatment and demanded more, which encouraged Charlotte to go in for medicine in a big way. She gave orders for a consignment of drugs, her father got the bill, and that ended her dream of becoming a doctor.

Charlotte remained a problem child, restless, unstable and possessing intelligence beyond her years. When her mother died, Colley went to live in London, for his fortunes had vastly improved, and he now controlled Drury Lane. The great man took a house in Berkeley Square and with him went Charlotte, who was enjoined to behave herself. It was like asking a volcano not to erupt, and as between the father and daughter it is difficult to guess who disliked the other the most. With womanhood and a new restlessness upon her, Charlotte began to hang about the theatre of which her father was the patentee, and there she met Richard Charke, its musical director. He was handsome and charming, and to Charlotte he personified the glamour of the stage. What she did not know was that he was a rake, without resources of his own, and who could contemplate marriage only with an eye to the main chance. Had Charlotte's mother been alive, or had Colley been more of a father to her, she might have avoided the disaster that befell her. Instead she ran away with Charke and married him. Colley, however, saw through Charke's scheming and threw the couple out of his house, to which they had returned expecting to be cordially received. It didn't take Charlotte long to discover her marital mistake, for when her husband realised that being Cibber's son-in-law was indeed no great shakes he began to neglect his wife for the company of the frail ladies who frequented the theatre and brothel-infested neighbourhood.

Whatever her faults, Charlotte had never lacked courage, and she chased her husband out of these places, brawled with him in public and even came to blows. Their quarrels became a scandal in Theatreland and must have greatly incensed dignified Colley Cibber, Patentee of Theatre Royal and a member of White's Club.

The curtain was due to fall on this ill-starred marriage, for Charke sailed for the West Indies with his latest charmer just as Charlotte was about to fulfil her womanhood in a way that should have given her husband joy, had he not been the thorough scoundrel he was. Charlotte, little more than a child herself—she was barely seventeen—went through the agonies of birth alone and was delivered of a daughter, born to a world of woe. She arose from the confinement a hardened woman, knowing that she had to face a hostile world alone, but she had pride and would neither bewail her fate nor ask for charity. She felt that the Theatre was in her blood and that she, too, could make her mark on the stage.

To this end, Charlotte went not to her father but to Nance Oldfield for guidance. The great actress was nearing her end, but she took pity on the young mother and gave her what tuition she could. It led to her getting a part in *The Provok'd Wife*, the very role, in fact, that Oldfield herself had once played. At that time Theophilus, Charlotte's brother, was managing Drury Lane for Highmore, to whom Barton Booth, Colley Cibber's erstwhile partner, had sold his share in the Patent. Theophilus saw to it that his sister was taken on as a general understudy, which meant that she had to be ready to go on in any role at a moment's notice. Colley Cibber, who loved Drury Lane and was so bitterly disposed towards his daughter, must have smiled wryly as Charlotte took over the role of Alicia in *Jane Shore* when Mrs. Porter broke her leg.

Charlotte was never a brilliant player, but she was competent, and when Theophilus revolted against Highmore, and led the players to the Little Theatre in the Hay, Charlotte went with them. Again she did fairly well, even to creating the part of Lucy in the first production of *George Barnwell*, which became a celebrated drama. It was shortly after this modest success that Charlotte took to breeches in a variety of roles, and clearly she loved wearing them. She knew they suited her and soon she took to wearing them in the street. It was a brief but comparatively happy period in her life, for her stage earnings brought her four guineas a week, which seemed enormous wealth to her. She spent it on finery and dressed her little daughter very smartly. Colley Cibber began to soften towards her, especially when he was informed of the death of Charke. Charlotte's success suggested that she might, after all, become a daughter of whom he could be proud and he sent for her, probably without knowing that she was beginning to get into debt. But the truth of the matter was that Cibber could not avoid being pompous with her and did not know how to handle this spirited filly he had bred. He made the mistake of preaching to her and Charlotte took the bit between her teeth, tossed her head, and said that as a married woman and a mother she knew something of the world and was well able to look after herself. Colley, who possessed the self-same spirit that she was displaying, couldn't forgive her and turned his back upon her. He was, of course, riled by the knowledge that she had played one of his famous parts and had had the effrontery to imitate him. The breach was wide and it was opened further by Charlotte's sister, who disliked her intensely and poisoned Colley's mind against her.

Shortly after Charlotte had clashed in this way with her father she found there was no more work for her on the stage and although she haunted the few theatres in search of employment, she did so dressed as a man, and that went dead against her. Managers were accustomed to actresses and their tantrums, but to have one who wore male clothes in the street—that was really asking for it! The stage closed its doors to Charlotte, and she knew she had to make a fresh start, so she pawned her few belongings, pledged the little credit her name was still good for and set up as a grocer in Long Acre. For this effrontery her father cast her off for ever. Charlotte didn't care, and found the shop a lot of fun. She had little stock and knew nothing about the business, but she put up a brave show, and friends of the family, some of them quite maliciously, came to buy.

The business began to founder and Charlotte, casting about to avoid ruin, decided that as she was a superb horsewoman she would ride round the countryside collecting orders and thus increasing the business. Up to now she had done most of her trade by selling torches to linkboys, and as she gave them a drink when they made a purchase, more often than not the transaction showed a loss instead of a profit. When a customer wanted something she did not stock—and she stocked very little—she would pop out to another retail shop and buy it and then re-sell it at a loss. She was going to put an end to all that with new methods and canvassing on horseback, but in the meantime a grubby linkboy made an amorous advance on the woman grocer in breeches. She threw him out of the shop, but he had his revenge a little later when, aided by his friends, he broke into the shop and stripped it of all Charlotte's scanty possessions, even to the scales and weights. It was a deadly blow, and Charlotte must have been in a very bad way, for she wrote to her father for help, but got no reply.

She had, however, an aptitude for making friends, and in her extremity someone lent her a few pounds with which she bought a bankrupt puppet show, situated in a top floor over a tennis court in St. James's Street. Charlotte paid much more for it than it was worth, spent more money on advertising the attraction than she could afford and redressed and repainted the puppets to resemble celebrities of the day, whom she proposed to burlesque and hold up to ridicule. The idea caught on, for the "quality" loved anything that savoured of scandal and could not keep away. Charlotte on her part was the soul of indiscretion and could not keep quiet about her success, so that her former creditors, who had written her off as a bad debt, now began to press her. Bailiffs began to hang around her little upstairs playhouse and they frightened away many of her clients, who had debts of their own. In the end Charlotte had to admit she was beaten and although the show was worth £500 she sold it for a mere £20 and quietly disappeared. While the venture lasted she had discarded her beloved breeches and returned to petticoats.

London's underworld effectively hid all trace of Charlotte for some time, but during this period, when no one saw or heard of her, she married again and her second husband was as big a villain as her first. He too vanished, leaving her burdened with debts, and she became a hunted creature, able only to go out at night time dressed as a man, those being the only clothes she possessed. Until she was caught and taken to prison for debt she had managed to look after her young daughter. When her plight became known to the "ladies" of the town, who plied their trade around Covent Garden, they got her out of jail, but although free she was little better off, for she heard that bailiffs were again searching for her. One of them was touched by her distress and misery and lent her his clothes so that she might visit her little daughter, whom she believed was dying in a house in Great Queen Street, where a slattern of a housekeeper was in charge.

Charlotte wanted to take a doctor along with her, but she was penniless and, nearly out of her mind, she screamed her grief in the street. She was of course so dressed that the crowd which gathered round took her for a young man. A gentleman named Hallam listened to her story and was touched by it. He took her to his home and had nurses and doctors in attendance in readiness for Charlotte's child, whom he sent for. Hallam proved a real benefactor and rallied help from Theatreland itself. Peg Woffington came to her aid and so too did Garrick and his partner Lacy, and even Rich of Covent Garden. Cibber was still a name with which to conjure.

Grateful as she was to Hallam, Charlotte would not live on charity at any price and must earn her own living. The stage beckoned once again, but she was fearful of going out in the day and would wait until night-time before canvassing stage doors in her male clothes hoping for a chance. She even tried that queer little place where she had played her puppet show and which was now some kind of theatre where amateurs paid to perform and show themselves off. For Charlotte, however, there was nothing doing.

Courage and perseverance of the rarest kind paid a dividend at least, for on one of those evenings that Charlotte spent in anxious enquiry she heard that the actor who was to play Captain Plume in *The Recruiting Officer* had failed to turn up. The management was in a panic and Charlotte seized her chance with both hands. She strode up and assured everybody that she could play the part, and, taking her for a man, they accepted her at once. Charlotte, knowing the Theatre of her day, demanded a guinea before going on, and they had no option but to pay her. She proved an excellent substitute and found, as many others have done, that one job leads to another. The manager of the theatre confided in her that he was sick of the venture and since he ran a troupe of strolling players, and was going back on the road, asked Charlotte if "he" would care to come along. Charlotte was very much in favour of the suggestion if "he" could bring his little "sister" along! The request was granted and so off with the strollers went Charlotte—now known as Charlie Brown—and her little daughter, to leave behind the importunate bailiffs, who had for too long cast an ugly shadow on her life.

But somehow Charlotte attracted misfortune and the untoward, and she was fated to engage in adventures that could have befallen nobody but herself. The strollers opened their show and Charlotte as "leading man" was an outstanding success—too much of a success, in fact, for a young lady, a heiress, who loved the play, came to see the show and left her heart behind, at the feet of "Mr. Brown." She was not to be rebuffed, either, and, confessing that she was head over heels in love with the handsome "actor," she threw aside all modesty and proposed marriage. Charlotte, however, was no gay deceiver and there was nothing to do but confess her masquerade. She revealed her identity to the girl and told her the story of her life. The two women had a good cry together and parted never to meet again, but this extraordinary incident appears to have embittered Charlotte more than any of the other strange events in her life. She felt that she, who had the mind and feelings of a man, had been cheated in being born a woman.

The show moved on to St. Albans, and there Charlotte heard that her father was to pay a visit to a great house in the vicinity. She knew his weaknesses, his inordinate desire to impress everybody by wearing his elegant best, glittering with jewellery, and with his purse full of guineas. There had been many reckless actions in Charlotte's life, but none as daring as this one she planned. She secured mask and pistol, borrowed or stole a horse, and held her father up on the road in the real manner of the High Toby, bidding him stand and deliver with the time-honoured alternative. Colley was not one to imperil his life and delivered, with admirable promptitude, all his money and valuables. But this did not satisfy Charlotte. She had her father get out of his coach and kneel down before her and it was then that she revealed that she was his daughter and bitterly and vehemently denounced his parental neglect and cruelty. She retained everything she had taken from him, for she knew that she not only possessed his purse but a story that would humble him to the dust, should it ever become public. Colley Cibber looked at his daughter with hatred and he certainly could hate, but he had at last met his match.

The strolling players disbanded and Charlotte took a job as valet to an Irish Lord, with whom she remained until he discovered her sex. He was horrified and got rid of her on the spot. Her next venture was the manufacture of sausages which nobody would buy, and it is more than likely that Charlotte dissipated on this ill-conceived scheme the last of the money she had looted from her father. In turn, she became a waiter at the King's Head Tavern in Marylebone, started her own troupe of strollers and then found herself reduced to starvation, albeit she starved as a man.

One of her relatives, an uncle, came to her aid when all seemed lost and set her up in a tavern hard by Drury Lane, but poor Charlotte was not fated to succeed and she was glad to take a job as a kind of property-man for a puppet show in what was then known as Hickford's Great Room, off Brewer Street. While the job lasted she got a guinea a day, but she was soon out of work again and hard up. To give Charlotte her due, though, she was willing to try anything, even to writing her autobiography, in which she made the most astonishing admissions without a thought of sparing herself. Her frankness and refusal to plead for sympathy told against her and helped to alienate the few friends she still possessed. On this occasion, when she did not know which way to turn for a shilling, she wrote her father the following letter:

> HONOURED SIR,—I doubt not you are sensible I last Sunday published the first number of a Narrative of my life, in which I made a proper concession into those unhappy miscarriages which have for many years justly deprived me of a father's fondness. As I am conscious of my errors, I thought I could not be too public in sueing for your blessing and pardon; and not only blush to think my youthful follies should draw so strong a compunction in my mind in the meridian of my days, which I might so easily have avoided. Be assured, Sir, I am perfectly convinced I was more than to blame, and that the hours of anguish I have felt have bitterly repaid me for the commission

of every indiscretion which was the unhappy motive of being so many years estranged from that happiness I now, as in my duty bound, most earnestly deplore. I shall, with your permission, Sir, send again to know if I may be admitted to throw myself at your feet and with sincere and filial transport, endeavour to convince you that I am, Honoured Sir,

Your truly penitent and dutiful daughter

CHARLOTTE CHARKE.

Her old father was then on his deathbed and he would probably have seen Charlotte, and given his blessing, but her elder sister intervened, and when Charlotte called for an answer there was none. She never saw her father and he died without being able to forgive her.

She was still battling with dire poverty and that year had written a novel which, by some means, she had got a publisher to look at. He must have thought something of it, for he deemed it worth while to go and see her and perhaps hear her read from it. She was then living, if it can be called that, in an appalling hovel in Islington, not far from the New River Head and at a spot where all the garbage was dumped. The approach to it was nearly knee deep in mud, and the publisher, who was accompanied by a friend, had to struggle through this morass to reach Charlotte's shelter.

The door was opened by a gaunt, ragged woman who quickly explained she was not Mrs. Charke and drew their attention to a figure seated on a broken chair crouching over a tiny fire before a wretched hearth. It was the authoress, back in female attire again, with a dog at her feet, as thin and starved as she herself was. On the back of her chair perched a magpie and on her lap was a pair of broken bellows which served as a writing desk. A pen worn to the stump and a broken cup containing ink made up her literary stock in trade. The visitors leaned against a three-legged bench and Charlotte began to read. Her voice was unimpaired and her indomitable spirit undefeated. When the reading came to an end, Charlotte gazed into the fire and there was silence. . . . Who could see into her heart or know the misery of forlorn hope? But she was not done with yet and she turned to the battle when the publisher enquired how much she wanted. "Thirty guineas," she replied without a moment's hesitation. The publisher looked at her and saw her stark poverty. "Five guineas," he said. Charlotte crouched deeper in her chair. She had savoured the bitter tang of disappointment all too often: she knew what to expect. But she would not have been the flaunting wearer of breeches, and old Cibber's daughter, if she had not put up a fight, so she pushed the price up guinea by guinea until she got the figure to ten pieces and then surrendered with a sigh.

That was not quite the end of Charlotte, for she appears to have secured some stage work afterwards and to have received a benefit in 1759 in which she is said to have played Marplot in *The Busybody* and worn breeches again. She was only fifty when she died on April 6, 1760, but she lived every moment of those unquiet years and mostly in breeches too.

No actress of greater modesty ever stepped on the stage than the daughter of Charles Macklin but like Charlotte Charke her weakness too was wearing breeches and the habit, sad to relate, proved her undoing, if that can be said without suggesting a *double entendre*. Macklin had married the widow of a Dublin haberdasher and taught her to become an actress. When the fiery Macklin became the father of a daughter he was not only determined to make a star out of her but a lady to boot. Both parents devoted themselves to this child and Macklin actually spent £1,200 on her education, an unheard of sum in those days. He would not have her sent to school until he felt she was safe enough to resist the temptations of a sordid world, and engaged expensive tutors, on whom he kept a watchful eye. He would have had no hesitation in killing anyone who sought to do her a mischief. Miss Macklin grew up to become a very accomplished girl and was able to speak French and Italian, paint and sketch and dance and sing. Her father launched her at Covent Garden in 1751 as Athenais in *Theodosius*. The girl did not set the Thames on fire, but audiences warmly welcomed her, particularly when she played Polly in *The Beggar's Opera* and Lucinda in *The Englishman in Paris*, which was tailor-made for her talents as a linguist and entertainer. But she was a minor star among the brilliant constellation of the stage, and the truth of the matter was that she had been too strictly brought up, and was a young lady first and an actress second. She was also religious and would sometimes miss a rehearsal because of her devotions. It was easy to bring the blush to her cheek, and when the talk became bawdy in the Green Room, as it nearly always did, she would take flight as quickly as a bird.

Yet for all her modesty, and sweet and unassuming character, she loved to don a pair of breeches and thus take the stage in male attire. Perhaps she inherited this trait from her father. Anyhow, it was breeches whenever possible and, since she had a pretty figure, and the nicest pair of legs imaginable, theatregoers found her attractive and came along to admire her. She was extremely particular about her appearance and wrinkled stockings, or breeches that sagged at the knees, were abhorrent to her, and she strapped them up so tightly that one of her legs began to swell just under the knee and caused her excruciating pain. A doctor was called in, but Miss Macklin, who didn't mind publicly exhibiting her legs swathed in hose, regarded with horror the prospect of one of her bare limbs being seen or handled by a male —it was an indignity not to be borne. Miss Macklin's excessive modesty finally killed her, for in the end she had to undergo an operation and she couldn't forget that masculine hands had been laid upon her and died at a comparatively early age, leaving her father to lament his loss until death, too, called him at the great age of 107.

The fate that befell poor Miss Macklin fitted into the tragicomedy of the eighteenth-century, a period of great individualism in the Theatre, in which players brought their own interpretations and stamped indelibly every play with their art. In a free and easy atmosphere the producer was eclipsed by custom, and it was not until Garrick began to insist on proper rehearsals, and word perfection, that discipline was at all exercised.

Garrick's influence on theatrical life was tremendous, for he knew too well that many players lived from hand to mouth and often died in penury. The Drury Lane Fund he founded exists even today and does good work and the greatest of the Theatrical Charities, the Royal General Theatrical Fund—so often unrecognised by those it is designed to serve—is a notable institution that maintains a fine tradition and encourages thrift in "the profession."

The bogus manager has always been a major curse to a precarious calling and although men of his kidney are not so numerous as they once were, the breed has not been entirely stamped out. In the old days salaries, as often as not, were in arrears and poor players found it hard to live. Few could have been reduced, however, to the straits of a Mrs. Burden, a sound actress of the second rank who lived in the eighteenth century. She had the misfortune at one time to work for Mossop, a weird character who was an erratic actor and an extremely bad manager. He was always hard up and his company suffered with him. In 1764 he was running a season in Dublin and doing as badly as ever. Despite his poverty, he imitated his betters in the theatre by holding a levee in his quarters, when callers were admitted to his presence, although such visitors had to fight their way through a crowd of tradesmen angrily pressing for the money that was owed to them.

Mrs. Burden was pretty desperate for she was to play Andromache in *The Distressed Mother* on the following day and she, too, was in debt and in distress since she had not received her salary for several weeks. She forced her way into Mossop's sanctum and, determined to give her employer a real performance "in character," threw herself at his feet and cried, "Oh sir. For God's sake assist me. I am starving and shall be turned out into the street." Mossop knew all about her plight, but brazenly reminded her that her salary was £5 a week. "Wo-man," he said, "you have five pounds a week." It was true only on paper and, thinking to rally him as an artist, she asked him how she could play Andromache without possessing a pair of black satin shoes. He must know it was unthinkable. But Mossop was not to be caught this way and thundered: "Wo-man begone. I insist on Andromache wearing black satin shoes." Poor Mrs. Burden fled when Mossop had the temerity to threaten her with the forfeiture of £10 should she dare importune him for her salary again.

They were a hardy race, those early actresses. They dragged themselves from town to town and village to village and brought up their families as best they could. All too often on the verge of starvation, they played on. They could never afford to be ill. Perhaps the palm for an example of doggedness goes to a company that arrived back from America and decided to stay in

Portsmouth, there for a time to restore their depleted finances. Transatlantic travelling was no luxury in those days, for the players crossed by cargo boats, taking their own scanty rations with them and suffered from every vagary of the weather. Among the company was a Mrs. Osborne, and when the company opened she played the lead in a piece called *The Mourning Bride*. The first four acts proceeded smoothly, but in the fifth the leading lady missed her entrance and the curtain came down in a hurry. After a brief delay the manager appeared in front to beg the audiences kind indulgence. Mrs. Osborne, he explained, having made her last exit, had just given birth to a child, and as certain arrangements had to be made the play would be continued with the minimum delay. The story goes that the young mother was able to return and complete her part, which sounds incredible, but who would say that the theatre is not the place where the seemingly impossible so often happens?

CHAPTER SIXTEEN

Kind Hearts and Coronets

ON the frosty morning of Christmas Day, 1769, and much too early for the good citizens of Salisbury to be astir, a little boy stood in the market place of that ancient city and watched the approach of a young girl carrying on her head an earthenware bowl and moving with great caution on the slippery road. But dexterous as she was, she found she could go no further and, stopping, gazed around her in despair. Her dilemma aroused the chivalry of the little boy, who at once ran towards her to give her a helping hand, but mistimed his approach and almost fell with her. They clutched at each other despairingly, managed to stave off disaster, and then, with the ease of the very young, at once became friends.

The little girl, pinched and cold in threadbare clothes, confided that her name was Elizabeth Farren and that she was on her way to the lock-up to give her father (who had been accommodated there on account of his Yuletide celebrations) his breakfast of a bowl of milk. The boy went along with her and lifted her up in his arms so that she could call through the window of the detention cell to her father, who told her he would be home in time for Christmas dinner, whatever that was in their poverty-stricken home.

It is heartening to know that the little boy in this story prospered exceedingly and became a Chief Justice. As for the little girl, well, she became one of England's best loved actresses and the heroine of a romance that defied time and temptation and in the end made her a Countess of Derby.

Elizabeth's father was a jovial drunk who left the responsibility of rearing his two daughters to his harassed wife. He had been an apothecary in Cork before joining a troupe of players and trailing all over Ireland with them and leading a wretched existence. He turned up in Liverpool eventually and getting a job on the stage did fairly well, although often beginning a performance sober and ending up tipsy. On one occasion when he was well in his cups actor Farren had to declare his intention of tearing up a letter, but he was suffering from multiple vision and made several unsuccessful grabs at the document. When finally he was able to seize it he was not too far gone to be able to realise that he was incapable of his simple task, so altered the line to "And thus, I throw the letter away," which saved the situation, more or less.

A great lapper-up of beer, Farren not surprisingly married a barmaid and then left Liverpool to tour the country. In his more sober moments he fancied himself as a poet and made a habit of scratching his verses on window panes. They were not bad at all, and one of them read:

How different David's fate from mine
His blessed, mine is evil.
His shepherd was the Lord Divine
My shepherd is the Devil.

Whether Mrs. Farren unshipped her husband or became a widow is not known, but she found times difficult for her and put her two girls, Margaret and Elizabeth, with a company of strollers. Elizabeth was a fair, blue-eyed girl who played boy roles in Shakespeare. The players would as often as not have to carry the scenery and wardrobe on their backs, and Elizabeth is said to have beaten the drum with which the company announced its presence.

Later the fortunes of the Farren family improved, for Elizabeth secured a regular job at the Wakefield Theatre and, although still only a child, played Columbine so charmingly, and sang so prettily, that she became a favourite with her audiences. Younger, who ran the theatre at Liverpool, was much taken with her and decided to give her a chance. The family moved with her, and on her fifteenth birthday she played Rosetta in *Love in a Village*, which was the first of many successes she notched in Liverpool.

They did not turn the girl's head either and there was no question of becoming a star overnight, for she was still immature and had a lot to learn. Under Younger's guidance, and her mother's watchful eye, Elizabeth worked hard for four years in every type of role imaginable, but it was not until 1777 that Younger judged that his protégée was ready to be introduced to the critical folk of London. He told George Colman of the Haymarket Theatre about her and could not have done better, for Colman was ever on the look-out for new talent and did not mind taking a chance with an unknown player. The Haymarket had been the first to introduce many players who were to catch the public fancy, Mrs. Powell, Henderson, Elliston (The Great Lessee), to mention only a few.

Elizabeth, now a tall, willowy girl, certainly not ravishingly beautiful, but with a most expressive face across which the moods of her role would ripple like a breeze ruffling the surface of a pool, made her Haymarket début as Kate Hardcastle in *She Stoops to Conquer*, and London at once recognised her for the fine actress she undoubtedly was. There was, of course, some criticism over her first appearance, but nothing serious, certainly nothing that could not be eliminated by a little extra polish and the correction of certain youthful faults. Elizabeth lacked neither vivacity nor sparkle, and although slightly marked by smallpox, was still attractive enough to command the attention of those with an eye for a charming girl.

Her mother, however, would allow no undue trespassing, not that she feared any indiscretion by her daughter, who had served her apprenticeship in the rackety company of strolling players and had a keen regard for respectability. Her salary was still very small and she knew that only by improving her acting could she hope to earn more. She and her mother occupied quite humble lodgings in Suffolk Street, just round the corner from the Haymarket Theatre, and lynx-eyed Mrs. Farren not only scared the wolves away, but saw to it that Elizabeth remained healthy enough to cope with the hard work she was called upon to do, constant new roles, daily rehearsals and nightly performances.

Mrs. Farren's greatest concern was to see that Elizabeth ate regularly, but in the midst of rehearsals it was not always possible for the girl to slip home for the meal that her mother had ready for her. And that was how Colman came to give Mrs. Farren the nickname of "The Pocket." At rehearsal one day Colman became aware of the savoury odour of cooked meat and traced it to Mrs. Farren, whom he found had had a special pocket made under her voluminous skirt. The pocket was lined with tin and this enabled her to carry about with her a good solid meal for her daughter, something that was really warm, nutritious and comforting. Colman could not help but admire a woman who was so very obviously the best of mothers, but ever afterwards Mrs. Farren was always "The Pocket" to him.

Among Elizabeth's most ardent admirers was no less a person than Charles James Fox, who became one of the greatest parliamentary figures of his generation, and but for his intemperate habits might have become Prime Minister. This elegantly bred *bon viveur* not only refrained from making Elizabeth improper proposals, but, by his conduct, showed that he probably contemplated proposing to her. He had, of course, never seen her in anything but the full skirts and flowing draperies that women then wore and he was among the audience that night when Elizabeth appeared in breeches for the first time, in the leading role of a new comedy called *The Suicide*. Unluckily for Elizabeth, she had neither the figure nor the legs for breeches, and Fox was horrified at the poor figure she cut. "Damn me," he said disgustedly to a friend, "she has no prominence either before or behind. All is a straight line from head to foot. And look at her legs, they are shaped like a sugar-loaf." Fox could never forgive Elizabeth for shattering his illusions and he would have nothing more to do with her.

Despite her legs, Elizabeth got to Drury Lane in 1778, for it was an age of youth at that theatre and none of the leading ladies there exceeded twenty years, with the exception of the redoubtable Mrs. Abington, who was the girl's closest rival. When Elizabeth appeared as Lady Townley the public forgot what she had looked like in breeches and closely followed her battle for supremacy.

The playing of tragedy was beyond Elizabeth. Her *métier* was unquestionably comedy, and from 1778, until she left the stage, she played only at Drury Lane, except for an occasional performance at the Haymarket. When Mrs. Abington went to Covent Garden Elizabeth reigned supreme and she was its leading lady when Sheridan opened the third building, also fated to be unlucky. In the prologue she spoke occurred these lines:

The very ravages of fire we flout,
For we have wherewithal to put it out.
In ample reservoirs our firm reliance
When streams set conflagrations at defiance.

To illustrate this jingle a property man then strode onto the stage, hammer in hand, and smote hard at the curtain that hung behind Miss Farren. Greatly to the astonishment of the audience, they realised it was made of iron, and it was indeed the first safety curtain ever seen. When it ascended it was revealed that the stage had been converted into a lake upon which boats were being rowed. From the "flies" a great cascade of water splashed into it. The year was 1794 and Drury Lane appeared to be safe from fire at last, but in 1809 the theatre went up in flames, all this water notwithstanding.

Elizabeth had a narrow escape there herself, for in brushing against a sconce one of the candles ignited the gauze of her dress and before she had realised the danger one of her fellow players, an excellent actor named Jack Bannister, whipped off his cloak and threw it over her and beat out the flames with his hands. Elizabeth probably owed her life to this split-second thinking.

It is not to be supposed at this period of her career that Elizabeth had not her detractors, but they were hard put to give any weight to their criticism. Success often provokes enmity and the scandal-mongers looked hungrily around for something with which to destroy the girl's reputation for virtue. But she had led a clean and wholesome life and was not to be besmirched by idle and vicious tongues. They tried to make capital from her carefulness with money and then they whispered that she was a snob who sought the company of high society. The truth of the matter is that Elizabeth was immensely popular with the quality, in whose company her impeccable behaviour was greatly admired, and she was the same girl in a salon as she was on the stage. She had found an influential friend in the Duchess of Leinster, and when society became engrossed in amateur theatricals it was Elizabeth who helped to organise these entertainments.

Among all the men who vainly sought her favours Elizabeth liked none better than the Earl of Derby, and it was at an entertainment given by the Duke of Richmond that she reached an understanding with him. The Earl was eager to possess Elizabeth, for he was greatly in love with her, but he had a wife, and she was the barrier that stood between them. On no account would Elizabeth enter into an irregular relationship, even though Derby's wife was a confirmed invalid, living in retirement and a spouse in name only. Only by marriage could the Earl make Elizabeth his own, and until that was possible they agreed to an intimate, but platonic, friendship. They became lovers without giving themselves to each other, and moral rectitude was the basis of their association.

Every morning without fail the Earl sent his servant to Miss Farren's lodgings to enquire after her health and the messenger had to be ready to inform His Lordship of her condition, and how she had slept, the moment he awoke. Never did their affection for each other wilt, and their understanding survived twenty years of waiting, for it was not until March, 1797, that the Earl's wife gave up the ghost and left him free to marry his matchlessly virtuous Elizabeth. The Earl and his beloved, having set for all time a pattern to all lovers, at once started making arrangements for their wedding and on April 7 of that year Elizabeth made her farewell stage appearance by playing Lady Teazle. The theatre was packed for the occasion, for everybody knew the story of Elizabeth and her Earl—their idealised romance and devotion to each other. Elizabeth was her stylish and brilliant best, but as the play drew to its end, and she spoke the last lines of the part that were indeed so apt to the occasion, she began to falter and suddenly dissolved into a flood of tears. She was leaving everything for a greater love, but she still loved the Theatre and her work.

Sir Peter Teazle came to her help, but she was still sobbing when the epilogue was spoken and the house rose to its feet to wish her luck. It was while the cheering was still sweeping the theatre that the Earl stepped on to the stage to take the arm of his weeping bride-to-be and lead her away. Sheridan met them in the Green Room and, kissing the hand of Elizabeth, said, "God bless you; Lady Teazle is no more and *The School for Scandal* is broken up for the holiday." Rumour says that Elizabeth responded by asking him to refund some fines he had imposed, but there was apparently nothing doing.

Elizabeth was thirty-eight when she became the Countess of

Derby, and she was married by special licence on May 1, 1797. Her honeymoon, spent at Epsom, lasted only two days, as she was anxious to be received at Court. She got her wish, although it was not customary for actresses to be thus honoured, even if married to a peer. The story goes that when Elizabeth appeared before the Queen she was possessed with an overwhelming desire to talk, and told Her Majesty that she felt the most blissful moment of her life had come in being accorded the honour of appearing before Her Majesty in a new "character part." The Queen was not amused and, staring at the actress, said, "Cannot your Ladyship forget her breeding?" an ungracious remark that might well cause doubt as to the breeding of the Royal Lady herself. The Countess took this rebuff like a thoroughbred, but from that moment the stage became a closed chapter in her life and she never spoke of it again.

Elizabeth never forgot how much she owed to her mother's devotion, and when she and her husband took up residence in Grosvenor Square Mrs. Farren joined them. As if to rebut the Queen's rebuke, Elizabeth took her mother with her everywhere and never disguised the pride she felt for her. She was an exceptional wife in every way and presented her husband with three children, one son and two daughters. Elizabeth's son could not inherit the title, because that went to the Earl's son by his first marriage, but it made no difference to the Earl and Countess of Derby, for they lived a life of perfect wedded bliss, with not a cloud on the horizon. Elizabeth Farren, daughter of an actor and a barmaid, and once a stroller, who stepped from obscurity to become one of the most popular actresses of her day, died at the age of seventy in 1829, at Knowsley, the county seat of the Earls of Derby. Her husband survived her by five years.

The ambition to act can burn in the most unexpected breast and if a Drury Lane grocer had not felt the impelling call of the Theatre perhaps one of the most charming romances between the stage and the peerage would never have been realised. The grocer in question was a certain Mr. Brunton who had come to London from Norwich, where he had been a soap-dealer. He dabbled awhile in rice, treacle, sugar and spice, and in the midst of it caught stage fever, so that in 1774 he played at Covent Garden, even to appearing as Hamlet. He was not a man, though, to allow his ambitions to outrun his ability, and having the good sense to realise that he was not just good enough, returned to Norwich. But his affection for the Theatre remained undimmed, and eventually he secured control of all those theatres in what was then known as the Norwich Circuit.

Brunton was the father of eight children, two boys and six girls, and his youngest daughter was Louisa, who was born in 1785. She was a striking little personality even as a child and she grew up to be a bewitchingly lovely creature with that rare grace without which beauty becomes only skin deep. Louisa had brains, too, and compensated for her father's lack of histrionic power by displaying stage talent that promised a brilliant future. After a good, solid provincial training, she went to Covent Garden and played Lady Townly and later Beatrice in *Much Ado About Nothing*. London playgoers took her to their hearts for her acting, not less than for her looks.

Miss Brunton was nobody's fool, for she had been happily brought up in a decent family, and, although she found that the men flocked round her, she kept her head and kept all-comers at a distance all very charmingly. Virtue again met its due reward, for Viscount Uffington of the County of Berkshire and Earl of Craven of the County of Yorkshire, a double peer, who had been A.D.C. to the King, was lately back from the wars with the rank of Major-General and saw Louisa queening it on the stage. He knew this was one conquest he must make at all costs.

He evidently believed in a frontal attack and at once proposed marriage to Louisa, who, being a dutiful daughter, said he might speak to her papa. Mr. Brunton could see no valid objection, and the lovely Louisa went to the altar in 1807, when she was twenty-two, with a bridegroom who was fifteen years her senior. They made as handsome a couple as one could wish to see. Of course, it was the end of Louisa's stage career and in 1815, the year of Waterloo, she had the honour—if honour it were—of being hostess to the Prince Regent at her husband's country seat in Warwickshire. Ever the dutiful wife, Louisa gave her husband three sons and a daughter. The Earl and Countess of Craven were indeed a very happy couple, and it was a thousand pities that their delight in each other was summarily ended by the death of the

Earl, from gout, at Cowes, Isle of Wight, ten years after their marriage. Louisa, ever gracious and charming, lived to the fine old age of seventy-eight and her death in 1860 was deeply felt by the many friends she had made, and kept, throughout her lifetime.

Yet another actress to find happiness with a husband acknowledged by *Debrett* was Mary Bolton, born in 1790 at 100 Long Acre, over the premises of Windover's, the famous coachmakers. Her father was an attorney and shared his wife's liking for music and the theatre and, almost as soon as the child could walk and talk, she was being tutored for the stage, especially for the lyric stage. Mary, pretty and with a lilting voice, was only sixteen when she appeared at Covent Garden as Polly in John Gay's famous light opera, and during that season she played the role on fourteen occasions. It was a heady success for a girl of her tender years, but before she had time to get any false notions about herself the end of the season arrived and the end of her engagement. It was disappointing, but she was soon re-engaged, although at a smaller salary. The step down didn't discourage Mary, for she was a courageous young woman who braced herself for hard work and hoped for the best. She was never in the first flight of players, but Harris, then running Covent Garden, was pleased with her progress and both raised her salary and gave her a five-year contract. She was a good singer of oratorio and her services were in demand by a choral society in Liverpool.

In the company of Kemble, she played Ariel in *The Tempest* and Ophelia in *Hamlet* and, without being an inspired performer, she was nevertheless adequate to her parts. Her "fate" appeared in the person of Edward Howell Thurlow, son of a divine who was Dean of St. Paul's before becoming the Bishop of Durham. Actually Edward Thurlow became Baron Thurlow in 1806, the year of Mary's stage début. He was a rather solemn young man who was born with a golden spoon, and he rather fancied himself as a poet. Anyhow, it must be admitted that he displayed excellent taste and judgment when he fell passionately in love with Mary Bolton, a graceful girl, extremely fair and appealing. They married on November 13, 1813, and the double thirteen evidently brought them luck, for they lived in perfect harmony and content. Related to the Lord Chancellor, the Baron Thurlow had long enjoyed sinecures heaped upon him, with which excellent emoluments he had not a financial care in the world. He was able to publish five volumes of poetry and write for *The Gentleman's Magazine*, while Mary managed his domestic affairs and became the mother of three sons. After sixteen years the marriage came to an end with the death of Baron Thurlow at Brighton in 1829. Little Miss Bolton that was, Lady Thurlow as she became, followed her husband to the grave within twelve months, at the early age of forty.

When Kitty Stephens, who became the Countess of Essex, was an earnest young pupil, whose brilliant future was unguessed even by those aware of the thrilling promise of her lovely soprano voice, a professor of music fell in love with her. He was one of her teachers, and her family, particularly her father, a carver and gilder in Park Street, Grosvenor Square, thought it an excellent match and readily gave his consent when his daughter's hand was asked for. Kitty's objections to the proposal were overruled, very persuasively, of course, and the day came when the eager groom stood awaiting his bride at the altar for a ceremony many had assembled to watch. Kitty, a beautiful but unsmiling bride, was led up the aisle on the arm of her proud papa and came at last to a halt. It seemed all over bar the congratulations, but when Kitty was asked to stand by the man she was to take for better or worse, etc., etc., she looked at him almost in surprise, gave a girlish giggle that finished up as a peal of laughter and, gathering her skirts, turned and sprinted down the aisle and out of the church to the street that led to her home. Neither the cajoling or the tearful expostulations of her mother could persuade her to return to the church to accept the bonds of holy matrimony, and so the wedding had, reluctantly, to be called off.

Kitty, who was born Catherine Stephens on September 18, 1794, and made her theatrical début at Covent Garden when she was nineteen, was, to give her her due, always more interested in music than men. She had a voice that was pure soprano and she disciplined herself as only the real artist can, for she would practise anything from eight to ten hours a day. Her stage appearance was an immediate success and when she played Polly and then Rosetta in *Love in a Village* her name was on everybody's lips.

She sang at Covent Garden for seven years and was held to be the peer of Catalini and Mrs. Billington, the supreme singers of their day. A great singer of ballads, Kitty commanded even the admiration of her rivals and Mrs. Billington, in a generous eulogy, said Kitty sang some songs as they would never be sung again. She also played at Drury Lane between 1823 and 1827 and though concert singing suited her best the crowds followed wherever she went. It is recorded that one man attended for fifteen years every performance at which she sang. He would wait for the pit doors to open and rush in to secure his favourite seat, in the middle of the third row. There he sat silent and enchanted until the show was over, when he would make a wild dash to see Kitty leave. Having seen her drive off in her carriage, he himself would vanish. He followed her everywhere, even when she went to Dublin to sing. He never attempted to approach or speak to her, and was content to admire her from a respectable distance. Although the poor fellow ended up in an asylum, he was not too mad to be enthralled by a beautiful voice.

Kitty was a handsome and attractive woman who led a blameless life. Men were drawn to her, but it was a one-way traffic and she is said to have refused the marriage offers of a Lord and also a Duke. Perhaps that early escape deterred her, but she finally surrendered, when she was an extremely well-to-do woman of forty-four and still able to command her public. There was no question of love on her part, for she married, in his eighty-first year, the Earl of Essex, an octogenarian who had buried his wife a few months previously. Kitty was wed on April 18, 1838, and she settled her own considerable means on her relations and was amply compensated by her husband. He died the following year, but Kitty was satisfied to remain a widow. As the Dowager Countess of Essex she became a popular hostess and society figure and entertained at her home at 9 Belgrave Square. She retained her interest and affection for her old profession and, quite remarkably, her good looks. She died in 1882 and was buried in Kensal Green.

Most men will, particularly if they happen to be on the wrong side of fifty, forgive beauty its failings, and this was the case when Lord Harrington married beautiful Maria Foote and made her his Countess. Heaven alone knows he needed all his charity to forget, for his wife had engaged in many torrid affairs, which were apparently known to everybody, including his Lordship. Maria was very, very lovely, with luxuriant light brown hair, the most eloquent blue eyes and a perfect figure which the art of deportment had enhanced. She was the daughter of Samuel Foote, who claimed descent from the English actor and dramatist whose caricature comedies had inspired his admirers to call him the English Aristophanes.

Maria's father was not eminent, but was an odd character and was in theatrical management when he launched his daughter whose attractiveness was obvious to the audiences at Covent Garden in 1814. She was then very young, but not at all inexperienced in the ways of the world. Her father was not above a bit of blackmail. It so happened that a gentleman named Haynes, who rejoiced in the nickname of "Pea Green" for obvious reasons, fell in love with Maria but was unaware that she had been living with a Colonel Berkeley and had borne him a child. He was rash enough to confide his feelings to her father, who explained that he would have been enchanted but Maria happened to be engaged to Berkeley. Haynes thought he still had a chance and invited Mr. Samuel Foote down to his country home and there Maria's father, while negotiating a "loan" for £1,150 from his host, who was certainly living up to his nickname, promised to do what he could to advance his cause. He persuaded his daughter to entertain Mr. Haynes and although the girl was anxious to confess to her new suitor her relationship with Berkeley, her father told her to keep a still tongue. But Haynes met Colonel Berkeley and was told the truth. Even then his infatuation was as ardent as ever and he asked Maria to marry him and hand the children—they were now plural—over to the Colonel, who had promised to look after them. Maria did so but by then Haynes had had time to reflect and called off the arrangement. So Maria, doubtless inspired by her father, brought an action for breach of promise and the case became a *cause célèbre*. Haynes had been indiscreet enough to write many letters of devotion, containing offers of marriage, and the cards were stacked against him The plaintiff failed to get all she claimed, a cool £10,000, but she was awarded £3,000.

Maria was then appearing in *The Belle's Stratagem* and every line of the play was considered by the public to relate to her court action and applauded or hissed as the occasion warranted. It was very heartening to Maria who was a great favourite, but Haynes could not keep away from the theatre and was spotted hiding in a box. Maria saucily began to sing "Where are You going to, My Pretty Maid?" and when she reached the line "I cannot marry you" she brought the house down.

Five years later Maria married fifty-one-year-old Lord Harrington, a tall, handsome man who had seen military service and had been a leader of the bucks in society and was certainly no innocent wandering abroad. He spoke with a lisp, had two great passions—snuff-boxes for every occasion, and tea. Maria, despite her reputation, was his ideal of womanhood and he lived very happily with her for twenty years until he died in 1851. They had one daughter. His Lordship left a vast amount of his personal possessions lying around, suits, canes, tea caddies and snuff-boxes. The firm of Fribourg and Treyer—still in the Haymarket—sent part of their staff to assess the snuff-boxes and their contents. Maria survived until she was seventy and she might have become the wife of Haynes, or "Pea Green," if the holder of that unenviable title had not heard her father boasting that he was a pigeon for the plucking and a real chump.

CHAPTER SEVENTEEN

Perdita and the Prince

LEAVING the peeresses, pure and (perhaps not so) simple, for the time being, the stage must be cleared for the appearance of some other great actresses, who have claims to the precedence of "ladies first." The fact that none of them was of exalted birth is apparently in the true tradition of theatrical success on the distaff side. Foremost amongst this new galaxy shines the name of the woman who left her mark upon theatrical annals in many ways but whose greatest impression was on the first playbill of a comedy produced at Theatre Royal, Drury Lane on May 8, 1777. The line on that bill, which contains so many famous names and an original of which now hangs above the present writer's table (the name he bears is on it too)—the line on that bill which matters at the moment is one which reads "And Mrs. Abington." For Mrs. Abington, born Frances Barton, will ever be remembered as the creator of the leading lady's role in that immortal comedy of manners *The School for Scandal.* Richard Brinsley Sheridan, its author, wrote it for her when she was at the height of her fame, but it must be recorded that she reached fame the hard way. Her father was an ex-soldier of the Guards, who, when his daughter was born, was cobbling shoes in Windmill Street, where he had a stall. Her brother was a hostler and a waterer of horses, performing that lowly if useful function for the steeds of the Hampstead stage, at the corner of Hanway Street, near where the famous hostelry "The Horseshoe" now stands. The mother died when little Fanny—her baptismal name was Frances but everyone called this little motherless girl Fanny—was just fourteen. There was no normal childhood for her, no time for play; poverty gripped the little family and she had to work, earning what she could, getting a few coppers here and there selling flowers. They nicknamed the pretty little thing "Nosegay Fan." She would sing or even recite in the various taverns, which was early evidence of her natural bent, and now and again she actually managed to get the proprietors of the more important coffee-houses, the meeting-places of wit, fashion and money, to allow her to entertain the quality therein.

Then she became apprentice to a French milliner in Cockspur Street, and she was quick to observe the great ladies who came to buy. She learned some French and she also learned about dress—above all how to dress herself to the best advantage, which was something to stand her in very good stead later on. Then for a time she was a servant in the house of old Robert Baddeley, the pastry-cook-actor who bequeathed the famous cake to Drury Lane, and it is an irony of fate that years later when she was the queen of *The School for Scandal*, Baddeley played Moses to his erstwhile cook-maid's star role.

There is an uncanny similarity between her career and that of Nell Gwynne, for both started in the depths, both queened it at Old Drury, both had many lovers, though Fanny Barton never had a king whose dying words breathed her name. . . .

Fanny Barton rose above the circumstances of her lowly environment and in her early struggles she was fortunate to find one avenue of advancement open to her, a profession which takes people at their own valuation, and one for which she knew she had an aptitude—the stage. She had got to know Theophilus Cibber, that bad son of a great father, brother of Charlotte Charke and husband of Susanna Maria. How they became acquainted, to what lengths the acquaintance ran, is irrelevant. The important point is that he offered "Nosegay Fan" the part of Miranda in *The Busybody*—to play opposite him as Marplot. Though she knew little about stage-craft, and was scared, Cibber coached her with such determination and patience that she was ready to step on to the Haymarket stage on August 21, 1755, and it has to be recorded that on that August evening a new light shone on the English stage. This young, inexperienced girl conquered at her first attempt. The audience rose to its feet and cheered her to the echo. Critics, professional and self-appointed, beaux *en route* for the coffee-houses and gossip, rushed round to praise and congratulate her, and though she was both frightened and bewildered she knew she had made good. Cunning Theophilus rubbed his oily hands with glee. This was indeed a scoop! Everyone predicted big things for this pretty girl, with which he agreed, and did not hesitate to mention that he had found her, which of course, he had. He had discovered what is called a "natural"! They are few and far between, but Frances Barton—Frances Abington to be—certainly was one. David Garrick was another.

From triumph to triumph went she who once was called "Nosegay Fan." At the end of her performance as Desdemona, Shuter, representing the management of the Bath Theatre, then the centre of fashion, the show-place of England, offered her an engagement and with hesitation she went to Bath, and there she conquered too. Lacy, who was later to be Garrick's partner, engaged her for the Lane itself. Truly this was a meteoric rise the like of which had seldom been known.

She played first at Drury Lane on October 29, 1756, being announced as a young lady appearing for the first time, a little theatrical fiction that was quite usual and not altogether false, since the management were careful not to say in such cases, "for the first time on any stage." It was a sort of alibi: if the aspirant succeeded, all was fine; if she failed, it mattered little—no names no pack drill! Frances Barton played Lady Pliant in *The Double Dealer*, and now this young and obviously inexperienced (theatrically speaking) girl was up really against something big, for in the cast were Mrs. Pritchard and Kitty Clive, two great stars who were hardly likely to let any young novice get away with too much. Nevertheless, the girl made a very tolerable début, even by the Lane's standards, and when later she played Lucy in *The Virgin Unmasked* her name was duly announced and she did well. Ambitious Frances began to get some education, improved her smattering of French, took elocution and singing lessons for which she paid out of her meagre salary. Perhaps the music lessons did not cost her much, for she was tutored by Mr. James Abington, a handsome man of military bearing, who had been a Royal Trumpeter and whom she married in 1759 when she was barely 21. The marriage was not happy, for they were both highly strung, temperamental people, he very jealous of his attractive young wife and the attention she received from men. He bullied her, but she had courage, high spirits and independence of mind needing no husband to lean upon. So the marriage ended in a legal separation, she undertaking to pay him a kind of pension, in return for which he promised not to molest her and both kept their bargain. He drew his money for many years but is lost to sight. She took his name, kept it and made it famous.

Mrs. Abington, as she was now known, left Drury Lane at the end of the 1758-9 season and went to Dublin, the happy hunting ground for those in search of Thespian fame. She was a big success, but she had to battle hard. She played Kitty in *High Life Below Stairs*, at the benefit of Tate Wilkinson and thenceforth she blazed across the life of Dublin like an electric flash. The house raved over her and the very next day she was the talk of the town, the rage of Dublin, London's rival in the art of the Theatre. Playgoers flocked to see her and it was then that her inspired taste in dress, which she had learnt as an apprentice to the French milliner, came to her aid. She set the fashion; whatever she wore became the mode. The hat she wore as Kitty was copied by all women who would be in the fashion . . . the Abington cap filled all the milliner's windows. She was uncrowned Queen of Dublin, and her own benefit was an amazing affair that brought her in a shower of guineas. Mrs Abington remained in Dublin for five years playing alternately at both the Smock Alley and Crow St. Theatres, and the crowds followed her from one to the other. An Abington night meant a packed house at increased prices. She could do no wrong, for indeed she was an excellent actress and a superb player of comedy. All the while she constantly improved herself, finding out her faults and correcting them. She even checked her tendency towards a harsh squeak in moments of emotion—like Peg Woffington's, and although Peg never got over it, Frances Abington conquered it. She had some mannerisms which charmed, particularly a gesture with her wrist towards her waist—a fascinating little trick which delighted her audiences. And she was a past-mistress at the art of handling a fan, at a time when fans were as essential to women as handbags are today. Her diction was perfection. Would that the younger players of today could realise what an asset that is to a stage career!

David Garrick, who missed nothing, alive to what this former odd-job girl at Drury Lane had achieved, decided it was time she came to him at Old Drury, so he offered her an engagement at Theatre Royal in 1765, at a salary of £5 a week.

He put her on as The Widow Belmour in *The Way to Keep Him*, broad comedy which was just her meat. She played it on November 27, 1765, and she scored as big a triumph as Old Drury Lane had ever witnessed. She played it off and on for over twenty-five years for playgoers could never have enough of it.

Always up against the impressions made by Mrs. Pritchard, Mrs. Porter, Peg Woffington, Kitty Clive, Susanna Maria Cibber, George Anne Bellamy and the rest, Mrs. Abington did not find it roses all the way but she was a great individualist, bringing something new to her renderings, some touch of her own, little flashes of novelty and freshness that captivated her audiences. Perhaps because of her early environment she shone in the parts of ladies risen from humbler degree, such as Lady Teazle. She was a Queen of Old Drury as she had been a Queen of Dublin, and in her private life she kept up great style, setting the fashions for London as she had for Dublin. Let her import a petticoat from Paris and as soon as possible every woman with any claim to be in the fashion was wearing the like. Mrs. Abington, greatly daring, had her hair powdered red instead of white and in a day or two the streets of London were packed with red-headed ladies of fashion.

In the theatre she was "difficult" when she got to power. She put on airs, which, may be, was natural for one who has risen to fame the hard way, but she should have known better, for she was very intelligent. She was always a headache to Garrick, whom she never really trusted, believing that he had kept her back when young. As the years advanced, so did her tantrums, and she wrote long letters to Garrick, like Kitty Clive did—but with all Kitty's temper, she was amusing, whereas Mrs. Abington was overbearing and abusive. There is an endorsement on one of her letters in Garrick's own handwriting: "The above is a true copy of a letter of that worst of bad women, Mrs. Abington." On another occasion he referred to her as "Mother Abington"—probably getting some personal satisfaction out of that. She was still at the Lane when he retired, remaining there until 1782, when she went to Covent Garden as Lady Flutter in *The Discovery*. She made a great hit and a new dress she wore caused just as great a sensation.

Through all this time she had steered clear of scandal though there had been an *affaire* with a Mr. Needham under whose protection she lived for some years. He kept the unruly crowd of licentious admirers at bay, and they lived in great affection and respectability, apart from the lack of wedlock. When his health broke down she nursed him, being by his side right up to his death.

She was received everywhere and great ladies consulted her on questions of dress. Dr. Johnson, who thought highly of her, visited her often, immensely enjoying the fare she provided. He once told another hostess who was trying to lionise him, that Mrs. Abington's jellies were better than hers! He went to one of her benefits and unable to find a good seat perched himself at a point from which he could neither see nor hear. A few nights later a wag asked him if he had enjoyed the performance. "Did you see?" queried the man. "No, sir," said Johnson. "Did you hear?" "No, sir." "Why, then, did you go?" asked the persistent questioner. "Because, sir," thundered Johnson, "she is a favourite of the public, and when the public cares a thousandth part for you that it does for her, I will go to your benefit, too."

Mrs. Abington left the stage for some years—from 1790 until 1797—coming back, under pressure, to appear at a charity performance at Covent Garden, and such was the pleasure of the public at her reappearance that she returned as a regular performer once more. She kept on as long as she could but she made no formal farewell, just slipping quietly out of things. Her last actual stage appearance was for the benefit of her old friend and colleague, Jane Pope, on April 12, 1799. She lived in various places, according to her decreasing means—in Southampton Street, Strand, in Leicester Fields, now Leicester Square, and in Clarges Street, Piccadilly, and in 1807 she had but two rooms at 19 Eaton Square. Though never in want—she had a fixed allowance under the will of her *bon ami*, Needham—her craze for gambling always kept her short of ready money. She died at 62 Pall Mall in 1815, and was buried in St. James's Church, Piccadilly, her age being given variously as seventy-seven or seventy-eight. She who was a queen of the stage had come a long way since the days of tavern singing and selling nosegays in the streets.

Compared with Frances Abington, the story of Mary Anne

Robinson is in sharp contrast. Mrs. Abington put her faith in nobody but herself; Mary Anne Robinson, ignoring the Biblical exhortation, put her faith in princes—at least in one, a Prince—and suffered for it. This actress, born at Bristol in 1758, was of Irish descent, the family name, originally Macdermott, having been changed to Darby. She was proud of her ancestry, claiming descent from Locke, the philosopher, and also that she was related to Benjamin Franklin. One of a big family, she was apparently the plainest of the lot, she herself recording that she was dark and swarthy, whereas the others were fair, that she had eyes too large for her small round face and that her expression was sad and melancholy. She was a very precocious child, could read at a very early age and recite much poetry, she learnt music easily and sang sweetly. At finishing school she did little else but write plays and verses, and one tragedy from her pen so impressed her dancing master that he got her introduced to Garrick, who heard her recite and promised her a job on the stage, but her mother would not hear of it.

She grew more attractive, and when she was only thirteen, a naval officer, thinking her to be much older, offered her marriage. As her years increased so did her would-be lovers, and she herself fell in love with a lawyer's articled clerk named Robinson, who surrounded himself with a great deal of mystery. He said he had great expectations from a very wealthy uncle, and he promised Mrs. Darby that she could come and live with them if he could marry Mary Anne. They were married in April, 1774, but, to the astonishment of his bride and mother-in-law, he asked for the wedding to be kept secret, the reason being that he was not the nephew of the man from whom he expected a fortune, but his illegitimate son. The child wife, for she was no more, attracted men, and several good-for-nothing roués tried without success to seduce her away from her husband. Robinson heavily in debt was arrested just as his wife presented him with a daughter, and it emerged later that he had been led into extravagances by rich men who were really after his wife. He was in jail for £1,200, and his faithful wife went into the prison of King's Bench with him for ten months, spending her time writing poetry. Then the Duchess of Devonshire heard the story and gave her patronage. Then Mary Anne met Brereton, the Drury

Lane actor, and, remembering Garrick's early kindness, she got Brereton to speak to the great man. The upshot was that Richard Brinsley Sheridan gave her an audition in the Green Room at Drury Lane, and Garrick, who was present although in retirement, was most impressed. He coached her with infinite pains, and on December 10, 1776, this entirely inexperienced girl essayed one of the greatest of tragic roles. Something of that pathos which was in her, something of the wistfulness of her own personality got across to the audience and atoned for her obvious lack of polish. She was a success, Garrick was overjoyed, and Sheridan at once gave her a job. She was given a chance of creating a role, in a play that was a dressed-up version of *The Relapse*. The audience had expected a new comedy from Sheridan, and they hissed. Poor little Mary Anne, paralysed with fear and humiliation, stood motionless on the stage, not knowing what to do until the Duke of Cumberland, in the stage box, called out to her, "It is all right. It is not you, but the play they hiss," and then, recovering her confidence, she proceeded with her performance.

Then in 1778 she was chosen to play Perdita in a Royal Command performance of *A Winter's Tale*. She was still very much the amateur and she was terrified at the prospect of appearing before Royalty. To cheer her up, "Gentleman" Smith, a very good actor who was playing Leontes said, "My Gad, Mrs. Robinson, you will make a conquest of the Prince, for tonight you look handsomer than ever."

Little did he know what a prophet he was.

His Royal Highness the Prince of Wales and the rest of the Royal Family were present, but it is only "Prinny," later George IV who matters to this story. He was then a mere boy of sixteen, but he showed the promise that his manhood fulfilled. He was attended by Lord Malden (George Capel Coningsby, fifth Earl of Essex, who afterwards married Kitty Stephens) and General Lake. Mary Anne made her entrance, nervous and scared, and her agitation increased when she saw that the Prince of Wales was gazing ardently at her from his box right on the stage. He made remarks about her to his companions in a voice loud enough for her to hear, and though they were most flattering, they were disturbing to a highly strung actress. And everyone else noticed the Royal preoccupation with Mary Anne—who shall now be called Perdita—and when the players bowed and curtsied to the Royalty, at the end of the play, the Prince gave Perdita a special bow and a most meaning smile. She retired, full of blushes, to the Green Room, where she found Lord Malden, who paid her glowing compliments, telling her of the nice things the Prince was saying about her. As she was leaving the theatre, she encountered the Royal Party again (one wonders why they were detained) and she curtsied low, receiving again as low a bow from the Prince as well as a very knowing look.

A day or two later, Lord Malden came to the theatre to see her, and after some desultory conversation, during which he did not seem too much at ease, he gave her a letter—addressed to Perdita. It was in a hand she did not know, over the signature, "Florizel," and it contained only a few words, beautifully phrased and rather pointed, despite their politeness. She was mystified by the identity of the writer and Lord Malden promptly enlightened her. It was from the Prince. Confused, hardly able to credit the information, Perdita returned a formal and humble answer, and in a state of bewilderment went to her dressing-room. The Prince became almost a fixture in the stage box whenever she played. From that moment onwards his eyes never left her, and he made no secret of his infatuation. He sent her his miniature, set in jewels, and put a little heart cut out of paper in the parcel, on one side of which was written "*Je ne change qu'en Mourant*" and on the other "Unalterable to my Perdita through life." Naturally, Perdita was swept off her feet, and soon there developed a correspondence between them in which Florizel pressed for a closer association. She advised him to wait until he was his own master, which indeed was wise counsel, but he became more and more ardent and she was bound to conclude that he really felt a deep and abiding affection for her. The situation was a tragi-comedy. Her own husband, who took her money to spend on other women, was making her desperately unhappy, and here was a real live Prince Charming placing his heart at her feet. What could a girl do? At last the Prince and Perdita met, and they sealed the bond between them in love's own way. Then she received another bond from the Prince which took her breath away, for it was a genuine legal bond, bestowing £20,000 on her, payable when he came of age. Its legality was doubtful, since he was a minor, but anyway, it was in the nature of a post-dated cheque. He had already showered valuable gifts on her which she had returned, but this was different so the *affaire* proceeded, though it was kept as quiet as possible until 1781, when the Prince was set up with his own apartments and his own staff. His own master now, they went about together, driving in a carriage which he gave her, valued at £900 and probably never paid for, and she let herself go in the matter of dress, wearing a different gown, in different style, every day. She was the talk of the Town. The Drury Lane Management, anxious to keep her there because she drew money into the house, raised her salary considerably, but she decided to quit the stage to assume the role of Royal mistress. Although the money on the bond never seemed to mature, the Prince was still the complete lover, and she sunned herself in the reflected glory of her exalted status. Then one day the Prince failed to turn up and she drove alone in the Park, the crowds being quick to notice that the figure of the Heir to the Throne was no longer in the carriage. Days passed into weeks, and still the Prince was absent. She began to press for the reason, and at last she received a message. "His Royal Highness regretted that pressure of affairs . . . etc."—a cold formal note that was, in modern parlance, a polite brush-off. Refusing to accept this rejection, she wrote appealing letters, and receiving no answer, she rushed down to Windsor and begged an interview, which was refused. Lord Malden, who, it was said, was making love to her, received her, and she begged his intercession. He pleaded with the Prince, who at last agreed to a meeting, and she hastened to the rendezvous. He was, she thought, his old self again, but he advised caution; there were concealed enemies waiting to strike; they must wait until the trouble had blown over and all would be well, for he was still her devoted Florizel. She desperately wanted to believe it, but the very next day she met him in the Park and he cut her dead in full view of everyone.

Now she was truly cast off by her royal lover. She was heavily in debt, owed the rent on her house in Cork Street, Burlington Gardens and, unable to find money elsewhere, she presented her £20,000 bond for payment. It was promptly dishonoured by the Prince. At her wit's end, a woman scorned, she wrote to the Prince, threatening to publish his letters, and old King George III, hearing of it, put the matter into the hands of Lord North, the Prime Minister. A Colonel Hotham was deputed to settle the matter for £5,000, but Charles James Fox, the wily, brilliant schemer, got the job of negotiating. He knew stage folk. Had he not been in love with Miss Farren until he saw her in breeches and found her lacking in curves? In next to no time Fox got Perdita to accept a pension of £500 a year for life, with a £250 pension for her daughter when Perdita died. It was entered in the records, with the explanation that it was awarded to Mrs. Robinson because she had resigned a lucrative profession at the request of the Prince of Wales. It is highly probable that Fox, in view of his services to both parties, was suitably rewarded, for he and Perdita were seen everywhere together, and doubtless they were living together. George Selwyn, maker of epigrams, coined one on the subject. Charles James Fox was known as "The Man of the People," so Selwyn innocently asked if there was any reason why "The Man of the People should not live with the Woman of the People"? It went down well. . . .

Let it not be thought Perdita accepted the break with lamb-like resignation. She returned the Prince's presents, except some minor items not worth more than £100, but she did not return the bond for £20,000. And doubtless she was right to make the so-called First Gentleman of Europe pay for his fun, but she was never the deceived, outraged little creature she pretended to be. Her eyes were open wide. When Charles James Fox had got everything settled, she took her daughter to Paris, where her fame had preceded her, and it is said that the Duke of Orleans wooed her, though she averred that she rejected him.

She went on writing poetry, as she had done since a child, and some of it was published for her notoriety aroused interest. When she went to France she wrote an ode, a sort of public farewell to her Florizel, which ended thus:

> Fare thee well, ungrateful rover,
> Welcome Gallia's hostile shore,
> Now the breezes waft me over
> Now we part—to meet NO MORE.

That was the sort of poetess she was.

But she came back home, and found another lover, Colonel Tarleton, afterwards knighted. His financial affairs were in an awful state and, no doubt with Fox's help, she was preparing to put them right when she was stricken down with paralysis. She was still only twenty-four years old; although she was bed-ridden and hardly able to move, she could dictate her poems, stories and plays. They were published, but she got little out of it. "My mental labours have failed owing to the dishonest conduct of my publishers," she complained. "My works have sold handsomely, but the profits have been theirs."

Perhaps, lying helpless, she recalled that summer evening in 1780 when she dined with Lord Malden at an inn on an island on the Thames at Kew. Their eyes kept straying to the opposite bank—they awaited a signal. As dusk was falling, a handkerchief waved and she and her escort stepped into a boat, crossed the river in the scented evening and she went straight into the arms of her Royal lover—a despicable man.

She died at Windsor on December 28, 1800, and was buried in Old Windsor Churchyard. Perdita—the lost Princess—had lost her Prince, but now she rested near his royal abode.

CHAPTER EIGHTEEN

The Little Pickle

THE stage gave Dorothy Jordan the nickname of "The Little Pickle," and it fitted her only too well, for she was "in a pickle" most of her life. Try as she would, she could not avoid trouble and it stayed with her, even when she became the mistress of the Duke of Clarence, destined to become England's King under Pitt. The Little Pickle bore her misfortunes with exemplary fortitude, but in the end they became too great a burden and her mind gave way. She was a superb actress and her name is forever enshrined in the annals of the theatre.

Dorothy was the daughter of Grace Phillips, a provincial actress who claimed to have married a certain Captain Bland at a Roman Catholic church in Ireland. After becoming the father of nine children, the Captain deferred to parental pressure, deserted his brood and went home to marry a rich woman. His father was a lawyer, and it can hardly be suggested that he would connive at his son's bigamy, and the more likely explanation is that Miss Phillips had at no time been Mrs. Bland. She took no steps to bring her supposed husband to heel and, indeed, he died within a year. Miss Phillips then claimed that her marriage had been annulled, and it was while playing in Dublin that Dorothy, her tenth child was born. She was credited to Captain Bland. Debarred by poverty from a decent education, Dorothy, at the age of fifteen, became a milliner's assistant, but too many actresses came to the establishment for the youngster's peace of mind and she got a job at Ryder's Theatre in Dublin. She was careful not to use the name of Bland, because she hoped that the man said to be her father would one day return, or maybe that his family would do something for her, and she had no wish to sully their name —which shows what was thought of the stage in those days. Dorothy played the usual round of parts given to girls of her age and received sufficient encouragement from audiences to continue her career.

The manager of the theatre was a man called Daly, and he appears to have been the type of fruity villain much beloved by authors and playgoers. He was given to seducing young actresses, and Dorothy apparently was no exception so far as his desire went. She was quite a fetching young girl, with a graceful and lissom figure. Daly worked to a set plan in getting these young girls into bed with him. He would lend them money in the style of a good companion and then make a sudden demand for immediate repayment, knowing full well that it was an impossibility. It was then that he played his master stroke by offering "a fate worse than death" in cancellation of the debt. This was the first pickle poor Dorothy got herself into, for she, too, had borrowed money, probably to give to her mother. She would not yield, however, and when threatened with arrest and imprisonment called Daly's carnal bluff.

But the melodrama was yet to be played out and Daly had another trick up his dastardly sleeve! He rallied the aid of some of the "ladies" of his company, who tricked Dorothy into accompanying them to a brothel, where she was locked in a room with Daly and cajoled and threatened until she finally yielded. Daly then set her free and warned her not to open her mouth, otherwise he would ruin her, and one imagines that he was referring only to her career as an artist. Dorothy and her mother knew he was dangerous and not to be tampered with, so they packed their belongings and got out of Dublin. They turned up in Leeds and met Tate Wilkinson, now rich and famous, and in control of many theatres in the North, including the Theatre Royal at York. Like all men of the Theatre, Tate's memory was first-rate and he remembered seeing Dorothy's mother play in Dublin. But he was more interested in the girl, although he could see that she was in what was then known as a "certain condition." Dorothy told him what had happened and, knowing Daly, Tate knew he had been given the truth.

Tate asked what she wanted to play—Tragedy, Comedy or

Opera? He expected the usual reply, "Tragedy," but Dorothy replied quite simply, "All of them." Tate was astonished, not only at the unusual reply, but at the girl's calm assurance, and he took her at her word. By a stroke of irony, two of her first plays were *The Virgin Unmasked* and *The Fair Penitent*. Dorothy showed that she could handle drama and sing an excellent song, and the big hand she got from her audiences told Tate he had picked up a bargain—and that for 15*s*. a week. Dorothy played the circuit—Wakefield, Sheffield, Doncaster and Hull—but at the last-named she ran into trouble. She had now become Mrs. Jordan, because Tate had likened her crossing of the Irish Channel to the crossing of Jordan and she adopted the significant name. Hull apparently wanted to know, when she was delivered of a little Jordan, where Mr. Jordan was. The women of the company had, of course, gossiped, and they were jealous enough of the newcomer to make it hot for her.

She returned to the theatre as soon as she could and found a hostile audience hissing their moral disapproval. But she had plenty of pluck and no little charm, which she turned on to the full. She sang and let her lovely voice caress the strait-laced citizens of William Wilberforce's city. They found her irresistible, and those who came to mock stayed to cheer. Her tremendous benefit night did justice to her talent and winning ways. She apparently appealed to an old gentleman named Cornelius Swan, who fancied himself as an authority on the drama, called the girl his adopted daughter, and insisted on coaching her. The old man had money, and Dorothy thought he might remember her in his will. He didn't do that, but proved a good friend in another way. Success travels fast, and Daly, the Dublin villain, heard about Dorothy and decided to collect the cash that she still owed him. His emissaries turned up and demanded £300, loan and accumulated interest, and, to save her from the danger of imprisonment, old Swan paid it for her.

Altogether Dorothy stayed with Tate Wilkinson for four years and during that time had her salary trebled and she received two benefits each year. She had been expecting an invitation from Covent Garden, having struck up a friendship with "Gentleman" Smith, one of the actors there, who occasionally came North for a week's racing. He had reported favourably on the girl, but

Richard Yates, another London player, considered her mediocre, and Mrs. Siddons's verdict was that she would do well to remain where she was. Perhaps Sarah was prejudiced, for she never liked her fellow player. When Dorothy was offered £4 a week at the Lane, Tate would not stand in her way, for he remembered his own early struggles and was a very human person.

Dorothy was wise enough not to try to compete with the mighty Mrs. Siddons, although she had ample faith in her ability to become a great tragedienne. In the comedy line too she was not at that time anxious to challenge the supremacy of Miss Farren and Jane Pope, and compromised by asking to be allowed to play the smaller and more sympathetic roles in tragedy, the comedy parts in Shakespeare and the romps in farce. Her début on October 18, 1785, when she was nineteen, was as brilliantly successful as she could have hoped, and the unstinted praise she received as Peggy in *The Country Girl* showed that she had nothing to learn in putting an audience in rare good humour. Neither did she rest on her laurels, but quickly made Viola in *Twelfth Night* her rightful property. At the end of the season Dorothy went on a provincial tour and, laying siege to York, Glasgow and Edinburgh, ran up her standard at each of these cities.

She returned in triumph to Drury Lane and found good news awaiting her from the management. Her salary had been increased to £12 a week—riches indeed for a young actress who had done it the hard way. Mrs. Jordan at about this time lost her mother. She had promised to play in a benefit in aid of someone else, but failed to turn up and was accused of deliberately breaking her word. Actually she was nursing her dying mother and remained with her to the end. Those who were all too eager to condemn her had to withdraw their allegations when the truth became known. Mrs. Jordan, who had now become known by the affectionate nickname of the Little Pickle—from her part in *The Spoiled Child*—began to undertake many male parts, and it must be said that breeches suited her. When Mrs. Siddons stepped down from Tragedy's high pinnacle to play Rosalind, many shrewd playgoers, comparing her performance with that of the Little Pickle, decided that the great Sarah had come off second best by a wide margin. Mrs. Jordan enjoyed conquests elsewhere, and one of them turned out to be the son of Sir Richard Ford, Chief

Magistrate at Bow Street and a Drury Lane shareholder. She was pretty enough in those days, with a dainty figure and an excellent disposition. They began to live together and liked people to believe they were married, especially when two children came along. But Ford was a ne'er-do-well who didn't mind being supported by his wife and attended the theatre on "treasury nights" to keep himself in funds. The association led to trouble for the Little Pickle, who was accused of being Ford's mistress and found the truth rankled. Ford's excuse for not marrying her had been that his father would disinherit him, but Mrs. Jordan determined to have the matter settled one way or the other, told him that she was maintaining the two children and contributing to his comfort and didn't mind continuing to do so, provided he made her his wife. Ford began to side-step, but the would-be Mrs. Ford gave him a few days to make up his mind, and that brought the affair to an end.

Mrs. Jordan soon found consolation in distinguished company, and it gradually dawned on her that whenever she was on the stage the theatre was graced by the Royal presence of the Duke of Clarence. He was a somewhat simple soul, this son of George III who was to ascend to the throne as William IV, and, having been a sailor, was probably vulnerable to women, particularly someone as bewitching as the Little Pickle. Anyhow, he fell in love with her and offered his Royal protection, a splendid establishment and an income of £1,000 a year. For a woman of her time and profession, Mrs. Jordan had not been promiscuous, but she had been decidedly unfortunate, what with being seduced by one and deserted by another. She must have been immensely flattered by this Royal proposition, which she had no hesitation in accepting.

The arrangement could not, of course, be kept a secret, and Mrs. Jordan's enemies—she had her share of them as a successful actress—saw to it that the more scurrilous newspapers were informed of what was going on. The object of all this was to turn the theatre-going public against Mrs. Jordan, and her career was in the balance for some little time. She lived with her Royal lover in a fine house at Bushey Park, of which the Duke was the Ranger. It was an idyllic setting for romance, for they were in midst of tree-lined avenues and lovely woodland that gave shelter to herds of deer.

When the affair came to the ear of the Duke's father, poor old, afflicted George III, he promptly sent for Clarence, and it is not difficult to imagine what must have taken place. "Clarence, Clarence, what's this I hear, hey? Do you keep an actress, an actress, hey?" The Duke must have owned up like a man and tried to tell his father what a delightful mistress Mrs. Jordan was proving, but the King wasn't interested in romance; he was too businesslike for his son. "How much, how much d'ye give her, hey?" The thrifty old monarch was appalled by the answer. "A thousand a year! Ye must be mad. It's not to be thought of, y' understand, hey? Give her £500; it's more than enough; it's ample, ample, hey?"

The audience came to an end and the Duke withdrew. He was a dutiful son and he reported to his charmer that he had been under fire from his Royal parent. Mrs. Jordan listened quietly and then asked, "How much did he say?" and Clarence explained that his father considered £500 was ample for her. "Oh, he did, did he?" she said before slipping out to her bedroom and returning with a playbill. She thrust it under the regal nose and drew the Duke's attention to the warning it contained: "No money returned after the rise of the curtain." That put an end to any question of reduced terms.

Mrs. Jordan was not only happy with her Royal lover, but she was faithful to him and, what is more, presented him with ten children, five boys and five girls, which indicates a nice sense of balance. The Duke was very fond of them and also of Mrs. Jordan's three children, who were part of the family, and not treated any differently. Mrs. Jordan sat at the head of the table and dispensed hospitality for the Duke's guests, and nobody, had they not known it, would have guessed that the union had not had the benefit of clergy. Although she remained a great actress, the Little Pickle, deeply involved in maternity as she was, could not avoid being absent from the stage on many occasions and audiences became vexed at this. She was booed on one of her reappearances, but reminded her followers that they knew quite well why she had been away: she had been doing her duty as a woman and as a loyal subject of the realm. That really got them, and she walked off to a storm of cheering.

The Duke, too, was not a whit less interested in her career, for he always read her new plays and proffered his advice on the suitability of the parts offered to her. It is certain that Mrs. Jordan donated her earnings to the family purse, for the Duke had not a lot of money. With waspish ill-will, somebody suggested that the Duke even went to the theatre to collect his wife's wages. Criticism or not, and despite the fact that she put on a lot of weight, Mrs. Jordan held the Theatre and her career in a firm grip. The idyll at Bushey Park lasted for twenty years and there was hardly a cloud on the horizon in all that time.

When the blow fell, Mrs. Jordan had not an inkling that the happiest years of her life had run their course. She was playing at Cheltenham when she opened a letter from the Duke, expecting to read of news of himself and the children, but the letter, with brutal simplicity, asked her to meet Clarence at Maidenhead to take farewell of each other. The poor Little Pickle shuddered and nearly lost her reason, but she was above all a "pro" and she had one more night to play. The show must go on. Before a packed house, and almost beside herself, Mrs. Jordan took her punishment bravely, but in one scene in which a conjuror was supposed to make her drunk and go off into fits of laughter, Mrs. Jordan found the task beyond her, and to the amazement of the audience she broke down and began to sob. The actor playing opposite her had the presence of mind to change his lines at once. "Why, Nell," he exclaimed, "the conjuror has not only made thee drunk; he has made thee crying drunk." That line got a laugh and saved the situation. When the show was over Mrs. Jordan ran to a carriage and, still in her comic stage costume, went to play the final act in her own drama. What passed between the Duke and his discarded mistress that night was never told, but without a shadow of a doubt Mrs. Jordan behaved as admirably then as she did afterwards. She was forty-nine and had lost much of her attractiveness, and this separation wounded her deeply, but she would not involve the Duke in public recriminations and, in fact, defended him to her friends. The terms of the settlement were that the Duke should look after the elder children and that Mrs. Jordan should have the care, until a certain age, of the four youngest daughters and be paid £1,500 yearly for their upbringing. There was an additional £600 for a house and carriage for their use. Mrs. Jordan received £1,500 for herself, and another £800 to enable her to make provision for the three daughters of whom the Duke was not father. She was forbidden to continue her stage career on pain of losing the custody of the children. The Duke gave his offspring the name of Fitzclarence and all secured titles and various sinecures, with the exception of one, who died in India. The arrangement cost the country a lot of money.

As matters turned out, Mrs. Jordan did forfeit the custody of the Duke's children, because she was anxious to secure the future of her other children and it was her ambition to give £10,000 to each of them as a marriage dowry. She returned to the stage and was most affectionately received. She is reputed to have earned £21,000 during the following three years and nobody would have guessed that the Little Pickle was not the happy, carefree woman she had always been. But away from the stage she was miserable and unhappy, the prey of a depression she could not shake off.

In 1815 she vanished suddenly and was next heard of in France, where she began to entertain the notion that she was ruined financially. She had had some reverses, but was far from being broke. Her only companion was a Miss Ketchley, who had been with the family at Bushey, and who had accompanied her mistress on the Duke's orders. Mrs. Jordan adopted the name of James and took a large and decaying house at St. Cloud. She, who had been so bright, now rarely spoke and she never smiled. She was obsessed with the idea that news of a secret and intimate character was on its way to her and was in despair when a letter failed to arrive. When it did she was no better and not even Miss Ketchley was told of its contents. There came a time when the poor creature found herself completely isolated and one day her condition, always pitiable, became worse.

She lay on a couch gasping for breath and convulsed, but it was a day she expected a letter and, unable to bear the suspense, sent a messenger to await the arrival of the post. She was half-demented by the time he returned and, as he entered the room, she raised herself up to receive the much expected missive. The messenger was empty-handed and she stared at him unbelievingly. Then with a groan she dropped back and death came upon her beneficently to end her suffering.

London lost a great friend when they carried Mrs. Jordan to the grave at St. Cloud and the Duke a faithful and loving mistress. He is believed to have designed a memorial for her, but it never left the mason's yard.

The Little Pickle was in her way a great humanitarian, for she loved her fellow creatures and would never willingly hurt a soul. Once when playing in Chester she heard of a poor woman, the mother of three children, who had been thrown into prison for a small debt. Mrs. Jordan paid it and, meeting the little family in the street one day, was embarrassed by their thanks, for they went down on their knees to her. A preacher who had witnessed the scene offered his hand to Mrs. Jordan and said, "Lady, pardon the freedom of a stranger, but would to the Lord the world was all like thee." Mrs. Jordan did not take the stranger's hand, and told him she was certain he would not have offered it had he known she was an actress. The preacher looked at her and again offered his hand, saying, "The Lord bless thee, whoever thou art; His goodness is unlimited; He hath bestowed upon thee a rare portion of His Spirit. As to thy calling, if thy soul upbraid thee not, why should I." He had spoken words that deserve to be the Little Pickle's epitaph.

CHAPTER NINETEEN

The Faithful Heart

JANE POPE, one of the most accomplished actresses ever to grace the stage, shared her warm and constant heart between a fellow actor and her theatre. The lover betrayed her, and is dead and lost in the mists of obscurity, but the theatre lives on in glorious perpetuity at Drury Lane. Few people remember Jane Pope's name and to many it is completely unknown, even though she was a comedienne who scintillated in the palmy days of great acting and was David Garrick's leading lady and Richard Brinsley Sheridan's twinkling star.

Her memory deserves the reward of honour, for with truth it can be said that she was of the Theatre and had always been, for her ancestry went back to the real birth of our Theatre in Tudor times. Both her parents were of the Drury Lane Company, and if she just missed being born in the theatre she could claim to have slept as a baby in one of the dressing-rooms while her mother was on the stage, an experience that befell Ellen Terry when her father was acting in the provincial theatres.

Jane's father, Alexander Pope, had gone to the Lane as a young man and quickly proved his worth as a tragedian. He shared with James Quin the distinction of being asked to give an encore! That rare request to a tragedian occurred at Drury Lane on January 6, 1720, in *Jane Shore*, in which Pope played Hastings, and so magnificently did he put over the great speech that the audience recalled him and made him do it all over again. Pope had a rare talent for making wigs, and when he retired from the stage he set up business in Great Queen Street, near to the theatre he loved.

PLATE XIII

LOUISA, COUNTESS OF CRAVEN

HESTER SANTLOW

MRS. HUGHES

MISS FOOTE

PLATE XIV

MRS. STIRLING

MARIE BANCROFT

MRS. KENDAL

The first of several children, Jane played in the theatre as a child, her first appearance being in *Lilliput*. In those days a popular entertainment was the performance of certain adult plays by children, and in this connection Jane appeared as Lethe in *The Fine Lady*, in *Miss in Her Teens* and many such others. Garrick thought very highly of Alexander Pope's young daughter. In 1759—to be precise, on September 27—Jane was given her first big chance, being entrusted with the role of Corinna in *The Confederacy*. She did not appear on the bill, but was identified as "A Young Lady," the usual custom with a player who still had to prove herself. Jane rose to the occasion like a lark climbing in the sky and Garrick promptly put her on the strength of the company. Jane had the week-end to muse over her triumph, made all the sweeter by the knowledge that the play was being retained and that further opportunities awaited her. It was a starry-eyed young woman who went down to the theatre the following Monday, confident in her ability, but she knew her place, and took it in a humble corner of the Green Room, to which she now had the entrée.

She had not long arrived there when in swept mercurial Kitty Clive, the Queen of Old Drury, whose entrance silenced the idle chatter. Kitty looked around her until she espied Jane and with an imperious wave of her fan she signalled the girl over. Poor Jane wondered what was wrong, for something must be amiss for that regal actress to condescend to speak to a nobody like herself. "My dear Pope," began Kitty, "you played peculiarly well on Saturday night, considering that you are, as yet, but a novice in the profession. Now take a piece of advice from me. . . . Do not be surprised when I tell you that tonight you must endeavour to act better and yet at the same time make up your mind to meet with less applause, for if you suffer your young heart to be too sanguine and place too much dependence on the caprice of public commendation and should find your hopes disappointed, you will foolishly let it cast a damp over your spirits, and thus, instead of improving, you will sink beneath yourself. Therefore, take my advice for your future progress. The violent thunder of applause which crowned your first appearance last Saturday was not, in strict justice, deserved. It was only benevolently bestowed by the audience, to give you the pleasing information that they were well satisfied by your efforts. You must therefore consider it as an earnest of their wishes that you will, by your future exertions, merit the distinguished kindness that they have manifested towards you."

Kitty, with a kind smile, then dismissed the young beginner and, murmuring her thanks, Jane curtsied and went to await her cue. She never forgot the advice, and it was the best that one actress ever gave to another. How well the girl responded to it is indicated by the fact that when Kitty Clive retired, shortly afterwards, her mantle fell on Jane Pope, and she wore it nobly and well. The meeting achieved yet another purpose, for it forged a bond of friendship between the two women that was never broken. Jane sought the advice and friendship of Kitty and they were generously given.

The time soon came when Jane, now receiving £8 a week, no mean salary, thought she deserved £10 in her pay packet and wrote suggesting this to David Garrick in the politest terms possible. Garrick, who at all times found it hard to part, replied in like vein and regretfully refused the request. Now, although they met every day in the theatre, rehearsing and playing together, such a mundane matter as salary was never discussed between them. There was therefore a protracted correspondence on the subject, carried out on both sides in a manner that would have done justice to international diplomats. But Garrick would not budge and in a fit of temper Jane resigned from Drury Lane and took a holiday. She soon began to miss the great playhouse which was "home" to her and although Covent Garden made her a most tempting offer she could not bring herself to go there. She began to fret without knowing that Drury Lane missed her, for Garrick was disturbed by her absence.

Jane took her troubles to Kitty Clive at Twickenham and begged her to intercede with Garrick. Kitty, who maintained a lively correspondence with Garrick throughout her retirement, wrote to him and asked him to take Jane back to the Lane before she broke her heart. Garrick must have grinned to himself on receiving this plea from a woman who was not given to asking favours, but he was thankful to get Jane back—at her old salary, of course. But having shown himself to be the undisputed master of the situation Garrick gave Jane the salary she had wanted and received full value in return. She had been doing that for some years, for quite early in her career John Churchill, a most trenchant critic, had written of her:

> With all the native vigour of sixteen
> Among the merry groups conspicuous seen
> See lively Pope advance to jig and trip
> Corinna, Cherry, Honeycombe and Snip
> Not without art, but yet to nature true
> She charms the town with humour, just, yet new
> Cheered by her promise, we the less deplore
> The fatal time when Clive shall be no more.

Jane became so eminent an actress that she was chosen by Garrick to play Beatrice opposite his Benedick on the extremely important occasion of his return to Drury Lane after a long absence abroad. She had no pretence to beauty, but she had personality and unlimited talent and her gay raillery had the delightful spontaneity known only to the true artist. Her ability was never in question at any time; it was simply a matter of being able to judge at what she excelled in most.

But Jane, for all her gaiety and high spirits, hid a wound that never healed throughout her life, for she had given her heart wholly to a Drury Lane actor named Holland. He was extremely handsome, and David Garrick watched the progress of the affair with some misgiving, since he knew the extent of Jane's infatuation and knew too that Holland, wayward and unreliable, could easily break her heart. Garrick warned Jane that the man she loved was capable of destroying her happiness, but she could not believe that and lived for the day when she would be his wife.

Disillusionment came to Jane one fine summer's day when she took the Richmond coach and travelled down to Twickenham to see Kitty. On the way down a postchaise swept by and Jane's heart stood still, for she could have sworn that it contained Holland and a lady, a very good-looking creature. Worried out of her wits, Jane left the coach at Richmond Bridge and walked through the riverside meadows towards Strawberry Hill. She was filled with doubt, for she remembered Garrick's warning. She tried to dismiss these thoughts, for lovers, both men and women, usually try to believe what they want to believe. Jane never reached Twickenham that day. She came across her faithless lover as he was fondling a fair but frail siren in a boat sheltering beneath a willow tree, and she fled from the scene, her romance shattered.

The following day she met Holland at rehearsal and, sensing that he had been discovered, he was prepared to be defiant and high-handed. The opportunity never arose, for Jane cut him dead and never spoke to him again. Holland was a born philanderer and came to an untimely end. Although she never again mentioned him, Jane forgave him, for she knew he had never been really happy and she could still shed a tear for him when youth had long passed her by.

As the years advanced, Jane grew rather portly and was involved in an amusing incident while playing with Mrs. Jordan, another actress inclined to be beefy. On the stage one had to pass a note to the other, but when it fluttered to the ground neither dare stoop to pick it up. They looked at each other knowing perfectly well that they shared the same handicap and amidst laughter and sympathetic cheers from the audience Jane pretended to call a maid from offstage.

Jane was too sensible to try to defy *Anno Domini* and, with her increasing weight, she readily relinquished her old parts and accepted those more suitable to her figure and years. She made the rafters ring with her interpretation of Mrs. Malaprop and by general consent her Duenna was superb.

When Garrick left Drury Lane she stayed on with Sheridan, and when he was writing *The School for Scandal* in his slow, leisurely manner she was one of the company waiting anxiously day by day for the play to be completed. Many a caustic message did she send to the dilatory playwright, and many a display of temper did she treat him to, but her tantrums were devoid of malice. It was Drury Lane over which she was worrying, for when bad times came, and there was precious little in the kitty because Sheridan spent it faster than it came in, Jane played for as little as £2 a week, saying she would do all in her power to aid the theatre she loved. Sheridan wrote the part of Mrs. Candour specially for her. She was, of course, candour personified.

She created Tilburina in *The Critic*, and to see her enter "stark mad, in white satin" was something with which to conjure in the way of acting. Ever mindful of the advice given to her when she was a young girl, she would refuse to play parts which she believed were unsuited to her and even risked a Royal rebuke for so doing. George III admired her acting, and in commanding a performance of *The Clandestine Marriage* expressed the wish that Miss Pope would play Mrs. Heidelberg. Now, she had played Mrs. Sterling in the play, but not Mrs. Heidelberg, and she doubted her ability to do so, and, greatly daring, addressed a petition to the King saying that she was afraid she would not do herself justice and would not affront His Majesty by giving anything but her best. The old King replied saying that whatever she did and however she played it, could not fail to give the greatest delight and satisfaction to himself and to the Queen. Thus strengthened, Jane played Mrs. Heidelberg and gave a grand performance.

In 1806 she made only one appearance, in Garrick's *Bon Ton*, which she had first played in 1775. She realised she had reached the end of her long career, and, refusing to hang on as a mere shadow of her former self, made her farewell appearance on May 26, 1808. It was characteristic of Jane that she would not impose on her last audience by going through a part she knew backwards, but she certainly astounded her friends by playing Deborah Bowlas in *The Heir at Law*, a part she had never previously undertaken, and she was her old brilliantly inventive self. For good measure, she rounded off a splendid evening with Audrey, and in that character spoke her goodbye: "And now poor Audrey bids you all farewell." It was the curtain on fifty years of acting.

Having lived for forty years in a house in Queen Street—the site is now occupied by a great Masonic building—Jane moved her residence to Newman Street, and she did not lack friends. Among her guests were several of His Majesty's judges, and even the Royal carriage had been known to set down there. The walls of her charmingly appointed rooms were covered with the portraits of celebrities, and prominent among these pictures was one of Holland, the faithless sweetheart of her youth. When she died on July 30, 1818, there passed a great actress and a great lady whose life glowed like a good deed in the naughty world of her time. At the Lane they always called her "Popie" and there is one there today who answers to the same nickname. And, just for the record, ninety-eight years and a day after Jane Pope left this world another Miss Pope slipped into it to tread those same boards and to answer also to the name of "Popie."

Coincident with the reign of Jane Pope at Drury Lane was the career of Mrs. Mattocks at Covent Garden, for although she was never as accomplished an actress as Jane, she was still a fine artist with an unerring sense of what the Theatre demanded. And that was not surprising for she, too, was of the blood, her father having been a comedian and her uncle once the manager of the Theatre in Goodmans Fields, Whitechapel, where Garrick made his first appearance. Like Jane, Mrs. Mattocks remained loyal to one theatre, for she never played anywhere else in London but at Covent Garden. Never could she bring herself to play at the Lane, because the Green Room of that theatre was where old Macklin slew her grandfather.

Mrs. Mattocks was born Isabella Hallam in 1746, and the family were related to John Rich. Her father, to escape his creditors, went to America, where he managed theatres in New York, Charleston and Philadelphia and is believed to have amassed a fortune worth £10,000, which he lost in the Civil War. Isabella was left in the care of Mrs. Barrington, her aunt, who was herself a good actress and planned her niece's stage career. The child appeared at her uncle's benefit performance at Covent Garden in a play entitled *What D'ye Call It*? She was so tiny that a gentleman in the pit remarked, "I can hear her very well, but damme, I can't see her without a glass." Isabella remained at Covent Garden playing child parts, and she was only fifteen when she was given the mature role of Juliet and was announced "as a young gentlewoman," it being her first appearance as a woman. It is quite surprising how Isabella's career closely resembled that of Jane Pope, for as Garrick gave Jane her chance on her first big part, so did Covent Garden do likewise for Isabella, who now joined the company there.

Isabella did well in tragedies and she also sang and made a niche for herself in ballad opera. She became a great favourite at Covent Garden, and hereabouts Isabella married a fellow actor named Mattocks, but his early death makes him a figure of little importance to her story.

It was Mrs. Mattocks who created the part of Betty Blackbury in O'Keefe's comedy, *The Farmer*, while she was the original Mrs. Racket in *The Belle's Stratagem*. She was never a good tragedienne, but in comedy she gave the audiences what they wanted and never threw a line away. She bade farewell to the stage on June 7, 1808, only a few days after Jane Pope had done likewise. She chose Flora in *The Wonder* to say "goodbye" to her many friends, and George Frederic Cooke, that fine but tipsy actor, recited an ode in her honour.

Mrs. Mattocks had led a thrifty life, and when her daughter married a barrister named Hewitt she was able to provide a handsome dowry. She wanted peace and quiet and she retired to a small place in Kensington. She also wanted security, and not being desirous of living on her capital, she handed over to her son-in-law for investment in gilt-edged securities about £6,000, which was a tidy little fortune. Hewitt had power of attorney over her affairs, and since Mrs. Mattocks duly received the interest on her capital, she felt that at sixty-two she had nothing to worry about. She became a grandmother, and when Hewitt died it was revealed that he had sold and converted to his own use all the stock belonging to Mrs. Mattocks, continuing to pay the interest to hide his machinations, and there was absolutely nothing to be salvaged.

The actress and her family faced destitution, but she belonged to a profession the members of which help each other in time of distress and a benefit was arranged for her at Covent Garden on May 24, 1813. The play was the *The Wonder* and was one in which Garrick said farewell. There was a full muster of stars, and Quick, Fawcett, Palmer, Bentham, and, above all, Mrs. Jordan was there to help, as she always was when somebody was in trouble. She played Violante. With rare good taste the presence of Mrs. Mattocks was neatly explained as a natural desire to return just once more to express thanks to her old friends, and this she did in a fine epilogue, although it was obvious that she felt her position most keenly. A vast sum for that period was raised—over £1,000, in fact—and the money was invested in an annuity. In the remaining years of her life Mrs. Mattocks had to endure much illness, and she was eighty when she died on June 25, 1826.

Her not-so-private life made Becky Wells more famous than did her stage career, but she was undoubtedly quite a good comedienne and a brilliant mimic. Her real name was Mary Davies and she was the daughter of a Birmingham gilder and carver who, with his partner, made the box in which Garrick enshrined a piece of the root of Shakespeare's mulberry tree at Stratford-on-Avon. When Mary's father was driven out of his mind by finding the brokers in for money he owed his partner, Mary, then a little girl, played boy parts on the stage and thus drifted into a life that took her all over the West Country. She married an actor who played Romeo to her Juliet when she was about eighteen. Then one day Mary returned home with a note from her husband to her mother. It read: "Madam,—As your daughter is too young and childish, I beg you will for the present take her again under your protection; and be assured I shall return for her soon, as I am now going on a short journey, Yours sincerely." That short journey lasted for the remainder of Mary's life, for she never again saw her husband.

Four years later, in 1871, the deserted young wife was invited to play at the Haymarket and at once she hit the high spots. She quarrelled violently with Miss Farren and later at Drury Lane with Mrs. Siddons, both of whom refused to appear with her until they discovered they were legally bound to do so. Becky considered that she was a better actress than Mrs. Siddons and explained this fantastic boast by asserting that when she played Isabella, one of Mrs. Siddons's great roles, she was able to scream louder than Sarah! Becky was a great eccentric and would wear muslin in winter and furs in the summer. She was rumoured to have been in an asylum and she had certainly been in prison for debt more than once. She was a prisoner in the Fleet when she met a Moorish gentleman named Sumbell. She was supposed to have married him at a ceremony of barbaric splendour, but for some reason Becky imagined that she had not embraced the Mohammedan religion, but had become a Jewess. They lived in Pall Mall in much style. Sumbell was a very jealous individual and if Becky happened to glance anywhere but at the stage when he took her to a theatre he would create a scene and thrash her when he got home. He was expecting to be recalled to Morocco either as Prime Minister or Grand Vizier, and would instruct Becky as to the duties that would be expected of her. They lived in a state of alternate strife and love-making, and when Becky ran away to save herself from further violence, she had Sumbell bound over to keep the peace. He tried to edge her into an asylum and sent her a slip of paper explaining that it was a bill of divorcement. She then sued him for maintenance, but rather than pay, Sumbell left her and went to Denmark, and apparently stayed there. Becky then toured the country as an actress, but she was quarrelsome and managers fought shy of her, and she must have had a tough time of it. Her nickname was "Cowslip," after a famous part of hers. Perhaps part of it was apposite. She abjured the Jewish faith but could find no other to suit her. At one time she was in a mental home, but got out again.

The last anyone saw of her was when a friend met her on Westminster Bridge in the company of a young man. Becky was in great form and sang a popular ditty for the entertainment of passers-by. Then she grabbed the arm of her escort and strolled away, never to be seen again. She was sixty-two then, but she had found a new lover—or husband.

CHAPTER TWENTY

A Gossip of Georgians

TO take a few pages from the lives, loves and adventures of a galaxy of famous Georgian actresses is like playing host at a dinner party at which it is not possible to offer more than a dish of *hors d'œuvres*—it would be just teasing the appetite of your guests without hope of satisfying it, and that would be an inexcusable discourtesy. Apropos of those Georgians, what is a poor author to do when he could fill a book about them and yet can afford only a chapter? He must hope for the best and trust his readers will appreciate his selectivity.

Of all the stories of from rag to riches, few can rival that of a certain Miss O'Neill, the daughter of a penniless brace of players who never conquered poverty and brought a child into the world in the plenitude of want. The youngster first saw the light of day in Drogheda some time in 1791, a pitiful mite, bare-footed and ill-clad, possessing an appetite that was never satisfied. It was devil take the hindmost in those hungry days, but somehow young Miss O'Neill managed to survive, and when her father was made stage manager of what passed for the local theatre, Miss O'Neill received her baptism on the boards by playing child parts until she was twelve.

She graduated to adult roles more as a matter of expediency than merit, but she was intelligent and malleable and, what was more important to her future, she possessed an Irish beauty which rendered her a ravishing creature. Anyhow, what with her good looks and native wit it was not surprising that somebody told Talbot, an enterprising actor-manager, that there was a flower in Drogheda worth picking. He soon introduced her to Belfast theatregoers, who gave her a most cordial reception and a little later to Dublin, where she made her début in comedy and again pleased her audiences. As luck would have it, a Miss Walstein, then Ireland's most prominent tragedienne, quarrelled with the management over her salary and withdrew, thus permitting Miss O'Neill to step into her shoes for the time being. It was valuable experience for the newcomer and she made an excellent Juliet although having to contend with a stage that was too small. What with the balcony being too low, her lover too tall and no rope ladder needed, the declaration "Oh that I were a glove upon that hand, that I might touch that cheek" made nonsense of the actual situation. It encouraged a voice from the gallery to roar to Romeo, "Get on wid your blarney; why don't ye touch her then, an' not be praychin all the while." Undismayed, the couple played on and Miss O'Neill and her Romeo, an excellent actor named Conway, received a warm ovation at the end.

In London about this time Edmund Kean was triumphant and packing them in at Drury Lane, but Covent Garden, having lost Mrs. Siddons through retirement, was in a poor way, despite all attempts to discover a successor. Miss O'Neill apparently arrived at a most opportune moment. She had lost her place to Miss Walstein, and the management at the Garden were well aware of this, but decided to take a chance with her. She was accompanied by Conway, and gossips hinted that he was more to her than just a fellow player, but it is doubtful if this was so. The young Irish girl cheerfully accepted the most modest terms and made her bow as Juliet on October 6, 1814. By the time the curtain came down on the first act she knew that she had conquered, and it was not long before her earnings were raised to £30 a week.

The lovely Miss O'Neill triumphed in new roles and in plays that became a success because of her.

She began to be compared with Mrs. Siddons, and her more enthusiastic admirers even went as far as to say that she was the better actress, which was a fulsome exaggeration, to say the least. Still, it is a tribute to any actress to be even compared with Siddons, and Miss O'Neill's youthful passion had a tenderness that was always most touching. She could make women weep unrestrainedly, and as for the men, they had been known to faint with emotion. There are actresses who could do the same today except that audiences, sated with too much entertainment, have lost the finer edge of enjoyment.

Miss O'Neill never spared herself, and when she played Mrs. Beverley in *The Gamester*, and had to throw herself on the body of her husband in hysterical despair, she did it so realistically that she was still gripped by hysteria half an hour after the curtain had fallen. Doctors shook their heads ominously when they were called in and said such nerve strain could prove fatal.

Once when she was rehearsing *The Grecian Daughter*, Fawcett and other experienced members of the company tried to advise Miss O'Neill about a scene in which she was called upon to stab one of her fellow players. "Gentleman," she said, "I am greatly obliged to you for the trouble you have taken, but you must excuse me when I tell you that I mean to kill him in my own way." She got her own way, too.

If Miss O'Neill drew the theatre crowds, she was not a whit less successful in attracting to her side many ardent admirers. They fluttered round her in the Green Room like moths attracted to a light, but Miss O'Neill was well protected by one or another of her family, her father or one of her brothers. The bucks of the town found it difficult to whisper to her sweet allurements the while her guardian stood guard on her other flank. There were those, including an Irish nobleman, quite prepared to offer marriage, but Miss O'Neill was choosey and not to be won easily. For innocent relationship, she enjoyed the friendship of many, including the Kemble family, for it was Charles Kemble who now played Romeo to her Juliet.

In 1816 Miss O'Neill probably did a little personal accounting, and on the debit side came across a few disturbing items, as a result of which she made her last stage appearance on July 13 of that year, and married William Wrixon Becher, Member of Parliament for Mallow, a wealthy suitor and landowner. He had wooed her with passionate persistence, and she was very happy to become Mrs. Becher, this former child of poverty; happier still when her husband inherited a baronetcy and more estate. Years later, as Lady Becher, she called upon Fanny Kemble and there met Charles Kemble as he hurried from his study. Charles extended his arms crying, "Ah, Juliet." She ran to receive his embrace and clasped her arms round him as she had so often done on the stage.

It presented a delightfully spontaneous tableau, for she was still a graceful and exquisite woman, even at sixty, and Kemble white-haired, was as handsome as ever at seventy.

Except for that charming incident, Lady Becher played the role of patrician without reference to her former career. She was a popular hostess, an admirable wife and mother, and this she remained until her death on October 29, 1872, at the age of eighty-one. She was unquestionably one of the best Juliets the stage has ever known, and in all her long career she never used her Christian name on the bills or in the theatre. It was Eliza.

And reluctantly we must pass over the history of Fanny Kelly, the first woman to really build and manage a theatre, leaving her to be written about on another occasion; while we record the story of Mary Ann Orger who, by marrying a Quaker, probably achieved greater distinction than did the "peerage" actresses. Mary was born in London on February 25, 1788, of theatrical parents named Ivers, who toured the provinces, taking their baby along with them. She had her stage baptism when she was carried on the stage in *Henry VIII* as a babe in arms, and it is to be hoped that she comported herself more satisfactorily than that youngster whom Charles Hart borrowed from a mother in the audience at Drury Lane, and who never ceased howling until the worried parent rushed on the stage, snatched her baby from the embarrassed actor, to the accompaniment of loud cheers from the house. As likely as not, Mary was on the stage as soon as she could walk, for she crops up on bills of obscure country theatres in 1793, particularly in a role in *The Children in the Wood*, which we now know as a pantomime. She played this part long after she had outgrown it and was probably only prevented from continuing because it took too many leaves to cover her!

Mary then joined Henry Thornton's stock company and played at Croydon, Reading, Windsor, Gosport and Chelmsford. Thornton was honest, but eccentric and absent-minded, with his thoughts anywhere but on the matter in hand. When his company played at Newbury, the old Margravine of Anspach, who lived close by, often "bespoke the play," as the picturesque phrase goes. Thornton could not have been more delighted had he received the Royal Command. Requested to play *Othello*,

Thornton discovered that the Margravine was preparing to leave after the murder of Desdemona and it was his duty in those days of badly lit theatres to "light her out," which he did, candle in each hand, walking backwards still in his stage costume, for he had had no time to change. The eternal dreamer, he could not resist closing his eyes probably to conjure up a vision of performing his present duty for a truly great personage. Whereupon the wind blew the candles out and the old lady had to grope along in the dark. Thornton was still in his seventh heaven when the show ended and, forgetting to change, went home still in Moorish dress, his face blacked with grease and lampblack. Thus, it was an ebon Thespian that his wife found as her bedfellow when she awoke the following morning.

Which brings to mind the night when little Mary Ivers was playing Miss Blandford in *Speed the Plough* and the actor who should have played her father was missing. Thornton, taking a pull at his nose, a habit when perplexed, said he would play it himself. As he dressed someone read the part to him but he finished before hearing it completed. "That will do," he said. "Let's see, a murder, a castle. I know enough to go on." He floundered through somehow until he came to the point where he had to describe his great crime, but instead of saying, "With one hand I tore the faithless woman from his damned embrace and with the other stabbed my wretched brother to the heart," Mr. Thornton, over-confident and unable to resist embroidery, declaimed, "I tore the faithless woman from his damned embrace, with one hand I stabbed my wretched brother to the heart, and what do you think I did with the other?" Nobody told him!

Such experiences added piquancy to the exciting if arduous life that Mary Ivers would not have exchanged for any other, for she was certainly becoming a competent actress. Growing up a pretty and delightful girl, she was the recipient of many "offers," and at High Wycombe she made an extraordinary conquest, for Thomas Orger, a good classical scholar and a man of some fortune, fell in love with her. He could not have seen the fifteen-year-old girl at the theatre, because he was a Quaker and observed the strict ordinances enjoined on him. It seemed incredible to him that one of such genteel mien could be a play actress, and though Mr. Orger may have suffered greatly in the spirit, love triumphed, and he left the Society of Friends to marry Mary, a tall girl of fine carriage, with a real cream and roses complexion and masses of lovely light brown hair. She left the stage and settled down to a quiet, secluded life, but after a year she began to miss the stage—the immemorial smell of sawdust, oranges and humanity, the fascination of candle-lit drama. Mr. Orger seems to have been a most understanding man, for, when Mary told him how unsettled she had become by her nostalgic yearning for the theatre, he agreed to her returning to the stage.

Mary reappeared at Glasgow with Master Betty, the infant Roscius, whose reception there was as riotously enthusiastic as was his appearance in London. Later Mrs. Orger came under the management of an extraordinary character named Beaumont who was given to tall stories. Once he regaled the company with a story about his scene painter, whose work, he said, approached genius. He had painted a snow scene so realistically that a man in the audience was struck down with agonising rheumatism. The man's wife complained to Beaumont about her husband's condition, and he told her to bring him to the theatre well wrapped in blankets and he would be admitted at half-price and cured. The wife did as she was advised and Beaumont put on a scene from *Don Juan* representing Hell. It was so effective that on beholding it the rheumatic victim broke into a profuse sweat and was cured on the spot. Or so the incorrigible Mr. Beaumont said!

Mrs. Orger played at Drury Lane and at the Lyceum, and the reason she never reached the heights was probably because she had the misfortune to be versatile, a quality that is often mistaken for mediocrity. It is the specialist who gets to the top and stays there, being in the enviable position of having a say in the casting.

Mrs. Orger, who was the mother of a beautiful daughter, dearly loved a gossip, and she was in the Green Room one evening, discussing with pretty Mrs. Humby and Mrs. Glover the forthcoming marriage of Charles Matthews to Madame Vestris, a person of brilliance, scandal and lovely legs. "It is said," chattered Mrs. Humby with wide-eyed innocence, "that before accepting him Vestris made a full confession of all her lovers," to which Mrs. Orger sniffed and said: "What needless trouble." The last word was, however, with Mrs. Glover. "But what a wonderful memory," she miaowed.

The men in her life—a father with the habits of a leech and a husband as voracious as a vampire—ruined all chance of happiness for Mrs. Glover, one of the best actresses of her time. Born in Newry on January 8, 1781, she was the daughter of a man named Betterton, himself an actor and no mean performer. Julia Betterton's mother died early and her father got her on to the stage as a toddler, and by the time she had reached six she had probably played more roles than many actresses today achieve at the age of sixty. Tate Wilkinson was the first to give her a real chance, and she was only eight when she played the young Duke of York in *Richard III* with George Frederick Cooke, who, drunk or not, knew an actress when he saw one and prophesied a great future for her. She was appearing in Bath at the age of fifteen when she came under the notice of Harris of Covent Garden and was offered £10 a week for a year or a three years' engagement, to be increased by £1 every twelve months. On her behalf her father refused and after considerable haggling she went to the Garden for five years, starting at £15 and rising to £20 a week. While she was establishing her reputation, her father was spending her earnings, and she was dependent upon him for everything, despite the fact that she was the breadwinner. She was eighteen, virtuous, and already a celebrated actress when a young man named Glover paid court to her and was rebuffed.

Glover then turned to the father, to whom he confided that he was wealthy and had great expectations. Julia's father, unable to secure any ready money from the young man, agreed to help him on the understanding that he would enter into a bond for £1,000, to be payable when the marriage took place. Dominated by her father, Julia married Glover on March 20, 1800, but it was only exchanging one villainous guardian for another, for when Glover's family found he had married an actress he was cut off with the proverbial shilling. Needless to say, the bond was promptly dishonoured. She played with Kean in *A New Way to Pay Old Debts* and her professional success was all an actress could desire, but she had a husband and a family to keep. Also she discovered that the money she gave Glover was being used by him to maintain another woman, who in turn was crediting him with a second family. Julia Glover left him, taking with her the four children that had survived out of eight, but in law a man's wife

PLATE XV

SARAH SIDDONS

perhaps the greatest tragedienne in the history of the British stage

Four stages in the career of the incomparable Ellen Terry, to whom the author pays a moving tribute in Chapter 25

was his chattel and Glover was able to secure £6 out of her weekly salary of £10. He actually sued Drury Lane in this connection for back pay and got a farthing damages. He continued to make life hell for his wife, and when Queen Victoria learned of this persecution she gave her patronage to a benefit for Julia and years later, when Julia fell ill, provided a carriage so that Julia in her convalescence could get the fresh air she needed. Julia died in harness in 1850, for she had just finished a performance when Death dropped the curtain on her own personal drama.

In her early days as an actress, Mrs. Mardyn could neither read nor write and her parts had to be read over to her for her to memorise. She was not destined to become a great actress, for her lack of education defeated that possibility, but she had the gift of playing from within herself and this together with her unfailing vitality, gave her far more natural charm than any polished mannerisms could have produced. She is believed to have been born in Ireland in 1789, but whether she was a child of love or not cannot be confirmed. What is certain is that she was brought up in poverty and seems to have been at one time in service in Portsmouth. Apparently a naval officer wanted to marry her, but was drowned before he could place a wedding ring on her finger, and then she seems to have been falsely accused of theft. She met a no-account actor named Mardyn and married him, later becoming wardrobe mistress for the company he worked with. She was then nineteen, and very pretty, and of course became stage-struck. Her first appearance was in 1808 in a farce called *The Jew and the Doctor*, but after further experience she turned up in London and played in breeches in a booth attached to a public-house in Kensington. It was a hand-to-mouth existence and Mrs. Mardyn had often, child in arms, to follow her drunken husband from tavern to tavern in order to get some money out of him. She was very attractive and audiences liked her, and ultimately, in 1815, Drury Lane, in search of new blood, engaged her. She played Amelia Wildenhaim in *Lover's Vows* and her high spirits and girlish romping, although very ingenuous, endeared her to theatregoers.

She left her husband and allowed him two guineas a week, but that wily gent got a friend to report his death and asked for the expenses for the funeral. Mrs. Mardyn gratefully paid up, only to meet her "dead" husband at the stage door a few nights later, roaring drunk.

At that time Lord Byron was a power at Drury Lane and Mrs. Mardyn wanted to meet him about a part she desired in a play. She may not have been aware of His Lordship's domestic difficulties, but she knew she had precious little chance of speaking to him at the theatre and asked for an interview at his home. It was granted, and as it was raining heavily when she prepared to leave, Lord Byron sent for his carriage and ordered the coachman to drive her to the theatre. Lady Byron's maid then spread a tale of an assignation under the very roof that sheltered Her Ladyship and although there was not a word of truth in it when Mrs. Mardyn played at Drury Lane she was cat-called and castigated. She burst into tears at this cruel calumny and appealed to the audience to whom she told the true story. They believed her and that was the end of the demonstration. After a spell at the Haymarket she went on a Continental tour and came back to accept the protection of an eminent person and repair the holes in her ragged education. Kemble said of her that she could look a volume but scarcely speak a word, and that about summed it up. She had the makings of a fine actress but not the opportunity, and her beauty and personal appeal had to suffice. She deserved the happiness that she found after leaving the stage and her last years were spent in contentment.

CHAPTER TWENTY-ONE

The Merry Heart

SHE was Shakespeare's merry heart that went all the way and left the sad to tire in a mile; she was lowly-born but loved laughter and reward led her along the golden path to riches and happiness; she was Harriet Mellon, the girl from nowhere, who married millions and later became the Duchess of St. Albans at whose festive table Royalty was pleased to sit.

The truth about Harriet's parentage was never fully disclosed. Her mother stuck to the story that her daughter's father was a Lieutenant Matthew Mellon of the Madras Infantry who was inconsiderate enough to die before he could proclaim to the world that Sarah Mellon was his wife. Sarah hinted that far from being a mere lieutenant he was highly born, but Harriet never saw him and it may well be that neither did her mother, for she had nothing with which to support her story. Sarah's background was certainly of the humblest. She was the daughter of an Irish peasant woman who had never learned to read or write. The prayers and little poetry she knew had been learned by heart. She was of striking appearance and though she was never much good as an actress she joined a little company of strollers as dresser, wardrobe mistress and money taker. Somehow she managed to get to London and on November 11, 1777, in poor lodgings at Lambeth gave birth to Harriet, father unknown until Sarah thought up Lieutenant Mellon. She had previously worked for a man named Kena, whose company she rejoined, taking her baby along with her. During a tour of the North a young man named Entwistle was engaged as violinist and four years later Sarah became his wife.

She was a tall, handsome young woman with an oval face, laughing dark eyes, jet black hair and a tender mouth. She had the gift of blarney and was too much of a handful for her husband, a weak and lazy individual, whose only merit was that he loved his little stepdaughter. He would not work until driven by hunger.

Often they tramped from town to town taking turns in carrying the child and their next most precious possession, the violin, and Sarah saw to it that the youngster got some kind of schooling whenever the opportunity presented itself. Harriet possessed her mother's good looks and, though often naughty at school, could read at an early age and thanks to her mother knew a good deal of poetry and could recite speeches from plays by the yard. She evidently surprised her teachers with her knowledge of Shakespeare and they kept her behind after school hours for further instruction and to teach her something about manners and conduct. Years later when she came to London Sheridan declared that she had a better command of language in ordinary conversation than that of any young woman he had ever met.

Sarah's one thought was for her little Harriet and, although she would on occasion storm and rage like a tornado, she won the child's heart, and Harriet throughout the whole of her life remembered her with the deepest affection. When the Entwistles left the strolling players they were taken on by another company at Preston for 17*s*. 6*d*. a week. Sarah looked after the wardrobe and her husband played in the orchestra and both were expected "to take characters in the processions." In the meantime Harriet was taught to sing by her stepfather and just before she reached the age of ten enjoyed the warming experience of a miniature triumph that must have seemed tremendously important to her. She played Mrs. Jordan's famous part in *The Spoiled Child*, which was staged in a barn adjoining the White Hart Hotel at Ulverstone. Harriet had by then a delightful speaking voice and so well did she do that the management made her a present of ten shillings and promised her another part.

Mrs. Entwistle's maternal instincts had never needed prodding, and although she was probably unaware that a swan sheltered beneath her wing, she still felt that Harriet was capable of rising above the life of hardship that she herself had had to endure. Anyhow she came to a satisfactory arrangement with another troupe playing at Stafford and controlled by a man named Stanton. She and her husband were to carry out their usual duties and Harriet was to play all the juvenile leads for a round payment of 30*s*. a week. Stanton was a bit above the ordinary type of provincial manager and was friendly with the county families and this suggested to Mrs. Entwistle the prospect of social advancement for her daughter. And so it turned out, for Harriet became a popular member of the company and friendly with the daughters of a banker named Wright. She visited their home and they lent her a pony to go riding, a recreation restricted by Mrs. Entwistle's unwillingness to give her a penny to pay the turnpike. Although Harriet was earning most of the money that came the way of her family, Mrs. Entwistle was in control and the only money she gave her daughter was a few coppers to put in a box to help those unfortunate enough to be imprisoned for debt. That had long been a sacred rite. While playing in *The Belle's Stratagem* and *The Romp*, at Stratford, Harriet was seen by Sheridan, then Member of Parliament for the town, and he promised to give her a chance.

When playgoers scanned the bill for a performance of *The Rivals* at Drury Lane one night in September, 1795, it was seen that an unknown actress named Harriet Mellon was playing Lydia Languish. Her voice and appearance came in for favourable comment, but that was about all, and after she had played out the season there the newcomer went on a tour of the provinces, for she still needed lots of experience and was wise enough to realise it. Still, she was progressing and saving money, and was able, at her mother's suggestion, to set Entwistle up in Cheltenham in a little music shop of his own. Sarah wanted him out of the way because he drank. Back at Drury Lane once more, Harriet made many friends for she was, above all, a merry girl who brought her own happiness with her and it was infectious. Her friends respected her chastity and even Miss Farren, a difficult person to deal with, liked her. She came across Harriet one day humming a tune and tapping out the rhythm with her feet and said to her "You happy girl, I'd give worlds to command a heart as light as yours."

For some time Harriet and her mother lived in Little Russell Street on a second floor above a milk-vendor's. They moved in on St. Patrick's Day, and all her life Harriet cherished the memory of those humble lodgings, to which she paid a yearly pilgrimage. When she felt that it was safe to leave her daughter in London, Mrs. Entwistle returned to Cheltenham, but would return periodically, perhaps to borrow money, and always to nag her daughter, despite the affection between them.

Opportunities did not come freely to Harriet at Drury Lane but as an understudy to the bigger names there she got her chance now and then, particularly when Jane Pope fell ill. Mrs. Entwistle, who was again short of cash, suggested that Harriet should visit Cheltenham for a benefit performance and she agreed, going down there with Miss Gifford, her closest friend who, incidentally, helped to push the tickets, even to sending a letter of invitation to Thomas Coutts, an elderly banker of immense wealth known to be staying in the town. Harriet and her friend thought no more of it until they went for a stroll along the Long Walk a few days before the performance was due to take place, and were stopped by a shabby old gentleman of frail build. Harriet did not know him, but he knew her and said he had seen her at Drury Lane and introduced himself as Thomas Coutts. She gave him a ravishing smile and he told her he had just sent along to the theatre a donation of five golden guineas, straight from the Mint, and trusted that they would prove lucky to her. Harriet in those days was twenty-four, and she looked more like a healthy girl from the country than an actress; she must have appeared that way to Coutts, who was seventy and looked it. No wonder Mrs. Entwistle began to dream afresh over her daughter's future.

Coutts was full of contradictions. He was the moving spirit behind the bank that bore his name, but, liking to be taken for almost a pauper, he went about in clothes that were no credit to his tailor. He would practise all sorts of small economies and also give away princely sums to charity. He had married the domestic servant of his brother and was the father of three daughters, but the family wealth enabled them to marry into the aristocracy. One was the wife of Sir Francis Burdett, another married the Earl of Guildford and the third took the Marquis of Bute for her husband. Mrs. Coutts had become mentally deranged and no doubt old Coutts was a lonely man. His private life was irreproachable and his friendship with Harriet Mellon beyond all criticism. He had taken an instant liking to her and probably felt he could use a little of the sunshine she radiated. Her reputation, too, was something to be proud of and no doubt Coutts was aware of this and he began to visit her at her lodgings. He preferred the lunch and simplicity of the place to his own home in Stratton Street, Piccadilly.

Mrs. Entwistle thought she saw possibilities in the friendship between them and took to coming up to town. She saw the woeful state of the banker's clothes and mended, darned and washed for him, much to the delight of his frugal soul. Harriet could afford to laugh at the sly hints she received in the Green Room, for scandal had never touched her and nor did malice. She was above hurt from either. Her salary was excellent and she had just won a fat prize in a lottery. Coutts introduced her to his daughters, and if they looked at her questioningly at first they soon dismissed their suspicions and admitted her to the intimacy of the family, either at Stratton Street or at Holly Lodge, Highgate. Eleven happy years went by in this way with Harriet still in demand as an actress, particularly when Mrs. Jordan left Drury Lane.

In January, 1815, Mrs. Coutts died and the old man turned to Harriett. He told her that he knew they had been the subject of gossip and that, however baseless it was, he felt he owed it to her to make her his wife. Their friendship had been based on mutual kindness and he would take no refusal. Harriet ran to her bedroom and came back with the five golden guineas in her hand which he had given her at Cheltenham. She asked him if he remembered the occasion and the old man was deeply touched.

Harriet knew that love did not enter into it. She was thirty-five and he was eighty, but she was very fond of him and determined to devote herself to the remaining years of his life. A fortnight after Mrs. Coutts was buried, Harriet was secretly married at St. Pancras Church, and she went back to the stage without anyone being the wiser. In the February of the same year she played Audrey in *As You Like It*, and although she may not have resembled Audrey as Shakespeare had conceived her, she looked absolutely enchanting in a yellow jacket trimmed with black lace, a striped petticoat and her well-shaped legs encased in yellow silk stockings. On her small feet she wore black silver buckled shoes and her husband, watching her from a box, decided that in future he was going to keep this lovely creature to himself. Harriet offered no objection. At that time, because of their secret, they were not living under the same roof, and a few days later when Harriet went to visit her husband at Stratton Street she found he was very ill and in the hands of his doctors. She demanded to know the truth about his condition, and thus the fact slipped out that she was his wife. Their marriage could no longer be kept dark and an announcement was made in *The Times*.

It was everybody's affair but their own, and Coutts was derided as a lecherous old man and Harriet as a shameless hussy who had sold herself to him for gold. Nothing could have been further from the truth, but it suited the scandalmongers to see it in this way, although Coutts could afford to ignore them—and so too could Harriet, as the wife of a millionaire. The management at Drury Lane then discovered how great was Harriet's talent, and how grievous the damage caused by her sudden departure, and exacted a solatium of a thousand guineas. The Coutts family naturally did not take kindly to the news, but Harriet quelled their fears and so too did their father—at least they knew and had admired the woman he had married.

Harriet became her husband's nurse and she did more for him than could his doctors. Her opulent good health and cheerfulness provided just the tonic he needed, and old Coutts seemed to draw vitality from her mere presence. She knew she was under the surveillance of every scandalmonger in town, so she sought out for her husband a middle-aged doctor who was married, but even this precaution failed, for his wife became jealous and insisted on his giving up the lucrative appointment. Harriet's mother died four months later. She had seen her fondest wishes come true and her daughter, now one of the richest women in London, had the chance of displaying the breeding she was supposed to have acquired from her mysterious father. True Mrs. Entwistle had been a rare schemer and avaricious as soon as her daughter began to earn money, but the girl had been brought up respectably, and, unless she had been remarkably discreet, appears never to have had an *affaire*.

Entwistle was offered an annuity of £500 and a cottage on the Thames, but he declined to leave Cheltenham, and knew he would never be short of money while Harriet lived. Old Coutts made the most of his marriage and entertained on a grand scale, and there was that occasion when four Royal Dukes, York, Clarence, Kent and Sussex, came to dine and be entertained by as gracious and as merry a hostess as ever graced a mansion. Harriet was really a great lady in her own right, for she was as much at ease with the quality as she was with her stage friends, whom she still met. Once when the house was packed with titled people, two of her stepfather's sisters visited her who were each given to smoking clay pipes, but Harriet welcomed them and society thought the better of her for it.

She loved Holly Lodge, a fine old house with lovely grounds, and, being superstitious, as most stage folk are, she had two old horseshoes affixed to the marble steps outside. They must have appeared rather dreadful to those who saw them, but nothing in the world would induce her to have them removed. She observed all the old customs and ate the right dishes on their right day and, if she ate an egg, always punctured the other hole to prevent the Devil from taking possession of the shell. She rewarded a hairdresser and a coachbuilder years after they had interpreted dreams that eventually became true. On March 2, 1822, seven years to the day of the announcement of their marriage, Coutts passed away peacefully and left his enormous fortune solely to his wife. It created some ill feeling with his daughters, despite the fact that their father had treated them generously when they married. They need not have worried, for Harriet called them together and dealt munificently with them out of her huge inheritance

Her vast wealth aroused envy, and several people tried to blackmail her by demanding money for the suppression of scurrilous accounts of her life. One of them, a clergyman, was brazen enough to call on her and suggest a payment of £100 for keeping quiet. Harriet Coutts, who could be as formidable as her mother when roused, took the manuscript from him and tossed it on the fire. She kept alive the memory of her husband: a statue stood in one room, his portrait hung over her bed and she slept on the pillow on which he had breathed his last. On the anniversary of his death she would go to the bank where he had worked and kiss the desk he had always used. She was grateful for what her husband had done for her and, although she did not go into a widow's retirement, she neither forgot, nor had the desire, to forget the old man.

Now forty-four with a fortune of a million and a half, even after making handsome gifts to her stepdaughters, she could have taken her choice of a score or more distinguished suitors. Even Elliston, the actor-manager, proposed and there was a rumour that His Royal Highness the Duke of York—who was also hard up—had offered his hand.

Harriet, however, remained a widow, and when mourning was over began to entertain and be entertained. She was a guest at a dinner at which it was hoped that young Lord Burchett (a descendant of Nell Gwynne and Charles II) would overcome his shyness sufficiently to propose to a certain young heiress who had agreed to accept him. But the young nobleman ignored the unfortunate girl and had eyes only for the radiant widow Coutts. His father, the Duke of St. Albans, was not at all displeased by his son's choice, and asked permission to call on Mrs. Coutts. She consented and he brought his son along. Before any arrangement could be reached, the father died a few weeks later and the new Duke of St. Albans then called and placed his hand and title at her disposal. Harriet reminded him that she was twenty years older and asked him to wait a year and speak to her again.

She then went off on a tour of Scotland and visited Sir Walter Scott, whom she asked for advice, the Duke having proposed a second time. Mrs. Coutts said that although she was not in love with him she entertained the friendliest feelings. Scott replied that friendliness was akin to love and therefore advised her to accept him. Sir Walter was impressed by Mrs. Coutts and, being a diarist, he noted how natural she was and free from pride. Harriet married the Duke by special licence on June 16, 1827, at her house in Stratton Street. The gossips would not be denied and said she was a snob who could not resist a title. The Duke was branded as a fortune-hunter, although his wife made no settlement on him in proportion to her means, but is said to have given him £30,000 as a wedding present.

When he was alive old Coutts had always maintained a house at Brighton, and now that she had become a Duchess, Harriet spent part of her time there, and tried to make the place livelier than it was. She organised many parties and revived the old sport of hawking. On the Downs she could be seen dressed for the part and looking regal on horseback. She wore a sweeping hat of black feathers, a green velvet dress, while from her belt hung a replica of a hawk in diamonds. Beside her rode the Duke resplendent in the costume of the Grand Falconer. Harriet liked to entertain her guests with stories of her experiences as a strolling player and her drollness was always admired. She made few demands on her guests, but she liked them to be punctual, because she retired early and disliked being kept up late by dilatory arrivals. Her invitation cards bore the time of assembly in large letters doubly underlined and, on one occasion when unpunctuality was the order of the evening, she ordered the doors to be closed and nobody admitted afterwards. Later in the evening there was a great rumpus, for a party of military men, determined not to forgo the festivities, hammered on the door and then got in through another entrance.

In the beginning of June, 1837, she collapsed at her Town house and must have received a premonition of her approaching end, for she ignored the advice of her medical advisers and ordered her carriage to be brought round. She was driven to Holly Lodge, and she then told her coachman to take her round the grounds of that splendid estate, where she had found so much happiness. She was saying goodbye and returned to Stratton Street afterwards. For some little time her bed was made up in the drawing-room, but soon she felt she must return to her own room—the room in which Thomas Coutts had spent his last hours. And it was there that she died on August 6, 1837. In her will she left the Duke £10,000, an annuity for a similar amount, and two of her houses, but stipulated that if he allowed his uncle, Lord Amelius Beauclerk or any of Lord Amelius's family, or the Duke's brothers, Lord Frederick and Lord Charles Beauclerk, to live with him in either of them, or elsewhere, the gift would be rescinded and the annuity as well. There must have been a terrific family feud at some time. In addition there were annuities and gifts to her friends and domestic staff, but the bulk of the huge fortune went to Angela, a favourite niece, on the understanding that the name of Coutts would be added to the name of Burdett.

It can be said of Harriet Mellon that she did a great deal of good in her lifetime and harmed nobody. She was sixty years of age when her merry heart stopped beating.

CHAPTER TWENTY-TWO

Immortal Sarah

WHAT can be said of Sarah Siddons that has not already been said? Biographies of varying value, critical surveys, articles which have probed into her art and reputation—artistic not social—are without number. And the consensus is that of all the ladies who came first, that is, all who shone before the nineteenth century merged into contemporary times—Sarah Siddons was immeasurably the greatest. There is little doubt that she was the greatest tragedienne our country ever produced, some would say the greatest the world has ever produced, although that would be contested by the supporters of that other Sarah, whose name was Bernhardt, as well as by devotees of Duse and other tragediennes of renown. Though unique and peerless in her own realm Siddons was not the greatest British actress of all time; the undisputed claimant to that title still remains Ellen Terry, whose all-round gifts transcended those of Siddons. Terry was infinitely human, lovable, and approachable; Siddons inspired awe, admiration and immense respect. Such an aura surrounds the memory of Siddons that a famous actor hearing about the preparations of this book and learning that it would begin with the first English actress, said at once, "Ah, Mrs. Siddons, of course." He knew little of those who went before, or he had forgotten; Mrs. Siddons, in his estimation, filled the past.

What set Siddons apart from all the rest was that she was entirely of the Theatre, possessing virtually no life outside it. She was a wife, and a mother many times over, but to her all this was incidental, something between the acts; the stage was everything, the Theatre was her Universe. What happened there was real, all else was Illusion. She expressed her whole being in her art; she carried with her the very spirit of the Theatre and indeed, from the time when she first came into prominence, she never ceased acting for a moment, on or off the stage. It was no pose, no trick to catch the notice of the public; it was a complete obsession with what, to her at all events, was the reality of Life—the Illusion of the Theatre. Her very speech was blank verse. To the careless waiter who brought her the wrong refreshment she would declaim:

> I asked for porter, boy
> You bring me beer.

To the girl in the shop, offering her a choice of umbrellas she would announce:

> This likes me well
> The cost? The cost?

the while she handled the gamp with a flourishing sweep. It was not exhibitionism or affectation; she just could not help it. That was her normal attitude and way of life.

In a human chain of players which stretched from Betterton right down to Macready, Sarah Siddons was an enduring link. Her grandfather, Ward, who had acted with Betterton toward the end of that wonderful man's career, was manager of a strolling troupe and his daughter (Sarah's mother) was a leading lady therein. They were people of considerable respectability and integrity, and old Ward did not want his daughter to marry an actor. Born in Clonmel her name, too, was Sarah, and in due time Sarah Ward fell in love with a good looking young man who was hairdresser to the little company of players and also "went on" in small parts. Roger Kemble was a pretty bad actor, but possessing good manners, good looks and a certain amount of grace he won the heart of Sarah, his manager's daughter. Father Ward, who had himself been a well-known actor in London, having appeared with Betterton and with Barton Booth, utterly forbade his daughter to mate with a hairdresser and player of small parts. So the young couple ignored papa's objections and eloped.

The time came when Ward forgave the errant couple, salving his conscience by saying "I forbade her to marry an actor and she didn't. He will never be an actor."

But Ward's prophecy was not quite accurate for though Roger Kemble never gained great fame as actor he achieved the rank of actor-manager and gave a good account of himself. His wife, an excellent actress in her own right, said Roger was the most gentlemanly Falstaff she had ever seen. That was meant for praise and she spoke truer than she knew for the fat knight is a gentleman though he is seldom played as such.

Kemble and his wife started an itinerant company of their own, playing and struggling in the smallest towns and villages but making a living and maintaining a high standard of respectability, both personal and managerial. They endured amazing hardships, and as the years went on their little company became their own in almost a literal sense, for the family increased until at one time, almost every member of it was son, daughter or relation by marriage. The first recruit to the family and the company was a daughter, born July 5, 1755, in Brecon at the Shoulder of Mutton Inn. The place can still be seen; indeed it was there that a celebrated actor, Owen Nares, died in 1948 while visiting the birthplace of that child who was destined to become so famous.

The baby was christened Sarah, and little Sarah Kemble was barely out of her cradle before she was put on the stage; indeed the appearance of the infant prodigy evoked a protest from the audience.

Sarah's mother saw to it that her child received the best education which their nomadic life permitted. She attended a day school wherever the family was currently located and was treated with a good deal of scorn by the prim young ladies of the neighbourhood, because she was the child of a player. But Sarah Kemble (the Siddons to be) never lacked pluck and she endured her humiliation courageously.

She played the young Princess Elizabeth at Worcester in 1767 in a celebrated play about Charles I. Her father played General Fairfax; her mother was Lady Fairfax; James, Duke of York was Master John Kemble; the Duke of Gloucester was Miss Frances Kemble. Sarah's sister wore the breeches, which was a form of attire Sarah herself never cultivated.

Sarah also played Rosetta in *Love in a Village*, so very popular for beginners (though she was hardly that, even at the age of twelve) and she was Ariel in *The Tempest* performed in a barn behind the King's Head public house in Worcester. Four years later she was at Wolverhampton acting in good parts. She was now sixteen and she was beautiful in her own way—a thing of classic, stately grace brightened by youth. The young men were aware of her—she had plenty of eager squires offering entertainment and there were rumours of an earl's interest too. But Sarah Kemble was not that sort of girl. Besides, there was a very handsome young actor from Birmingham in the company, one William Siddons, who had fallen in love with this handsome girl—and she with him. Family history was repeating itself. Mr. and Mrs. Kemble, it will be recalled, had defied parental authority and eloped, so it might be reasonable to expect they would permit their daughter to follow the dictates of her heart. But parents are not like that. They desired, understandably, that their daughter should do better than they had done, although they were happy enough. Thus the couple were told that marriage was out of the question and Mr. Siddons was bluntly informed that he would not be acceptable as a son-in-law. Nor was he a good actor either, little better indeed than Roger Kemble had been when he ran away with his Sarah.

But Mr. Siddons was not without resource. He wrote and recited a little ode, at his benefit show, which put the audience in full possession of the romantic facts and won him a good deal of sympathy, though it infuriated the sweetheart's parents. So he left the company, and young Sarah, who was disconsolate, left the company too. She shook off her parents, left the stage and took a job as lady's maid with a family named Greathead, titled people who lived at Guy's Cliffe, Warwick. Siddons pursued his Sarah to Warwick. They were married in Coventry in November 1773, the parents, in the meantime, having capitulated. She was eighteen, he was twenty-nine.

The couple returned to the Kemble's company, and young William apparently deserved his place, for the audiences in the tiny towns liked him. He had good looks, a pleasant manner and a gift of being able quickly to learn any part, no matter how long, being absolutely word perfect at the performance but forgetting every word the very next day. The young pair, entirely dependent upon the salary paid them by Roger Kemble, wanted advancement so they joined a company run by Crump and Chamberlain, two provincial managers of disrepute, at Cheltenham. The night came when she was to play Belvidera in *Venice Preserv'd*, the famous tragedy by Otway. Whilst young Sarah was dressing in the disgraceful room provided for that purpose—a ragged blanket separated the men and women—she was told that a party of important people from London itself were "in front," and that they had come chiefly to have a good laugh at the efforts of the strolling actors. This put Sarah on her mettle and she played as she had never played before—giving a performance of great tragic intensity. But from the box containing the London party came sounds which she took for derision, and she left the stage in a rage of despair.

She was wrong. It was not jeering she had heard; it was heartfelt sobbing, for she had so worked on their emotions that those who came to mock were melted in tears. They called upon Sarah Siddons, gave her praise, and presents and something she was in sore need of, clothes. The leader of the party, Lord Bruce, promised to speak to David Garrick about her, and Garrick, who so loved a lord, sent King, that fine actor, to have a look at this girl. He saw her play Calista, and much impressed, he advised Garrick to send for her. Garrick had his doubts, but he kept track of her.

Meanwhile Mrs. Siddons had gone into production on her own account. Her first child was born, so she now had to keep a baby as well as its father, for that was what the situation amounted to. But motherhood awakened latent emotions in her. Her powers of concentration increased, and a rekindling of imagination and a dynamic energy now possessed her. Studying the part of Lady Macbeth, she became absorbed in the character, saw it come to life, experienced what the murderous Lady was feeling, and with the realisation, fear came to her. She was so moved by the assassination scene—which now she appreciated clearly in all its implications—it seemed she was living the part, not acting it. She was in a panic, and seizing a candle she ran upstairs, the rustling of her own dress seeming to her to be pursuing, shadowy footsteps. She threw herself into bed, without undressing, seeking a sanctuary where she could elude the phantoms she had called up. She hardly slept but she continued to work on the part all through the next day and she played the role in the theatre at night. From that time on, all the parts she played obsessed her; once in costume, she ceased to be Sarah Siddons any more. She would go from her dressing-room on to the stage oblivious to all around her, completely in the thrall of her creation, almost in a state of trance. A step on the stage and the metamorphosis was complete. It was more a case of the part playing her than she playing it.

Eventually Garrick decided to try her out, sending one of his scouts, Dr. Henry Bate, to see the person whom he called "the woman Siddons." Bate was a remarkable character, being a clergyman, proprietor of the *Morning Post*, sportsman, duellist and a renowned boxer, but the role in which he fancied himself most was that of dramatic critic. "The woman Siddons" was playing Rosalind on a stage about nine feet wide, in a Worcester barn. She was also very obviously in "an interesting condition," but Bate was enthusiastic, and sent a glowing report to Garrick, advising that despite her shape at the time she nevertheless had "a good breeches figure." The great David was tired and getting near his retirement, after leading the stage for forty years. He had been plagued by his leading ladies, he had fought with, and triumphed over, many rivals—and he had raised the status of his profession to a height hitherto undreamed. Weary of the back-stage rows, he felt that here was a girl from the country, raw and green, he could control and have some peace for the time he had left.

Garrick offered Mr. and Mrs. Siddons, jointly, an engagement at Drury Lane for £5 a week, and Mr. Siddons accepted, allocating the salary as £3 to his wife and £2 to himself. But trouble sprang up. Their provincial management tried to stop them going to London and Covent Garden came forward with more tempting offers, which was the way of the Theatre then and, still is, for that matter.

An artist, an author, a composer may languish unrecognised for years. Then somebody takes a chance and immediately all the competitors try to cash in. In the Theatre they do not watch the public, they watch each other, which is probably why the proportion of failures so outweighs the number of successes.

All these complications occasioned delays which the Siddonses could ill afford and Siddons was constrained to fall back on that old theatrical dole—a "sub." Garrick advanced him £20 and immediately Mrs. Siddons gave birth to a daughter. She used her brief period of lying-in to make a list of her parts for Garrick to choose, and of the twenty-three submitted, she herself laid stress on seven, all contrasted. Amongst them were Belvidera, Portia and Rosalind.

He chose Portia and it was in that character that Sarah Siddons first appeared at Drury Lane. She came to town in November, weak and ill, after her confinement, with her husband and two children trailing after her. As Portia she faced a big audience on the night of December 29, 1775. There was a strong supporting cast, including King himself as Shylock and Bensley as Bassanio. The rest were the strength of the Drury Lane company and Garrick's standard was high. It was evening fraught with nerves for everyone in the ancient, renowned playhouse, and the two chief sufferers were Garrick and Sarah. It was soon apparent that someone had blundered. The new actress was not getting over. She was failing all along the line, obviously not suitable to the part, and a prey to fright, due to the vastness of the auditorium so alien to her, who had been used to the smallest of "barns." She was scared to death, her voice was stifled by nervous tension and above all, she was badly dressed. Also she was playing comedy, an ill choice for the début of one who was to be the greatest tragedienne of all time. Only her good looks, the handsome classic features and her rather delicate appearance were in her favour but quite definitely she failed.

Garrick tried again, again miscast her as Epicene in Johnson's *Silent Woman*, and again she failed. Her third venture nearly caused a riot . . . not on her account but because of the worthlessness of the play, a piece called *A Blackamoor Washed White*, written by her "discoverer," Bate. A critic wrote: "All played well except Mrs. Siddons, who, having no comedy in her nature, rendered that ridiculous which the author evidently intended to be pleasant."

As Mrs. Cowley in *The Runaway* and Mrs. Stickland in *The Suspicious Husband* she added further black marks to the miserable record. Then came her last chance. She appeared with Garrick himself, playing Lady Anne to his Richard III, one of his greatest creations. It was a dreadful ordeal for the sick, half-distraught woman, conscious of her record of failure and now playing opposite the greatest of all actors. Alas, she could not stand up to it. She forgot all she had been told and was conscious only of Garrick's angry, menacing eye upon her. In the solitary notice her performance received the critic said she was "lamentable." She blamed Garrick for her failure, believing he had miscast her purposely, which was not the case, though undoubtedly he had made an error of judgment.

So she went back to the provinces, the simple truth being that she was not yet ready for London.

She continued to play on, she also added to her family. Offers from other managements invited her to come to Town. She refused, saying she had made up her mind not to play in London again. She triumphed everywhere in the Provinces, and on her benefits she took calls, with her children around her, for Siddons the Matron was good publicity. She was never a favourite back stage; she did not "mix," being aloof and enwrapt in the work in hand. She was the quintessence of Theatre, only eschewing the social side and the gaieties and gossip of the Green Room.

Mrs. Siddons made a few friends, nevertheless, and Henderson, the great actor on whom the mantle of Garrick later fell, recommended her to Sheridan, who now had Drury Lane, but it is probable that the word of the Duchess of Devonshire, Sarah Siddons's greatest devotee, also carried weight with "Sherry." After his usual procrastination he made her an offer which she accepted, for she had never been serious about her threat not to play in London again. Indeed she was burning to avenge the shame of defeat, and yearning to triumph over Garrick, even if he was not there to see. No longer poor, for as a great provincial star her benefits had brought her big money, she came to town again—for Sheridan—once more to enter the arena of the Theatre Royal and fight it out. That was the sort of woman she was.

She now had vast experience, poise and her classical, if coldly statuesque, beauty. It was a very different Sarah Siddons. That year 1782 was to be a memorable one for the Theatre.

Coming to town a fortnight before she was due to open at The Lane, on October 10, Siddons and the family took lodgings at 149 Strand. This time she selected her own part, Isabella in *Isabella*,

or The Fatal Marriage, a part with which she felt she would win victory. She soaked herself in the study of the role, building it up in her mind, letting it seize her imagination, letting it suggest its own way to her emotions, so that when it came out, it issued of its own accord naturally.

Her voice, once weak, now rang forth to the uttermost corner of the enormous auditorium during the rehearsals and the company, watching her, was moved to tears. These rehearsals were long and arduous for with this return of a once defeated actress it was hoped to build the fading fortunes of Old Drury. Actually she had only two rehearsals. That sounds incredible now, but those were the days when actors and actresses had to be "up" in scores of parts and ready to perform them at a moment's notice. She had played Isabella many times before but this time she must transcend all previous efforts, for another defeat meant extinction.

The second rehearsal held the company spell-bound and King could scarcely find words to express his amazement, for while he had always believed in her, this was now Siddons past belief. She was so realistic that her eight-year-old son Henry, who had a child part in the play, actually thought that she had died in the death scene and he howled the place down until she rose and took him in her arms.

That night panic again seized her when she found her voice had become hoarse. Exhausted, she slept all night and when she awoke next day, the grey skies had cleared, the sun was shining, and this she took as an omen, for she had her superstitions. Though her voice was better she begged to be excused from the last run-through that had been called, and for most of the day she sat gazing at the sunshine, in an agony of mind with alternating hopes and fears. Relentlessly the clock ticked on towards the hour when she must put her fortune to the test, and she was still terrified, when her old father came round to support and calm her and to escort her to the theatre. William, the husband, who was in a nervous state, was told to keep away, and so father and daughter, provincial actor and potential Queen of Drury Lane set forth together, to meet the supreme challenge.

Siddons went into her dressing-room—the room is still there, much the same as it was when she used it—and one of her moods of depression descended on her, although she was outwardly calm and tranquil, her "desperate tranquillity" as she called it. Without speaking one word to a soul, only heaving a sigh from time to time, she let Isabella invade her, take possession of her, until she was Sarah Siddons no longer, but the tragic character she was about to portray on the stage.

She passed her father in the wings on her way to the stage without a sign of recognition for she was not his daughter, she was Isabella, and as her cue came a pang seemed to shoot through her whole body and her brain—she never forgot the moment, and her transition into Isabella was complete.

It was one of the great nights of Theatre history, comparable only to the débuts of Garrick before her and Kean not long afterwards. The excitement was tremendous and Siddons's triumph was staggering. The audience refused to let the players complete the play after Isabella was dead and there was almost pandemonium in the house. Nothing could be heard above the roar of human voices, yelling, cheering, acclaiming Siddons. It was a scene comparable only, for noise and enthusiasm, with the winning goal in a modern Cup Final. Exhausted by the terrific nervous strain she was unable to speak the epilogue that had been written for her. She was as solemn as a mourner and quite speechless in her hour of triumph; indeed she reacted to success exactly as she had done to failure, with dumb resignation. She went home with her father, and together with her husband they sat down to a very frugal supper which had all the ear-marks of an Irish wake. Her father shed tears of joy, the husband's attempt at chatter died on his lips and at last Mrs. Siddons, who had hardly spoken, went to bed. She lay awake for a long time reliving in her mind the unforgettable evening over and over again . . . and as the echoes of the frenzied applause receded from her senses the sleep of exhaustion claimed her. The dawn filled the sky with a new day—her first day as Queen of the Theatre—but Siddons slept on. . . .

All London went mad about Sarah Siddons. No wonder knowledgeable old Tate Wilkinson always referred to the year 1782 as "The year when Mrs. Siddons came to London and raised the price of salts and hartshorn." Henceforth after this astonishing night the crowds were phenomenal; people fought at the pit doors, many were taken away stunned or hurt, and Siddons went on to new triumphs, triumphs that were all the sweeter because she had tasted the bitterness of defeat. She never forgot . . .

So much has been written about the wonderful career of Siddons that there is no need here to recount the milestones. She hardly had a failure; only when she essayed comedy did she encounter trouble; in tragedy Siddons reigned supreme and unchallenged.

Some glimpses of the woman herself gleaned from contemporary records are worth recording. Let Dr. Johnson have his say: "Mrs. Siddons in her visit to me, behaved with great propriety and modesty, and left nothing behind her to be censured or despised. Neither praise nor money, the two powerful corrupters of mankind, seem to have depraved her." Probably the best Johnson story about her is the one concerning a call she made on the Doctor. She was unable to find a chair vacant and the contretemps was quickly seized upon by Johnson. "Madam," said he, "you who so often occasion a want of seats to other people will the more easily excuse the want of one yourself."

Tate Wilkinson, who has been so often quoted, adds his tribute. It is succinct. "If you ask me, What is a Queen? I should say, Mrs. Siddons."

And that famous Henderson summed her up as "an actress who never had an equal, nor would ever have a superior." Another fine actor, Charles Young, treasured a memory which deserves reiteration: "I remember her coming down the stage in the triumphal entry of her son, Coriolanus, when her dumb show drew plaudits which shook the house. She came alone, marching and beating time to the music, rolling (if that be not too strong a term to describe her motion) from side to side, swelling with the triumph of her son. Such was the intoxication of joy which flashed from her eye and lit up her whole face, that the effect was irresistible. She seemed to me to reap all the glory of that procession to herself. I could not take my eye from her. Coriolanus, banner and pageant, all went for nothing to me after she had left her place."

Now, that was not simply a case of an actress "hogging" the limelight, it happened to be precisely what Shakespeare had intended for Volumnia.

Lord Erskine, a notable orator, said that Siddons's performances were a school for oratory, and that he studied her cadences and intonations and that the harmony of her periods enabled him to improve his own eloquence. Thomas Campbell, a critic not to be despised, said that her lofty beauty, her graceful walk and gesture and her potent elocution marked her down for stage supremacy. But what mattered most was her judgment, and how she welded all her gifts into a perfect whole enabling her to give sustained performances of characters right down to the smallest details. Her secret was the consistency of her excellence: there were no spasmodic outbursts of brilliance.

She possessed indeed all the attributes of theatrical greatness. Just above middle height, she never showed the slightest signs of corpulency, the symmetry of her figure never altered and she had beauty of countenance and feature, a face that mirrored the emotions and moods of the character she was impersonating. Her eyes were large and eloquent; her voice always perfectly controlled, was in the main plaintive, often melancholy—but it could ring like a clarion call or be sonorous as an organ diapason. She could utter a shriek at moments of doom which pierced the very soul of her audiences.

Hazlitt apostrophised her thus: "The enthusiasm she excited had something idolatrous about it; we can conceive nothing grander. She embodied in our imaginations the fables of mythology of the heroic and deified mortals of elder time. She was not less than a goddess or a prophetess inspired by the gods. Power was seated on her brow; passion radiated from her breast as from a shrine; she was Tragedy personified."

And let Lord Byron have the last word: "Of actors, Cooke was the most natural, Kemble the most supernatural, Kean the medium between the two. But Mrs. Siddons was worth them all put together. . . ."

Few great actresses could excel her in "making an entrance." She showed how it should be done in a rather bad play *The Earl of Warwick*. There was an archway, centre, through which poured a regiment of soldiers, guarding a captive. They divided into two ranks, and immediately in that entrance stood the figure of the prisoner, Margaret of Anjou—Mrs. Siddons—motionless. She had appeared as if from nowhere yet timed to a split second. There she stood, bound in chains, head erect, her eyes sending out flashes of fire, doing nothing except simply being there, dominating the entire stage, indeed the entire theatre, with her astonishing personality.

Not only did Siddons spell-bind her audiences, she also had a profound effect on the actors playing on the stage with her. That same Young already quoted came under her spell in *The Gamester*. He was so choked with emotion at her performance that he could not speak. His throat contracting, he lost all control, and the prompter, thinking he had dried up, supplied the lines, but to no purpose, for all Young could do was to stand and stare mesmerised by Mrs. Siddons. She understood, and touching him on the shoulder said a stage whisper, "Mr. Young—recollect yourself." The spell was broken.

Once, an unfortunate actor who was playing the Surveyor to her Queen Catherine was so terrified by her glance of scorn and hatred that he fled off the stage and vowed he would never play with her again if he had to meet that look.

Of the countless parts she played, her enduring fame rests largely on her Lady Macbeth. When she first played it at Drury Lane she sat as usual in her dressing-room slowly immersing herself in the spirit of the part. Sheridan was nervous about the "business" of washing the hands which Siddons, breaking with tradition, had introduced into the sleep-walking scene, and greatly daring, he invaded her dressing-room to argue his point. She listened, though doubtless annoyed by his interrupting the metamorphosis of Mrs. Siddons into Lady Macbeth, but she resolutely refused to alter her "business." That sleep-walking scene would be played her way—and every actress has played it so since. . . .

She bade farewell to the stage at Covent Garden in that very part on June 29, 1812—the year of Waterloo. At the end of the sleep-walking scene, which that night she played as never before, an enormous roar of acclaim broke from the vast audience as the curtain fell. People stood on the benches and they demanded that the play should end there and then so that they might carry away with them the memory, undimmed, of that amazing climax. It was an unprecedented request but their wishes were obeyed. At the end although the final curtain remained down for twenty minutes—the house still cheered and clamoured for her. Then—

the curtains rose again revealing Mrs. Siddons sitting at a table, dressed in white. Pandemonium broke loose once again. She rose, came down to the footlights and a great hush fell upon the excited house. And to an adoring audience that had hung upon her every syllable she ended her farewell thus:

> Judges and friends, to whom the magic strain
> Of nature's feeling never spoke in vain,
> Perhaps your hearts, when years have glided by
> And past emotions wake a fleeting sigh
> May think on her whose lips have poured so long
> The charmed sorrows of your Shakespeare's song;
> On her who, parting to return no more
> Is now the mourner she but *seemed* before
> Herself subdued, resigns the melting spell
> And breathes, with swelling heart
> Her last, her long Farewell.

Kemble came upon the stage and led his sister off. She moved slowly away, as if in deep dejection, but there was no sign of a tear or trace of emotion for as soon as the last words were spoken, she seemed to have shed the raiment of the actress and become Sarah Siddons the woman.

They tried to persuade her to come back, after her retirement, but the utmost she would do was to give readings from Shakespeare, which always drew crowds.

In her retirement, she retained all her dignity. She was an honoured guest everywhere, and enjoyed Royal hospitality. There had never been a trace of scandal in her life although, years before, an attempt had been made to link her name with no justification whatever in an *affaire* with a fencing master. Sarah Siddons was incapable of infidelity and no man breathing would have had the courage to make the slightest advance to her.

She died June 8, 1831, at the age of seventy-six, a white-haired, distinguished old lady, looking like a Queen to the end. She was buried in Paddington Church Yard. After many years, the statue on her grave has been mended—her memory could never be defaced.

Garrick said, when Susanna Maria Cibber died, that Tragedy had died with her. It might well have been said of Sarah Siddons. Something of her genius as a tragedienne has been recaptured by an actress who graces the stage today. In recent times, at Edinburgh she played a long neglected part of Sarah Siddons' in the old play *Douglas*, and Sarah Siddons seemed to live again in the person of Dame Sybil Thorndike. . . .

Sarah Siddons was more than the immortal actress of the British Stage; she was an example to all who succeeded her, in her methods, her care, her complete immersion in her profession and in every character she played, and also in the fact that she had failed and then, never losing heart—she triumphed.

CHAPTER TWENTY-THREE

Vignette of Victorians

WHEN that great peak which was Siddons was veiled in the mists of retirement and eventual death, the lesser eminences around came into focus but, with one exception, they failed to dominate the theatrical landscape as she had done.

There were many noteworthy actresses on the stage of Victorian times and among the few who can make an entrance here was Helena Faucit—who became Lady Martin. She shed radiance on the stage from 1833 until she retired. Her retirement was made gradually and her final appearance as a professional actress seems to have been at Manchester in the year 1871. She had made a pact with her husband by which she should give certain performances every year, in order to maintain three relations of hers—all delicate and poor. She wanted the responsibility to be hers alone, and the money she earned by these little provincial tours she devoted to her charitable undertaking.

Her last professional role was as Portia. She held the house enthralled, and at the conclusion of the Court scene, when she should have said to Antonio, "I wish you well, and so I take my leave"—she turned and spoke those lines to the audience. It was the only sign of farewell she ever gave. . . .

Helena Faucit—she dropped the final "a" when she took to the stage—was born in London in 1817, five years after Siddons retired. She was of theatrical stock. Her grandfather, a merchant named Diddear who was of French extraction, had lost money in the East Indies, and started business in London as a silk mercer. He failed again, and turned to the stage. This was a curious quirk of Fate, for he became a good actor and later a successful provincial manager. He ran the Margate Theatre and it was there that an actor named Saville Faucit fell in love with Mr. Diddear's daughter Harriet. They were soon married and the couple did well. He was a good actor and dramatist, and she became a leading lady at both Covent Garden and Drury Lane. They had four sons and two daughters, and three of the boys became excellent actors. Helena the youngest of the family, and her elder sister Harriet (named after her mother), also went on the stage and became quite famous. Helena, a delicate affectionate child, was called "Birdie," and because of her parents' profession, she had to live mostly at boarding school where she felt lonely and unwanted. Her parents had separated; she sometimes saw her mother, but her father not at all. Books became her friends, and she steeped herself in an acting edition of Shakespeare, as used by John Philip Kemble. She knew much of "The Inferno" by heart as well and she was transported with delight when Imogen fell to her lot in a school reading. The Theatre, which was in her blood, became the paramount interest in her life and since she was not allowed to go to the play, so she acted to herself. She loved her sister, who was already an actress, and drank in all the stories she told. They spent holidays together at Richmond and it was on Richmond Green that she met one of the greatest actors the Theatre has ever known—Edmund Kean. He was failing and very ill when she glimpsed him, a small, pale sick man, shivering in a fur cap and cloak. His black piercing eyes frightened her, but her sister spoke to him and his voice—that voice which had swayed myriads—seem to her to come from a long, long way off, as if he had to summon it from a cavern inside him. He enquired, "Who is the little one?" and he gave her a wonderful smile which she never forgot. They sat on a seat and talked together for a long time. Her shyness gone, she had prattled on—telling him of her love for poetry and Shakespeare. When she told him her name was Helena, Kean smiled again. "Oh, the old ballad," he said. "Do you know it?—it begins

> O my Helen
> There is no tellin'
> Why love I fell in
> The Grave, my dwellin'
> Would I were well in. . . ."

He laid his hand, shrunken and thin, upon her arm and asked her to come to see him and recite to him. And then, he went away—very soon to that grave of which he had spoken. She never saw him again. But what an experience for a stage-struck child—to have chatted with the great Edmund Kean, to have had him recite to her and her sister—no wonder it lingered all her life.

The Theatre was forbidden her—but not her sister. They used to sneak in through the stage door, and once, when nobody seemed about, they crept on to the stage which was set with a balcony scene. Her sister said, "Go up, Birdie, and I'll be your Romeo." The child went up to the balcony and they played the scene. They thought they were alone, but away in the dark recesses, the lessee of the Theatre listened to them. He was much taken by the voice of the girl who spoke the lines of Juliet, he was impressed by her grace and figure, she was tall for her age. The lessee, Willis Jones, insisted that she should make a début and with a little plotting it was arranged. Announced simply as "A Young Lady" she was to play Juliet and her sister Lady Capulet. She dressed in the room which had been Kean's and which in 1833 still held the relics of things he had used. Her mother came down to stand by her daughter—little Helen, who was conscious of nothing at all but the role of Juliet. She went through the evening in a kind of trance. She remembered little of it and at the end she fainted. But she was an immense success and when she played again she was even better. Helen was only sixteen and she had to return to school. But she had tasted the thrill of stage success: nothing could stop her. And two years later, in 1835, she was at Covent Garden! She was to play Juliet, and no less a person than Charles Kemble, who had watched her rehearse, decided to play Mercutio on the occasion of her début. A snag arose. They could find no actor young enough to be Romeo to this youthful Juliet, so they changed the play to *The Hunchback* in which little Helen Faucit would be Julia. Though carefully trained by her mother and by a friend, Percy Farren, elder brother of William Farren, the great actor, she suffered agonies during rehearsals. When the actual night came, she was terrified. She went through with it, determined not to be defeated, and she was not. She had quite a triumph, an excellent Press and received a three years' engagement as a result. She played opposite to Charles Kemble for the rest of his career, and was his leading lady at his farewell performances in December, 1836.

William Charles Macready, who dominated the theatrical horizon, fired the imagination of Helen Faucit. When he became actor-manager at Covent Garden, he found Miss Faucit installed there and the management insisted that he took her over. He was absolutely astounded at her salary of £30 a week. But Miss Faucit was a popular favourite—and the management, politely but very firmly, informed Mr. Macready, the eminent tragedian, that if he desired to take over Covent Garden he must take over the leading lady too. He had a personal talk with her and found her charming and reasonable. After he explained his risks and his hopes, she met him halfway—accepting £15 a week instead of £30. So from 1837 onwards she remained with Macready, going with him to the Haymarket and to Drury Lane. At the Haymarket she played, as well as created, many parts, including Clara Douglas in Lytton's famous play, *Money*, which had such a struggle to get produced. Macready in his diary recorded that she was "a sweet girl"—and he even took her on for a call when they appeared together in *The Duchess de Vallière* at Covent Garden—a rare thing for Macready to do. Miss Faucit was a remarkably versatile actress with an immense range of parts. She was the original Pauline in *The Lady of Lyons*. A great part of her career was bound up with Macready's. She partnered him during his visit to France, where King Louis Phillippe presented her with a costly bracelet for her performance as Ophelia. For her Antigone, the Royal Irish Academy and Society of Ancient Arts presented her with a brooch of Irish gold, four inches in diameter. The public adored her, her personality was lovable, and there was never any scandal about her. Miss Faucit conformed exactly to the Victorian definition of a lady, a definition which took some living up to, and she contrived to be a very good actress as well. No less a person than Mrs. Kemble's father said that her rendering of the line "Dost thou love me? I know thou wilt say, 'Ay,'" afforded him the most exquisite pleasure. She asked the question slowly and with anxiety—and then answered it for Romeo, in the way she desired. De Quincey likened her Antigone to the perfection of the finest Grecian sculpture; it was said of her sleep-walking Scene in *Macbeth* that "to witness it was worth a thousand homilies against murder! There was in it such a frightful reality of horror, such terrible revelation of remorse, such unrepenting struggles to wash away, not the blood from the hands but the blood from the soul, that it made people shudder and their hair stand on end." It is of such things that acting is made.

As Rosalind she sparkled, she was joyous and gay, she took her audiences with her into the glades of Arden and all that she did seemed so natural and of the situation that she lived the part, not acted it.

Miss Faucit battled against ill-health and conquered it, as she did against difficulties with her voice. What she regarded as the greatest compliment she ever received was when she was playing Pauline in *The Lady of Lyons*. Noticing an empty chair in the wings, she asked why it was there, and was told that Mrs. Glover —the famous actress—always sat in it to watch her play certain scenes. . . .

Miss Faucit married Sir Theodore Martin, K.C.B., K.C.V.O., the eminent author who wrote a life of the Prince Consort. They were a most devoted couple, and amongst their friends must be counted Queen Victoria herself, who showed Miss Faucit many favours. On one occasion she sent the Royal yacht to bring her to the Isle of Wight, to give some performances at Osborne. The Queen presented her with a handsome bracelet, and during the actress's last illness, she kept up constant enquiries. And this was at a time when actresses were not received in polite Society. But Miss Faucit, Lady Martin, was different, for she was a lovely person to look at and she shed charm around her. She was one of those rare people as popular with the public as with members of their own profession. When she drove away from that Manchester Theatre after her informal farewell, crowds held up the carriage. A working-class woman with a baby in her arms, in the very front rank of the crush, kept knocking on the closed window. Helen Faucit opened it, and her humble admirer said she wanted her child to look upon "the dear lady" so that she, the mother, might tell her about it and remind her of it when she grew up. Helen Faucit kissed the child and the mother nearly swooned with delight. When she appeared in Edinburgh at the Theatre Royal, the manager and proprietor, Robert Wyndham (of the famous partnership of Howard and Wyndham), always gave her the

Green Room as her dressing-room. He met her at the stage door, lighted candles in hand, and bowed her into the room, for all the world as if she had been royalty. And indeed she was royalty of the Theatre.

When *Money* finished its first long run—it ran for eighty consecutive nights, an amazing thing in 1840—it had a revival the following year. Helen Faucit was unable to play her original part because of illness, so Clara Douglas was performed by another great Victorian actress, Mrs. Stirling. The lives of these two women ran together, and yet there was no enmity between them at any time. There are plenty of people still alive who saw Mrs. Stirling, for she survived until 1895, aged eighty-two.

Miss Faucit died on October 31, 1898, aged eighty-one.

Her rival and friend, Mrs. Stirling, was a most remarkable woman. She was born Mary Anne Hehl in Queen Street, Mayfair, in 1813. Her father, Captain Hehl, was Third Captain in the Regiment of Foot Guards and Assistant Quartermaster-General at the Horse Guards, London. A Freeman of the city of Dumfries, he was a portly, well-dressed gentleman of tremendous dignity and appears to have been a very honest man, for despite his job as Assistant Quartermaster-General, he got into severe financial straits. He had three children, a son who became a bank clerk, and two daughters, one who became Lady Superior of a Convent in Bruges—and Mary Anne Hehl. The latter received a good education, but when she finished school she had to earn her living. It was not easy then for a girl to make a career. Nor was marriage the refuge for a penniless girl, even though pretty, and Mary Anne was that. Fortunately, she had a mind of her own, and an ambition to go on the stage, a rather dubious calling for the daughter of a Captain in the Foot Guards. But needs must when the devil drives. The stage at that period was going through a difficult phase. There is no authentic note of Mary Anne's début, and while it is believed she started at the Coburg, now the Old Vic, there is no trace of it on any bill. The City Pantheon, nick-named the Grub Street Theatre, also claims the honour of introducing her to the public. This theatre, formerly the City Chapel, Fore Street, Cripplegate, E.C., was a very minor play-house, also used for displays by students of the musical and theatrical arts. Mary Anne probably had some lessons there.

It is pretty well authenticated that Mary, in her desire to act and earn money, applied to Amherst, the Manager of the East London Theatre, who was struck by her manner and her appearance. She got a job and took the name of Fanny Clifton.

By January 9, 1832, she was at the Pavilion Theatre with Farrell, earning £3 a week. Farrell was a robustious type of actor, popular in the lesser theatres of early Victorian times. He shouted his words and his part became three times as large as life, which his audiences loved, for they wanted escape from the Victorian way of life. Fanny Clifton started by playing Mdlle. Aubry in *The Man in the Iron Mask*. A Press critic described her as "a pretty piece of uninteresting matter, with just enough ability to speak her lines and no more." Well, critics are not prophets; they can only write of what they see. Did not one scribe have the temerity to report that "as Lady Anne, Mrs. Siddons was lamentable"? Probably at the time the critics were right. They have a knack of being right, even today. And, proverbially, managers are always wrong. A worthy gentleman who was for years an ardent first-nighter, used to demand of all and sundry, "What are the managers thinking of?" In due course he became a manager. Now he knows.

For a while Miss Clifton made little headway. She was badly cast and harshly treated by the critics.

But if managers and reviewers were being unkind, Fate was taking a hand. At the Pavilion there was a young actor named Edward Stirling who promptly fell in love with and married Fanny Clifton. Neither was established in the profession when they went on tour; they had a pretty bad time, being without money. Stirling organised benefits and wrote special pieces for them, they played in all the towns, but it was in Birmingham that Fanny Clifton's talent—now maturing—first really received notice. She was getting a sure touch, she was learning her business the hard way—but she was learning and mastering it. Managerial London became aware of her, and in January, 1836, at the age of twenty-three, she was invited by the Adelphi to play Biddy Nutts in the popular melodrama by J. C. Buckstone called *A Dream at Sea*. Though she had to follow a redoubtable actress, Mrs. Nisbett, she succeeded. Mrs. Stirling, as she was now known, was acclaimed by the critics. Exclaimed one: "She possesses in an eminent degree every requisite for a low comedy performer; she uses all with admirable tact and discretion, and she is withal, a very pretty woman."

The roles that followed, however, gave her little chance.

The Times was sorry for Mrs. Stirling. Its critic said on January 7, 1836: "Of Mrs. Stirling, who is a recent acquisiton, it is not too much to speak in terms of high encomium; she is a natural actress and imparts even to a character which never existed in nature an appearance of actual existence and life. It is to be regretted that her talents are not better employed." That critic was a perceptive writer for Mrs. Stirling's great gift was her ability to impart life and naturalness into all she touched, especially in her real line, which was comedy.

So far she had played only melodrama and low comedy. In 1837 she went to the Strand—which stood where the Aldwych Tube Station now is—and she played in comedy and farce. Her husband wrote one for her, called *Bachelor Buttons* and he gave her every chance, since she appeared as a tomboy schoolgirl, a jockey, a sportsman and a loquacious maid-of-all-work, being good in all of them. And to round off the evening, she played an officer in a burletta called *Venus in Arms*, a part in which she wore breeches. One critic was carried away. "What a handsome officer she makes, how genteel is her bearing—how amiable her little failings—how enchanting the symmetry of her person." At the St. James's, where Braham the unlucky had put his fortune to the test and was losing it all, Mrs. Stirling saved one show, *Natural Magic*, from utter condemnation. Nothing if not versatile, she played an aged countess and then a girl of eighteen. Then Braham staged a show called *Pascal Bruno* and cast her for a bandit chief. This pretty, fragile young woman was expected to make the public believe she was the current equivalent of the "Bad Man" of modern Western films. The whole thing failed, but further fiasco was to follow in *'Tis She; or Maid, Wife and Widow*, a play that was as bad as its name. Confused by a multiplicity of similar cues and quick changes, she appeared in widow's weeds when she should have been a bride! Only the quick-witted, inspired gagging of Ben Webster enabled her to get off, make the change and carry on with the play.

Temporarily, Mrs. Stirling quit the stage, to become, it is said, a governess. But she had left an impression in the minds and on the hearts of all who had seen her. Fanny Stirling did not stay away for long. On April 1, 1839—an ominous date—she was playing at what is now the Lyceum, but was then the English Opera House, in a play called *Lady Mary Wortley Montague, or Courtship and Marriage in 1712.* The play was not a success, but she was. She signed a contract for three years with W. J. Hammond, hoping thereby to get on the Drury Lane Pension Fund, but alas, the manager's tenure at the Lane did not last for three months.

There are some amusing contemporary pen-pictures of Mrs. Stirling. "In person, she is about the middle stature, with a figure approaching, from the waist upwards, to harmony and fair proportion. Her foot and ankle were fabricated for a larger structure and do not exactly assimilate with other adjacent beauties. Her teeth are regular and white and are set within two ruby lips, that even an anchorite might sigh to hear confessions from. Her eyes are small and dark, but vivid in their expression and sweetly penetrating in their glance." Thus one captivated critic. But what about that critic who found her so perfectly symmetrical in male attire?

She went to the Olympic in *The Ladies' Club* with Mrs. Glover, and she took up that actress's part when she left. She became a great friend of Mrs. Glover and of old William Farren, who correctly prophesied success for her.

At the Haymarket with Macready she made rapid progress. That tyrant put her through her paces, and in her old age she paid tribute to what she had learnt from him. It was at the Haymarket that she had to follow Helen Faucit as Clara in *Money*. She had something to follow—talent as well as beauty. The beauty of Helen Faucit, De Quincey was never tired of praising: "He who has seen the Coliseum by moonlight, the Bay of Naples by sunset, the Battlefield of Waterloo by daybreak and Miss Helen Faucit in Antigone has only to thank God and die, since nothing else remains worth living for." Fanny Stirling had to follow that.

Macready said he was much pleased with her as Clara. "She speaks with a freshness and truth that no other actress on the stage can now do," he declared. She played on, at the Haymarket, at Drury Lane, at the Strand, and Bunn engaged her to play Lady

Anne to Kean's Gloucester. Siddons had failed in that part the first time she played it at the Lane, and so did Mrs. Stirling.

Then she went to the old Princess's in Oxford Street, which stood on the spot now occupied by Woolworth's, and there she found great success, as she did, later, at the Lyceum with Vestris. The tide was flowing her way. But it was at the Olympic in 1849 that she gained her first triumph, and fortune stayed with her ever afterwards. She played Laura Leeson in *Time Tries All*—a play adapted from a story in the *Family Herald*—and she stepped at one bound into the front rank. It was not a great play, not even a good one, but that talent of Mrs. Stirling's for giving life to lay figures lent magic to the show. From then on she was a star, though nobody called them stars then. She even scored in tragedy in 1849, as Adrienne Lecouvreur, in a part to which she gave a splendour far beyond the merit of the play itself. She regarded it as her finest performance. It was a part in which Rachel had triumphed, and Fanny Stirling more than held her own. That was her vintage year, for she scored as Kate Hardcastle in *She Stoops to Conquer* and as Iolanthe in Sir Theodore Martin's play, *King Rene's Daughter*.

She stepped into Mrs. Glover's shoes when that lady retired, as Jane Pope had done into those vacated by Kitty Clive. Mrs. Stirling and Jane Pope had something in common, for Fanny Stirling was said to be the best Mrs. Candour since Jane Pope, who created the role.

In 1851 there came on the scene a dramatist who could write parts for Fanny Stirling, by now one of the leading ladies of the Victorian stage. He was Charles Reade, Vice-Chancellor of Magdalen College, Oxford. He adapted *The Ladies' Battle* from the French of Scribe and sent it to Mrs. Stirling. It was not a big success, but from it sprang something which was to be real and enduring, for, in 1852, Reade, who never stopped thinking about plays for Mrs. Stirling, conceived the idea of writing one about Peg Woffington for her to recreate. She brought him into touch with Tom Taylor, who knew all about stagecraft, which Reade did not at that time, and the two of them, spurred on by the actress, collaborated in a play. It was a tough job. They fought and they argued, but she kept the ring and made them stick to the job, for she knew it would be worth while. It was. The play was

Masks and Faces—over-written and badly made, maybe—but so much of the Theatre that it could hardly fail in those days of illusion and unreality in stage affairs. It was just what the mid-Victorians wanted. She knew it, and so did wise old Ben Webster at the Haymarket. It was theatrical history treated in the real theatrical way—twice as large as life—but who cared? Staged at the Haymarket on November 20, 1852, it was an immense success and as Peg Woffington Mrs. Stirling scored the hit of her career.

She worked on, this wonderful woman. She even put her daughter Fanny on the stage and appeared with her; but Fanny Junior had not her mother's genius.

As the nineteenth century turned its corner, Mrs. Stirling played less and less. She did not like the condition of the stage; she no longer felt at home; she resented the new methods. But she came out of semi-retirement now and again to show them her art and her wonderful gift of creating a character. She was received everywhere; there had never been any scandal attaching to her name, and she was in great request as a public speaker. She always appeared at benefits and the farewell performances of other people, but she never announced her own. She had been on the stage for fifty years and had travelled a long way since pretty little Fanny Clifton had been "a piece of uninteresting matter" in the East End.

Like Mrs. Siddons and Helen Faucit, she gave public readings from Shakespeare, and she would come back now and again to show the modern young things how parts—suitable to her age—should be played.

She came to the Lyceum under Sir Henry Irving's management and, with Ellen Terry as Juliet, she played the Nurse. Mrs. Stirling, who had played Shakespeare's heroines with Macready, now came to play for the man who had put the Theatre on the highest pinnacle it had ever occupied—Garrick not excluded—and to play with the greatest actress of the time. She had not the genius or the wide range of Ellen Terry—she belonged to a different school, almost another age—but she possessed the quality from which actresses are made. Irving, like all the true actor-managers, put quality first. He had asked Mrs. Stirling to play the Nurse to the finest Juliet within memory—perhaps ever. It was the zenith of the Victorian stage—and the year was 1882

—with Irving as Romeo, Terriss Mercutio, Ellen Terry Juliet and Mrs. Stirling the Nurse. There was another old-timer, Tom Mead, who played the Apothecary. The rehearsals were amazing, but Mrs. Stirling thought them very short and inadequate. She had some battles with Ellen Terry, over traditional business and rendering of lines, but in the end all was smooth and well. Let Ellen Terry herself tell the result:

> She played it splendidly. Indeed, she as the Nurse and old Tom Mead as the Apothecary—the two "old 'uns"—romped away with the chief honours, had the play all to nothing. . . . She was the only Nurse I have ever seen who did not play the part like a female pantaloon. She did not assume any great decrepitude. In the cords scene, where the Nurse tells Juliet of the death of Paris, she did not play for comedy at all, but was very emotional. Her parrot scream when she found me dead was horribly real and effective. . . . When she played the Nurse at the Lyceum, her voice had become a little jangled and harsh, but her eye was still bright, and her art had not abated—not one little bit, nor had her charm. Her smile was the most fascinating, irresistible thing imaginable. . . .

Mrs. Stirling played on, with the Bancrofts in *Caste*, even creating a new role in Pinero's *Lords and Commons* at the Haymarket in 1883—at the age of seventy. And she went back to the Lyceum again in 1884, to play the Nurse to the Juliet of lovely Mary Anderson. Just before this performance began, that eminent Victorian, W. E. Gladstone, said to Mary Anderson: "You will be seeing Fanny Stirling tonight. Please tell her from me she was my first love. No harm telling her that now." He had first seen her forty years previously.

Mrs. Stirling's very last part was played at the Lyceum in 1885, again with Irving and Ellen Terry, when she played Martha in the wonderful production of *Faust*. It was her final effort, and she was nearly blind when she played it. . . .

Her husband, Edward Stirling, had died in 1894, and in that same year, when she was eighty-one, she married a very old friend who had become a devoted companion, Sir Charles Gregory. He was a most courtly gentleman, and the home of the distinguished old couple at 3 Duchess Street, Portland Palce, became a rendezvous for all the great ones of the Theatre.

She died at the age of eighty-two on December 28, 1895. To her, all the world was a stage whereon one played many parts —as she had done, giving always of her best, staunchly faithful to her profession, and proud of its dignity. In truth she played many parts during that long life of hers, two hundred and sixty-five in London alone, to say nothing of the provincial roles. She had all the indomitability of the Victorians, she never gave up—and she triumphed mightily.

Amongst our great comediennes—in the best sense of the word —Fanny Clifton, Mrs. Stirling, Lady Gregory has a place of her own, but always, first and last, she was an actress and proud of it.

CHAPTER TWENTY-FOUR

Eminently Respectable

AT the time when Charles II paved the way for women to enter the theatrical profession on terms of equality with male actors, respectability was not regarded as the highest of virtues, and it has to be conceded that the majority of those ladies who seized the opportunity to enter the profession were by no means without blemish. Players, generally, retained some traces of what might be termed the outlawry of the road, added to which the morals of the time were notoriously loose. But customs alter and the evolutionary processes that change the character of all things began to have an effect on the modes and manners of the Theatre. A leavening was at work especially among some of the wilder and more unruly spirits and although it did not proceed quickly, it nevertheless worked surely.

Sarah Siddons was a monument of virtue and a symbol of the respectability that was later to permeate the Theatre and indeed the whole nation when Victoria came to the throne. It was a swing of the pendulum. The advent of a Queen after a long succession of kings wrought a fundamental change in the social life of the country. The licence, debauchery, gambling and fantastic fashions of the Regency and George IV periods began to disappear as the young Queen, with her purity of thought and wholesome outlook, gradually set new standards. If the evils were not wholly stamped out, they certainly went under cover, for apart from anything else the old way of life was no longer considered fashionable, and fashion is a potent weapon in the armoury of reform. The new Court set the fashion and respectability became fashionable.

It did not sweep the Theatre in a wave of revolutionary zeal, but it had a profound effect on the type of plays presented. They had to hold the mirror up to Nature and reflect the mood of contemporary life.

Professional actors and actresses were still not considered in some circles as being people "nice to know," but it is significant that within the first few years of the Age of Respectability two Ladies of the Theatre were recruited from the ranks of eminent respectability, and both eventually attained titles—a thing no actress had done before. One achieved the honour because her husband was given a knighthood; the other gained it herself, becoming in her later years a Dame of the British Empire. The first was Marie Effie Wilton, who became Lady Bancroft; the other Margaret (Madge) Robertson, who became Dame Madge Kendal. They were notable members of their profession, and they demonstrated that it was perfectly easy to be both a respectable woman and a superb actress.

Both, in theatrical parlance, were "born in a basket"; they were of theatrical stock. The stage claimed them as small children, they graced it for many years, and continued to shed lustre on it even in retirement. They were eminent actresses and they were eminently respectable. Dame Madge Kendal, indeed, could not tolerate anyone who was not respectable around her.

Neither was a tragedienne, tragedy having already gone when they began to shine, but both were queens of comedy in the highest sense of the word and both were versatile. They reached a ripe old age—Lady Bancroft eighty-two and Dame Kendal eighty-seven, and both left a mark on their profession for they possessed that finest attribute in the whole of the Theatre—quality.

Marie Effie Wilton, Lady Bancroft, was born in Doncaster in the year 1839, when Queen Victoria had been only two years on the throne. She died in 1921 under George V and saw the beginning of the new age which followed the First World War. Her father was intended for the Church, but he became stage struck, though his family, of eminent respectability in Gloucestershire, soon stopped that. So he went to sea. This he liked less than the idea of the Church. He tried the Law, which he found just as bad, and then enlisted in the Army—after a quarrel with his father, but twenty-four hours of soldiering found him beseeching his paternal parent to buy him out. That stern gentleman refused, but his mother managed to do it. And so he became an actor, which was the end of his family ties, for his father cast him out, since he had publicly abandoned "respectability." His only brother never spoke to him again, and only his fond mother grieved for her prodigal son. He married a girl who later became an actress, but neither ever achieved the slightest notability. They had six children who survived, all girls, and Marie Effie was the one who brought lustre to the name. She made her first appearance when she was either four or five, and all by herself this little tot would go on the stage and recite. She never had any childish fun, and at night, when her sisters were in bed, she was at the theatre with her father, playing children's parts. Her father wrote little sketches for her, and she would recite and sing as a little jockey, or as a tiny sailor in white trousers and a blue jacket, in the latter role dancing a hornpipe with immense success. She worked seven days a week, for on Sundays she was made to rehearse, and thus she never got a proper education. But her mother was her best teacher, and under that lady's care she learnt long recitations and many of the Shakespearean heroines in totality. It was from her mother that she learned the cardinal lesson for all actresses and actors—to be always completely audible in the largest theatres, the voice reaching the remotest recesses—and Marie Wilton never forgot this. Once she gave a recitation in aid of a church repairing fund, for which she got no fee, but she so delighted the ladies of the church that a little whip round to buy the mite a toy was suggested. Then some evil fate inspired one of the ladies to ask whose child she was, and out came the truth that not only was she a child of the Theatre, but her parents too were professional players. The purses snapped shut at once. The ladies, with expressions of horror, shook their skirts and quickly removed themselves from the presence of the little outcast. That was how the stage was regarded.

In those days, being an actress was not a glamorous job: it was as near hard labour as made no difference, and such a thing as comfort was unknown. Actresses today would be horrified at the sort of dressing-rooms then provided, or the general conditions which existed. But those Ladies Who Came First just carried on and Little Marie Wilton was a typical specimen. She shone at Norwich, Bristol and Bath, and on September 15, 1856, when she was seventeen, she made her first appearance in London, something of a veteran, with fourteen years of experience behind her. She played at the Lyceum, the part being the boy Henri in that fine old drama, *Belphegor*, with that splendid but drunken actor Dillon in the title role. On the same night she also played the title role in a burlesque by William Brough, entitled *Perdita, or the Royal Milkmaid*, which had its first performance that evening too —a double début, as it were. Dillon had seen her at Bristol, and though her mother wanted her to play comedy and had trained her to be natural, not barnstorming or stagey. Dillon insisted she play the part his way. She, however, had her own ideas, and she won, the result being that she had to take a special curtain call. Thus successfully launched in London, she went to the Haymarket and played in Talfourd's burlesque, *Atlanta*, again with success. The critics liked her not less than did the public, and in 1857 she was at the old Strand Theatre in *Court Favour*, put on specially for her so that she might play the part created by Madame Vestris. She was again a success. Now managements competed for this bright, vivacious girl, small in stature, but large in talent, a star of burlesque, farce, and extravaganza, who was able to make the house rock with laughter. It was at the Strand that she scored her biggest successes.

Touring with the Strand Theatre Burlesque Company, she was playing at Liverpool when a young actor in the Liverpool Stock Company saw her. He had played everything from Shakespeare to melodrama, but with only four years of stage work to his credit, London was not for him yet or so young Squire Bancroft thought up to the moment he saw Marie Wilton play in Liverpool, for he fell in love with her at first sight. Marie Wilton was going back to London; she was going into management with H. J. Byron, the dramatist, having already taken a terrible little theatre off the Tottenham Court Road, a graveyard of hopes which had brought ruin to many. It was, indeed, a "blood tub" given up to the worst form of melodrama at the lowest possible prices, but Marie Wilton was going to take the risk. Young Bancroft got a job in Miss Wilton's company and that settled his doubts about playing in Town.

Marie Wilton took that awful little Queen's Theatre, previously the Fitzroy and a string of other names, but popularly known as

"The Dust Hole," and which is now the Scala. She had £1,000 capital and the exclusive services of H. J. Byron as playwright, but he put up no money. Everyone warned her against the venture, but she persisted, for she remembered that a gipsy had once told her mother that little Marie would be one of the luckiest women in the world. She rechristened the little playhouse the Prince of Wales's by special permission of the Heir to the Throne, she had it redecorated, and, with only £150 left in the bank, she opened it on April 15, 1865, with a little comedy, a burlesque and a farce. Her fashionable audience had followed her, and the venture was a success from the word "go." Hansoms drove to the theatre for the first time for over twenty years. The only person disgruntled was an orange woman, whose wares were despised by the smart audiences. "If these are yer Haristocrats, give me the roughs. I've only took fourpence," she wailed.

The gipsy's prophecy was coming true. Her enterprise succeeded, even though the theatre had a narrow escape from being burned down on the very first night.

Fame came to Marie Wilton and her venture when her life became entwined with the family of the other eminently respectable Victorian who shares this chapter with her, and when Tom Robertson began to write his plays for her. She married that reliable and modest young actor, Squire Bancroft, and their lives and their management became a joint affair. With their author, they began to revolutionise not only stage methods and forms, but the very basis of English comedy. Those plays which Robertson wrote—nearly all had titles of one word: *Society*, *Ours*, *School*, *M.P.*, *Caste*—were something new; they were akin to life, yet had the romance of the stage. The Bancrofts, as they were now known, gave them wonderful casts and settings. All London went to the Prince of Wales's Theatre, the once despised Dust Hole, proving that it is not position which makes a theatre, but rather what is happening on its stage. Soon the Theatre world was talking; fame was gathering for the Bancrofts. Everything they did was of the highest quality and strictest respectability. *Caste* was a milestone in theatrical history, and Marie Wilton (Mrs. Bancroft) was never better than as Polly Eccles nor her husband than as Captain Hawtree. *Diplomacy*, the adaptation of the Sardou play, made history too, and was another acting triumph for the two of them, especially Mrs. Bancroft as Countess Zicka. And in that cast was Mrs. Kendal, sister of Tom Robertson, whose fame had been made by the Bancrofts, and her husband.

Success for the Bancrofts marched on, and soon they were the leaders of their profession, as well as the darlings of Society. How Mrs. Bancroft must have laughed when she recalled her earlier outcast days.

By 1879 they found their little kingdom in Tottenham Street rather too small for them. They yearned for that perfect theatre, the Haymarket, and Mrs. Bancroft's luck being what it was, that lovely place fell into their hands. They made it even lovelier than it had been. It was redecorated, given a new auditorium, and the pit abolished. The opening night of this distinguished couple in their new home was marked by one of the last of the old-fashioned riots, to say nothing of a real "London Particular" pea-soup fog outside, but the Bancrofts triumphed over both Nature and malcontents. That old gipsy had prophesied well.

They opened at the Haymarket on January 31, 1880, and they reigned there in glory until July 20, 1885. Then they said farewell to management, and almost farewell to the stage, except for a few appearances afterwards, mostly for charity. They were held in the greatest respect by all, and Bancroft was knighted—an honour which was as much for his wife as for himself, for always they had been a joint concern. As Lady Bancroft, she must have chuckled when she met Society folk at charity performances and remembered her first appearance at a charity performance, when she was scorned because she was a Theatre child.

She was for most of her life a tiny, dainty woman, with immense charm and tremendous talent. She was an actress of the natural school, which does not mean she underplayed. Her clarity of diction was remarkable, her ability to give point to lines and her timing were superb, but above all she had the gift of laughter. She could mix a smile and a sigh with the skill of a *cordon bleu* making a sauce, in exactly the right proportions.

It may be that both she and her husband, in later life, were a little stiff and pompous, a little ultra-Victorian in their eminent respectability; maybe she was inclined to forget occasionally that Lady Bancroft had once been Marie Wilton, queen of burlesque and extravaganza amongst the big-thighed beauties in tights at the old Strand. But who shall blame her—she who had known poverty, and hard toil and had conquered? She and her husband rendered inestimable service to the English stage, and their names endure—even though a young lady in the Drama Section of the B.B.C. might blandly confess to the present author that she had never heard of them! The Bancrofts are forever secure in the memory of true Theatre-lovers.

The life of that other eminently respectable lady of our Theatre, Mrs. Kendal, *née* Margaret Robertson, was just as remarkable as Marie Wilton's, except that no gipsy was on hand to foretell amazing luck. She was born in a Grimsby hostelry, where her theatrical parents were lodging, on March 15, 1848. Those parents were provincial players of good repute, and she thus had the calling in her blood.

She made her first London appearance long before her friendly rival, Marie Wilton, for little Margaret Robertson, always called Madge, went on at the Marylebone Theatre as the Blind Child in *The Seven Poor Travellers* at the mature age of four—in 1852. She was given a pair of new shoes of which she was inordinately proud, and when she entered, she skipped down to the footlights, caught sight of her nurse in front and cried out, "Nursie, look at my new shoes." There was a roar of laughter and rounds of applause. The Blind Child was a success all right, and she played several other parts at the Marylebone. In her memoirs she says that the first part she played was Marie in *The Struggle for Gold*, but even Ellen Terry disputed which house in Coventry she was born in—and records have a habit of being right, not that it matters very much.

Before she was seven, her parents took Madge to Bristol, a town from which much greatness has come, and not the least of it was Madge Robertson, Mrs. Kendal. Bristol has a long and proud theatrical history, and in letters of gold thereon is inscribed the name of James Henry Chute. Before he took over the Bristol Theatre he had been a provincial actor. So Madge's mother wrote to him, saying: "You were an actor once in our theatre. Let me be an actress in yours." Thus they went to Bristol, and Mr. Chute saw to it that little Madge got stage chances. She made her début as Little Eva in a dramatised version of *Uncle Tom's Cabin*, sang two or three little songs and hymns, died most affectingly, and was hauled up to heaven by a rope fastened round her waist. Everyone agreed it was beautiful.

Madge really began to learn her business with Chute at Bristol and Bath, playing with all the visiting stars, the great ones of the period. She appeared in all sorts of parts in all sorts of plays, and after ten years' gruelling experience in many provincial places, she was judged fit for London. Buckstone of the Haymarket offered her a contract for three years, starting at £10 a week and rising to £15. She was a very handsome girl, with clear-cut features, a fine figure and splendid voice, capable of expressing every emotion. When she got to the Haymarket, Buckstone had sub-let to Walter Montgomery for a short season, and she made her first mature London appearance on Saturday, July 29, as Ophelia to Montgomery's Hamlet. He did not please the public, but young, handsome and appealing Miss Robertson did. Then came a bit of a staggerer. She played Desdemona to the Othello of Ira Aldridge, a Negro actor. Now, a few years ago, between the wars, there was a storm when a young, beautiful and extremely talented English actress was announced to play Ophelia to the Othello of a very eminent Negro actor-vocalist. The association was not considered quite respectable. Yet there was no such outcry when the extremely respectable young Miss Robertson played Ophelia to a really black actor; indeed it was quite an occasion. Montgomery played Iago. Mrs. Kendal recalls that these performances were successful, and that Aldridge got applause by a clever trick of taking her own very white hand in his and marking the contrast of their colour. She remembered also that in the smothering scene he made her wear stockings with painted toes, so that it appeared as if she were really undressed, and he dragged her round the stage by the hair of her head. The audience hissed heartily at what seemed to them needless brutality, but Miss Robertson was not in the least put out.

After the Haymarket engagement, she went on tour again, and then to Drury Lane, where she appeared in 1867 in *The Great City*, playing the heroine at the age of nineteen. In 1868 she was back at the Haymarket and had become a first-class leading actress. And then, remarkable to relate, this star of Shakespeare and comedy, this very delightful and respectable young lady, became the first leading lady the Gaiety Theatre ever had, starring with Alfred

Wigan in *On the Cards* on the opening night of the theatre, December 21, 1868.

She was there in another play, *Dreams*, written by her famous brother, but he had not by then reached his full stature. Madge Robertson went back to the Haymarket, where the sun shone for her. She appeared in a play by Tom Taylor and Dubourg called *New Men and Old Acres*, a piece that creaked a bit, but Madge lifted it into success. She had the gift of laughter and tears, a gift she shared with Mrs. Bancroft, for they were both great comediennes. There was probably no other actress on the English stage who could cry like Madge Kendal could. It was not merely an outburst of emotion; the tears came as tears do in real life. No need for the glycerine of Hollywood; this was the real thing: a woman really crying, as women really do cry. One has seen many actresses do this, but nobody ever did it like Mrs. Kendal, not even Dame Marie Tempest, who came nearest. Madge added to her laurels with *New Men and Old Acres*. She was a splendid Lydia Languish in *The Rivals*, she was magnificent in Gilbert's *The Palace of Truth* and many people regarded her Galatea in *Pygmalion and Galatea* as her masterpiece, though others preferred her in *The Wicked World*.

Pygmalion was destined to change the course of her life, for she played opposite to a young actor named W. H. Kendal, whose real name was Grimston. They fell in love, though it was no whirlwind courtship. He was just as respectable as she was, a tall, well-set-up man, good-looking according to Victorian standards and a good actor—dependable and efficient rather than brilliant. Their engagement lasted for two years, and they were wed in Manchester on August 7, 1869.

Their life became a wonderful partnership, they never played apart, and their respect for the institution of marriage and its responsibilities was terrific. They became a prominent management, playing in the West End and in America, bringing luck to the then unfortunate St. James's Theatre in association with their friend John Hare, who was afterwards knighted. They took their talent to the provinces, along with a supporting cast of young people whom they had trained actually on the stage. They were hard taskmasters, especially Mrs. Kendal, who not only insisted on the very highest standards, but imposed on her company a rigid discipline. There was no nonsense, on or off the stage, no wild parties, nothing but hard work and the utmost respectability. Her companies held her in respect mingled with fear, and only one man ever defied her—the completely irrepressible Seymour Hicks, though he too held her in admiration and awe. Long after she retired she sent him a command to come and see her at her country house. Hicks could not refuse, but he was scared, and rather than go alone he made the author of this book accompany him, the better to cope with this formidable old lady. The author, it so happened, was in her good books, for, as a member of the Committee of Warrior's Day, he had once suggested that a good way to raise funds would be for prominent ladies of the stage to hold tea parties actually on the stage and charge visitors for the privilege of taking tea with such eminent hostesses. Mrs. Kendal was the first of these hostesses, and she sat in state on the stage at Wyndham's whilst a never-ending line of guests passed before her, each receiving a handshake and a smile. Few worried about the tea for which they had paid 5*s*. It was enough to be in company with Mrs. Kendal, a memory they could cherish for ever. The old lady was delighted. She radiated benevolence on that occasion, her customary rather frigid air being replaced by a genuine warmth. She was charm itself, and everybody was delighted. Thus Seymour Hicks had a good ally when he was summoned to the presence. Nevertheless, she put Seymour through a strict cross-examination, and though he was past middle age then, she treated him like a young recruit. He sat on the edge of his chair like a school-boy and answered all questions with great decorum and politeness. It was typical of the awe and respect Mrs. Kendal always engendered.

Perhaps as an actress (and certainly as a woman) she lacked the gift of passion, though she possessed practically everything else. She was far too respectable to rise to heights of passion, even in simulated form, and even her clothes were respectable. Her costume as Rosalind would have evoked laughter today, yet she was a very delightful Rosalind. It is not possible to record a hundredth part of her triumph or recount a thousandth part of what she achieved.

Mr. and Mrs. Kendal did yeoman service for the Theatre, in keeping the high level of acting constantly before the eyes of provincial playgoers.

If in their later years they seldom produced anything new, it did not matter, the public never tired of them in *The Elder Miss Blossom*, *The Ironmaster*, *A Scrap of Paper* and *Still Waters Run Deep*. They were Victorian plays played by masters of the art of Victorian acting. If, towards the end, Mrs. Kendal seemed a bit mature for some of the parts, a bit matronly for the shrinking virgin, the slighted, tender-hearted sister, she nevertheless played them so perfectly that nobody minded, and nothing seemed incongruous.

No scandal ever attached to the Kendals, nothing to tint the cheeks of "the young person," so preciously guarded in Victorian times. They were still acting when King Edward ruled, and they did not change at all. Kendal died in 1917. Sincerely mourned both as actor and man, he left each of the four children £5,000.

An extraordinary thing about this couple was that they did not get on very well with their children, despite that last bequest.

But this is no place to go into the whys and wherefores of the only crumpled rose leaf in the record of a remarkable man and woman. The world always said that Kendal was his wife's leading man; she always maintained that she was his leading lady. They left the stage a better place than they found it. She stands as one of the finest comedy actresses in our great Theatre history, one who played with the greatest of the Theatre—as their peer. Nobody privileged to see her and Ellen Terry as the Merry Wives of Windsor at His Majesty's, with Sir Herbert Tree as Falstaff, will ever forget the heights which English acting can reach. Perhaps she was not a very happy woman (and she was a very difficult one), but she was an institution, a monument of respectability. Queen Victoria was her friend and gave her presents; George V created her a Dame of the British Empire; Queen Alexandra condoled with her on her widowhood.

The Kendals had retired quietly and unobtrusively some time before Mr. Kendal died. She lived on to be eighty-seven, dying in 1935, a year after that interview with Seymour Hicks. In retirement, she had never lost her power and her name remained a standard for all that was best in our Theatre and for all that is encompassed in the term "respectability." A glance at her picture shows it all—a great actress, a beautiful woman—and the very essence of true Victorianism in every sense.

CHAPTER TWENTY-FIVE

A Great and Gracious Lady

THE most gracious lady our stage ever knew and one of the greatest actresses in the rich tapestry of our Theatre was born on February 27, 1847.

Her birthplace was Coventry, Warwickshire, in the very heart of green England, and in the same county as William Shakespeare, whose heroines she was to adorn with new glory. Her name was Alice Ellen Terry. She came within the category of those who, in Shakespeare's definition of greatness, are born great. It was not the greatness of ancient lineage, nor of worldly position, but that innate greatness of which she herself was quite unconscious, though apparent to everybody else. For even if you had never met her, but only sat and worshipped her from the public side of the footlights, you saw, felt and recognised that you were in the presence of true greatness. It is a quality which transcends all others.

She was a great woman, a great lady and a great actress. She came of actor parents, and before Ellen Terry ever trod the boards she was quite at home in theatres, for she would sleep as a small baby in her mother's dressing-room whilst that lady was on the stage playing her part.

She adored her parents. Her father taught her the first great lesson which all players should learn—to put quality first—and as soon as she could talk he taught her to speak clearly and well, tolerating no slipshod pronunciation even in her baby days. Believing that only the best is good enough, he taught her to take the greatest pains over every trifle, to let nothing go by chance, to realise that everything she did on the stage was of vital importance, and it must be said that she never forgot those lessons.

Naturally, she went on the stage and Glasgow nearly had the honour of her first appearance. Her parents were playing in that city and a small child was wanted for the pantomime, *The Spirit of the Mustard Pot.* Her father suggested tiny Ellen for the part; the stage-manager was agreeable, but Ellen Terry was not. It meant her being put into a mustard pot, from which she had to spring, and when they tried to "pot" her, as it were, she resisted violently and screamed the place down. Tearful, sobbing Ellen was taken home, and thus pantomime in Glasgow just missed Ellen Terry's stage début. It was reserved for a more distinguished field of action, for she actually made her first appearance as Mamilius in *A Winter's Tale* with Charles Kean at the Princess's Theatre in Oxford Street, the site of which is now covered by a Woolworth's emporium. Thus Shakespeare claimed her at once and thus she found herself surrounded by the best that the stage could offer in 1856, the year of her début.

The actor-manager was just coming into his own, and let the moderns say what they will, those were the best and palmiest days of our Theatre, when quality and the personal touch ruled, when men who practically lived in the Theatre ran the Theatre with understanding. Such a one, David Garrick, had reformed the stage and raised it to a height greater than it had achieved even under that famous triumvirate of actor-managers, Wilks, Doggett and Colley Cibber. John Philip Kemble had continued the good work, and Macready had gone a step further; he did wonderful pioneering work in décor, following the example set by an actress-manageress named Madame Vestris, who is remembered far too often only for her lovely legs and sultry reputation. And now had come Charles Kean to lay the foundation stone for the edifice that would be created by the Irving productions.

Ellen Terry's younger days—her most impressionable days—were spent in an environment in which quality was the rule for living, and it conditioned the whole course of her future career.

Charles Kean, when he controlled the Princess's Theatre, contributed to theatrical history, and although he had not the fire and genius of his wonderful father—the immortal Edmund Kean—he was generally sound, and indeed excellent in certain parts. As a manager he gave the stage the most lovely productions which London had ever seen until then—both scenically and artistically. There had been a bad period in the Theatre—a patch of slovenly production, indifferent plays and bad acting—and Charles Kean at the Princess's changed the course of things. It was a magnificent training ground for young Ellen Terry. Her father having taught her elocution, she now learned the technicalities of her work in the finest school of actual experience. Kean had a ballet master who taught the players how to walk. He pinned on to them a blanket which trailed behind their feet for a good six inches and hung down before them, and in this garment they had to walk with dignity. Ellen Terry mastered it almost at once. The actors also had to walk the plank, like pirate's victims. Long, narrow planks were laid across the stage, at some height above it, and along these they had to go, faster and faster, until they could achieve the passage without swerving from the straight line or looking down at their feet. Thus they learned balance, poise, upright carriage and certainty of gait. There were no breaks for lunch in the long rehearsals. Performances began at seven and went on until midnight. Players then earned their salaries, and rarely thought of taking a holiday. We could do with some of this spartan régime in the Theatre today.

Such was the training and groundwork of Ellen Terry's stage career. She drank it all in, wide-eyed and active; everything she saw was new, entrancing and delightful; everything she did gave her interest and joy. Those feelings she never lost. To the end of her days, she constantly found new joys, new delights, and nothing ever bored her for she was in love with life and the Theatre.

She travelled about with her family after those days at the Princess's like a real strolling player, sometimes walking from town to town. And during one of those tramps—it was from Bristol to Exeter—she appeared so silent and rapt that her parents were constrained to ask what she was thinking about. She replied, "Only that I should like to run wild in a wood forever." Well, that she did, for the world became her wood, and she roamed it in enchantment, filling it with her radiance, dispersing all shadows and creating a perpetual springtime.

There is little need to discuss her career, her great triumphs, her tremendous versatility: she was a woman who could play anything with perfection. Here was the ideal Lady Macbeth, Beatrice, Imogen, Portia and Madame Sans-Gêne. Here was the woman for whom Shaw wrote *Captain Brassbound's Conversion*, here was a Juliet who compelled the tears, a Mistress Page who evoked laughter. Here was the whole art of acting in one woman's frame, in one woman's creative imagination. Here was the body completely subservient and obedient to the mind in any given role, and each role was a masterpiece. The parts she played with Irving at the Lyceum are alone superb portraits in the Royal Academy of the World's Stage. Volumes have been written about them, and they are limned in imperishable colours in the memories of those privileged to see them. Tens of thousands of people still alive treasure those memories. No matter at what period of her career you were lucky enough to see Ellen Terry, you still saw her in her prime. Age never touched that charm, that beauty, that genius, that wholly feminine loveliness. How could it, when she herself was always young? All the Terry family had great charm: Marion and Kate possessed it in full measure, as did Fred Terry, who was one of the best and certainly the most graceful actor who ever walked the stage. But the quintessence of it was expressed in the personality of Ellen. When she made her entrance something happened to the audience, the like of which one has never seen happen since her time. It was mass surrender —the whole house fell immediately under her spell. Sir John Martin-Harvey spoke of her "witchery," but he meant bewitchery —enchantment—for she was a sorceress, if you like, but hardly a witch. Circe must have been such a creature as Ellen Terry, though Ellen could never have changed men into swine; she just bound them in unseen fetters of complete adoration. Perhaps Titania was nearer her prototype. Yet Titania quarrelled and fought with Oberon and Ellen Terry never quarrelled with anyone; nobody ever heard her speak ill of a living soul, for she saw only the good side, and it was all she wanted to see.

It was not her physical beauty which captivated her countless admirers, for there have been more beautiful women by classical standards. But there can never have been another person who so radiated beauty. Nor have there ever been anyone else who was so completely gracious.

She was a great actress in a period of great acting. Sarah

Siddons had died only sixteen years before Ellen Terry was born, and at that time the memory of her was clear and vivid. It seems as if the gods who guard the Drama could not bear a vacuum and sent little Ellen to fill the void.

During Ellen Terry's career there were before the public such great actresses as Helen Faucit, Mrs. Stirling, Mrs. Kendal, Lady Bancroft, Duse, and the great Sarah Bernhardt herself, to mention only a few. She transcended them all, and it is not to their detriment to say so. Even Siddons failed in Comedy, but Ellen Terry took both the Comic and the Tragic Muse in her stride. Sarah Bernhardt, magnificent as she was, had not the humanity or the femininity of Ellen Terry, and if other of her compeers had their limitations, she never betrayed hers. Her recipe for playing Juliet was not to study other actress's readings or critics' ideas, but to go to Verona, and *imagine* it all, and translate it into terms of her performance.

At forty, she was the finest Cordelia in *King Lear* the stage has ever seen. She literally became the youngest daughter of the old King, glowing with unspoken love and devotion, and investing this difficult part with the tenderness which Shakespeare intended, but so few manage to achieve. She understood that the reason why Lear treated Cordelia as he did was because his reason was already unhinged, and that is something which not all those who play Lear himself seem to realise. But then she understood everything she did. She played the vulgar, good-hearted Sans-Gene with the same sure touch that she brought to Ophelia or to Portia. She once played Portia at a Shakespeare Festival when her last husband, James Carew, whom she had married not long before, was playing Shylock for the first time, and when she came to the words, "Here's thy money offered thee," she moved towards him, laying her hand on his arm. The purists were amazed, even shocked, for no such piece of business had ever been seen before. Lady Benson, an old friend and actress, asked her why she had done it. Ellen Terry maintained that she had not put her hand on Shylock's arm. But Lady Benson persisted: she had the evidence of her own eyes and could call plenty of corroboration. Ellen Terry smiled. "No, Constance," she said. "I did not put my hand on the Jew's arm, but on my husband's." She had sensed his fear and tension on that trying occasion, and she made that charming little gesture of support, encouragement and sympathy. For none knew better than she what first-night nerves were. She herself admitted that the only comfortable first night she ever had at the Lyceum was when she played Olivia, a part she had played so often elsewhere that she had not the burden of creating it.

Another instance of her complete understanding of a player's feelings was when she engaged Matheson Lang, then a young actor, to play Benedick to her Beatrice in *Much Ado About Nothing*. She was running that lovely but unlucky theatre, the Imperial in Westminster, and not even she could exercise the hoodoo, though she came very near doing so. She wanted someone to play Benedick, and at short notice. Lang's wife, Hutin Britton, a gracious lady and good actress too if ever there was one, was playing Hero. While Lang was watching the play, he was told that Miss Terry wanted to see him. He went to her dressing-room and paid her what compliments he could on her Beatrice, a part in which she was incomparable, despite her age. She asked him if he had ever played Benedick, and he said he had not. "But of course you know every line of it?" she enquired and he shook his head. She in her turn, shook her finger at him. "Young man, when I was your age I knew every leading part in Shakespeare, whether I had played them or not." Lang, a Bensonian, tried to explain that it took him all his time learning the parts assigned to him, but she cut him short. "How soon could you play the part?" she asked. "In three days?" Astounded, he said that he could. "Then go home and study it," she commanded. "I want you to play it with me in three days from now." At rehearsal the great actress and the young player sat on a bench discussing points. Suddenly she said, "Young man, how old are you?" Lang told her, and she threw up her hands. "Heavens! You are younger than my own son. I can't play love scenes with you." But rehearsals went on all the same, and Lang thought it over and devised a make-up which added years to his age. Ellen Terry made no further comments on his age; she appreciated the mind which had followed her subtle suggestion. She guided him through his part, yet never seeming to instruct, for she knew he had it in him, and like a magnet she drew it out. Would there were producers today like that!

A few nights afterwards, the Manager of the theatre said to Matheson Lang, "What has happened to you, Lang? When you first played Benedick you were good enough, but now, in so short a time, your performance has improved not only by leaps and bounds, but out of all measure." Lang's own words should be quoted in reply: "That is Miss Terry. Without ever appearing to do so, simply by a hint there, a suggestion here, she has guided and developed my performance night by night." Typical of Ellen's understanding was an incident one night when Lang observed Ellen whispering to some members of the cast. He overheard her say "Now remember, not a word to Langy." That was the name she always called him and he was quite mystified by the cryptic message. So during one of the waits he went up to Ellen and demanded to know what it was they were keeping from him. "Oh, you poor dear," she said, "has that worried you? Well, I had better tell you now. Henry is in front."

And when Lang went on for his next entrance he glanced around and there, sitting back in a box, was Sir Henry Irving —he who had played Benedick with Ellen at the Lyceum. How well she understood that the presence of the great actor might have disturbed Lang in his opening scene. He acknowledged that the influence of her spirit was overwhelming, that it was impossible not to respond to the life and sparkle of such a performance as her Beatrice. To Lang the play seemed a living thing, and he went down to the theatre every night to live a new and enchanted life. He was with her for two years, and swore he learnt more in that time than in all the years before or after. She had her faults and her failings; her memory often played her false, a thing common to all of the Terry family. Once she made Lang play a minor comedy part because that part was with her on the stage a great deal and she wanted him to prompt her. He did it sacrificing the lead to play it. Scripts would be hidden from the public under cushions, behind pieces of furniture, for her aid, but her charm and her supreme genius always got her through with few people being aware of the subterfuge. It was only in new parts that the trouble occurred. She had a delicious vagueness, as witness the occasion in her old age when she was making two pictures at once at Elstree. Coming off the set after a little scene which had brought tears to the eyes of Constance Collier, Gladys Cooper and Ivor Novello, who were watching her with adoration, she gaily enquired which picture she had just been filming? She did not know—but she knew the scene and what to do with it. Another time when she was filming, the scouts tried to find a place for location shots not too far from Elstree. They found it in the grounds of an old house in which lived another very lovely and gracious old lady. Permission was given to shoot the scenes, the lady never dreaming of asking for payment. The day for "shooting" arrived and with it came hordes of cameramen and executives, masses of players and an army of "extras." The lady of the house came out to see the fun, and up the drive came a victoria containing another old but very beautiful and gracious lady. It was Ellen Terry. Now, the lady of the house knew Ellen Terry and went forward to greet her, Ellen being overjoyed at the reunion. Her dear Elizabeth must get into the victoria and have a chat, and that chat went on and on, both the ladies being oblivious of time. The film folk fumed and fretted: the light was going; expenses were piling up. But nobody dared disturb that blissful, unconscious *tête-à-tête*. The lady of the house suggested tea—and the great actress and her hostess went into the house and continued their talk over the tea-cups. No filming was done that day. When the director at last uttered a gentle protest, Ellen Terry was horrified. Why had they not interrupted before? It was all her fault. Let them make a start at once. But the light had gone so it was decided to do the filming on the following day, and this time the chat between the two old friends was delayed until after the "shooting" had taken place. And Ellen Terry laughed happily over the whole thing, but scolded herself unmercifully.

She always had an eye, too, for the other person's advantage. Sylvia Grey, when quite a girl but a divine dancer, used to arrange the gavottes, minuets, country dances and the like which Irving wanted in his productions, and for this she got an infinitesimal reward. She acted in some of the plays too, for she was as good an actress as she was a dancer, which is saying a very great deal. Ellen Terry made friends with the little dancer, found out what she was earning and was quite cross about it. Electing herself Sylvia Grey's business manager, she got a much better fee out of Irving than he would have paid otherwise, and Sylvia Grey, who still graces this world of ours with the beauty, charm and dignity of days gone by, has never forgotten the kindness which the great actress had shown her. Sylvia became the dancer of her time, and she could have shone equally well as an actress, for they all wanted her to go into straight plays—Wyndham, Hawtrey and all the rest—but she remained faithful to her art of terpsichore.

Those who saw Ellen Terry in what, by the calendar, was her old age saw the same Ellen Terry whom their fathers and grandfathers had seen. Was there ever a gayer, more mischievous Mistress Page than when she played the part in *The Merry Wives of Windsor* at His Majesty's Theatre with Sir Herbert Tree? Mrs. Kendal, who played Mistress Ford, is said to have described Sir Herbert as a star between two ancient lights, though the same story is attributed to Lady Tree in the following connection. A rehearsal was called for the two veteran actresses, Ellen and Mrs. Kendal, to play their scenes together. Nobody was to be allowed on the stage whilst these special "run throughs" were on. One morning Lady Tree arrived, and as usual walked straight on to the stage. The stage manager tried to restrain her, explaining that the two stars were rehearsing privately. "Stars," said Lady Tree with a smile. "Don't you mean ancient lights?" Lady Tree meant no harm by the remark—she had the same biting wit as her husband and she could never resist the opportunity for a "gag." It was witty, but it was untrue. You cannot diminish starlight—light years are incalculable to the ordinary mind—and it was starlight which Ellen Terry for ever radiated. Her Alice-Sit-by-the-Fire in Barrie's play at the Duke of York's was another thing of beauty, and she was fifty-eight then. She played Hermione in *A Winter's Tale* fifty years after her début in that play, and her role was still something at which to wonder. Her Lady Cecily Waynflete in *Captain Brassbound's Conversion* was the character as Shaw himself conceived it, for it was perfectly done. Truly age could not wither her, nor custom stale her infinite variety.

The secret of her eternal youth and eternal interest was that she kept abreast of everything, and was delighted by every new experience. One very foggy night in the November of 1917, she came to the Globe to see Gaby Deslys, and at the end of the show her escort was in a dilemma as to how to get her home, the car being hopelessly fog-bound. Unperturbed, she sat in the vestibule, which was full of people in the same plight grumbling and cursing their luck. But Ellen Terry was smiling brightly. It was an adventure, and at the age of seventy she was still ready and eager for adventure. The crowd, aware of who she was, gathered around her, and she chatted to them with delight, while plans for getting her home were being made. There was nothing for it but the Tube, a mode of travel she was unfamiliar with, but she adored the chance—the crowds, the pushing, the hurrying and the admirers who surged around her—and when she got back home she said she had never enjoyed an evening more.

How would most women react if a box of chocolates hit them on the head? Certainly not the way Ellen Terry did when an eager upper-circle-ite, leaning over to catch a glimpse of her in the stalls, knocked a box of chocolates off the ledge. Down it hurtled, right on to Ellen Terry's lovely head, with chocolates spraying around like shrapnel. The girl upstairs who was responsible nearly fainted with horror. But Ellen picked up the box, waved her hand in a gesture of thanks, flashed up one of her dazzling smiles, and—ate what remained of the chocolates with every sign of enjoyment.

Once a young man sent a telegram to her house at Smallhythe in Kent, saying that he would call to see her at a certain time on a certain day. He signed the wire with his name—Barker. On the day appointed, when he alighted at the station, he found Ellen Terry's car waiting for him, and on the way to her home the chauffeur handed him a note saying that he was to have lunch. Then, to his horror, he saw that the note was addressed to Granville Barker, the famous author-actor-producer. In considerable confusion, he scribbled a note in reply, explaining the mistake, and waited outside whilst the chauffeur delivered it. The answer came—he was still invited to lunch, for there was no disappointment in Miss Terry, only joy at a new acquaintance and a delightful contretemps. Indeed, she apologised for the lunch because Granville Barker was a vegetarian. She made the whole situation a joy. They chatted and they played with Miss Terry's juvenile relations, she herself revelling in the game, until the time came for the young man to go. Then she gave him a photograph signed by herself inscribed "To the boy who was not Granville." Actually he was Eric Barker, "The Stroller" of *The Evening News* and as fine a newsgetter as Fleet Street ever had.

To mark her Stage Jubilee, Ellen Terry was given a great

celebration performance at the Theatre Royal, Drury Lane, on June 12, 1906. The whole profession did her homage, the most famous personalities appearing in her honour. Caruso sang, Duse hastened from Florence, and said she would have come from South Africa to lay her tribute at Ellen's feet.

The patrons of the pit and gallery waited outside the theatre all night so as to be sure of being present on such an occasion. And Ellen Terry came to see them at two o'clock in the morning, to thank them. She had been told they were there and she insisted on visiting them. That was the sort of thing Ellen Terry always did. If it was good enough for them to wait all night, it was good enough for her to join them.

She was indeed much beloved. Of her marriages, of the happiness and the unhappiness they brought, no need to ponder here. These were her own affairs and no concern of others. To the public she brought joy and let nothing interfere with it.

The most remarkable thing about her was that immense yet unconscious power of attraction. She literally compelled attention —she drew all eyes. She would come into the stalls of a theatre completely unheralded, but instantly the audience would stand up and applaud her to the echo. And they would smile, for she conveyed happiness to all around her. Her sense of gaiety and laughter was contagious. It was a radiance which flowed from her, which surrounded her like an aura, the greatest example of personal magnetism which the present writer, who has seen much and known so many, has ever observed. There was a land of perpetual sunlight around her, and on the stage she hardly seemed to need the help of artificial lighting. Irving had similar magnetism, but not the same radiance. When he entered a scene, with as many as three hundred people on the stage, it was only at Irving one looked.

Ellen Terry loved flowers, and the daffodil most of all, which was in itself symbolic, for she was born in the lap of spring, and she was endowed with the strength and immense vitality that is possessed by those green lances of the daffodil which pierce the frostbound earth and climb towards the sky. Her own shining radiance gleams in the golden trumpet of that flower, which, in the words of the play wherein she first appeared, "comes before the swallow dares and takes the winds of March with beauty."

Ellen Terry was herself truly a day in the English spring—the spring which never grows old. Hers was the gentleness, the tenderness, and the charm of those inexpressibly lovely April days which often herald the merry month of May, days which are so breath-takingly beautiful that only the poets can capture their magic in words. And in the dark days we remember them and our hopes revive. They are rare, it is true, but so too was Ellen Terry of blessed memory.

She was made D.B.E., a Dame of the British Empire—a fitting honour—and had it been possible to bestow a greater honour on a woman, it would undoubtedly have been hers too. But she did not seek such recognition; she was perfectly happy to be herself—Ellen Terry. She died on July 21, 1928, at the age of eighty-one, which was the total of her years, but she was as young in heart as ever she was.

Her ashes lie in a silver chalice in the Church of St. Paul, Covent Garden, the Actor's Church, whose small archway has been the last stage door through which so many members of her profession have passed. The date on the inscription is wrong by a day, but that was in character too, for what did she ever care for dates, she whom time did not touch?

On the hundredth anniversary of her birth, a service in her honour was held in that Parish Church of the acting profession. Dame Sybil Thorndike, Dame Edith Evans, Peggy Ashcroft, Sir Ralph Richardson, Leon Quartermaine, E. Harcourt Williams and so many others participated. Sir Bronson Albery, the Old Vic organisation and the present author also contributed something to it. Scenes from Shakespeare were played before the altar, and Peggy Ashcroft recited from the Sonnets. They might have been written with Ellen Terry in mind. A choir sang her favourite hymns, especially "All things bright and beautiful," which was her best beloved. The Rector, the Rev. Vincent Howson, himself an old Bensonian, officiated, and the address was given by the Bishop of London. It was a ceremony full of brightness, with nothing of the usual memorial note and so much of the spirit of the woman in whose honour it was held. But it was not the presence of celebrated members of her profession which impressed most on that occasion, magnificent as they were. Rather was it the homage paid by the general public. The date

February 27, 1947, fell in one of the worst winters in human memory. Arctic cold had gripped these islands for months; frozen snow covered everything in a deathly pall; the leaden grey of the skies never lightened; and there was grave lack of heating and light in many homes. Yet the People who had loved Ellen Terry and whom she had loved came in their thousands to pay tribute to her memory and her greatness. The church, far too small for the occasion, though eminently suitable in every other way, was packed to capacity. The churchyard itself was filled to overflowing, filled with people whom the name and memory of Ellen Terry had gathered together in a bond of reverence. Some were up to their knees in snow; all braved the biting cold of the wintry day. They stretched through the arches on either side of the churchyard into the thoroughfares beyond, and when the services started, the church doors were thrown open, despite the freezing temperature, so that those outside could at least hear, even if they could not see, and thus enjoy a spirit of participation. Her daughter, Edith Craig, had come with some of the oldest friends, travelling up from the home in Smallhythe, Tenterden, which now stands as a memorial to its great occupant and to which the members of the Ellen Terry Fellowship make an annual pilgrimage. Edith Craig was ill and should not have come, but she had her mother's spirit and none could gainsay her determination to be present on that wonderful occasion. She died soon afterwards and her friends mourn the passing of another great lady who carried on the family tradition with pride and dignity.

People of all ages, from all parts of the Kingdom, stood bareheaded at the great memorial service, impervious to the cold, for the spirit and radiance of her whom they had loved was upon them all. Winter's blast was defeated. The gloom had vanished, for it was no mourning crowd which stood uncovered in the snow. It was a Festival occasion, and they constituted that which she had always loved, an audience. A hundred years had passed since she came to earth, but it was as though she had never left it. As in life, her presence could be felt.

And when it was all over, the crowd, unwilling to depart, filed slowly through the church, admiring the spring flowers, which reminded all of Ellen's own spring-like beauty, gazing not with sadness but with the recollection of former happiness, at the silver chalice in which her ashes were encased. Close by grim old Macklin, who lived for 107 years, has his lasting monument. He was the actor who first played Shylock as we know that character today, as grim as Ellen Terry had been gay—and now their memories were enshrined together within the walls of that ancient church which Inigo Jones had built. And not far away is the plaque to the memory of Dr. Arne, another parishioner of the Land of Illusion, whose bones lie in the resting place of the heroes and heroines of the Theatre, under the very shadows of the two great Theatres Royal, Drury Lane and Covent Garden.

It was hours before the last of the pilgrims left.

The ashes of Ellen Terry repose in the heart of Covent Garden, whose great market laps her round, and where the seasons come and go, as easily observed as in a country woodland or a Devonshire lane. For to that market come the flowers in their profusion—the deep richness of the summer posies, the glory of autumnal tints, and the delicate, gay whites and yellows of those spring flowers which typify the lady who is embowered amongst them. Masses of golden daffodils come to Covent Garden before they go elsewhere in this land, and they are piled high, like golden sunshine, all around the spot where she rests, those daffodils which were her favourites and which are so very, very like what she was.

There she is enshrined for ever. Even when those of the generation which was the last to behold her in the flesh have moved on, her name will still glow, for it is inscribed indelibly in the annals of the British Theatre—the finest Theatre in the world—not only as an actress, but as the reincarnation of one of the women whom Shakespeare created. For her gracious person and being encompassed all that is meant by that magic and compelling word—Woman. Ellen Terry, incomparable actress, was womanliness personified.

Index

OF NAMES & PLAYS